1985

W9-ADS-757

3 0301 00053171 1

PASCAL

An Introduction to the Art and Science
of Programming

R. Billstein, S. Libeskind, and J. Lott
Problem Solving with Logo (1985)

G. Booch
Software Engineering with Ada (1983)

D. M. Etter
Structured FORTRAN 77 for Engineers and Scientists (1983)
Problem Solving with Structured FORTRAN 77 (1984)
Structured WATFIV for Engineers and Scientists (1985)
Problem Solving with Structured WATFIV (1985)

P. Linz
Programming Concepts and Problem Solving: An Introduction to Computer Science Using Pascal (1983)

A. Kelley and I. Pohl
A Book on C (1984)

W. J. Savitch
Pascal: An Introduction to the Art and Science of Programming (1984)

R. W. Sebesta
VAX 11: Structured Assembly Language Programming (1983)

R. W. Sebesta
PDP-11: Structured Assembly Language Programming (1985)

PASCAL

An Introduction to the Art and Science of Programming

Walter J. Savitch
University of California, San Diego

The Benjamin / Cummings Publishing Co., Inc.
Menlo Park, California · Reading, Massachusetts
London · Amsterdam · Don Mills, Ontario · Sydney

LIBRARY
College of St. Francis
JOLIET, ILL.

Sponsoring Editor: Alan Apt
Production Coordinator: Charles Hibbard
Book Designer: Marilyn Langfeld
Cover Designers: Marilyn Langfeld and Betty Armstrong
Cover Illustrator: Betty Armstrong

Acknowledgments:

Chapter 7, ending quotation from F. P. Brooks, Jr., *The Mythical Man-Month*, *Essays on Software Engineering*, p. 116. Addison-Wesley Publishing Company (1975). Reprinted by permission of the publisher.
Chapter 12, opening quotation from John R. Ross, *Constraints on Variables in Syntax*, p. i, Ph.D. dissertation, Massachusetts Institute of Technology (1967). Reprinted by permission of the author.
Chapter 12 ending quotation, from Jorge Luis Borges, "The Garden of Forking Paths," in Jorge Luis Borges, *Selected Stories and Other Writings*, p. 25. New Directions Publishing Company (1964). Reprinted by permission of the publisher.
Chapter 14, ending quotation from Niklaus Wirth, *Algorithms + Data Structures = Programs*, title. Prentice-Hall (1976). Reprinted by permission of the publisher.
Chapter 15, ending quotation from B. W. Kernighan and P. J. Plauger, *The Elements of Programming Style*, 2nd ed., p. 117. McGraw-Hill Book Co. (1978). Reprinted by permission of the publisher and Bell Laboratories.

UCSD Pascal is a trademark of the Regents of the University of California.

Copyright © 1984 by The Benjamin/Cummings Publishing Company, Inc.

All rights reserved. No part of this publication may be reproduced, stored in a retrieval system, or transmitted, in any form or by any means, electronic, mechanical, photocopying, recording, or otherwise, without the prior written permission of the publisher. Printed in the United States of America. Published simultaneously in Canada.

Library of Congress Cataloging in Publication Data

Savitch, Walter J., 1943–
    Pascal, an introduction to the art and science of programming.

    Includes bibliographies and index.
    1. PASCAL (Computer program language) 2. Electronic digital computer—Programming. I. Title. II. Title: Pascal.
QA76.73.P2S28   1983   001.64′24   84-303
ISBN 0-8053-8370-0

ABCDEFGHIJ-HA-8987654

The Benjamin / Cummings Publishing Company, Inc.
2727 Sand Hill Road
Menlo Park, California 94025

001.6424
8268

2-7-85 Joan Rametta # J

To Sis

113,348

Preface

This book was designed for use in introductory programming courses that use the Pascal language. It can be used for courses as short as one quarter or as long as one academic year. The book includes both a thorough introduction to programming techniques and a complete description of the Pascal language. It assumes no previous knowledge of computers and no mathematics beyond high school algebra. Some additional details about the book are summarized below.

Emphasizes Problem Solving and Programming Techniques

Chapters 1, 11, 12 and 15 are dedicated exclusively to problem solving and programming techniques. Every other chapter includes sections dedicated to such topics as top-down and other algorithm design techniques, programming style, testing techniques and debugging techniques. For ease of reference, these sections are tabulated in a separate table of contents. Additional discussion of these topics is integrated into the presentation of Pascal language constructs.

Designed for Interactive Programming

This book can be used by those running programs in batch mode. However, the emphasis is on interactive use. All the programs were designed for use in an interactive environment.

Many Sample Programs

Complete programs are presented very early. Thereafter, concepts are always illustrated with complete programs and procedures, rather than small fragments of code. Sample input and output are displayed along with the program text. Both long and short programs are presented. The longest program occupies four pages of text; the input and output extend to another two pages. Program displays of two or three pages are common.

Introduces Procedures and Parameters Early

Like most newer texts on programming, procedures are introduced early, the reason being that this facilitates the teaching of modularity and top-down design.

Unlike other texts, this book adopts the approach without reservation. Not only procedures, but also a detailed discussion of parameters are presented very early, even before such basic Pascal constructs as *if - then* and loops. This allows virtually all the sample and exercise programs to be written using completely modular procedures. Programming without parameters invariably violates generally accepted modular design principles, and so forces students to practice techniques that must later be unlearned. Introducing parameters early eliminates the need to teach programming techniques that will later be rejected.

When we tested this approach in actual classes we found that it was not only possible to introduce parameters this early, but that the students found this approach easier than the traditional approaches. At the early stages of a programming course they have fewer new concepts to integrate and can thus concentrate without distraction on the notion of parameters.

Self-Teaching Style

The chapters were designed so that they can be read by students before they attend lectures on the material. Material is covered completely, problems and questions are anticipated, and typical examples are given. This allows students to read ahead at their own pace and to come to lecture already primed to digest the material quickly. (This also makes the book suitable for self-teaching outside a classroom situation.)

Covers Both Standard and UCSD Pascal

This book can be used in either a standard Pascal or a UCSD Pascal environment. All the UCSD Pascal detail is isolated into separate sections. Hence a standard Pascal user can read this book without seeing any reference to UCSD Pascal details. All the programs satisfy the ANSI/IEEE770X3.97-1983 Pascal standard (except for two short programs in optional sections about UCSD Pascal). They have all been compiled and tested using the Berkeley Pascal compiler and interpreter with the standard Pascal option. For a few programs dealing with files, alternative UCSD Pascal versions are needed and are given. However, those cases are the exceptions rather than the rule. If one programs with a view toward portability, the two dialects of Pascal are simply not that different. This does mean that the programming style in this book tends a bit more toward standard Pascal than UCSD Pascal. Still, a complete treatment of UCSD Pascal constructs is given in the appropriate chapters and not relegated to a brief appendix.

The point of including both versions of Pascal is not simply a compromise between two alternatives. One important programming technique that needs to be taught is portability. The two dialects of Pascal are close enough that they can both be taught without confusing the student. Yet they contain enough differences to illustrate portability techniques. If time permits, it is a good idea to cover some aspects of the "other" Pascal, whichever dialect that may be.

Flexibility

The dependency chart on p. xxiii shows the possible orders in which the chapters may be covered without losing continuity. A bit more than the first half of the book is a core course that must be covered first. The rest of the book contains topics such as recursion, some software engineering topics, some numeric programming techniques and a substantial amount on data structures including records, files and pointers. These later chapters may be covered in almost any order, or a subset of the chapters may be chosen to form a shorter course. The chapter on text files has been divided into two parts to allow for two possibilities, either postponing the topic entirely until later in a course or briefly introducing it early and giving more detail later on. To add even more flexibility, sections with optional topics are included throughout the book.

Self-Test and Interactive Exercises

Each chapter includes self-test exercises with answers in the back of the book. In addition to these self-test exercises, students should be encouraged to learn by trying out small test programs; that is, by "playing" with the system. Unfortunately, most beginning students have trouble thinking of things to try out. For this reason, interactive exercises are also included. They consist of suggestions for writing short programs that help give a feel for the concepts presented in the chapter. More traditional exercises are also included. The book contains more than 370 exercises of various kinds.

Support Material

A chapter-by-chapter instructor's guide is available. All the programs in the text are available in machine readable form. Thus it is possible to have all the programs available for students to run without having to type them in.

Acknowledgments

I have received much help and encouragement from numerous individuals and groups while preparing this book. I am very grateful to the University of Washington (Seattle) Computer Science Department and to the EECS Department at the University of California, San Diego for providing facilities and a conducive environment for writing the book. My thanks also go to the following individuals for suggestions and comments on the book (unfortunately the size of the list makes it impractical to catalogue the many important contributions that each individual made): Guy Almes, Bill Appelbe, Andrew Black, Jim Bunch, John Donald, Mike Denisevich, Patrick Dymond, Klaus Eldridge, Jim Gips, Richard Kaufmann, Alean Kirnak, Keith Muller, Vijay Rao, Robert Rother, Gary Sackett, Joe Sandmeyer, Robert Streett, Sue Sullivan, Martin Tompa, Dennis Volper, Ann Wilson and Chin Wu. Special thanks go to the many students in my programming classes who tested and helped correct preliminary versions of the book. Finally, I express my appreciation to all the individuals at Benjamin/Cummings who organized the reviewing and production of the book; in particular Charlie Hibbard, Jo Andrews and my Editor Alan Apt contributed much to the final product.

Contents

Chapter 10
More on Data Types   255

Chapter 11
Program Design Methodology   291

Chapter 12

Using Recursion

Chapter 13

Text Files and Secondary Storage

Chapter 14

More Structured Data Types 373

Chapter 15

Solving Numeric Problems 413

Chapter 16

More File Types 437

Chapter 17
Dynamic Data Structures   461

Chapter Sections Dedicated to Problem Solving and Programming Techniques

Dependency of Chapters

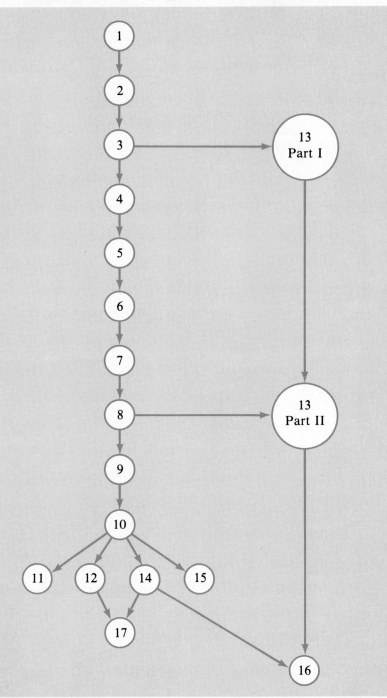

1

Introduction to Computers and Problem Solving

The arithmetical machine produces effects which approach nearer to thought than all the actions of animals. But it does nothing which would enable us to attribute will to it, as to the animals.

Blaise Pascal

2
Introduction to
Computers

Chapter Contents

In this chapter we outline some of the basic concepts common to all computer systems and all programming languages. The theme here and throughout this book is that there is a methodology of effective programming that is relatively independent of the particular programming language used or the particular computer used. In fact, this chapter presents no details of the Pascal language.

What a Computer Is

Computers are encountered regularly in the everyday business of our lives. They keep track of our financial transactions. For better or worse, they allow government agencies to keep track of certain details of our lives that we ourselves may lose track of. Computers control games sophisticated enough to keep intelligent players entranced for hours or even days at a time. Computers also control most of the technology that surrounds us. They control manufacturing processes, keep track of airline reservations, predict weather, compute government economic forecasts, control space probes—the list goes on seemingly without end. But just what are these things called *computers*?

One could say that a computer is a complicated arrangement of silicon, wire, plastic and various other materials, but this answer would miss the point of the question. A better answer would explain what a computer "really does" and what it is like to work "directly" with one. In this sense, computers are surprisingly simple. They are machines that perform very simple tasks according to specified instructions. Their ability to perform so many of these simple tasks with such great speed and with a high degree of accuracy is what makes computers so useful. One may think of a computer as a clerk who does nothing all day but sit and perform trivial, routine tasks according to some set of instructions and who does so with perfect accuracy, infinite patience, a flawless memory, and unimaginable speed.

The Modern Digital Computer

A set of instructions for a computer to follow is called a *program*. The collection of programs used by a computer is referred to as the *software* for that computer. The actual physical machines that make up a computer installation are referred to as *hardware*. In this book we are concerned almost exclusively with software, but a brief overview of how the hardware is organized will be useful.

software / hardware

Most computers are organized as shown in Figure 1.1. They can be thought of as having four main components: the input device(s), the output device(s), the central processing unit (CPU), and the memory.

An *input device* is any device that allows a person to communicate information to the computer. For readers of this book the input device is likely to be a keyboard rather like a typewriter keyboard, but it could be some other type of device or could consist of a variety of devices. Another common input device is a card reader for reading punched cards.

input

keyboard

An *output device* performs the opposite task. It allows the computer to communicate information to the user. One of the most common output devices consists of a *display screen* which resembles a television screen. This display screen is sometimes referred to as a *CRT* screen or *monitor*. (The initials CRT stand for cathode ray tube.) Quite often, there is more than one output device. For example, in addition to the display screen there may be a typewriter or typewriterlike device to produce printed output. One commonly used typewriter-

output

display screen

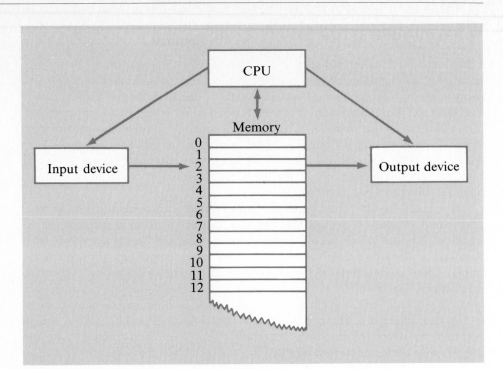

**Figure 1.1
Main components
of a computer.**

memory

like device is called a *line printer* because it types an entire line of text at one time. The keyboard and display screen described above are usually combined into a single unit that serves as a combination input and output device. This combination unit is called a *video display terminal* or simply a *terminal*.

In order to store input and to have the equivalent of scratch paper for performing calculations, computers are provided with *memory*. The memory is very simple. It consists of a long list of numbered locations, frequently called *words* or, more descriptively, *memory locations*. The locations are numbered starting with zero; that is, they are numbered $0, 1, 2, \ldots$ rather than $1, 2, 3, \ldots$. The number of memory locations varies from one computer to another, ranging from a few thousand to many millions. In fact, memory may be added to a computer almost without limit, although once the memory size exceeds certain thresholds, the computer system must be a bit more sophisticated. Each memory location or word contains a string of zeros and ones. The contents of these locations can change. Hence, you can think of each memory location as a tiny blackboard on which the computer may write and erase. In most computers, all locations contain the same number of zero/one digits; some typical sizes are 16, 32, and 64 digits. A digit that assumes only the values zero or one is called a *bit*. Hence, if somebody tells you that you are working on a 32 bit machine, they mean that each memory location in your computer can hold 32 bits, that is, 32 digits, each either zero or one.

That the information in a computer's memory is represented as zeros and ones need not be of great concern to a person programming in Pascal. The reasons for using only zeros and ones have to do with the physics of hardware design. Computers using larger repertoires of digits can and have been designed.

The use of zeros and ones does, however, have a few implications that you should be aware of. First, the computer has to do its arithmetic in something called "binary notation." We will discuss binary arithmetic further in Chapter 15. A more important point is that the computer interprets these strings of zeros and ones as numbers or letters or instructions or other types of information. The computer performs these interpretations automatically according to certain codes. A different code is used for each different type of item that can be stored in a location: one code for letters, another for whole numbers, another for fractions, another for instructions and so on. For example, in one commonly used set of codes, 1000001 is the code for the letter "A" and also for the number 65. In order to know what the string 1000001 in a particular location stands for, the computer must keep track of which code is currently being used for that location. Fortunately for us, the programmer seldom needs to be concerned with such codes and can safely reason as though the locations actually contain letters, numbers or whatever is desired.

The memory we just described is called *main memory*. Most computers have additional memory called *secondary memory*, also frequently called *secondary storage* or *auxiliary storage*. Main memory serves as a temporary memory that is only used while the computer is actually following the instructions in a program. Secondary memory is used for keeping a permanent record of information after (and before) the computer is used. On small computers secondary memory is likely to consist of something called a *floppy disk* and on larger computers is likely to be something called a *hard disk*. Magnetic tape units are also commonly used for secondary memory. A typical computer installation with different kinds of memory is diagramed in Figure 1.2. We will not be concerned with secondary memory until we reach the topics in Chapter 13.

secondary memory

disks

The *CPU* is the "brain" of the computer. It tells an input device when to place information in memory. It tells an output device when to output information from memory. It is the CPU that follows the instructions in a program and performs the calculations specified by the program. The CPU is, however, a very simple brain. All that it can do is follow a set of simple instructions provided to it by the programmer.

CPU

Typical CPU instructions say things like "interpret the zeros and ones as numbers and then add the number in memory location 37 to the number in memory location 59 and write the answer in location 83" or "read a letter of input, convert it to its code as a string of zeros and ones and place it in memory location 1298." The CPU can do subtraction, multiplication and division as well as addition. It can move things from one memory location to another. It can interpret strings of zeros and ones as letters and send the letters to an output device. The CPU also has some primitive ability to rearrange the order of instructions. But that is about all it can do. Needless to say, CPU instructions vary somewhat from computer to computer, but they are all about as simple as we have described. The CPU of a modern computer can have as many as several hundred available instructions, but these instructions are just minor variants of the simple operations we mentioned above.

At this point you may be wondering where in the computer the program is kept. The answer is: in the memory. Thus, the memory serves both as a place to

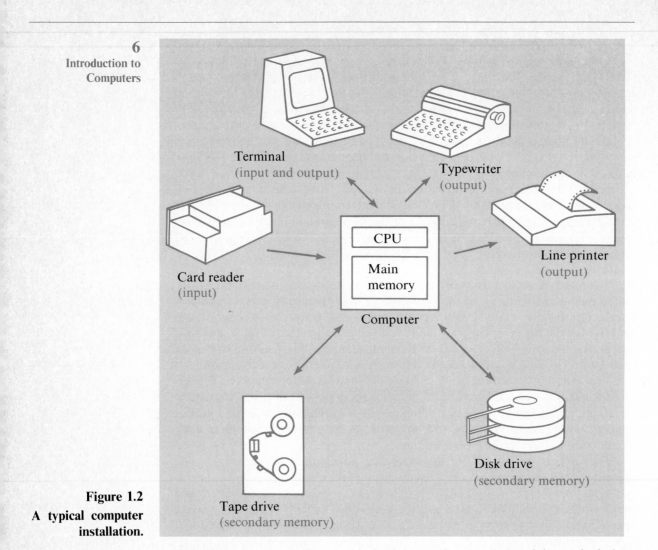

**Figure 1.2
A typical computer
installation.**

store the program and as a kind of "scratch paper" for doing calculations. Usually, we conceptualize the program as something outside of memory but occasionally we will need to be aware of the fact that it resides in memory.

That is it. That is all there is to a computer. Conceptually it is a simple machine. Its power comes from the size of its memory, its speed, its accuracy and the sophistication of its programs. Your computer may not be configured exactly as we have portrayed it, but it will be similar and, more importantly, will behave exactly as if it were the very machine we have just described.

The Notion of an Algorithm

algorithm

program

When learning your first programming language it is easy to get the impression that the hard part of solving a problem on a computer is translating your ideas into the specific language that will be fed into the computer. This most definitely is not the case. The most difficult part of solving a problem on a computer is coming up with the method of solution. After you come up with a method of solution, it is routine to translate your method into the required language, be it Pascal or some other programming language. When solving a problem with a computer, it is therefore helpful to ignore temporarily the computer programming language and to concentrate instead on formulating the steps of the solution and writing them down in plain English, as if the instructions were to be given to a human being. A set of instructions expressed in this way is frequently referred to as an *algorithm*. Some approximately equivalent words are "recipe," "method," "directions" and "routine." The instructions may be expressed in a programming language or a human language. Our algorithms will be expressed in English and in the programming language Pascal. An algorithm expressed in a language that a computer can understand is called a *program*; Hence, computer languages are called *programming languages*.

The word "algorithm" has a long history, but its meaning has recently taken on a new character. The word itself derives from the name of the ninth-century Arabic mathematician and astronomer Al-Khowarizmi, who wrote an early and famous textbook on the manipulation of numbers and equations. The similar sounding word "algebra" was derived from an Arabic word in the title of this text. Indeed until very recently, the word "algorithm" usually referred to algebraic rules for calculating numbers.

Today the word "algorithm" refers to a wide variety of instructions for manipulating symbolic as well as numeric entities. The properties that qualify a set of instructions as an algorithm now are determined by the nature of the instructions and not by the things they apply to. To qualify as an algorithm, a set of instructions must specify the steps to be taken and must give the order in which they are to be performed. Moreover, the instructions must be completely and unambiguously specified. They cannot rely on any intelligence on the part of the person or machine that will follow the instructions. The follower of an algorithm does exactly what the algorithm says, no more and no less.

An example may help to clarify the concept. Figure 1.3 contains an algorithm expressed in rather stylized English. The algorithm determines the number of times a specified name occurs on a list of names. So, if the list contains the winners of each of last season's football games and the name is that of your favorite team, then the algorithm determines how many games your team won. The algorithm is short and simple but is otherwise very typical of the algorithms we will be dealing with.

*sample
algorithm*

The instructions numbered 1 through 5 in our sample algorithm are meant to be carried out in that order. Unless otherwise specified, we will always assume that the instructions of an algorithm are carried out in the order in which they are given (written down). Most interesting algorithms do, however, specify some change of order, usually a repeating of some instruction again and again such as in instruction 4 of our sample algorithm.

This simple example illustrates a number of important points about algorithms. Algorithms are usually given some information. In our example, the algorithm was given a name and a list of names. The information that is given to

*input or
data*

begin
 1. Request the list of names and call it **NameList**.
 2. Request the name being sought and call it
    KeyName;
 3. On a black board called **Count** write the number
    zero;
 4. Repeat the following for each name on **NameList**:
       if the name on **NameList** is the same as **KeyName**
          then add one to the number written on **Count**;
          {the old number is erased, leaving only one num-
          ber on **Count**}
 5. Announce that the desired answer is written on
    Count
end.

**Figure 1.3
An algorithm.**

an algorithm is called *input* or *data*. Algorithms usually give an answer, or answers, back. In the example, the answer was a number. The answers given by
output   an algorithm are called *output*. In addition to being able to remember input and output, algorithms typically need to remember some other information. In the example, a single number was remembered; the number changed as the algorithm proceeded and only the last value of the number was output.

One final observation about the algorithm above: it always ends. No matter how long the list is, the algorithm always gets to the end of the list and announces an answer. There are algorithms that never terminate. Common examples are the algorithms used by computerized airline reservation systems. They never terminate; they just keep adding and deleting reservations forever, or until the airline goes bankrupt or changes its computer system. An algorithm that might not end is called a *partial algorithm*. An algorithm that is guaranteed to end is called a *total algorithm*. Some authors, especially in more advanced texts, reserve the word "algorithm" for what we called total algorithm. However, we will use the word to mean any algorithm, whether or not it is guaranteed to terminate.

Programs and Data

running   As we already noted, a program is just an algorithm written in a language that
a program   can be fed into a computer. As shown in Figure 1.4, the input to a computer can be thought of as consisting of two parts: a program and some *data*. The data is what we conceptualize as the input to the algorithm that the computer will follow. In other words, the data is the input to the program, and both the program and the data are input to the computer. The word "input" is thus being used in two slightly different ways. This does require some care to keep from getting confused, but this is standard usage and you may as well get used to it. For the sample

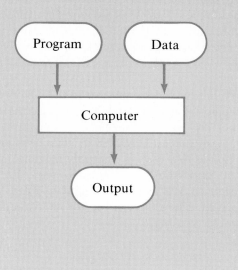

Figure 1.4
Simple view of
running a program.

algorithm of the previous section, the data was the name sought and the list of names to be searched. In order to get a computer to carry out the algorithm, both the algorithm (translated into some programming language) and that data are given as input to the computer. Whenever we give both a program and some data to a computer, we are said to be *running* the program on the data, and the computer is said to *execute* the program on the data.

The word "data" also has a much more general meaning than the one we have just given it. In its most general sense it means any information available to the computer or to some part of the computer. The word is commonly used in both the narrow sense and the more general sense. One must rely on context to decide which meaning is intended.

High Level Languages

The language Pascal is a *high level language*, as are most of the other programming languages you are likely to have heard of such as FORTRAN, BASIC and COBOL. High level languages resemble human languages in many ways. They are designed to be easy for human beings to write programs in and easy for human beings to read. As a typical example of a high level language, the language Pascal uses English words combined in ways that resemble English sentences. For

high level
language

example, the following is a line from a Pascal program:

```
if (X = Y) and (Z = W) then write('the answer is 42')
```

You can read and understand this instruction almost without any explanation.

*low level
language*

A high level language like Pascal contains instructions that are much more complicated than the simple instructions a computer's CPU is capable of following. The kind of language a computer can understand is called a *low level language*. A typical low level instruction might be the following:

ADD X Y Z

This instruction might mean "add the number in the memory location called X to the number in the memory location called Y and place the result in the memory location called Z."

*assembly
language*

The above sample instruction is written in what is called *assembly language*. In order to get a computer to follow an assembly language instruction, the words need to be translated into strings of zeros and ones. For example, the word "ADD" might translate to 0110, the "X" might translate to 1001, the "Y" to 1010 and the "Z" to 1011. The version of the above instruction that the computer ultimately follows would then be:

0110100110101011

*machine
language*

Programs written in the form of zeros and ones are said to be written in *machine language*, because that is the version of the program that the computer (the *machine*) actually reads and follows. Assembly language and machine language are almost the same thing and the distinction between them will not be important to us. The important distinction is that between machine language and a high level language such as Pascal.

Do not bother to memorize our assembly language instruction to add two numbers, nor its translation into a string of zeros and ones. The exact assembly language instructions and their translation to zeros and ones will differ from machine to machine. The only point to remember is that any high level language must be translated into machine language before the computer can understand and follow the program.

compiler

A program that translates a high level language, like Pascal, to a machine language is called a *compiler*. A compiler is thus a somewhat peculiar sort of program in that its input or data is some other program and its output is yet another program. To avoid confusion, the input program is usually called the *source program* and the translated version is called the *object program* or *object code*. The word *code* is frequently used to mean a program or a part of a program, and this usage is particularly common when referring to object programs.

Now, suppose you want to run a Pascal program. In order to get the computer to follow your Pascal instructions, proceed as follows. First, run the compiler using your Pascal program as data. Notice that in this case the Pascal program is not being treated as a set of instructions. To the compiler your Pascal program is just a long string of characters. The output will be another long string of characters, which is the machine language equivalent of the Pascal program.

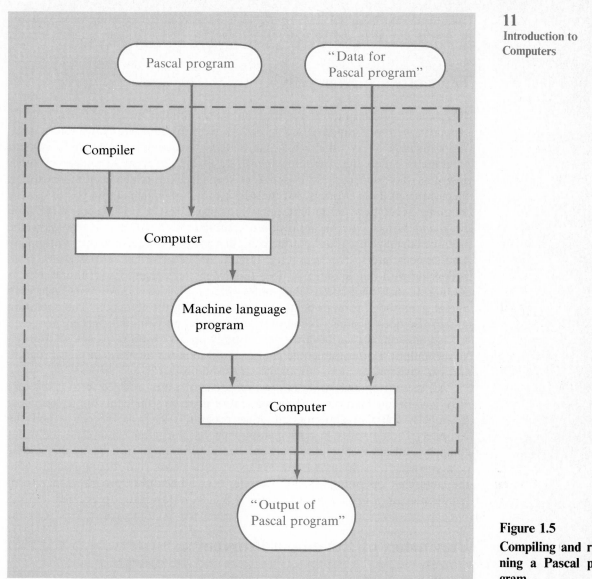

Figure 1.5
**Compiling and run-
ning a Pascal pro-
gram.**

Next, run this machine language program on what we normally think of as the
data for the Pascal program. The output will be what we normally conceptualize
as the output of the Pascal program. The process is easier to visualize if you have
two computers available, as diagramed in Figure 1.5.

In reality, the entire process just described is facilitated on one computer by
special programs called *systems programs*. Although there is but one computer,
the systems programs make it appear as though a big box, represented by the
dotted line in Figure 1.5, were built around two computers. You simply place
your Pascal program and data in the box and the rest is usually taken care of
automatically. Hence, you can think of the computer as actually running the

Pascal program. None of this is peculiar to Pascal. The translation process is the same with any high level programming language.

The Software Hierarchy

operating
system

The preceding description is a correct but oversimplified picture of what actually happens when you run a Pascal program. Systems programs on modern computers include many other programs besides the compiler. The main systems program is called the *operating system*. It is the program in charge of other programs, the "manager" so to speak. It keeps track of which program is run on which piece of data; it brings out the editor program, which allows you to use the computer as a typewriter in writing up your programs; it puts the editor program away and brings out the appropriate compiler when needed; it also runs the machine language program that the compiler produces. On a computer with many simultaneous users, the operating system also keeps the various users from interfering with one another. It does this by moving resources from one user to another at such high speeds that, unless the number of users is very high, each user is given the illusion of being the only one using the computer. The operating system also does whatever accounting and security checking are needed. While all this is going on, the various programs usually produce various pieces of information as output. For example, the compiler will look for mistakes in your program and will give one or more output messages should it find any errors.

All these programs working together are sometimes referred to as a *software hierarchy*. In this hierarchical arrangement of programs the operating system is at the top. It controls a number of other programs, such as the editor and the compiler. The compiler in turn manipulates your program, and, on a multiuser computer, other Pascal programs. Your Pascal program in turn manipulates some data. Viewing a computer system in this way, there are four identifiable levels in the hierarchy: operating system, compiler and other utility programs, user programs, such as your Pascal program, and finally, data for user programs.

Pragmatics of Running a Program

editor

files

We have outlined the basic tasks involved in running a program. They are common to all systems. However, the details will vary from system to system and you must find out all these details before you can run a program. Your system will have a program, called an *editor*, that lets you use the computer as a typewriter. The system will also allow you to store programs and to retrieve them at a later time. The program that controls this storing and retrieving is usually called a *file manager*, or some similar term such as *file system* or *filer*. You will need to learn how to use both the editor and file manager. Finally, you will have to learn how to get the compiler program to translate your program into machine code and how to run the machine language program. (On many systems the processes of compiling and then running the program are combined into a single process.)

None of this is difficult, but there can be a lot of details to learn. Your best sources of information for these details are manuals, your instructor if you are in a course, and friends who already know the details. Although you will need to find out these details about your computer system, at this point you do not need to know anything about how to write a program in Pascal or in any other programming language. The rest of this book is devoted to teaching you how to go from a problem to a Pascal program to solve that problem.

Designing Programs

Designing a program is frequently a difficult task. There is no complete set of rules, no algorithm to tell you how to write programs. Program design is a creative process. Still, there are some useful hints, some guidelines that can help the creative process along.

The first step in designing a program is to be certain the task to be solved is completely and precisely specified. Do not take this step lightly. If you do not know exactly what you want as the output of your program, you may be surprised at what your program produces. Be certain that you know what the input to the program will be and exactly what information is supposed to be in the output, as well as what form that information should be in. For example, if the program is a bank accounting program, you must know not only the interest rate, but also whether it is to be compounded annually, monthly, daily or whatever. If the program is supposed to write poetry, can the poems be in free verse or must they be in iambic pentameter or some other meter?

problem definition

Once the problem is completely defined and understood, the basic algorithm can be designed and expressed in ordinary English or some stylized version of English. This is the hardest part of designing a program. In the next section we outline a plan of attack for designing this algorithm. The last and easiest step is to translate the algorithm into Pascal or some other programming language.

Top-Down Design

A good plan of attack for designing an algorithm is to break down the task to be accomplished into a few big subtasks, then decompose each big subtask into smaller subtasks, then replace the smaller subtasks by even smaller subtasks and so forth. Eventually the subtasks become so small that they are trivial to implement in Pascal or whatever language you are using. This method is usually called *stepwise refinement* or *top-down design* or more graphically *divide and conquer*. Occasionally, the method is referred to as *structured programming*, although the latter usually refers to a larger theory of which stepwise refinement is a key idea.

stepwise refinement

Not only is stepwise refinement an efficient design method, it also produces a good algorithm in the sense that the algorithm is easier to understand and subsequent modifications are relatively easy to make. This is very important as most programs are changed at some time, and some of them are being changed constantly. For example, a simple computerized airline reservation system might be expanded to keep track of seat as well as flight reservations. As another example, a program designed to interact with English-speaking users might be modified to produce a version that interacts in Spanish.

As a concrete example of stepwise refinement, let us consider the design of an algorithm to compute the amount of state income tax owed by an individual. The state in question has the following graduated tax rates. (Net income is computed to the nearest dollar.)

1. No tax is paid on the first $15,000 of net income.

2. A tax of 5% is assessed on each dollar of net income from $15,001 to $30,000.

3. A tax of 10% is assessed on each dollar of net income over $30,000.

For example, if a person's net income is $38,000, then the first $15,000 is tax free, the next $15,000 is taxed at a rate of 5% and the last $8,000 is taxed at a rate of 10%. So this person's tax liability is $0 plus $750 plus $800, for a total state tax bill of $1,550.

One way to divide the computation into subtasks is the following:

```
begin
    1. Determine the net income;
    2. Determine the amount of tax due at the 5% rate;
    3. Determine the amount of tax due at the 10% rate;
    4. Add the amounts calculated in steps 2 and 3
        {The result is the total amount of tax owed.}
end.
```

Step 4 is already very small and can be left for direct translation into the programming language. Subtasks 1, 2 and 3 can be refined further. When designing an algorithm for one of these subtasks, you need not be concerned with the other subtasks. Each subtask is treated as a separate design task.

Analyzing subtask 1 we see that it can be decomposed into:

```
begin
    1a. Determine gross income;
    1b. Determine adjustments to income;
    1c. Subtract adjustments to income from gross income
        {The result is the net income.}
end.
```

Subtask 2 is subjected to a separate design effort, which produces the following decomposition:

```
begin
    2a. Compute the fraction of net income in the range $15,001 to $30,000
        and call this amount FirstChunk;
    2b. Multiply FirstChunk by 0.05
        {The result is the amount of tax due at the 5% rate.}
end.
```

These smaller subtasks may need to be further subdivided into even smaller subtasks. For example, subtask 2b is small enough, but subtask 2a can be decomposed as follows:

begin
    2a-1. If the net income is $30,000 or less, then **FirstChunk** is the net income minus $15,000;
    2a-2. If the net income is over $30,000, then **FirstChunk** is $15,000
end.

Subtask 3 is handled in a manner similar to subtask 2; it decomposes into:

begin
    3a. Compute the amount of net income over $30,000 and call this amount **SecondChunk**;
    3b. Multiply **SecondChunk** by 0.10
        {The result is the amount of tax due at the 10% rate.}

Subtask 3a, in turn, decomposes into:

begin
    3a-1. If the net income is $30,000 or less, then **SecondChunk** is zero;
    3a-2. If the net income is over $30,000,
          then **SecondChunk** is the net income minus $30,000
end.

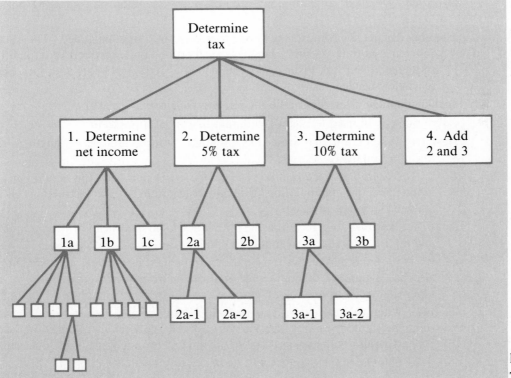

Figure 1.6
Top-down design.

To get a complete algorithm, some of the tasks require further refinement. For example, determining gross income would be decomposed into the subtasks determine wages and salaries, determine interest income, determine dividend income, determine capital gains and so forth. Moreover, some of these subtasks may need still further refinement. As an example, the capital gains computation divides into computing long-term and short-term capital gains. This decomposing of tasks into subtasks is diagramed in Figure 1.6.

The diagram in Figure 1.6 will also help to explain why stepwise refinement is also called *top-down* design. The various tasks shown are formulated starting at the top of the figure and proceeding down the page.

◇

There was a most ingenious Architect who had contrived a new Method for building Houses, by beginning at the Roof, and working downwards to the Foundation...

Jonathan Swift, Gulliver's Travels

◇

Summary of Terms

algorithm   Detailed, unambiguous, step-by-step instructions for carrying out a task.

assembly language   Almost the same thing as machine language. The only difference is that assembly language instructions are expressed in a slightly more readable form, instead of being coded as strings of zeros and ones. See **machine language**.

auxiliary storage   Another name for *secondary memory*.

code   Sometimes used to mean a program or part of a program.

compiler   A program that translates programs from a high level language to machine language.

CPU   The *central processing unit* of a computer. It performs the actual calculations and the manipulation of memory according to the instructions in a machine language program.

data   The word has two meanings: (1) the input to an algorithm or program; (2) any information that is available to an algorithm or to a computer.

editor   A program that allows the computer to be used as a typewriter. An editor also has a number of commands that are more powerful than those of a typewriter, such as moving an entire piece of text from one place to another.

execute   When an instruction is carried out by a computer, either directly or in some translated form, the computer is said to execute the instruction. When a computer follows the instructions in a complete program, it is said to execute the program.

file manager   Also sometimes called a *filer* or *file system*. A program that allows the user to store and retrieve objects called files. Among other things, a file can contain a Pascal program. Hence, a file manager is the program used to store and retrieve Pascal programs.

hardware   The actual physical parts of a computer or computer system.

high level language   A programming language which includes larger, more powerful instructions and, typically, a grammar that is somewhat like English. Programs in a high level language usually cannot be directly executed by computers. See **machine language**.

machine language   A language that can be directly executed by a computer. Programs in machine language consist of very simple instructions, such as "Add two numbers." These simple instructions are coded as strings of zeros and ones. See **assembly language**.

main memory   The memory that the computer uses as temporary "scratch paper" when actually carrying out a computation. See **secondary memory**.

object program   The translated version of a program produced by a compiler. See **source program**.

operating system   A program that is part of the system software of a computer. It is the program that controls and manages all other programs.

program   An algorithm that a computer can either follow directly or translate and then follow the translated version.

running a program   When a program and some data are given to a computer in such a way that the computer is instructed to carry out the program using the data, that is called running the program (on the data).

secondary memory   The memory a computer uses to store information in a permanent or semipermanent state. (When the computer does not have sufficient main memory for a computation, then it is also used as an addition to main memory.) See **main memory**.

software   Another term for programs.

source program   The input program to be translated by a compiler is called the source program. See **object program**.

system software   Refers collectively to all the programs that handle user programs. Included under this heading are such programs as compilers and operating systems.

Exercises

The exercises are divided into two classifications. The Self-Test and Interactive Exercises are to help you get the feel of the material. They should be done first, and they need only be done quickly and casually. When they are programming assignments they need not have as nice a style as the Regular Exercises. Many of the Self-Test and Interactive Exercises have answers in the back of the book so that you can check your answers. The

Regular Exercises should be done carefully. In classes, they are suitable homework to be assigned and graded. It is not necessary to do all the exercises. However, you should do most of the Self-Test and Interactive Exercises and at least some of the Regular Exercises.

Self-Test and Interactive Exercises

1. A good illustration of an algorithm is the instruction set for the U.S. Internal Revenue Service's long form 1040. If you have a copy readily available, read it through, noticing how very explicit the instructions are.

2. Most individuals have income tax deducted (withheld) from their pay check. Change the outline of our algorithm for computing tax so that it also accounts for tax withheld.

3. Write an algorithm to add two whole numbers. The input to the algorithm is to be two strings of digits representing the two numbers. For example, the number 1066 is thought of as the four symbols 1-0-6-6. The algorithm should be capable of being followed by a child who has not yet learned to do addition.

4. Write an algorithm to subtract one whole number from another. The rules are the same as in the previous exercise.

5. Write an algorithm to tell if an input word is a palindrome. A *palindrome* is a word which is the same spelled backwards and forwards, such as "radar."

6. Write an algorithm to count the number of occurrences of each letter in an input word. For example, the input word "pop" contains two p's and one o.

Regular Exercises

7. Write an algorithm to multiply two whole numbers. The rules are the same as in Exercise 3.

8. Write an algorithm to divide one whole number by another whole number. The rules are the same as in Exercise 3.

9. Write an algorithm that takes a page of text as data (input) and corrects the spacing according to the following rules: there should be exactly one space between two adjacent words, except that there are two spaces between adjacent sentences and paragraphs are indented by exactly three spaces. Define the start of a paragraph as one or more spaces (indentation) at the start of a line. The data may contain any number of spaces, except that you may assume that there are no spaces inside of words and that there is at least one space between any two words on the same line. The output is to be written onto a second sheet of paper.

10. Many banks and savings and loan institutions compute interest on a daily basis. On a balance of $1000 with an interest rate of 6%, the interest earned in one day is 0.06 times $1000 and then divided by 365 because it is only for one day of a 365 day year. This yields $0.16 in interest, so the balance is then $1000.16. The interest for the second day will be 0.06 times $1000.16 divided by 365. Design an algorithm which will take three inputs: the amount of a deposit, the interest rate and a duration in weeks. The algorithm should then calculate the account balance at the end of the duration specified.

11. Negotiating a consumer loan is not always straightforward. One form of loan is the discount installment loan, which works as follows. Suppose a loan has a face value of $1000, the interest rate is 15% and the duration is 18 months. The interest is computed by multiplying the face value of $1000 by 0.15 to yield $150. That figure is then multiplied by

the loan period of 1.5 years to yield $225 as the total interest owed. That amount is immediately deducted from the face value leaving the consumer with only $775. Repayment is made in equal monthly installments based on the face value. So the monthly loan payment will be $1000 divided by 18 or $55.56. This method of calculation may not be too bad if the consumer needs $775 dollars, but the calculation is a bit more complicated if the consumer needs $1000. Design an algorithm that will take three inputs: the amount the consumer needs to receive, the interest rate and the duration of the loan in months. The algorithm should then calculate the face value required in order for the consumer to receive the amount needed and should also calculate the monthly payment.

References for Further Reading

K. Bowles, *Beginner's Guide for the UCSD Pascal System*, 1980, Byte Books, Peterborough, N.H. If you are using a version of UCSD Pascal, this reference will explain how to use the editor, filer, compiler and similar utility programs.

L. Goldschlager and A. Lister, *Computer Science—A Modern Introduction*, 1982, Prentice-Hall International Series in Computer Science, Prentice-Hall, Englewood Cliffs, N.J. Discusses many of the issues in this chapter in more detail. Is written at the introductory level.

T. Kidder, *The Soul of a New Machine*, 1981, Avon Books, New York. This is a popular description of the engineering effort that went into designing a specific computer. It is entertaining and you do pick up a few technical facts as well.

M. Overgaard and S. Stringfellow, *Personal Computing with the UCSD P-System*, 1983, Prentice-Hall, Englewood Cliffs, N.J. An alternative reference to the Bowles book.

I. Pohl and A. Shaw, *The Nature of Computation*, *An Introduction to Computer Science*, 1981, Computer Science Press, Rockville Md. Discusses many of the issues in this chapter in more detail. Is written at the introductory level.

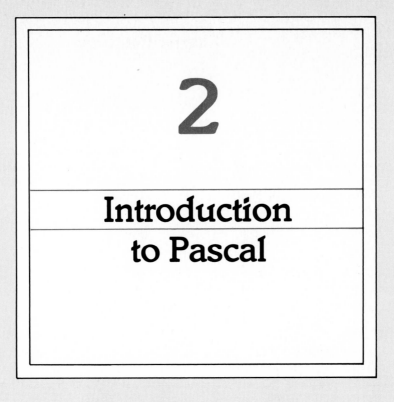

2

Introduction to Pascal

"Don't stand chattering to yourself like that," Humpty Dumpty said, looking at her for the first time, "but tell me your name and your business."

"My *name* is Alice, but—"

"It's a stupid name enough!" Humpty Dumpty interrupted impatiently. "What does it mean?"

"*Must* a name mean something?" Alice asked doubtfully.

"Of course it must," Humpty Dumpty said with a short laugh: "*my* name means the shape I am—and a good handsome shape it is, too. With a name like yours you might be any shape, almost."

Lewis Carroll,
Through the Looking-Glass

Chapter Contents

In this chapter we give an introduction to the Pascal programming language. We explain some sample programs and present enough details of the Pascal language to allow you to write some simple programs. We will also continue the discussion of algorithm design that we began in Chapter 1 and will illustrate these design techniques by developing a complete Pascal program. We begin with a brief overview of the origins and purposes of the Pascal language.

The Pascal Language

Pascal is a high level, general-purpose programming language. When we say Pascal is a *general-purpose language* we mean that it is suitable for a diverse range of applications. Indeed, it is commonly used to write programs for a wide variety of applications including programs for numeric scientific calculations, for business data processing, and for text editing, as well as to write various systems programs including compilers.

The Pascal language was developed by Professor Niklaus Wirth and his colleagues at the Eidgenossische Technische Hochschule in Zurich, Switzerland, during the late 1960's and early 1970's. Wirth designed Pascal to be a good first programming language for people learning to program. Pascal therefore has a relatively small number of concepts to learn and digest. It has a design that facilitates the writing of programs in a style that is now generally accepted as good standard programming practice. Another of Wirth's design goals was ease of implementation. He designed the language so that it is relatively easy to write a Pascal compiler for a new type of machine. This is one of the reasons that it has become available on so many different computers in such a short amount of time. Needless to say, Pascal does have its shortcomings, and they will become apparent as you learn the language. Still, it is a good, possibly the best, language to use for learning to program computers. Moreover, it does not lose its usefulness after you learn the rudiments of programming. It is widely available and is frequently used by professional programmers, and it is fast becoming the standard language for many computing projects and even entire firms. Also, a number of other popular programming languages are similar to Pascal and are thus easy to learn once you have mastered Pascal.

The Notion of a Program Variable

Pascal and most other common programming languages perform their calculations by manipulating things called *variables*. In a Pascal program a variable is written as a string of letters and digits that begins with a letter. Some sample names for Pascal variables are:

`X   Y   Z   SUM   N1   N2   SALLY   Joe   rate Time`

Pascal variables have some similarity to the variables used in algebra and related branches of mathematics, but they very definitely are not the same thing.

Pascal variables are things that can hold numbers or other types of data. For the moment, we will confine our attention to variables that hold only numbers. These variables are rather like little blackboards on which the numbers can be written. Just as the numbers written on a blackboard can be changed, so too can the number held by a Pascal variable be changed. Just like blackboards, variables might possibly contain no number at all, or they might contain the number left there by the last person or thing which used the variable. The words *hold* and *contain* when applied to variables are exact synonyms and, if you think in terms

*variables
and
values*

Program

```pascal
program Sample(input, output);
  var N1, N2, SUM: integer;
begin
  writeln('Enter two numbers');
  readln(N1, N2);
  SUM := N1 + N2;
  writeln(N1, ' Plus ', N2, ' Equals ', SUM);
  writeln('Enter another two numbers');
  readln(N1, N2);
  SUM := N1 + N2;
  writeln(N1, ' Plus ', N2, ' Equals ', SUM)
end.
```

Sample Dialogue

Enter two numbers
4 5
　　4 Plus　　5 Equals　　　9
Enter another two numbers
8 9
　　8 Plus　　9 Equals　　　17

Figure 2.1
A Pascal program.

---

of the blackboard analogy, refer to the item written on the figurative blackboard. The number or other type of data held in a variable is called its *value*.

memory locations and variables

Most compilers translate variables into memory locations. A memory location is assigned to each variable, and the value of the variable, in a coded form consisting of zeros and ones, is kept in that location. For example, Figure 2.1 contains a Pascal program that uses the three variables **N1**, **N2** and **SUM**. When that program is compiled, the compiler might assign the locations 1001, 1002 and 1003 to the variables **N1**, **N2** and **SUM**, respectively. When the value of a variable is changed, the coded number in its assigned memory location changes to the new number. Whether or not your particular compiler actually makes this assignment of memory locations to variables is irrelevant, since it will make the program act as if just such an assignment had been made.

To illustrate how program variables can change their value, we will give a step-by-step explanation of the program displayed in Figure 2.1. In this example and throughout this book, we will assume that input is via a keyboard and that the output is via a display screen.

Stepping through a Program

statements

In Figure 2.1, the eight lines between **begin** and **end** contain eight instructions to be carried out by the computer. Such instructions are called *statements*. The semicolons at the ends of the statements are used to separate the statements and strictly speaking are not part of the statements. That is why the last statement is not followed by a semicolon; there is no subsequent statement that it needs to be separated from. Minor points of punctuation like this need not be a serious concern for us yet. For now, simply note that the semicolons must be there. If you prefer, it is perfectly acceptable to add a semicolon after the last statement and thereby make things uniform. The program will perform identically with or without the extra semicolon.

The word **writeln** in the first line is pronounced "write-line." This first statement does not affect any variables. It simply causes the following phrase to appear on the display screen:

Enter two numbers

Suppose that, in response to this, an obedient user types two numbers on the keyboard, say **4**, followed by a space, followed by a **5**, followed by pressing the return key. (The return key is the one which starts a new line, much like the carriage return on a typewriter.)

The next statement, which is shown below, tells the computer what to do with these numbers.

readln(N1, N2)

(We will usually not bother to show the final semicolon when displaying lines out of a program like this.) The word **readln** is pronounced "read-line." This statement is an instruction to the computer to "read" the two numbers into the variables **N1** and **N2**. It causes the value of the variable **N1** to become equal to the first number typed in, namely **4**, and the value of **N2** to become equal to the second number typed in, namely **5**. Recall that our hypothetical compiled translation of the Pascal program assigned memory location 1001 to **N1** and 1002 to **N2**. This means that location 1001 in the computer's memory will contain a coded version of the number **4**. Similarly, location 1002 will contain the code for **5**. Prior to this time, the variables **N1** and **N2** had no value.

The next statement in our sample program is:

SUM := N1 + N2

The meaning of the part **N1 + N2** is what you might guess. It instructs the computer to add the value of **N1** to the value of **N2**. In other words add **4** to **5** and get **9**. When the translated version of this statement is executed, the computer (the CPU, to be precise) will retrieve the **4** from location 1001 and the **5** from location 1002 and add them together to obtain **9**. This statement also says what is to become of the resultant number **9**. It becomes the value of the variable **SUM** and so goes into the location, namely 1003, assigned to **SUM**.

The symbolism **:=** is called the *assignment operator*, and statements such as the one under discussion are called *assignment statements*. The assignment operator is composed of two symbols, a colon and an equal sign, but it is considered to be one item and is always treated as a single unit. In particular, there should not be a space between the colon and the equal sign. The assignment operator has no

assignment operator

113,348

College of St. Francis Library
Joliet, Illinois

standard pronunciation. Many people pronounce it "gets the value," which describes the action; others simply pronounce it "assignment operator." Some people even read it literally as "colon equals," but the meaning of the assignment operator is not derived from the usual meaning of the colon and equal symbols. The meaning of **:=** is that it changes the value of the variable on the left-hand side to whatever value is given on the right-hand side. We will say more about the assignment operator shortly, but first let us explain the rest of our sample program.

The next statement in our sample program is:

```
writeln(N1, ' Plus ', N2, ' Equals ', SUM)
```

It shows the result of the assignment statement by causing the following phrase to appear on the screen:

```
4 Plus    5 Equals    9
```

For the moment, do not worry about why the word **write** is embellished with a funny ending or why words like **' Plus '** are written with single quotes and blanks before and after them. We will come back to those details shortly. For now, simply note that the values of the variables and the words in quotes are output to the screen in the order in which they occur in such **writeln** statements.

*changing
the value
of a
variable*

The rest of the program is almost a repetition of what we have just discussed. The program requests another two numbers with the statement:

```
writeln('Enter another two numbers')
```

This time, let us suppose that the user types in **8** and **9**, again separated by a blank and with the line terminated by pressing the return key. The two numbers are read when the program executes the next statement in the program:

```
readln(N1, N2)
```

This second read-line statement sets the value of **N1** equal to **8** and the value of **N2** equal to **9**. The old values of **4** and **5** are lost.

Next comes the second assignment statement:

```
SUM := N1 + N2
```

This changes the value of **SUM** to the value of **N1** plus the value of **N2**. In other words, the value of **SUM** is changed to **8** plus **9**, or **17**. The old value of **SUM** is lost. The final **writeln** statement outputs these new values of **N1**, **N2** and **SUM**.

Figure 2.1 also shows the complete dialogue between the computer and the user as it would appear on the screen. The material typed in by the user and the output produced by the program are shown in different typefaces, which will help to clarify where the different lines came from. In reality, they would appear in the same typeface.

Now that you have one complete Pascal program, you can type it up and run it.

College of St. Francis Library

More about Assignment Statements

An *assignment statement* always consists of a variable on the left-hand side of the assignment operator and an expression on the right-hand side. This statement instructs the computer to evaluate the expression on the right-hand side and to set the value of the variable equal to that value of the expression. A few more examples may help to clarify the way these statements work.

The expression on the right-hand side of an assignment operator may use the subtraction sign or the multiplication sign instead of the addition sign. The Pascal multiplication sign is nontraditional and is represented by an asterisk, like so:

expression

```
SUM := N1 * N2
```

This statement changes the value of **SUM** to the product of the values of **N1** and **N2**. Of course that makes **SUM** a poor choice for the name of our variable, but the program will still run. When the computer sees the identifier **SUM**, it will know it is a variable capable of storing numbers, but it does not know or care that it spells an English word indicating addition. The computer is perfectly willing to use it for differences or products as well as sums.

The expression on the right-hand side of an assignment statement can simply be another variable. The statement

```
N1 := N2
```

changes the value of the variable **N1** so that it is the same as that of the variable **N2**. The value of **N2** is not affected. This example is illustrated in Figure 2.2.

As yet another example, the following changes the value of **N2** to **3**:

constants

```
N2 := 3
```

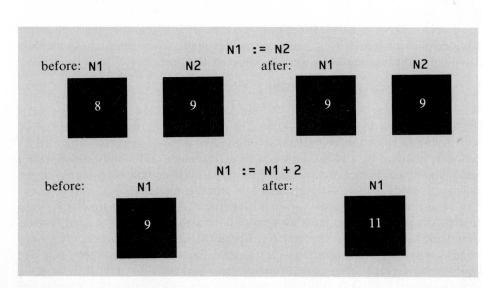

Figure 2.2
The assignment operator.

The number **3** on the right-hand side of the assignment operator is called a *constant* because, unlike a variable, its value cannot change.

Since variables can change value over time and since the assignment operator is one vehicle for changing their values, there is an element of time involved in the meaning of an assignment statement. First, the expression on the right-hand side of the assignment operator is evaluated. After that, the value of the variable on the left side of the operator is changed to the value that was obtained from that expression. This means that a variable can meaningfully occur on both sides of an assignment operator. As an example, consider:

```
N1 := N1 + 2
```

This statement will increase the value of **N1** by 2.

In the next chapter, we will have more to say about what expressions are allowed in an assignment statement. For now, let us move on to a discussion of some other types of data besides whole numbers.

Data Types—An Introduction

A *data type* is what the words say it is, namely a type or category of data. Each variable can hold only one type of data. In our sample Pascal program all variables were of type **integer**. That means that their values must be integers. An integer is any whole number such as:

```
38   0   1   89   3987   -12   -5
```

The value of a variable of type **integer** cannot be a fraction. The variables **N1**, **N2** and **SUM** in the program in Figure 2.1 can never contain fractions like 1/2 or 3.1416. Fractions are numbers of another data type called **real**, which we will discuss later in this section.

Every variable in a Pascal program must be *declared*, that is, the type of the variable must be stated. This is done at the beginning of the program. In our first sample program the variables were declared by the line:

```
var N1, N2, SUM: integer;
```

Here, as elsewhere in Pascal and virtually all programming languages, the rules for writing things down are very strict. The declaration must consist of the word ***var***, followed by one or more blanks, followed by a list of variables separated by commas, followed by a colon, followed by a type name, and finally ended with a semicolon. Extra blanks may be added so long as you do not insert blanks in the middle of words such as ***var***, **integer** or variable names.

There are two reasons for requiring these declarations: to clarify your thinking by reminding you of what type of data the variable will be used for and to provide information to the compiler. Recall that the computer has only strings of zeros and ones in memory. In order to treat these strings as integers, it uses a code to encode each integer as a string of zeros and ones. In order to treat these strings as letters, it uses a different code to encode letters as strings of zeros and ones. The declaration tells the compiler and ultimately the computer which code to use.

Numbers that include a fractional part, such as the ones below, are of type **real**:

2.71828   0.098   -15.8   100053.98

When such numbers appear in a Pascal program they are called *constants*. All number constants have a type, either **integer** or **real**, and must be written according to the prescribed rules for their data type. Constants of type **integer** must not contain a decimal point. Constants of type **real** may be written in two different forms. The above constants are written in the simpler of these two forms.

The simple form for **real** constants is like the everyday way of writing decimal fractions. **real** constants written in this form must contain a decimal point and must contain at least one digit before and one digit after the decimal point. No number in Pascal may contain a comma. Hence none of the following are allowed as constants of type **real** (or as constants of type **integer**):

1,000   .009   -.05   72.

A variable **Z** is declared to be of type **real** in the following way:

var Z: real;

In Pascal, division can be expressed using a slash. So, **N1 / N2** means divide the value of **N1** by the value of **N2**. When we were discussing expressions, we mentioned addition, subtraction, multiplication but not division. It was not an oversight that caused us to omit division. We omitted it because we had not yet introduced the type **real**, and an expression that is the quotient of two numbers always yields a value of type **real**. Hence, in the following assignment statement, the variables **N1** and **N2** might be of type **integer** or of type **real**, but the variable **Z** can only be of type **real**:

Z := N1 / N2

Conceptually, every whole number is both an integer and a real number. However, the computer makes a distinction between whole numbers considered to be of type **integer** and whole numbers considered to be of type **real**. In particular, the constant for the **integer** three is written **3** whereas the constant for the **real** number three is written **3.0**. We will have more to say about this distinction in the next chapter.

The type for letters or, more generally, any single symbol is **char**, which is short for "character". Values of this type are frequently called *characters* in books and in conversation, but in Pascal programs this type must always be spelled in the abbreviated fashion **char**. Two variables **X** and **Y** of type **char** are declared as follows:

var X, Y: char;

A variable of type **char** can hold any character on the input keyboard. So, for

reals

number constants

characters

char

Program

```
program Tricky(input, output);
   var X, Y: char;
begin
   X := 'A';
   Y := X;
   writeln('The first value of Y is:');
   writeln(Y);

   Y := 'X';
   writeln('The second value of Y is:');
   writeln(Y);

   writeln('I hope this helped to explain quotes.')
end.
```

Sample Dialogue

The first value of Y is:
A
The second value of Y is:
X
I hope this helped to explain quotes.

**Figure 2.3
Using single quotes
for characters.**

example, **X** could hold an ´**A**´ or a ´**+**´ or an ´**a**´. If both upper- and lower-case letters are available, they are considered to be different characters.

quotes   The single quotes indicate that we literally mean the letter. Hence, **X** is used for a variable named **X**, whereas ´**X**´ is used for the upper case version of the third from the last letter of the alphabet. This is an important distinction. For example, the statement

Y := X

changes the value of the variable **Y** to the value of the variable **X**. So, if **X** contains the letter ´**A**´, then this statement will change the value of **Y** to ´**A**´. On the other hand, the statement

Y := ´X´

changes the value of the variable **Y** to the letter ´**X**´, which is quite another thing. The program in Figure 2.3 illustrates this important distinction.

Unlike some printed texts, Pascal has only one kind of single quote; the opening quote and the closing quote are the same symbol.

Expressions consisting of a character in single quotes, such as ´**X**´, are also called *constants* and are in fact the same sort of objects as the number constants, such as **3** and **5.98**, except that they are of a different type, specifically the type **char**. There are constants of other types as well and we will discuss them as the opportunities arise.

It is perfectly acceptable to have variables of more than one type in a program. In such cases they are all declared at once following the format illustrated below:

```
var N1, N2: integer;
    Time: real;
    Initial: char;
```

Note that the word **var** is only used once, no matter how many variables are declared and no matter how many variable types are used in the declarations.

The variables need not be declared in any particular order. For instance, the above declaration is equivalent to the following one:

```
var Initial: char;
    N1: integer;
    Time: real;
    N2: integer;
```

The best order is the one that groups the variables according to how they are used in the program.

Simple Output

The values of variables as well as strings of text may be output to the screen with **writeln** statements, such as those used in our sample program. There may be any combination of variables of different types as well as strings to be output. The strings of characters are included in single quotes. The items to be output are listed in the order in which they are to appear on the screen. By way of example, consider the following piece of code taken from a Pascal program in which **LETTER** is a variable of type **char** and **NUM** is a variable of type **integer**:

```
NUM := 76;
LETTER := 'C';
writeln(LETTER, ' is a symbol ', NUM, ' an integer')
```

That **writeln** will cause the following line to appear on the screen:

```
C is a symbol   76 an integer
```

No extra space is inserted before or after strings or the values of variables of type **char**, which is why the quoted strings in the samples usually start and end with a blank. The blanks keep the various strings and numbers from running together.

When outputting numbers, the computer system follows an algorithm that is supposed to choose a number of spaces that will look good. On many systems it looks like too many spaces have been left. Other systems go to the opposite extreme and insert no blanks at all; on those systems you must explicitly insert a blank, or other separator, between any two consecutive numbers. In any event, if you are not happy with the spacing the system provides for numbers, then you can specify the spacing you desire inside of the **writeln** statement. The way to do that is discussed in the next section.

Values of type **real** are output in a form that requires some explanation. If **X** is a variable of type **real**, then the statements:

```
X := 1234.56;
writeln(X)
```

are likely to produce an output that looks something like the following:

1.2345600000000E03

This output is not an error but is another way of writing the number 1234.56. The *E* stands for exponent and means multiply by 10 raised to the power which follows the *E*. Hence, the above output means:

1.23456×10^3

To decode this sort of output, move the decimal point to the right the number of places written after the *E*. In the sample you take *1.2345600...* and move the decimal point *03*, that is three, places to the right. If the number after the *E* is negative, then move the decimal point the indicated number of spaces to the left, inserting extra zeros if need be. To take another example, the output

1.23456000000000E – 02

means the fraction 0.0123456.

The suffix **Ln** on the word **write** is short for "line." It is usually pronounced "line" but it is always spelled **Ln**. Including the **Ln** instructs the computer to start a new line for the next item output. For example consider the two statements:

```
writeln('First line');
writeln('Second line')
```

They will cause the following to appear on the screen:

*First line
Second line*

On the other hand, consider the two statements:

```
write('First line');
writeln('Second line')
```

They will cause the following to appear on the screen:

First lineSecond line

The last output statement in a program should always be a **writeln** rather than a **write**. This is because some systems require that the end of all lines, including the last line of output, be explicitly indicated.

While we are on the subject, we should note two minor but useful properties of **writeln**. First, you can use **writeln** without specifying anything to output. This simply causes the computer to skip to the next line, which is handy for skipping lines and when you do use **write**. Hence, the three statements

```
write('Line one');
writeln;
writeln('Line two')
```

are equivalent to the two statements:

```
writeln('Line one');
writeln('Line two')
```

The second, more minor but occasionally useful, property is that you can place expressions inside of a **write** or **writeln** statement. So the following is permitted and has the obvious meaning:

```
writeln(N1, ' Plus ', N2, ' Equals ', N1 + N2)
```

Formatted Output

When using **write** or **writeln** you can specify the exact number of spaces used to display each value that is output. To do so, simply add a colon and a number after the expression, variable or quoted string which is to be output. The number following the colon is called a *field width* and specifies the total number of spaces allocated for outputting the number or other type of value. For example,

field widths

```
N := 123;
writeln('Start-field', N:5,'End-field');
```

produces the following output (there are two spaces between the *d* and the *1*):

```
Start-field   123End-field
```

Any extra spaces are always in front of the value being output. If you allow too few spaces, it is not a disaster; the computer will allocate more space, but the format may not be what you desired.

In your first few programs it may be best to omit field width specifications and just settle for the spacing that the system decides on. Even after you become proficient at designing fancy output, it makes sense to omit such detail on your first version of a program. First get your program to work. Then go back and add the field widths if you want neater output. This is a good example of the divide-and-conquer strategy we introduced in Chapter 1. The task of designing a program can frequently be subdivided into two main subtasks: computing some quantities and displaying them in a neat and clear manner. When solving the problem of how to compute the quantities, there is no need to confuse the issue with questions about the number of spaces needed to output the quantities. That is a separate task.

In this book we will frequently omit field width specifications from the **write** and **writeln** statements in our sample programs. This is to keep the programs simple and to avoid cluttering the examples with details irrelevant to the point being discussed. In many cases, the program presented is only a solution to the task of computing quantities. In order to get a program with neat looking output, it may be necessary to add some field width specifications.

There is at least one case which definitely demands a field width and other related output *field specifications* in order to avoid looking ridiculous. When the output is an amount of dollars and cents, an output without a field specification usually looks absurd.

Total cost including tax is **$** *1.56347690000000E01*

The above screen display is a poor way to say the cost is $15.63. Some **writeln** statements with field specifications that avoid this problem are included in the sample program given in Figure 2.4. For example, one **writeln** statement uses a field specification of **:7:2**. The first number, the **7**, says to allow a total of seven spaces for the output. The second number, the **:2**, says to allow two digits after the decimal point. This second number is also preceded by a colon, and if the second number is present, that tells the computer not to use the *E* notation. As an

---

Program

```
program Cashier(input, output);
  var PRICE, TAX, TOTAL: real;
begin
  writeln('Enter PRICE of item, then press return');
  writeln('Do NOT type in a dollar sign, $');
  readln(PRICE);

  TAX := PRICE * 0.06;
  TOTAL := PRICE+TAX;

  writeln('Tax on $', PRICE:7:2, ' is $', TAX:6:2);
  writeln('Total cost including tax is $', TOTAL:7:2)
end.
```

Sample Dialogue

Enter PRICE of item, then press return
Do NOT type in a dollar sign, $
19.98
Tax on $ 19.98 is $ 1.20
Total cost including tax is $ 21.18

Figure 2.4
A program that uses output field specifications.

example, consider the following two lines from a Pascal program:

```
COST := 15.63;
writeln('Total cost including tax is $' COST:7:2)
```

These two lines will produce the following output (there are two spaces between the $ and the *1*.):

Total cost including tax is $ 15.63

Input

readln

read and **readln** are for input and are analogous to **write** and **writeln**. They are written the same way, namely with a list of items separated by commas and enclosed in parentheses. In this case all the items must be variables. They instruct the computer to read values typed in from the keyboard and to set the values of the variables equal to the values read in.

Variables of the types **integer**, **real** and **char** may be given values with a **read** or **readln** statement. Later we will introduce other data types besides these three. However, on most systems only values of type **integer**, **real**, and **char** may be read in from the keyboard.

*type
conflicts*

You may mix the types of the variables in a single **read** or **readln** statement, but the types of the values input must match the types of the variables listed in parentheses. Suppose, by way of example, that a program contains the following declaration:

```
var COUNT: integer;
    AVERAGE: real;
```

and the following **readln** statement:

```
readln(COUNT, AVERAGE)
```

Then it is acceptable to type in the following:

```
12   6.95
```

This will work fine since the first value is of type **integer** and the second is of type **real**. The value of **COUNT** will be changed to **12** and the value of **AVERAGE** will be changed to **6.95**. Suppose you do not type in the **12** first, but instead reverse the entries and type in:

```
6.95   12
```

There is then a *type conflict*. You have asked the computer to make **6.95** the value of **COUNT**. But that is against the rules. All values of **COUNT** must be of type **integer** and **6.95** is of type **real**. Similarly, there is a type conflict in your request to change the value of **AVERAGE** to **12**. All values of **AVERAGE** must be of type **real** and **12** is of type **integer**. This second conflict is not too serious, since the system will automatically convert an **integer** value to an approximately equivalent **real** value when filling a variable of type **real**. However, it will not automatically convert **real** values to **integer** values.

Just what happens when you make such a mistake varies from one computer system to another. Ideally, the computer should send an error message to the screen. In some, less ideal but unfortunately typical, installations the computer will set the values of **COUNT** and **AVERAGE** to some strange value and proceed with the program. In almost any installation your program becomes useless when this happens. Your only recourse is to start your program over again.

When entering numbers, you must insert one or more blanks between numbers on the same line so that the computer knows where one number ends and the next begins. The situation with characters is different. Anything you type in, including a blank, is a value of type **char**. Hence, there is no space before an input character that is intended for a variable of type **char**. To avoid problems, at least until you are more familiar with input, it is best not to use variables of type **char** except in **read** or **readln** statements that have only that one variable.

The difference between **read** and **readln** is that **readln** instructs the computer to go to the next line, causing the rest of the input on the current line to be discarded. The exact details are different for numbers and for character input.

When reading in numbers with either **read** or **readln**, the computer will automatically go to the next line when it runs out of values on the current line. The only difference between the two is that with **read** the computer does not go to the next line until the line it is on has been exhausted. On the other hand, after the computer completes a **readln**, it discards anything remaining on the current line, and hence, any subsequent **read** or **readln** will take its first value from the next line.

When reading in characters, **readln** causes a similar discarding of the end of the current line; any subsequent **read** or **readln** will take its values from the next line of input. However, with character input, the computer does not automatically go to the next line when the current line is exhausted. If it requires a character to fill a variable of type **char** and there are no more characters on the current line, then the results are unpredictable. For data of type **char**, there must always be at least as many symbols on a line as the program expects.

A simple **readln**, without any variables, instructs the computer to disregard the rest of the input on the current line. For example, the two statements

```
read(X, Y);
readln
```

are equivalent to the single statement:

```
readln(X, Y)
```

Uses for the unadorned **readln** will occur to you naturally as your programming skills develop.

When the computer executes a **read** or **readln** it expects some data to be typed in at the keyboard. If none is typed in, it simply waits for it. The program must tell the user when to type in data. The computer will not automatically ask the user to enter data. That is why the sample programs contain statements like the following:

```
writeln('Enter two numbers')
```

These output statements *prompt* the user to enter input.

When writing your first few programs, it is probably best to avoid **read** and **write** in favor of **readln** and **writeln**. Using **writeln** and **readln** to organize the screen display into alternating lines of input and output is usually easier and safer than trying to integrate **read** and **write** instructions.

Batch Processing
(Optional)

On some systems, programs must be run in what is called *batch mode*. On these systems both the program and data are prepared ahead of time, frequently on punched cards, and then input to the computer simultaneously. A program designed to run in batch mode should have a different style of input and output. Since all the input is waiting to be read, there is no need for prompt lines. Since the output is not available until after the computer program has run to completion, the output usually needs some additional information to make sure that it is understandable. The output should be labeled to indicate clearly what output is paired with what input.

Designing Input and Output Instructions

sample input and output

The program in Figure 2.5 does nothing except carry on a little conversation. Still, it illustrates a number of concepts. Pay particular attention to the **readln** statements. The program asks for the user's first name, but the **readln** statement contains a variable of type **char**. As a result, only the first letter of the name is read into the computer. A similar thing is done with the user's last name. This is a common technique. Frequently it is natural for the user to type in a whole word in a situation where the program need only read the first letter. A common example of this is yes/no type questions. The user can type in **'yes'** or **'no'**, but the computer need only read in **'y'** or **'n'**. In such circumstances the program could tell the user to type only **'y'** or **'n'** but there is no reason to trouble the user with unnecessary instructions.

In Figure 2.5, the **readln** statements with no variables serve to stop the program. At the points where the computer reaches such statements, it simply halts and waits for the user to press the return key. The user's response is ignored. In this case the **readln** is used to trick the user into thinking the program is waiting for a response and will do something with the response. Another reason for using such unadorned **readln** statements is to freeze the screen so that the

Program

```
program Talk(input, output);
  var FirstI, LastI: char;
begin
  writeln('Good day. My name is Ronald Gollum,');
  writeln('but you can call me R.G.');
  writeln('Please answer using the keyboard, and please');
  writeln('end your answers by pressing the return key.');

  writeln('First things first, as they say.');
  writeln('So, please tell me your first name.');
  readln(FirstI);
  writeln('A very nice name, indeed!');
  writeln('And what is your last name?');
  readln(LastI);
  writeln('Pleased to meet you ', FirstI, '.', LastI, '.');

  writeln('It gets lonely inside this box.');
  writeln('Will you tell me something about the outside?');
  writeln('Is it raining out now?');
  readln;
  writeln('That is interesting.');

  writeln;
  writeln('Oh dear! I just remembered.');
  writeln('What time is it?');
  readln;
  writeln('Oh my! I seem to have lost track of time.');
  writeln('I really must go.');
  writeln('Good bye ', FirstI, '.', LastI, '.');
  writeln('I enjoyed talking with you.')
end.
```

Figure 2.5
A friendly program.

Good day. My name is Ronald Gollum,
but you can call me R.G.
Please answer using the keyboard, and please
end your answers by pressing the return key.
First things first, as they say.
So, please tell me your first name.
Marilyn
A very nice name, indeed!
And what is your last name?
Monroe
Pleased to meet you M.M.
It gets lonely inside this box.
Will you tell me something about the outside?
Is it raining out now?
Not right now
That is interesting.

Oh dear! I just remembered.
What time is it?
quarter to three
Oh my! I seem to have lost track of time.
I really must go.
Good bye M.M.
I enjoyed talking with you.

Figure 2.5 (cont'd)

user can read the output before the program proceeds and produces more output. If the output will not fit on one screen and no such provisions are made, then the first part of the output will flash by too rapidly to be read by the user.

Names: Identifiers

In Pascal, variables are written as strings of symbols. The string of symbols serves as the name of the variable. Pascal programs also have names. The name of the program in Figure 2.5 is **Talk**. As we learn more Pascal, we will encounter other Pascal objects that have names.

A name used in a Pascal program is called an *identifier* and is defined to be any string of letters and digits, provided the string starts with a letter. With the one exception to be discussed shortly, any Pascal identifier can be used as a variable in a Pascal program, and nothing else can be used as a variable. As examples, the following are all Pascal identifiers:

names for
variable

X X1 Sample ABC123z7 SUM Data1 Data2 TEMP

The following are not Pascal identifiers:

```
12   3X   DATA.1   FILE.TEXT   DATA-GOOD
```

The first two are not identifiers because they start with a digit rather than a letter. The remaining three are not identifiers because they contain symbols other than letters and digits.

long
identifiers

There is no limit to the length of a Pascal identifier but some computers (strictly speaking, some compilers) will ignore all characters after some specified number of initial characters. A common situation is for the computer to ignore all but the first eight characters of an identifier. From now on, we will assume that the computer does ignore all but the first eight characters. Even under this assumption, the following is a perfectly valid identifier:

```
TheFinalAnswer
```

In some contexts it may be the most sensible identifier to use, but remember that with such long identifiers, you must be certain that there is no other identifier with the same first eight letters. For example, the following three identifiers are for all practical purposes equal, since their first eight letters are the same:

```
TheFinalAnswer   TheFinalResult   TheFinal
```

There is nothing special about the number eight but there usually is some limit. The first versions of Pascal used eight as the limit. Many implementations still do use this limit, and no system uses a limit of fewer than eight characters. For that combination of reasons, it is a good idea to pretend that your system uses eight, even if it does not.

moving
programs

In order to keep from getting confused, you should not use two different names for the same variable, even if the names are equivalent on your system. Hence only one of the three equivalent identifiers displayed above should be used in any one program. There is another compelling reason for the rule of one identifier per variable. If you move your program to a system that has a limit greater than eight, your program will still work; otherwise, you might need to rename some of the variables.

upper-case
and
lower-case

Unfortunately, there is little uniformity in how systems treat upper- and lower-case letters in identifiers. If lower-case letters are available, then they may or may not be treated as being distinct from upper-case letters when they occur in identifiers. The original definition of Pascal as well as the current "official" standard definition of the language both state that the distinction between upper- and lower-case letters is to be ignored by the compiler when it processes identifiers. On systems that follow that rule, the identifiers **SUM**, **Sum** and **sum** are all equivalent. On the other hand, some systems treat upper- and lower-case letters as being distinct when they occur in identifiers. On those systems the above three identifiers would be distinct. Needless to say, under these circumstances it is not a good idea to rely on the distinction between upper- and lower-case letters when choosing identifiers. If your system treats **sum** and **SUM** as distinct, there is little reason to think some other system will. So it is best to use only one of the two variants.

These remarks also apply to upper- and lower-case letters in identifiers like *program*, *begin*, integer, and so forth, which have a standard meaning in the Pascal language. Your system might require that all these predefined identifiers be typed in all lower-case or all upper-case letters. If your compiler lists an error in the first word of your program, that is, in the identifier *program*, then try changing to all upper-case letters for such predefined identifiers. A few minutes of experimenting or questioning will easily clarify your system's requirements about when to use upper-case letters and when to use lower-case letters.

If both upper- and lower-case letters are available, then they are always treated as being different when they appear in quoted strings or as the values of variables of type char.

This book uses a convention on upper- and lower-case letters that is designed to emphasize certain concepts: all identifiers whose meaning is defined by the Pascal language are written using all lower-case letters; all identifiers that the programmer must make up are written using at least one upper-case letter, such as in SUM and TheAnswer. We never use two spellings that differ only in the case of some or all of their letters.

There is a special class of identifiers, called *reserved words*, that have a predefined meaning in the Pascal language and cannot be used as names for anything else, such as variables. The following is a complete list of all the reserved words we have seen so far:

reserved words

> *begin   end   program   var*

In this book all reserved words are written in boldface italic. A complete list of reserved words is given in Appendix 2.

You may wonder why the other words that we defined as part of the Pascal language are not on the list of reserved words. What about words like integer, char and readln? The answer is that they have a predefined meaning, but you are allowed to change their meaning. Such identifiers are called *standard identifiers* and, in this book are written in roman (ordinary) lower-case, boldface letters. Needless to say, using standard identifiers as names for things other than their standard meaning can be confusing and dangerous and, thus, should be avoided. The safest and easiest practice is to treat standard identifiers as if they were reserved words.

standard identifiers

Putting the Pieces Together

You now know enough details about Pascal to write a program. When doing so, you must be careful to put all the pieces together in the right order and with the correct punctuation. Your best bet for deciding on these details is to follow the examples of the sample programs given in this chapter. When reading the rest of this section, check to see that you can find each of the details mentioned in one of the sample programs. They occur in all the samples, so it does not matter which sample program you use.

Pascal programs start with a line called the *program heading*. This consists of the reserved word *program* followed by an identifier to serve as the name of the program, followed by the standard identifiers input and output, which are

program heading

separated by a comma and enclosed in parentheses. Finally, the heading is terminated with a semicolon. For example, if the program name is **Arthur**, then the heading would be:

```
program Arthur(input, output);
```

There should be a space between the identifier **program** and the program name. Other spaces can be added so long as no spaces are inserted in the middle of an identifier.

body

After the program heading come the variable declarations. Next comes the *body* of the program. The body of the program consists of a list of statements that serve as the instructions to be followed. This is the algorithm part and is set off by the reserved words **begin** and **end**. The statements are separated by semicolons. As already pointed out, there is no need for a semicolon after the last statement, since there is no other statement that it needs to be separated from. However, if you do insert an extra semicolon there, it will cause no problems. Pascal programs end with a period. The period comes after the identifier **end**.

spacing

In Pascal any two identifiers or numbers must be separated either by one or more spaces or by a line break or by a punctuation symbol (such as a comma, semicolon or colon) or by a combination of two or more of these separators. Hence the above displayed program heading cannot start out **programArthur**. Otherwise, Pascal allows a wide range of possible spacings. For example, the following program opening is allowed:

```
program Arthur ( input , output ) ;
```

line breaks

Pascal allows similar latitude in deciding when to start a new line. Two or more statements may be placed on the same line. With one exception, a line may be broken anyplace that a blank is allowed. The one exception is that you cannot break a quoted string across two lines. So the following is not allowed:

```
writeln('You may NOT break a quote
across two lines like this.')
```

Almost any pattern of spacing and line breaks will be acceptable to the compiler. However, as we point out in the next section, programs should always be arranged so as to make them easy to read.

Introduction to Programming Style

All the sample programs were laid out in a particular format. For example, the statements were all indented the same amount. Similarly, the declarations were aligned. This and other matters of style are of more than aesthetic interest. A program that is written with careful attention to style is easier to read, easier to correct if it contains a mistake and easier to change.

indenting

A program should be laid out so that elements which are naturally thought of as a group are made to look like a unit. The standard way of doing this is to indent everything in that group by the same amount. Another way to make a

blank lines

program more readable is to skip a line between pieces that are logically thought of as separate. The important point is to make separations on the basis of indentations and line breaks. The exact number of spaces in an indentation is a matter of personal taste. Sometimes there are also natural break indicators, such as the words **begin** and **end**, which can be made to stand out and frame a group.

Variables, constants and even program names should at least hint at their meaning or use. It is easy just to use **X**, **Y** and **Z** again and again as variables for numbers. This can be done and still produce working programs. However, it is much easier to understand a program if the variables have meaningful names. Contrast

choosing names

```
X := Y * Z
```

with the more suggestive statement below:

```
Interest := Principle * Rate
```

The two statements accomplish the same thing, but the second is easier to understand. Humpty Dumpty's objection to Alice's name applies equally well to the names **X**, **Y** and **Z**.

Designing a Sample Program

To keep from getting confused when designing a program and to produce a readable, easy to change program requires patience and a systematic approach to the design process. In the first chapter we outlined one such systematic approach. It consisted of carefully analyzing the problem, designing an algorithm for a hypothetical person to follow, and then translating the algorithm into a Pascal program for the computer to follow. The algorithm design phase is best carried out by dividing the task to be accomplished into smaller subtasks. If need be, the subtasks are divided into yet smaller subtasks until the subtasks are small enough to be manageable. In this section we illustrate these techniques by designing a very small Pascal program.

design strategy

The program we design will play a simple game. The rules of the game are as follows: the user chooses two numbers and then tries to guess the average of these two numbers. The user could calculate the average with pencil and paper, but the idea is to choose relatively big complicated numbers and to really guess rather than compute the average. The program is supposed to let the user know whether or not the guess was correct. This is not much of a game; nonetheless, it can be used to illustrate a number of concepts.

The task of this program can be broken into three main subtasks:

subtasks

```
begin
    1. Get the user to input two numbers and a guess of their average;
    2. Calculate the average;
    3. Output enough information to permit the user to easily check if the
       guess is correct
end.
```

An algorithm for the first subtask is the following:

1a. Ask the user to type in two numbers;
1b. `readln(N1, N2);`
1c. Ask the user to guess their average and enter the guess;
1d. `readln(GUESS)`

pseudocode

Our algorithm for subtask 1 contains a mixture of Pascal and English. This is quite common. When the Pascal way to express a step is obvious, there is little point in writing it in English. When the steps are large or complicated, they are usually first expressed in English. This combination of English and Pascal is sometimes called *pseudocode*.

The algorithm for subtask 1 translates into the following Pascal code:

```
writeln('Enter TWO INTEGERS, separated by a SPACE');
writeln('Then press RETURN');
readln(N1, N2);
writeln('Now GUESS their AVERAGE,');
writeln('Enter your GUESS, then press RETURN');
readln(GUESS)
```

The second task is to compute the average of the numbers held in the variables **N1** and **N2**. The definition of average yields our algorithm:

2a. Compute the sum of **N1** and **N2**;
2b. Divide the sum by **2** to get the average

In order to translate this, we use two more variables, one of type **integer** to hold the sum and one of type **real** to hold the average. If we call the first variable **SUM** and the second variable **AVE**, then we get the following Pascal code for subtask 2:

```
SUM := N1 + N2;
AVE := SUM / 2
```

Designing step 3 requires some thinking. Since we are not yet experienced programmers, we will settle for a very simple-minded solution. The computer will simply announce the user's guess and the correct average. The user can then see if the guess matches the true average. This solution is simple enough to translate directly into Pascal:

```
writeln('You guessed ', GUESS);
writeln('The right answer is ', AVE)
```

The complete program is shown in Figure 2.6. A blank line separates the code for each of the three subtasks from the code for the other subtasks.

*program
enhancement*

A good strategy is first to design a program that works, and then to add embellishments to the input and output so that the program is easier and more pleasant to interact with. This is yet another way of dividing the entire programming task into smaller subtasks. The program in Figure 2.6 can be made more

Program

```pascal
program Game(input, output);
  var N1, N2: integer;
    GUESS: real;
    SUM: integer;
    AVE: real;
begin
  writeln('Enter TWO INTEGERS, separated by a SPACE');
  writeln('Then press RETURN');
  readln(N1, N2);
  writeln('Now GUESS their AVERAGE,');
  writeln('Enter your GUESS, then press RETURN');
  readln(GUESS);

  SUM := N1 + N2;
  AVE := SUM / 2;

  writeln('You guessed ', GUESS);
  writeln('The right answer is ', AVE)
end.
```

Figure 2.6
First version of the Game program.

pleasant to interact with by adding some personalized output and some output field specifications, as shown in Figure 2.7.

Blaise Pascal
(Optional)

The language Pascal was named after Blaise Pascal, a mathematician, engineer, scientist and religious philosopher. Pascal was born in 1623 in Auvergne in central France. At the age of 18, he designed a computing machine capable of performing simple arithmetic calculations. The machine was a type of adding machine and not the sort of programmable machine that would today be called a computer. Nonetheless, the machine did receive a good deal of attention and did serve as a prototype for a number of later computing machines. Pascal had a number of models built and attempted to market the machine. However, due to its high price, the machine was never a financial success.

His calculating machine was only one of Pascal's numerous scientific and engineering contributions. He designed Paris's first public bus system, which used horse-drawn carriages. He made important contributions to geometry, probability theory and hydrodynamics. Pascal was also a prominent figure in religious philosophy. He belonged to a controversial movement within the Catholic church

Program

```pascal
program Game(input, output);
  var FirstI, LastI: char;
      N1, N2: integer;
      GUESS: real;
      SUM:  integer;
      AVE:  real;
begin
  writeln('Enter your FIRST INITIAL, then press RETURN');
  readln(FirstI);
  writeln('Enter your LAST INITIAL, then press RETURN');
  readln(LastI);
  writeln('Hello ', FirstI, '.', LastI, '.');

  writeln('Enter TWO INTEGERS, separated by a SPACE');
  writeln('Then press RETURN');
  readln(N1, N2);
  writeln('Now GUESS their AVERAGE,');
  writeln('Enter your GUESS, then press RETURN');
  readln(GUESS);

  SUM := N1 + N2;
  AVE := SUM / 2;

  writeln('You guessed ', GUESS:7:2);
  writeln('The right answer is ', AVE:7:2);

  writeln('Hope you were right ', FirstI, '.', LastI, '.')
end.
```

Sample Dialogue

Enter your FIRST INITIAL, then press RETURN
J
Enter your LAST INITIAL, then press RETURN
B
Hello J. B.
Enter TWO INTEGERS, separated by a SPACE
Then press RETURN
56 99
Now GUESS their AVERAGE,
Enter your GUESS, then press RETURN
76.5
You guessed 76.50
The right answer is 77.50
Hope you were right J. B.

Figure 2.7
Enhanced version
of the program in
Figure 2.6.

known as Jansenism. His last and most widely read religious work is now
published under the title *Pensées*. The quotations of Pascal in this book were
taken from that work. Although the book was intended as a work on religious
philosophy, some of the remarks do seem to apply to the philosophy of computer
programming.

Summary of Problem Solving and Programming Techniques

Programs should be designed using the stepwise refinement (top-down) method
described in Chapter 1 and illustrated in this chapter. When using this method,
the early versions of the algorithm can be expressed in a combination of Pascal
and English known as pseudocode. Once the complete algorithm has been
designed, it is easy to translate it into Pascal. The pseudocode and the final Pascal
program should use meaningful names for variables and should have an indentation pattern that is similar to the sample programs.

◇

It is superstition to put one's hope in formalities; but it is
pride to be unwilling to submit to them.

Blaise Pascal

◇

Summary of Pascal Constructs

Each of the following chapters contains a summary similar in form to the following one.
The entries in the summary consist of three parts: (1) an outline of the syntax (form) of
the construct, (2) one or more typical examples of the construct, and (3) an explanation of
the construct. Occasionally, one or two of the parts are omitted.

identifier

Example:

SUM2

An identifier is any string of letters or digits that starts with a letter.

variable declarations

Syntax:

```
var ⟨variable list 1⟩: ⟨type 1⟩;
    ⟨variable list 2⟩: ⟨type 2⟩;
               ⋮
    ⟨variable list n⟩: ⟨type n⟩;
```

Example:

```
var N1, N2: integer;
    SUM: real;
```

Variable declaration section of a program. Each variable list is a list of variables separated by commas. All the variables on ⟨variable list 1⟩ are declared to be of type ⟨type 1⟩, all the variables on ⟨variable list 2⟩ are declared to be of type ⟨type 2⟩, and so forth. The types may be any type names. They may be in any order and may be repeated. The types we have seen so far are **integer** for whole number values, **real** for number values with a fractional part and **char** for values which are a single character.

assignment statement

Syntax:

```
⟨variable⟩ := ⟨expression⟩
```

Example:

```
SUM := N1 + N2
```

The expression ⟨expression⟩ is evaluated and the value of the variable ⟨variable⟩ is set to that value. The ⟨variable⟩ and the value of the ⟨expression⟩ must be of the same type.

write statement

Syntax:

```
write(⟨argument list⟩)
```

Example:

```
write('Answer is ', SUM)
```

Outputs the values of the items in ⟨argument list⟩ to the primary output device, usually a display screen. ⟨argument list⟩ is a list of variables and quoted strings separated by commas. The quoted strings may not be broken across two lines.

write-line statement
Syntax:

writeln(⟨argument list⟩**)**

Example:

writeln('Answer is ', SUM)

Same as the previous definition with the addition that it causes any subsequent output to appear on a different line.

read statement
Syntax:

read(⟨variable list⟩**)**

Example:

read(N1, N2)

Read statement. The ⟨variable list⟩ is a list of n variables separated by commas. There may be any number n of variables. This statement causes the computer to read n values from the primary input device, usually the keyboard, and to set the values of the variables in ⟨variable list⟩ to these values. The values read must correspond in type to the variable types.

read-line statement
Syntax:

readln(⟨variable list⟩**)**

Example:

readln(N1, N2)

Read-line statement. Same as the previous definition with the addition that it causes any subsequent input to be taken from the next line of input.

Exercises

Self-Test and Interactive Exercises

1. What is the output produced by the following three lines (when correctly embedded in a complete program)? The variables are of type **integer**:

```
X := 2; Y := 3;
Y := X;
writeln(X, Y)
```

2. What is the output produced by the following three lines (when correctly embedded in a complete program)? The variables are of type **integer**:

```
X := 2;
X := X + 1;
writeln(X)
```

3. What is the output produced by the following two lines (when correctly embedded in a complete program)? The variables are of type **char**:

```
A := 'B'; B := 'C'; C := A;
writeln(A, B, C)
```

4. Type up and run the following program:

```
program DoMeFirst(input, output);
  begin
    writeln('This line should appear on the screen');
    writeln('End of program')
  end.
```

5. The following program contains errors. What are they?

```
program (input, output)
  begin
    writeln("Hello");
    writeln('This program was written in a hurry');
    writeln('It contains a few mistakes');
    writeln('Can you find them?)
    writeln('The compiler can')
  end
```

6. Write a program that reads two **integer** values from the keyboard and then writes them back to the screen.

7. Add the field widths **4** to the output statement of the previous program, so the program will then allocate four spaces to hold each number on the screen. Run the modified program. Try running it a few times with numbers of different sizes. Try some numbers that are too large to fit in the field width, that is, numbers that are five or six digits long.

8. Which of the following are correctly formed constants of type **integer**:

```
3.5   4.0   4.   4   1,295   9 / 3   8 / 5   '7'
```

9. Which of the following are correctly formed constants of type **real**:

```
98.6   -33.4   .89   -.89   3,987.85   4.   4
```

10. What is the output produced by the following two lines (when correctly embedded in a complete program)? The variable **R** is of type **real**.

```
R := -1234.56789;
writeln('START', R:10:3, 'END')
```

11. Change the program of Exercise 6 so that it reads in values of type **real**. Add field specifications **:6:2** to the output statement that writes out the numbers. Run this new program a few times and try various decimal numbers as input. Try some whole numbers

without any decimal point. Remove the field specification and run it again on the same input.

12. What (if anything) is wrong with the following declarations?

(a)

```
var COUNT : integer ;
    ANSWER: char ;
    AMOUNT : integer ;
```

(b)

```
var TIME: integer;
var RATE: real;
```

(c)

```
var COUNT1; COUNT2: integer;
    RATE: real;
```

(d)

```
var N1, N2: integer;
    AVE: real
```

13. Type up and run the program given in Figure 2.1. Then modify the program so that it does subtraction instead of addition. Do not forget to change the string ` Plus ` to something appropriate. Run the modified program. Next modify the program so that it does multiplication instead of addition or subtraction. Run that program.

14. Modify your program from the previous exercise so that it uses data and variables of type **real** instead of type **integer**. Run the program. Modify the program again so that it does division instead of multiplication.

15. Modify your program from the previous exercise so that it outputs the equal sign symbol instead of the word ` Equals `.

16. Write a Pascal program that will read in a character typed in on the keyboard and then write it to the screen twice.

17. Do the same as the previous exercise but have your program read in two characters and then write them both out twice. Remember that the blank is a perfectly good character to the computer, and so things will go wrong if you separate the characters by a blank.

18. Type up and run the program shown in Figure 2.5. Try any modifications that suit your fancy.

19. Type up and run the program shown in Figure 2.7.

20. Modify the program from the previous exercise so that it also outputs one additional line giving the amount by which the user's guess missed the true average. For this problem, it is acceptable to output zero or a negative number as the amount by which the guess missed the true average.

Regular Exercises

21. Write a Pascal program that will read in two integers and will then output their sum, difference and product.

22. Write a Pascal program that will read in two integers, divide one by the other, place the result in a variable of type **real** and then output both the two numbers and their quotient. Be sure to include a **writeln** statement that warns the user not to give input that would cause the computer to try to divide by zero.

23. A class has four exams in one term. Write a program that will read in a student's four exam scores, as integers, and will output the student's average.

24. A company pays its employees one rate for ordinary hours worked and one and one-half times that rate for overtime hours worked. Write a program that will read in an employee's rate of pay, the number of regular hours worked and the number of overtime hours worked and will then output the amount of pay due the employee.

25. A Celsius (centigrade) temperature C can be converted to an equivalent Fahrenheit temperature F according to the following formula:

$$F = (9/5)C + 32$$

Write a Pascal program that will read in a Celsius temperature as a decimal number and then will output the equivalent Fahrenheit temperature.

26. The straight-line method for computing the yearly depreciation in value D for an item is given by the formula:

$$D = \frac{P - S}{Y}$$

where P is the purchase price, S is the salvage value and Y is the number of years the item is used. Write a program that takes as input the purchase price of an item, its expected number of years of service and its expected salvage value, and then outputs the yearly depreciation for the item.

27. An automobile is used for commuting purposes. Write a program that will take as input the distance of the commute, the automobile's fuel efficiency in miles per gallon and the price of gasoline and will then output the cost of gasoline for the commute.

28. Write a program that calculates change for a cashier. The program requests the cost of the item. The user then types in the cost as a decimal numeral. In a similar manner, the program next requests and receives the amount tendered by the customer. It then calculates the cost of the item including sales tax. (Use 6% as the sales tax value.) It also calculates the amount of change due the customer. Finally the program outputs the cost including tax, echos the amount tendered and outputs the amount of change. Be sure to use field specifications so as to produce reasonable looking output. (Figure 2.4 can be used for part of the program.)

29. Workers at a particular company have won a 7.6% pay increase. Moreover, the increase is retroactive for six months. Write a program that takes an employee's previous annual salary as input and that outputs the amount of retroactive pay due the employee, the new annual salary and the new monthly salary.

30. Write a Pascal program for the algorithm about discount installment loans that was given as Exercise 11 in Chapter 1.

31. Write a program that will display your last initial on the screen as a large block letter formed from an arrangement of asterisks, *.

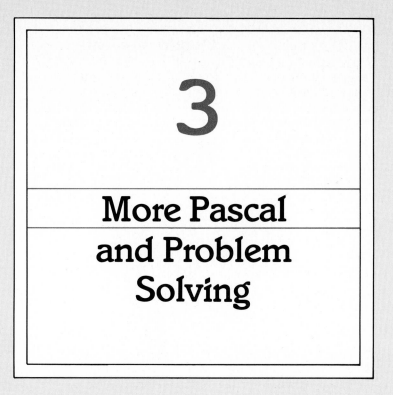

3

More Pascal
and Problem
Solving

"... —and that shows that there are three hundred and sixty-four days when you might get un-birthday presents—"

"Certainly," said Alice.

"And only *one* for birthday presents, you know. There's glory for you!"

"I don't know what you mean by 'glory,'" Alice said.

Humpty Dumpty smiled contemptuously. "Of course you don't—till I tell you. I mean 'there's a nice knock-down argument for you!'"

"But 'glory' doesn't mean 'a nice knock-down argument,'" Alice objected.

"When *I* use a word," Humpty Dumpty said, in rather a scornful tone, "it means just what I choose it to mean—neither more nor less."

"The question is," said Alice, "whether you *can* make words mean so many different things."

"The question is," said Humpty Dumpty, "which is to be master—that's all."

Lewis Carroll, *Through the Looking-Glass*

Chapter Contents

In this chapter we present a more complete and more precise description of types and expressions. We also discuss some new and important points about program style. We develop another sample program from the problem formulation stage through to a Pascal program. After that, we give some hints to assist you in locating and correcting mistakes in programs. One section is for UCSD Pascal users and describes some of the differences between UCSD and standard Pascal. We start off with a new but simple topic.

Naming Constants

There are two problems with constants in a computer program. The first is that they carry no mnemonic value. For example, when the number **10** is encountered in a program, the number gives no hint of its significance. If the program is a banking program, it might be the number of branch offices or be the number of teller windows at the main office. In order to understand the program you need to know the significance of each constant. The second problem is that when a program needs to be changed, the process of changing constants tends to introduce errors. Suppose that **10** occurs 12 times in a banking program, that four times it represents the number of branch offices and that eight times it represents the number of teller windows at the main office. When the bank opens a new branch and the program needs to be updated, there is a good chance that some of the **10**'s that should be changed to **11** will not be or some that should not be changed to **11** will be changed. Pascal provides a single mechanism to deal with both of these problems.

In Pascal you can assign a name to a constant and then use the name in place of the constant. This is done with a *constant declaration*. In Pascal, the constant declarations are placed between the program heading and the variable declarations.

constant declarations

A constant declaration consists of the reserved word ***const*** followed by the identifier that is to be the name of the constant, followed by the equal sign and then the constant. The declaration also includes sufficient blanks to separate the various pieces and is ended with a semicolon. In this case, an example is clearer than the definition. The following gives the name **BranchCount** to the number **10**:

```
const BranchCount = 10;
```

To declare more than one constant, simply list them all, separated by semicolons. Like so:

```
const BranchCount = 10;
      WindowCount = 10;
      InterestRate = 0.06;
      AccountCode ='S';
```

Any identifier that is not a reserved word may be used as a name. Any type of constant can be named in this way.

Once a constant has been given a name by a constant declaration, the identifier naming the constant can then be used anyplace the constant is allowed, and it will have exactly the same meaning as the constant it names.

To change a named constant, you need only change the constant declaration. The meaning of all occurrences of **BranchCount** can be changed from **10** to **11** by simply changing the first **10** in the above declaration.

The program in Figure 3.1 illustrates the use of a constant declaration. The constant declaration in that program gives the name **PI** to the constant **3.14159**. That is the approximate value of the number π (pi), which is then used in the

```
program UsesConst(input, output);
   const PI = 3.14159;
   var Diameter, Circum: real;
begin
   writeln('Enter the diameter of a  circle');
   readln(Diameter);
   Circum := PI * Diameter;
   writeln('A circle of diameter ', Diameter);
   writeln('has circumference ', Circum)
end.
```

Figure 3.1
Program with a
constant
declaration.

standard formula for computing the circumference of a circle. The assignment statement in that program is thus equivalent to:

```
Circum := 3.14159 * Diameter
```

string constants
You can also assign a name to a quoted string with a constant declaration. For example, the following assigns the name **Prompt** to a long string:

```
const Prompt = 'Now enter the Next Number';
```

The identifier **Prompt** can be used anyplace the string constant can be used and will have the same meaning as the constant. In particular, if the program contains this constant declaration, then the statement

```
writeln(Prompt, ' and wait for the answer')
```

will cause the following to appear on the screen:

Now enter the Next Number and wait for the answer

Do not enclose string constants like **Prompt** in quotes. That means something else.

Although unnamed constants are allowed in a program, you should almost never use them. Instead, you should name constants with a constant declaration and then use the name rather than the constant. This will make your programs easier to read and easier to change.

Syntax Diagrams

syntax
The rules of grammar for a programming language are called the *syntax* rules of the language. The syntax rules determine whether or not a string of characters forms an acceptable program, statement or other subpart of a program. There is a

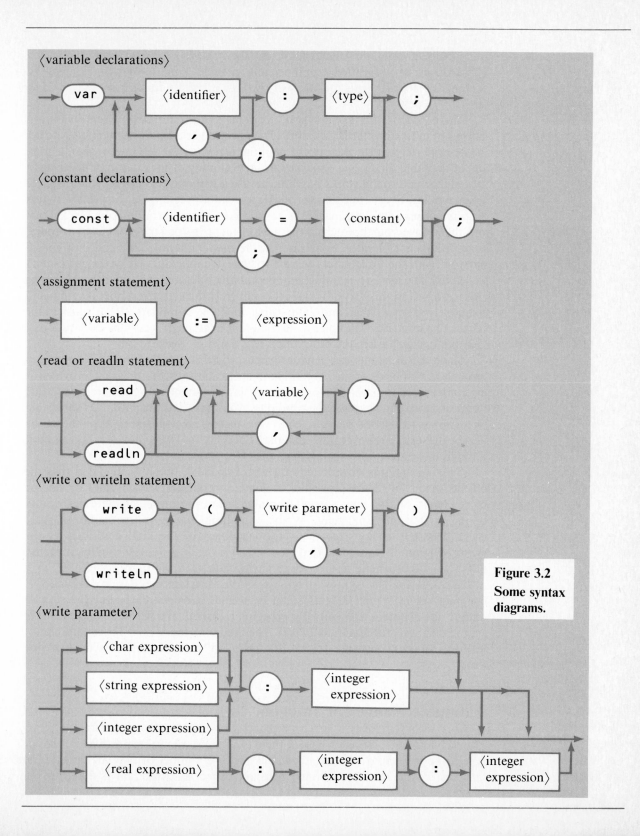

⟨variable declarations⟩

⟨constant declarations⟩

⟨assignment statement⟩

⟨read or readln statement⟩

⟨write or writeln statement⟩

⟨write parameter⟩

Figure 3.2
Some syntax
diagrams.

standard diagrammatic way to represent the syntax of programming languages. These diagrams are called, appropriately enough, *syntax diagrams*. Figure 3.2 contains syntax diagrams for many of the Pascal constructs we have presented so far.

The procedure for using syntax diagrams is quite intuitive. Each diagram is labeled to indicate what it describes. To test whether a string of symbols satisfies the description, start at the inward pointing arrow on the left end of the diagram and at the same time place a marker at the beginning of the questionable string; a mental marker usually works but you can use a real marker such as your finger or a pencil point. Every time you encounter a round or rectangular box in the syntax diagram, check that your marker is at an object of the form described in the box and then move your pointer to the next element in the string. Objects in round boxes are meant literally. For example, the box containing **var** can only match the word with the three letters **v – a – r**. Objects in rectangular boxes correspond to defined objects. For example, any Pascal identifier matches the box containing ⟨identifier⟩. If in this way you can get completely through the syntax diagram and completely through the candidate string, then the candidate string satisfies the syntax diagram. For example, if the diagram is labeled ⟨constant declarations⟩, then the string satisfies the description of a constant declaration.

Since the diagrams can have branches, there is usually more than one path through a syntax diagram. A candidate string satisfies the diagram provided it matches one such path. For example, an input statement may start with either **read** or **readln**. To check the candidate, you must find the path. It is somewhat like a maze puzzle. If there is some way through the diagram, then the string passes the test. However, the diagram does not tell you how to find a path through the maze of the syntax diagram.

Syntax diagrams do not tell you about spacing, but it is intended that the objects in the boxes be separated in some appropriate way, usually by one or more blanks. Syntax diagrams give an almost but not quite complete description of the programming language syntax. Anything that fails the syntax diagram check definitely is not a correctly formed object of the kind described by the syntax diagram. A candidate that passes the syntax diagram test usually must also pass some other simple tests, such as having blanks in the right places.

We will include syntax diagrams as we develop the Pascal language. A complete set of syntax diagrams can be found in Appendix 5, but the simpler ones in the chapters will probably prove more useful. We will always present the syntax diagrams for standard Pascal. The diagrams for UCSD Pascal are almost identical, and any variance for UCSD Pascal will be noted in the accompanying text.

Allowable Range for Integers

maxint

For each implementation of Pascal, there is a largest allowable positive number of type **integer** and a smallest allowable negative number of type **integer**. The language Pascal has a predefined constant called **maxint** that is equal to the largest value of type **integer** that can be used on the computer. You do not need to include it in a constant declaration. It is already defined for you. The smallest value of type **integer** need not be minus **maxint**, but it will be approximately that value. To discover the largest possible integer value for your machine, simply embed the following in a complete program:

```
writeln('Largest integer = ', maxint)
```

More about Real Values

The numbers that have a fractional part, like **7.56**, are values of the type **real**. Like the numbers of type **integer**, there is a largest positive and a smallest negative number of type **real** that the computer can handle, and these numbers will vary from one installation to another. There are no predefined constants for these values. So it is not as easy to discover these limits. However, the largest allowable number of type **real** is always much larger than the largest allowable number of type **integer**, and the smallest allowable negative number of type **real** is always much smaller than the smallest negative number of type **integer**.

Conceptually a whole number is a special kind of **real** number, namely, one that happens to have all zeros after the decimal point. If that were the only difference between the two types, then we would have no need to ever use the type **integer**. However, there is another important difference. Numbers of type **integer** are stored as exact values while numbers of type **real** are stored only as approximate values. Thus, if we know that some value will always be a whole number in the range allowed by our computer, then it is best to make it of type **integer**. The precision with which **real** values are stored varies from one computer to another, but on most computer systems, the following constant declaration is pointless:

*reals
versus
integers*

```
const PI = 3.14159265358979323846;
```

The program is likely to give exactly the same output, if the declaration is changed to:

```
const PI = 3.14159;
```

In addition to the simple notation that we have been using for **real** constants, there is another more complicated notation for expressing constants of type **real**. We have already had a brief introduction to this alternative notation. This alternative notation is the *E* notation, which is used by the computer to output values of type **real**. This notation is frequently called *scientific notation* or *floating point notation*.

Scientific notation is particularly handy for writing very large numbers and very small fractions. For instance, the numbers

$$3.67 \times 10^{17} = 367000000000000000.0$$

and

$$5.89 \times 10^{-6} = 0.00000589$$

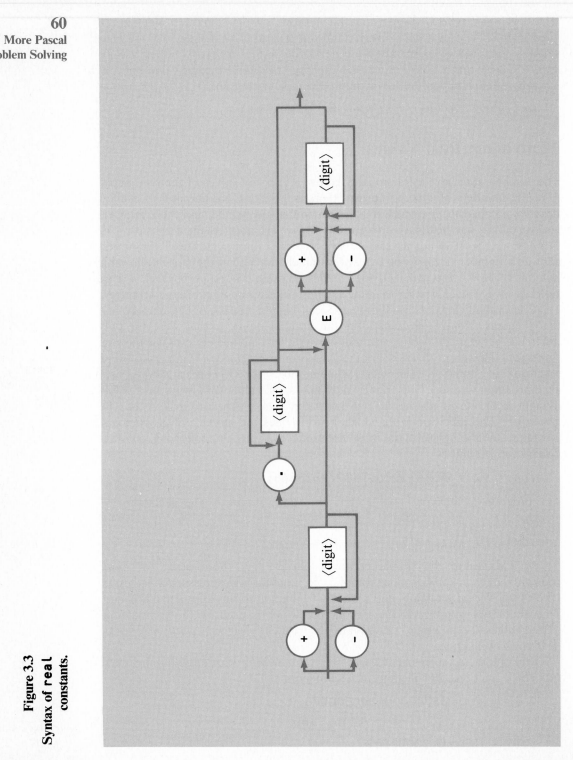

**Figure 3.3
Syntax of real
constants.**

are best expressed in Pascal by the constants **3.67E17** and **5.89E‑6**, respectively.

As with other Pascal constructs, the syntax rules for writing constants in the **E** notation are very rigid. The number before the **E** can be any decimal number, with or without a plus or minus sign. It need not contain a decimal point at all, but if it does, then there must be at least one digit before and at least one digit after the decimal point. The number after the **E** is called the *exponent* and must be a whole number, either positive, negative or zero. It can not contain a decimal point. Hence, the following are all correctly formed constants of type **real**:

9.34E13	**5E27**	**5E‑27**	**‑8.62713E21**
1.234E‑15	**‑6.783E‑12**	**1.0E+13**	**+34.78E56**

By contrast, none of the following is an acceptable constant:

.5E12   **‑.7E13**   **3.5E22.5**

The first two are incorrect because they have no digit before the decimal point. The last one is incorrect because it has a decimal point in the exponent. The syntax for **real** constants is summarized in Figure 3.3.

Type Compatibilities

In Pascal programs, **2** and **2.0** are different kinds of numbers: the first is of type **integer** and is an exact value; the second is of type **real** and represents an approximate value. This is not always an important issue, since the computer will perform an automatic type conversion, converting a number of type **integer** to an approximately equal number of type **real** whenever the situation demands a value of type **real**. Hence, if **X** is a variable of type **real**, then the following is allowed:

*integers
in place of
reals*

```
X := 2
```

The reverse situation is not allowed. If **Y** is of type **integer**, then the following is illegal in Pascal:

```
Y := 2.0
```

This sort of type conflict is not likely to arise in such a simplistic manner. However, the same principle applies in more subtle situations. To take a slightly more likely mistake, note that the following is illegal whenever **X** is of type **real** and **Y** is of type **integer**:

```
Y := X
```

The Types char and string

The two data types **char** and **string** are very closely related. Recall that the values of type **char** are single characters such as ´G´ and ´+´. Values of type

string consist of any number of characters, so long as they do not go across a line break. The constants of the two types are formed in the same way by enclosing the character or characters in single quotes. By way of example, the following are constants of type **string**:

`'Prompt'  'Sue'  '$A%+9Cb'  'Surf''s Up'  'A'`

quotes
in strings

Since a single quote is used to mark the end of a constant of type **string**, you must use a special mechanism in order to include the single quote symbol in a string constant. In order to include the single quote symbol in a string constant, you need to type it twice. The output of

`writeln('Surf''s Up')`

is the following:

Surf's Up

limited
use of
the type
string

A Pascal program can have all the usual things of type **char**: variables, named and unnamed constants in assignment statements, named and unnamed constants in **write** and **writeln** statements and other things still to be discussed. In standard Pascal, the only things of type **string** that are allowed are named and unnamed constants. Moreover, the only places these constants can be used in a standard Pascal program are inside of **write** and **writeln** statements. In particular, standard Pascal does not allow variables of type **string**.

Some implementations of standard Pascal have been extended to allow variables of type **string** and all UCSD Pascal systems allow variables of type **string**. The use of strings in UCSD Pascal is discussed in the section on UCSD Pascal.

The preceding definitions contain an ambiguity: constants consisting of one symbol, such as `'A'`, are of type **char** and are also of type **string**. This is a genuine ambiguity, but it causes no problems, since a constant of type **char** is allowed anyplace that a constant of type **string** is allowed. The constant `'A'` is considered to be of type **char**, but if it is used in a place that demands a constant of type **string**, then an automatic type conversion is performed. In other words, you need not worry about this ambiguity; the system always does the desired thing.

Arithmetic Expressions

Constants and variables of the types **integer** and **real** may be combined to form more complex expressions by using the operators **+**, **−**, ***** and **/** for addition, subtraction, multiplication and division, respectively. We have already used simple versions of such arithmetic expressions. By using parentheses, it is possible to build more complicated expressions from these simpler expressions.

As an example, suppose that **N**, **M** and **Y** are each either constants or variables and are each of type either **real** or **integer**. The right-hand side of the following assignment statement is then a well-formed arithmetic expression:

```
X := 2*(N + (M/3) + 4*Y)
```

The value of the expression is **real** because it contains a division and the result of a division is always of type **real**. Since the expression is of type **real**, the variable **X** on the left side of the assignment operator must also be of type **real**.

Any combination of the types **real** and **integer** may be combined using the operations **+**, **−**, ***** and **/**. The type of the expressions being combined determines the type of the resulting arithmetic expression according to the following simple rule: If the operation can ever be used on values of the types being combined so as to produce a number with something nonzero after the decimal point, then the resulting type is **real**; otherwise, it is **integer**. A more detailed statement of the rule is given in Figure 3.4, but this short rule is easier to remember.

*mixing
reals and
integers*

Notice that the type of an arithmetic expression is determined by the types of its subexpressions and by the operations it contains, and is not determined by the particular value of the expression. Whether or not an arithmetic expression evaluates to a "whole number" is irrelevant to the type of the expression. The quantity **4 / 2** is of type **real** despite the fact that the answer "comes out even."

There is a version of division that applies only to values of type **integer** and that returns values of type **integer**. It is essentially the "long division" you learned in grade school. For example, 17 divided by 5 yields 3 with a remainder of 2. The two numbers obtained from integer division in this way can be produced with the operators *div* and *mod*. The *div* operation yields the number of times one number "goes into" another. The *mod* operation gives the remainder. The operator *mod* is pronounced "modulo," or more simply "mod." In both

*div
and
mod*

How to determine
the type of an arithmetic expression:

1. Combining something of type **real** with something of type either **integer** or **real** always yields something of type **real**.
2. Combining anything with the division sign **/** always yields something of type **real**.
3. Combining two things of type **integer** with either the addition sign, **+**, the subtraction sign, **−**, or the multiplication sign, *****, yields something of type **integer**.
4. Placing a minus sign, **−**, in front of an arithmetic expression does not change its type.

**Figure 3.4
Type rules for
arithmetic
expressions.**

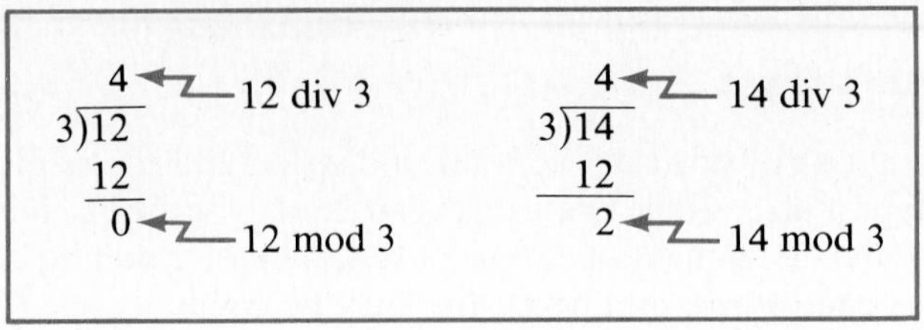

Figure 3.5
mod and *div*.

cases, the divisor goes second. For example, the statements

```
writeln('17 Divided by 5 is ', 17 div 5);
writeln('with a Remainder of ', 17 mod 5)
```

yield the following output:

```
17 Divided by 5 is   3
with a Remainder of   2
```

Figure 3.5 shows the relationship of these operations to grade school long division. Figure 3.6 illustrates the differences between the two kinds of division in Pascal.

Any reasonable spacing will do in arithmetic expressions. You can insert spaces before and after operations and parentheses, or you can omit them. Do whatever produces a result that is easy to read.

parentheses
The order of operations can always be determined by parentheses, as illustrated in the following two expressions:

```
(X + Y) * Z
X + (Y * Z)
```

To evaluate the first expression, add **X** and **Y** and then multiply the result by **Z**. To evaluate the second expression, multiply **Y** and **Z** and then add the result to **X**.

precedence
rules
If you omit parentheses, the computer will follow precedence rules similar to those used in everyday arithmetic. For example,

```
X + Y * Z
```

is evaluated by first doing the multiplication and then doing the addition. Except for some very standard cases, such as a string of additions or a simple multiplication embedded inside an addition, it is best to put in the parentheses, even if the intended order of operations is the one dictated by the precedence rules. The

Expression	Value	Expression	Value
16 *div* 5	3	17 *div* 5	3
16 *mod* 5	1	17 *mod* 5	2
16 / 5	$(3 + 1/5 =)$ **3.2**	17 / 5	$(3 + 2/5 =)$ **3.4**

Figure 3.6
The different kinds
of division.

Order of evaluation for arithmetic expressions:

1. If parentheses are present, then they determine the order of operation.
2. If the order is not determined by parentheses, then *****, **/**, **div** and **mod** operations are evaluated before **+** and **−**.
3. If there is still a question of which operation to do first, do the competing operations in their left to right order.

**Figure 3.7
Precedence rules
for arithmetic
expressions.**

parentheses make the expression easier to read and less prone to programmer error. For reference, the exact precedence rules are given in Figure 3.7.

Unlike some written and printed mathematical formulas which contain square brackets and various other forms of parentheses, Pascal allows only one kind of parentheses in arithmetic expressions. This is because keyboards typically have very few kinds of parentheses and the other varieties are needed for other purposes.

While we are on the subject of arithmetic operations, we should point out that Pascal contains no operator for exponentiation. There is no Pascal equivalent to:

exponents

$$x^y$$

Later on we will see how to define things that are equivalent to this kind of exponentiation. For now, you will simply have to use repeated products to get powers and to do without any equivalent of fractional exponents. So, **X** cubed is expressed as:

```
X*X*X
```

Standard Functions

Pascal includes a number of *standard functions* that can appear inside arithmetic expressions. As an example, **sqrt** is the square root function. It takes a value of type either **integer** or **real** and, in either case, yields a value of type **real**. The value of **sqrt(4)** is **2.0**, for example.

The value a function starts out with is called its *argument*. The value it produces is referred to as the *value returned*. In the sample, **4** was the argument and **2.0** was the value returned. These standard functions can be combined with other arithmetic expressions to obtain new, larger arithmetic expressions. For example,

arguments

value returned

```
X := 3 * sqrt(4)
```

sets the value of **X** to **6.0**.

Name	Description	Type of argument	Type of result	Example	Value of example
`abs`	absolute value	`integer` `real`	`integer` `real`	`abs(-2)` `abs(-2.4)`	+2 +2.4
`round`	rounding	`real`	`integer`	`round(2.6)`	3
`trunc`	truncation	`real`	`integer`	`trunc(2.6)`	2
`sqr`	squaring	`integer` `real`	`integer` `real`	`sqr(2)` `sqr(1.100)`	4 1.2100
`sqrt`	square root	`real` or `integer`	`real`	`sqrt(4)`	2.00

Figure 3.8
Some predefined Pascal functions.

Figure 3.8 is a list of some commonly used standard Pascal functions as well as their descriptions and an example of each. The functions **round** and **trunc** can be used to obtain an **integer** value from one of type **real**. The former returns the integer nearest to its argument. The latter returns the number you get by discarding the part after the decimal point. So, **round(4.8)** returns **5**, while **trunc(4.8)** returns **4**; **round(-4.8)** returns **-5**, while **trunc(-4.8)** returns **-4**. The function **sqr** computes the square of its argument. So, **sqr(X)** means the same as **X*X**. It is rather redundant, since you can use ***** to obtain the same effect. Occasionally it makes for neater notation, though. It allows you to express the square of a long expression without having to write it twice.

The function **abs** is the absolute value function. It leaves positive numbers unchanged and removes the minus sign from negative numbers. If the argument is **real**, then **abs** returns a value of type **real**; if the argument is of type **integer**, then **abs** returns a value of type **integer**.

A Sample Program Using Functions

The program in Figure 3.9 computes the hypotenuse of a right triangle given the two sides as input. It uses the Pythagorean formula:

$$a^2 + b^2 = h^2$$

In the formula the two sides are a and b, and h is the hypotenuse. (Traditionally c is used in this formula rather than h, but h seems more suggestive.) The program reads in the two sides, the a and the b, and computes the hypotenuse h. To get a formula for the hypotenuse, solve the Pythagorean formula for h and you will find:

$$h = \sqrt{a^2 + b^2}$$

Program

```
program Pythagoras(input, output);
  var Side1, Side2, Hypotenuse: real;

begin
  writeln('ENTER the TWO SIDES of a right triangle');
  readln(Side1, Side2);
  Hypotenuse := sqrt(sqr(Side1) + sqr(Side2));
  writeln('A triangle with sides of lengths:');
  writeln(Side1,' and ', Side2);
  writeln('Has a hypotenuse of length ', Hypotenuse)
end.
```

Sample Dialogue

```
ENTER the TWO SIDES of a right triangle
3.0 4.0
A triangle with sides of lengths:
    3.000000000000E0 and    4.000000000000E0
Has a hypotenuse of length   5.000000000000E0
```

Figure 3.9
Sample program using standard functions.

If perchance this is all new to you, do not be concerned. It is only an example. You can simply take it on faith that the formula works.

Comments

In order to make a program understandable, you should include some explanatory notes at key places in the program. Such notes are called *comments*. In Pascal and most other programming languages there are provisions for including such comments within the text of a program.

In Pascal a comment may be inserted almost anyplace as long as it is preceded by the symbol **{**, sometimes called a "brace" or "curly bracket," and followed by the matching symbol **}**. The compiler simply ignores anything between a matching pair of the curly bracket symbols **{ }**. Comments cannot appear inside a quoted string. Otherwise, there would be no way to include the symbols '**{**' and '**}**' inside a quoted string. Also, comments can not appear inside of other comments; the effect of a comment inside of a comment is unpredictable. Except for string constants and other comments, a comment can go anyplace that the blank symbol is allowed. It may go across more than one line, so long as it begins with the curly bracket symbol **{** and end with the matching symbol **}**. Pascal does not demand a pair of the symbols **{ }** on each line of a comment.

If the symbols **{ }** are not available on your keyboard, or if you do not want to use them for some reason, you can use the pair **(*** and ***)** instead.

when to comment

Each program unit of any substantial size or complexity should be explained by a comment. In particular, each program should open with a comment that explains what the program does, as in the following sample heading:

```
program Teller(input, output);
     {Accepts deposit amounts as input and writes out
      the value of the deposit plus interest after one year.}
```

In this book, comments will always be written in italic typeface in order to make them stand out from the program text. This is just an aid to the reader; keyboards and terminals do not ordinarily have a variety of type fonts.

It is a little difficult to say just how many comments a program should contain. The only correct answer is "just enough," and this answer does not convey a lot to the novice programmer. It will take some experience to get a feel for how and when it is best to generate comments. Whenever something is important and not obvious, it merits a comment. However, too many comments are as bad as too few. A program that has a comment on each line can be so buried in comments that it hides the structure of the program and it hides the critical comments in a sea of obvious observations. Comments like the following contribute nothing to understanding and should not appear in a program:

```
Distance := Rate * Time; {Computes the distance traveled}
```

Another Sample Program

Figure 3.10 is a sample program that makes use of most of the Pascal constructs discussed so far. It was designed for a new, not yet federally or state chartered, savings institution. This institution is installing an automated 24-hour teller and has a limited amount of capital to spend on hardware and software. The program in Figure 3.10 was designed to handle deposits.

use of constants

Since the board of directors is not sure that their current name represents sound marketing practice, the name has been placed in a constant declaration. This makes it easier to change the name if they later decide that they prefer something more dignified, such as "Nocturnal Aviators Savings and Thrift Assoc. Inc." A similar remark applies to the motto. Almost all constants in the program are named in a constant declaration. Even the field widths for formatted output are given names. For example, the fourth **writeln** is equivalent to:

```
writeln(Rate:5:2, '%  on deposits,')
```

Program

```pascal
program Teller(input, output);
{Accepts deposit amounts as input and writes out
the value of the deposit plus interest after one year.}
  const Name    'FLY BY NIGHT THRIFT';
        Motto = 'We''ll take your money any time.';
        BrCount = 2;
        CountLength = 2;
        Rate = 7.25;
        RateLength = 5; {Field Length for outputting the Rate}
        MoneyLength = 7;{Field Length for outputting the
                         Deposit and the Deposit plus interest.}
  var Deposit, Amount: real;

begin
  writeln('WELCOME TO ', Name);
  writeln(Motto);
  writeln('We currently pay:');
  writeln(Rate :RateLength:2, '% on deposits,');
  writeln('AND have');
  writeln(BrCount :CountLength, ' offices to serve YOU!');
  writeln;
  writeln('ENTER the amount of your DEPOSIT at');
  writeln('the keyboard and press the RETURN KEY.');
  writeln('PLEASE, do NOT type in a $ sign.');
  readln(Deposit);
  writeln('Next, put your money in an ENVELOPE,');
  writeln('WRITE your NAME on the envelope,');
  writeln('and slip it UNDER THE DOOR.');
  writeln('Thank you for your deposit of:');
  writeln('$', Deposit :MoneyLength:2);

  Amount := Deposit + (Rate/100)*Deposit;
  {The division by 100 changes the percent figure to a fraction.}
  writeln('In just one short year');
  writeln('your deposit will grow to');
  writeln('$', Amount :MoneyLength:2);
  writeln('Thank you for choosing ', Name, '!')
end.
```

Figure 3.10
**Sample of constants
and arithmetic
expressions.**

WELCOME TO FLY BY NIGHT THRIFT
We'll take your money any time.
We currently pay:
    7.25% on deposits,
AND have
    2 offices to serve YOU!

ENTER the amount of your DEPOSIT at
the keyboard and press the RETURN KEY.
PLEASE, do NOT type in a $ sign.
100.00
Next, put your money in an ENVELOPE,
WRITE your NAME on the envelope,
and slip it UNDER THE DOOR.
Thank you for your deposit of:
$ 100.00
In just one short year
your deposit will grow to
$ 107.25
Thank you for choosing FLY BY NIGHT THRIFT!

Figure 3.10
(cont'd)

The arithmetic expression includes parentheses in order to ensure that the division is done first, then the multiplication and lastly the addition. If the parentheses are omitted, the expression will evaluate the same way. This is because the order of the division and multiplication is left to right. However, it is poor style to rely on that convention. Doing so introduces errors on the part of the programmer and makes the program harder to read.

The assignment statement in this example was chosen to be complicated enough to illustrate a few important principles. In practice, however, it might be preferable to replace that single assignment statement with the following pair of assignment statements which are easier to read and understand:

```
Interest := (Rate / 100)*Deposit;
Amount := Deposit + Interest
```

The identifier **Interest** should then be declared as a variable of type **real**.

Designing a Sample Program

In this section we will design a sample program to make change. Given an amount of money, the program will tell how many of each coin, such as quarters, dimes and so forth, that it takes to equal the given amount.

The statement of the task to be accomplished by the program seems pretty clear, but before we go on let us make sure that as few details as possible are left unspecified. For example, what is the range of inputs for which the program must work? Does it need to give out dollars as change or not? If yes, what denominations of bills should it use? What should it do with an input of zero? The answers depend on the use to which the program is to be put.

*problem
definition*

For this example, we will assume that it is to be used by a cashier who has no trouble with dollars but needs to be told what coins to hand out and is at least smart enough to know that zero cents means no coins. Hence, we can assume that the change is some amount of change from 1 to 99 cents. Are there any other points left unspecified? What if the cashier runs out of some particular coin? After all, this cashier is not too smart. That is why we were asked to write the program. We inquire and discover that the cashier usually has very few if any half dollar coins and occasionally runs out of nickels but never runs out of any other coin. After consulting with the cashier's boss, we decide to ignore half dollar coins and nickels. These coins will just be brought to the bank at the end of the day.

Now that we understand the problem, we can start to design an algorithm. Our first attempt is the following:

*algorithm
design*

```
begin
  1. Input the amount;
  2. Compute a combination of quarters, dimes and pennies whose value
     equals the amount;
  3. Output the coins
end.
```

We have broken down our task into three subtasks. Now we must solve these subtasks and produce some Pascal code for the solutions. (In this context the word *code* means a part of a program.)

The first subtask is easy. We simply read the amount into some variable. To make our program easy to read, we choose the name **Amount** for this variable. Subtask 1 is accomplished by the following:

```
writeln('Enter an amount of change');
writeln('from 1 to 99 cents:');
readln(Amount)
```

The second subtask is still quite large and it will help to break it down into still smaller tasks. One sensible breakdown is:

2a. Compute the number of quarters to give out;
2b. Compute the number of dimes to give out;
2c. Compute the number of pennies to give out

These three subtasks are not completely independent. For example, the number of dimes given out will depend on the number of quarters given out. The number of dimes to give out will be computed on the basis of the original amount minus the total value of the quarters given out. To help keep our reasoning straight, we introduce a new variable called **AmountLeft**. At various points in

*interaction
of subtasks*

the computation **AmountLeft** will equal the amount left to be given out. After calculating the amount of quarters to give out, **AmountLeft** will be set equal to the original amount minus the value of the quarters given out. After computing the number of dimes, **AmountLeft** will be further decreased by the value of the dimes. The smaller tasks, into which subtask 2 is subdivided, can now be rewritten into the following more detailed decomposition of subtask 2:

2a. Compute the maximum number of quarters in **Amount** and set **AmountLeft** equal to **Amount** minus the total value of the quarters;

2b. Compute the maximum number of dimes in **AmountLeft** and decrease **AmountLeft** by the total value of the dimes;

2c. Compute the number of pennies in **AmountLeft**

*analysis of
possible
solutions*

Subtask 2a is already expressed as two smaller subtasks. The first one is to compute the maximum number of quarters in **Amount**. There are a number of ways to do that. We could subtract **25** from **Amount** as many times as is possible (without going negative) and count the number of times we do that. That would work, but before we jump to the keyboard and type it up, we should think about whether there is a simpler solution. There is.

The number of times we can subtract **25** from **Amount** is the number of times **25** "goes into" **Amount** and we have a standard Pascal operator for that. The number of times that **25** goes into **Amount** is:

```
Amount div 25
```

That is thus the number of quarters to give out and might appropriately be stored in a variable called **Quarters**. Hence the first part of subtask 2a can be accomplished by the Pascal statement:

```
Quarters := Amount div 25
```

The amount left over after giving out the quarters is:

```
Amount - 25*Quarters
```

That formula will work, but again there is a simpler expression for the amount. The amount left is just the remainder on dividing **Amount** by **25**, and in Pascal that remainder is written:

```
Amount mod 25
```

Hence, the complete subtask 2a can be accomplished by the Pascal code:

```
Quarters := Amount div 25;
AmountLeft := Amount mod 25
```

Subtask 2b can be accomplished by a similar piece of Pascal code:

```
Dimes := AmountLeft div 10;
AmountLeft := AmountLeft mod 10
```

The variable **Dimes** and the variable **Pennies** mentioned next have the obvious interpretation.

Program

```
program Change(input, output);
{Outputs the coins used to give an amount between 1 and 99 cents.}

   var Amount, AmountLeft,
       Quarters, Dimes, Pennies: integer;

begin
   writeln('Enter an amount of change');
   writeln('from 1 to 99 cents:');
   readln(Amount);

   Quarters := Amount div 25;
   AmountLeft := Amount mod 25;
   {AmountLeft now contains the amount left after
   giving out as many quarters as possible.}

   Dimes := AmountLeft div 10;
   AmountLeft := AmountLeft mod 10;
   {AmountLeft now contains the amount left after
   giving out as many dimes and quarters as possible.}

   Pennies := AmountLeft;

   writeln(Amount, ' cents can be given as:');
   writeln(Quarters, ' quarters');
   writeln(Dimes, ' dimes and');
   writeln(Pennies, ' pennies')
end.
```

Sample Dialogue

Enter an amount of change
from 1 to 99 cents:
67

        67 cents can be given as:
        2 quarters
        1 dimes and
        7 pennies

Figure 3.11
A program to make change.

Subtask 2c is very simple, since the remaining amount is given out as pennies. It is accomplished by:

```
Pennies := AmountLeft
```

Subtask 3 can be accomplished by a series of **writeln** statements that output the values of the variables **Quarters**, **Dimes** and **Pennies**. As a check to make sure that the original amount was typed in correctly, the value of **Amount** should also be output. The complete program is shown in Figure 3.11.

Testing and Debugging

By now you know enough Pascal to get yourself in trouble and may need some hints on how to get out of trouble. It is not possible to anticipate all the mistakes you might make, but we can warn you about a few very common mistakes and indicate ways to find them and repair them.

The compiler will catch certain kinds of mistakes and will write out an error message when it does find a mistake. The compiler will detect *syntax errors*. In other words, the compiler will tell you whether you have written a Pascal program or whether you have violated some syntax rule, such as omitting a semicolon or failing to declare a variable.

If the compiler discovers that your program contains a syntax error, it will tell you where the error is likely to be and what kind of error it is likely to be. If the compiler says your program contains a syntax error, you can be confident that it does. However, the compiler may be incorrect about either the location or the nature of the error. It does a better job of determining the location of an error, to within a line or two, than it does of determining the source of the error. As a general rule, the compiler is likely to be right about the location of the first syntax error in your program, but it may not know what the nature of the error is. This is because the compiler is guessing at what you meant to write down and can easily guess wrong. After all, it cannot read your mind.

Error messages after the first one have a higher likelihood of being incorrect with respect to either the location or the nature of the error. Again, this is because the compiler must guess your meaning. If the compiler's first guess was incorrect, this will effect its analysis of future mistakes, since the analysis will be based on a false assumption.

Programs tend to contain numerous matching pairs such as comment delimiters, quotes, parentheses and other delimiters to be discussed later. A common syntax error is to miss one end of some matching pair. The compiler will always detect such an omission, but the error message may be a little confusing.

As an illustration, consider the statement:

```
writeln('Answers are, W, X, Y Z, 'in miles')
```

The statement has a quote missing in the first quoted string. Yet the compiler will not find a mistake until it reaches the second quoted string. The error message will probably say the error is in the neighborhood of the word `in` and may or may not mention a missing quote. The reason for this is that the compiler perceives the quoted string

`'Answers are, W, X, Y Z, '`

as the first item to be written out. After all, it is a perfectly legitimate **string** constant. If you realize that the mistake is in the first constant and you add the quote, you will get:

`writeln('Answers are', W, X, Y Z, 'in miles')`

This will, of course, still produce a compiler error message pointing out the missing comma between the **Y** and the **Z**. In many cases, of which this is just one example, one mistake can hide another. In this case, the missing quote caused the compiler to ignore the missing comma.

Sooner or later you will come to a situation in which you are absolutely certain that your program is correct but yet the compiler will not accept it and insists that there is a mistake in a particular line. The natural assumption is that there is a mistake in the compiler and that your program is correct. Occasionally, there are mistakes in compilers, but they are rare and it is extremely unlikely that the fault is in the compiler. Frequently it is a mistake that you can not see for either physical or psychological reasons. You may have typed the letter "Oh" when you meant to type the digit zero. There may be a real and visible mistake that you automatically correct in your mind, and so you always miss the mistake. When you can not find anything wrong with the line, try retyping it. Amazingly enough, this will sometimes cure the problem.

There are certain kinds of errors that the computer system can only detect when a program is run. Appropriately enough, these are called *run-time errors*. Most computer systems will detect certain run-time errors and output an appropriate error message. The distinction between syntax errors and run-time errors is illustrated in Figure 3.12.

run-time errors

Many typical run-time errors have to do with numeric calculations. If an integer expression tries to evaluate to some value greater than **maxint**, the system should detect this fact when the program is run and should output an error message called an *overflow* message. A similar message should be output when real valued expressions get too large or too small. (Unfortunately, some versions of Pascal do not provide overflow messages.) The system will also provide a run-time error message if the program attempts to divide by zero or to take the square root of a negative number. Other run-time errors have to do with features of Pascal that we have not yet introduced. These errors will be discussed as the relevant Pascal features are introduced.

If the compiler approved of your program and the program ran once with no run-time error messages, this does not guarantee that it is correct. Remember, the compiler will only tell you whether you wrote a Pascal program. It will not tell you whether the program does what you want it to do. In order to test that, you should run the program on several sets of representative data and check the program's performance on those inputs. If the program passes those tests, you can

testing

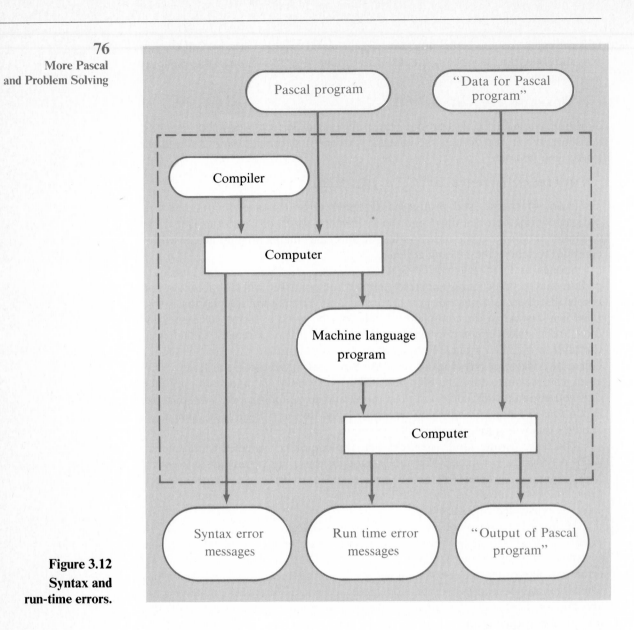

**Figure 3.12
Syntax and
run-time errors.**

have more confidence in it, but this is still not an absolute guarantee that the program is correct. It still may not do what you want it to do when it is run on some other data.

The only way to justify confidence in a program is to program carefully and so avoid most errors. That is far better than trying to fix a program that is riddled with errors. The errors may go undetected, and even if you do detect the presence of an error, it may not be easy to locate the source of the error.

A mistake in a program is usually called a *bug* and the process of eliminating bugs is called *debugging*.

UCSD Pascal*

UCSD Pascal was developed under the direction of Professor Kenneth Bowles at the University of California, San Diego, in the 1970's. It was based on Wirth's original version of Pascal but was specifically designed for use on small personal computers called *microcomputers*. It was designed to be easy to implement on these computers and to take advantage of the special properties of microcomputers. Although this produced differences in the compiler and other systems programs, the differences between UCSD Pascal and standard Pascal programs are relatively minor. In this section we will point out a few of the differences between UCSD Pascal and standard Pascal. We will encounter no other differences until we get to more advanced topics. Readers working in standard Pascal can omit this section entirely.

One difference between UCSD Pascal and standard Pascal is almost cosmetic. In UCSD Pascal it is not necessary to include the words **input** and **output** in the program heading. So, for example, if the first line of a standard Pascal program is

program `Sample(input, output);`

then the following will do as the first line of the equivalent UCSD Pascal program:

program `Sample;`

It does no harm to include the identifiers **input** and **output** in a UCSD Pascal program. The compiler treats them as though they were comments. So, both of the preceding lines are acceptable and they are equivalent in a UCSD Pascal program. In a standard Pascal program, only the first form can be used.

Another difference between UCSD Pascal and standard Pascal is also cosmetic, but of more import. In UCSD Pascal an identifier may contain the underscore symbol __. This is to aid readability. In UCSD Pascal the following is an acceptable identifier:

The _ Number

The compiler ignores the underscore, however, and so the above identifier is the same as the identifier **TheNumber**; the two names are completely interchangeable and hence can not be used to name two different identifiers. An identifier can not begin with the underscore symbol.

All the programs we have seen so far work for both UCSD Pascal and standard Pascal systems. In the few cases when that is not true, we will make note of the fact that the program only works on one of the two systems.

One advantage of UCSD Pascal is that it allows variables of type **string** and has a number of special functions especially designed for string manipulating.

A value of type **string** has a length which is the number of characters in the string. This number can be retrieved by using the function **length**, which takes

string variables

string functions

---

*UCSD Pascal sections are optional for Standard Pascal users.

an argument of type **string** and returns a value of type **integer**. For example,

```
length('Hi there')
```

returns **8** as its value. Notice that blanks are counted.

Two or more values of type **string** can be joined together using the **concat** function. The function's name is an abbreviation of "concatenation." This function takes any number of arguments, all of type **string**, and returns a value of type **string**. For example,

```
concat('DO ', 'BE ', 'DO ')
```

returns the value:

```
'DO BE DO '
```

Other functions for manipulating strings will be discussed later on in this book.

After learning more about Pascal, you will think of numerous uses for **string** variables and these special functions. However, remember that they only work on UCSD Pascal systems and so programs written using them will not run on a standard Pascal system. Figure 3.13 is a sample UCSD Pascal program that illustrates the use of variables of type **string** as well as the two functions **length** and **concat**.

inputting
strings

If they are not used with care, variables of type **string** can present some problems with input. To illustrate a problem that can arise, suppose **Name** is of type **string**, suppose **Age** is of type **integer** and consider the following pair of statements:

```
writeln('ENTER your NAME and AGE');
readln(Name, Age)
```

If in response to the prompt line the user types in the following all on one line:

Alice 12

and then presses the return key, then the variable **Name** will get the value:

```
'Alice 12'
```

Remember, blanks and digits are characters and so can be part of a value of type **string**. After giving **Name** the wrong value, the program will stop and wait for the user to type in an integer to use as the value of **Age**. Since, the user thinks that the value of **Age** has already been set, this is likely to produce serious problems. A safer sequence of statements is:

```
writeln('ENTER your NAME and press RETURN');
readln(Name);
writeln('ENTER your AGE');
readln(Age)
```

turtle
graphics

Many UCSD Pascal systems also have provisions for graphics commands that allow you to create programs that draw intricate pictures. These graphics packages, called *turtle graphics*, will not be discussed in this book. However, the

Program

```pascal
program UCSD;
{This program works in UCSD Pascal but not in standard Pascal.}
  const Blank = ' ';
  var FirstName, LastName, FullName: string;

begin
  writeln('ENTER your FIRST NAME then press RETURN');
  readln(FirstName);
  writeln('ENTER your LAST NAME then press RETURN');
  readln(LastName);
  FullName := concat(FirstName, Blank, LastName);
  writeln('Good day ', FullName);
  writeln('I like people with');
  writeln(length(FirstName), ' letters');
  writeln('in their first name.');
  writeln('Good bye ', FirstName)
end.
```

Sample Dialogue

ENTER your FIRST NAME then press RETURN
Blaise
ENTER your LAST NAME then press RETURN
Pascal
Good day Blaise Pascal
I like people with
  6 letters
in their first name.
Good bye Blaise

Figure 3.13
UCSD Pascal but
not standard Pascal.

UCSD Pascal graphics system is described in Appendix 6. That will provide enough information to give the graphics a try, provided it is available on your system. It is not available on all UCSD Pascal systems.

Summary of Problem Solving and Programming Techniques

We have introduced a number of techniques for making a program easier to understand: Almost all constants in a program should be given meaningful names in a constant declaration. Arithmetic expressions should include enough parentheses to make their meaning clear. Comments should be inserted to explain major subsections or any unclear part of a program.

When designing an algorithm for some task, the basic approach is to break the task into subtasks and to solve the subtasks separately. This does not imply that the subtasks do not interact. Typically, they do. You should make this interaction clear by inserting suitable comments in the program and even in the pseudocode.

◇

"In matters of grave importance, style, not sincerity, is the vital thing."

Oscar Wilde, The Importance of Being Earnest

◇

Summary of Pascal Constructs

constant declarations

Syntax:

const ⟨identifier 1⟩ **=** ⟨constant 1⟩**;**
⟨identifier 2⟩ **=** ⟨constant 2⟩**;**
.
.
.
⟨identifier *n*⟩ **=** ⟨constant *n*⟩**;**

Example:

```
const Rate = 7.25;
      Motto = 'We aim to please';
      Days = 365;
```

The constant ⟨constant 1⟩ is given the name ⟨identifier 1⟩, the constant ⟨constant 2⟩ is given the name ⟨identifier 2⟩ and so forth. The identifiers can be any Pascal identifiers that are not reserved words. The identifiers can then be used anyplace that the constants can be used and will have the same value as the constants they name.

the type integer

Syntax:

```
integer
```

The data type whose values are all the whole numbers (positive, negative or zero) that the computer system can handle. Constants of this type are strings of digits optionally prefixed with a plus or a minus sign. The values are stored exactly.

maxint

Syntax:

```
maxint
```

A predefined constant equal to the largest value of type **integer** that the computer system can handle.

Syntax:

real

The data type whose values are numbers that, when written in the usual decimal notation, have digits after the decimal point. The values are stored as approximate values. The constants of this type may be in either of the following forms, optionally preceded by a plus or a minus sign:

1. A sequence of digits containing a decimal point that has at least one digit before the decimal point and at least one digit after the decimal point.

2. A number followed by the letter **E**, followed by a constant of type **integer**. The number before the **E** must be either an **integer** constant or a **real** constant in form 1.

the type char (characters)

Syntax:

char

The type consisting of single characters. The constants are formed by placing the character in single quotes. For example, ´**A**´, ´**$**´, and ´**3**´

the type string

Syntax:

string

Examples:

´*Hi Mom*´   ´*Surf´´s Up*´

The type consisting of a string of characters. The constants are formed by placing the string in quotes. To include the single quote symbol, repeat it. In standard Pascal, constants may be of type **string** but there are no variables of this type. UCSD Pascal allows variables, as well as constants, of type **string**.

comments

Syntax:

{⟨text⟩**}**

Example:

{*This is a comment***}**

The text between the two symbols **{** and **}** is ignored by the compiler and so has no effect on the program. The pair **(* *)** may be used as an alternative to **{ }**. Hence, the following is also a comment:

(**This is also a comment****)**

The comment delimiters **{**, **}**, **(*** and ***)** may not be used inside a comment.

Exercises

Self-Test and Interactive Exercises

1. Write a program that outputs **maxint** to the screen.

2. Determine the smallest value of type **integer** that can be represented on your system. It is likely to be **−maxint** plus or minus two.

3. Determine the value of each of the following Pascal arithmetic expressions:

15 *div* 12	15 *mod* 12
24 *div* 12	24 *mod* 12
123 *div* 100	123 *mod* 100
200 *div* 100	200 *mod* 100
99 *div* 2	99 *mod* 2

4. Write a program that reads two integers into the variables **X** and **Y** and then outputs **X** *div* **Y** and **X** *mod* **Y**. Run the program several times with different pairs of integers as input.

5. Write a program that will convert a number of seconds to the equivalent number of minutes and seconds. Use the *mod* and *div* operators.

6. Convert each of the following (non-Pascal) arithmetic expressions into Pascal arithmetic expressions:

$$3x \qquad 3x + y \qquad \frac{x + y}{7} \qquad \frac{3x + y}{z + 2}$$

7. Determine the value of each of the following Pascal arithmetic expressions:

```
                 sqrt(16)       sqrt(4 + 5)
trunc(6.8)       trunc(-6.8)    round(6.8)    round(-6.8)
abs(-6.8)        abs(6.8)       abs(4)        abs(-4)
                 sqrt(abs(20 - sqr(2)))
```

8. Convert each of the following (non-Pascal) arithmetic expressions into Pascal arithmetic expressions:

$$\left(x + \frac{y}{x + z} + w\right)^2 \qquad \frac{2x^3}{4a} + b$$

$$\sqrt{\frac{x + 3z}{w} + y}$$

9. Write a program that reads in a number, computes the square root of that number using the standard function **sqrt**, then squares that value using the function **sqr**, and finally outputs all three values: the input number, the square root and the square of the square root. Run the program several times using a wide variety of numbers.

10. Write a program that reads in a decimal number, applies both the functions **trunc** and **round** to the number and then outputs both values.

11. Which of the following are correctly formed Pascal constants of type **real**?

    98.6, **4.0**, **.99**, **7.89**, **57**, **57E12**, **57E-12**,
    57E3.7, **57.9E3.7**, **-9.8E2**

12. Type up and run the program shown in Figure 3.1. Then change the constant declaration to the following and run it again:

    const PI = 3.1415926536;

Next change the last digit. The value of **PI** will then be slightly (more) incorrect. Run this modified program. Compare the results of all three programs when run on the same input.

13. Determine the smallest value ϵ such that your computer can distinguish between 1 and $1 + \epsilon$. Feel free to use trial-and-error methods.

14. Type up and run the program **Teller** given in Figure 3.10. Change the name of the institution, its motto and the interest rate, and then run it again.

15. (UCSD Pascal only) Rewrite and embellish the program **Talk** from Figure 2.5 using variables of type **string**.

Regular Exercises

16. The area of a triangle whose sides are a, b and c can be computed by the formula:

$$A = \sqrt{s(s - a)(s - b)(s - c)}$$

where $s = (a + b + c)/2$. Write a program that will read in the three sides of a triangle and output the area of the triangle.

17. A liter is 0.264179 gallons. Write a program that will read in the number of liters of gasoline consumed by the user's car and the number of miles traveled by the car, and will then output the number of miles per gallon the car delivered.

18. A metric ton is 35,273.92 ounces. Write a program that will read in the weight of a package of breakfast cereal in ounces and then output the weight in metric tons as well as the number of boxes of cereal needed to yield one metric ton of cereal.

19. A government research lab has concluded that certain chemicals commonly used in foods will cause death in laboratory mice. A friend of yours is desperate to lose weight but can not give up soda pop. Your friend wants to know how much diet soda pop it is possible to drink without dying as a result. Write a program to supply the answer. The input to the program is the amount of artificial sweetener needed to kill a mouse, the weight of the mouse and the weight of the dieter. To ensure the safety of your friend, be sure the program requests the weight at which the dieter will stop dieting, rather than the dieter's current weight. Assume that diet soda contains 1/10th of one percent artificial sweetener.

20. Write a program that will take as input an integer with seven, eight or nine digits and will then echo back the number written in the conventional way with commas inserted every three digits. (It is acceptable to have an extra space before or after a comma.)

21. The gravitational attractive force between two bodies of mass m_1 and m_2 separated by a distance d is given by:

$$F = \frac{Gm_1m_2}{d^2}$$

where G is the universal gravitational constant:

$$G = 6.673 \times 10^{-8} \text{ cm}^3/\text{g sec}^2$$

Write a program that will read in the mass of two bodies and the distance between them, and will then output the gravitational force between them. The output should be in dynes; one dyne equals a g cm/sec^2.

22. According to Einstein's famous equation, the amount of energy E produced when an amount of mass m is completely converted to energy is given by the formula:

$$E = mc^2$$

where c is the speed of light. Write a program that will read in a mass in grams and output the amount of energy produced when the mass is converted to energy. The speed of light is approximately:

$$2.997925 \times 10^{10} \text{ cm/sec}$$

If the mass is given in grams, then the formula yields the energy expressed in ergs.

23. The public utilities commission has decided that the electric company overcharged its customers for two months last year. To make up the difference to the customers, the commission therefore orders the company to decrease each of next month's bills by 10%. The city also levies a 3% utility tax, which is to be applied to the bill before it is discounted. Also, the 10% discount does not apply to the utility tax. Assume electricity costs $5.26 per kilowatt-hour. Write a program to compute next month's electricity bill given the number of kilowatt-hours consumed as input.

24. Rewrite the program **Change** in Figure 3.11 so that it takes as input any amount of dollars and cents (as a number of type **real**) and outputs the correct number of bills as well as coins to give as change. Use bill denominations of $1, $5 and $20 only.

25. An hourly employee is paid at a rate of $9.73 per hour for regular hours worked per week. Any hours over that are paid at the overtime rate of one and one half times that. From the worker's gross pay 6% is deducted for social security tax, 14% is withheld for federal income tax, 5% is withheld for state income tax and $6 per week is deducted for union dues. Write a program that will take the number of regular hours worked in a week and the number of overtime hours worked as input and will then output the worker's gross pay, each deduction, each withholding and the net take home pay for the week.

References for Further Reading

There are a large number of introductory Pascal books on the market. We have listed a few of the more popular ones below. They do not offer any more information, but it is sometimes useful to read another approach to the subject.

D. Cooper and M. Clancy, *Oh! Pascal!*, 1982, W.W. Norton, New York.

P. Grogono, *Programming in Pascal*, revised edition, 1980, Addison-Wesley, Reading, Mass.

E. B. Koffman, *Problem Solving and Structured Programming in Pascal*, 1981, Addison-Wesley, Reading, Mass.

G.M. Schneider, S.W. Weingart and D.M. Perlman, *An Introduction to Programming and Problem Solving with Pascal*, 2nd edition, 1982, John Wiley, New York.

The following are reference manuals rather than tutorial books. The first is specifically designed for UCSD Pascal. The second one describes the differences between various Pascal implementations. It is particularly useful if you are changing from one Pascal system to another.

R. Clark and S. Koehler, *The UCSD Pascal Handbook, A Reference and Guidebook for Programmers*, 1982, Prentice-Hall, Englewood Cliffs, N.J.

J. Tiberghien, *The Pascal Handbook*, 1981, SYBEX, Berkeley, Ca.

The following reference manuals are designed for individuals who already know some other programming language besides Pascal:

K. Jensen and N. Wirth, *Pascal User's Manual and Report*, 1974, Springer-Verlag, New York.

D. L. Matuszek, *Quick Pascal*, 1982, John Wiley, New York.

4

Procedures and Top-Down Design

Words differently arranged have a different meaning, and meanings differently arranged have different effects.
Blaise Pascal

Chapter Contents

A good way to design an algorithm to solve a task is to break it down into subtasks and solve these subtasks by smaller, simpler algorithms. Ultimately, the subalgorithms to solve these subtasks are translated into Pascal code, and the entire larger algorithm containing these subalgorithms is translated into a Pascal program. Since the subalgorithms are algorithms, it is natural to think of them as smaller programs within a larger program. Moreover, preserving this structure in the final Pascal program would make the program easier to understand, easier to change, if need be and, as will become apparent, easier to write, test and debug. Pascal, like most programming languages, has facilities to include program-like entities inside programs. The Pascal term for such program-like entities is *procedure*.

In this chapter we introduce procedures and give some guidelines for how to use them effectively.

Simple Pascal Procedures

In Pascal you can assign a name to a sequence of statements by means of something called a *procedure declaration*. You can then use the procedure name inside the body of the program and this will have the same effect as executing the sequence of statements. For example, the following is a sample procedure declaration that assigns the name **Compliment** to two **writeln** statements:

```
procedure Compliment;
  begin{Compliment}
    writeln('A lovely letter.');
    writeln('One of my favorites.')
  end; {Compliment}
```

In a program with this procedure declaration, the identifier **Compliment** can be used anyplace a statement can be used, and when it is executed, it will cause the following to appear on the screen:

```
A lovely letter.
One of my favorites.
```

Figure 4.1 shows this procedure declaration embedded in a complete program.

The syntax for a simple procedure declaration is as follows. The first part of the procedure is called the *heading*. It consists of the word **procedure** followed by any (non-reserved-word) identifier to serve as the procedure name, followed by a semicolon. This is followed by the *body* of the procedure. The body of the procedure is a list of statements separated by semicolons and enclosed between a **begin/end** pair, just like the body of a program. However, you end a procedure declaration with a semicolon placed after the final **end** and not with a period. In a Pascal program, procedure declarations are placed after the variable declarations and before the main body of the program. The order of declarations within a program is summarized in Figure 4.2.

A procedure name that occurs inside the body of a program is considered to be a special kind of statement called a *procedure call* or a *procedure invocation*. These procedure-call statements are treated just like any other kind of statement when it comes to semicolons and other syntactic features.

A Top-Down Design Example

In the previous chapter, we designed a change making program by dividing the program's task into subtasks as follows:

```
begin
  1. InputAmount: Input the amount;
  2. ComputeChange: Compute a combination of quarters,
       dimes and pennies whose value equals the amount;
  3. OutputCoins: Output the coins
end.
```

Program

```
program BriefEncounter(input, output);

var FirstI, LastI: char;

procedure Compliment;
   begin{Compliment}
    writeln('A lovely letter.');
    writeln('One of my favorites.')
   end; {Compliment}

begin{Program}
  writeln('Please enter your first initial.');
  readln(FirstI);
  Compliment;
  writeln('Now enter your last initial.');
  readln(LastI);
  Compliment;
  writeln('Pleased to meet you ', FirstI, '.', LastI, '.')
end. {Program}
```

Sample Dialogue

Please enter your first initial.
J
A lovely letter.
One of my favorites.
Now enter your last initial.
R
A lovely letter.
One of my favorites.
Pleased to meet you J.R.

Figure 4.1
Program with a
procedure.

Figure 4.2
Order of
declarations.

1. Constant declarations.
2. Variable declarations.
3. Procedure declarations.

Subtask 2 was further subdivided as follows:

begin
2a. **ComputeQuarters**: Compute the maximum number of quarters in **Amount** and set **AmountLeft** equal to the value of what is left after giving out that many quarters;
2b. **ComputeDimes**: Compute the maximum number of dimes in **AmountLeft** and decrease **AmountLeft** by the value of the dimes;
2c. **ComputePennies**: Compute the number of pennies in **AmountLeft**
end

*procedures
for subtasks*

By means of procedure declarations, we can assign a name to the Pascal code for each of these subtasks, as is done in the program shown in Figure 4.3. This program is equivalent to the one in Figure 3.11. The two programs will carry on exactly the same dialogue with the user, but the version with procedures explicitly shows the breakdown of the program into smaller subalgorithms.

As the example in Figure 4.3 illustrates, it is permissible, in fact frequently desirable, to have a procedure call inside the body of another procedure declaration. The only constraint is that a procedure call can not appear before the procedure is declared. Hence, the procedure declarations for **ComputeQuarters**, **ComputeDimes** and **ComputePennies** must be given before the procedure declaration for **ComputeChange**.

*procedures
calling other
procedures*

We derived the program in Figure 4.3 in an artificial, almost pointless way—that is, we first wrote the program without procedures and then rewrote it using procedures. We did this simply because we did not know about procedures when we first wrote the program. A more logical method for writing this program —and any other program—is to translate each subtask into a procedure and then to write a program like the one in Figure 4.3. The stepwise refinement of tasks into subtasks and the writing of procedures go hand in hand.

Commenting Procedures

Notice that we labeled the **begin/end** pairs in Figure 4.3 with a comment to identify them. Procedure declarations—and other constructs still to be introduced —contain numerous **begin/end** pairs, and it is important to keep track of which ones go together; otherwise, you might omit one or might misread a procedure.

You should include a comment with each procedure heading. The comment should explain everything a programmer using the procedure needs to know, including what the procedure does, what other procedures it calls and what variables it changes. One popular method for doing this is to frame the comment in a box to make it stand out. For instance, the following would be a good

```
program Change3(input, output);
{Outputs the coins used to give an amount between 1 and 99 cents.}
var Amount, AmountLeft,
    Quarters, Dimes, Pennies: integer;

procedure InputAmount;
  begin{InputAmount}
    writeln('Enter an amount of change');
    writeln('from 1 to 99 cents:');
    readln(Amount)
  end; {InputAmount}

procedure ComputeQuarters;
  begin{ComputeQuarters}
    Quarters := Amount div 25;
    AmountLeft := Amount mod 25
  end; {ComputeQuarters}

procedure ComputeDimes;
  begin{ComputeDimes}
    Dimes := AmountLeft div 10;
    AmountLeft := AmountLeft mod 10
  end; {ComputeDimes}

procedure ComputePennies;
  begin{ComputePennies}
    Pennies := AmountLeft
  end; {ComputePennies}

procedure ComputeChange;
  begin{ComputeChange}
    ComputeQuarters;
    ComputeDimes;
    ComputePennies
  end; {ComputeChange}

procedure OutputCoins;
  begin{OutputCoins}
    writeln(Amount, ' cents can be given as:');
    writeln(Quarters, ' quarters');
    writeln(Dimes, ' dimes and');
    writeln(Pennies, ' pennies')
  end; {OutputCoins}
```

Figure 4.3
Procedures calling
procedures.

```
begin{Program}
  InputAmount;
  ComputeChange;
  OutputCoins
end. {Program}
```

comment to add to the procedure **ComputeChange** in Figure 4.3:

```
procedure ComputeChange;
{**************************************************************
* Sets the value of Quarters, Dimes and Pennies to a number of each coin such *
* that the sum of the values of all the coins equals Amount. Also changes the *
* value of the variable AmountLeft. Calls the procedures ComputeQuarters, *
* ComputeDimes and ComputePennies. *
**************************************************************}
```

On large programming projects that involve more than one programmer, this comment should also contain the author's name and the date written, as well as the date and nature of any modifications to the procedure. In this book we will use a somewhat shorter comment format, in order to save space.

Testing Procedures

Because they divide big tasks into smaller tasks of more manageable size, procedures make programs easier to write and easier to change. You can solve each subtask separately, write it up as a procedure and then test it separately.

testing example

For example, consider the change-making program in Figure 4.3. We can test each of the procedures separately. We can check the procedure **InputAmount** by using a program such as the one in Figure 4.4. Having tested this procedure, we can go on to test the other procedures.

We can test the procedure **ComputeQuarters** with a program such as the one in Figure 4.5. The procedures **ComputeDimes** and **ComputePennies** can be tested by similar programs. Once these three programs have been tested, we can then test the procedure **ComputeChange**.

Each procedure in a program should receive a separate test. The method we outlined for testing the change program is called *bottom-up testing* and is one of two basic methods for testing a program. In the bottom-up testing strategy each procedure is tested and debugged before any procedure that uses it is tested. One possible order for bottom-up testing of our change program is given in Figure 4.6.

bottom-up testing

If you test each procedure separately, you will find most of the mistakes in your program. Moreover, you will find out which procedure contains the mistake. If instead you just tested the entire program, and if there is a mistake, then you will probably find out that there is a mistake but may have no idea of where it is. Even worse, you may think you know where the mistake is but be wrong.

```pascal
program Test1(input, output);

var Amount: integer;

procedure InputAmount;
  begin{InputAmount}
    writeln('Enter an amount of change');
    writeln('from 1 to 99 cents:');
    readln(Amount)
  end;{InputAmount}

begin{Program}
  InputAmount;
  writeln('Amount = ', Amount)
end. {Program}
```

Figure 4.4
Test 1.

Program

```pascal
program Test2(input, output);

var Amount, AmountLeft, Quarters: integer;

procedure ComputeQuarters;
  begin{ComputeQuarters}
    Quarters := Amount div 25;
    AmountLeft := Amount mod 25
  end; {ComputeQuarters}

begin{Program}
  writeln('Enter Amount');
  readln(Amount);
  ComputeQuarters;
  writeln('Amount = ', Amount);
  writeln('Quarters = ', Quarters);
  writeln('AmountLeft = ', AmountLeft)
end. {Program}
```

Sample Dialogue

Enter Amount
80
Amount =   80
Quarters =   3
AmountLeft =   5

Figure 4.5
Test 2.

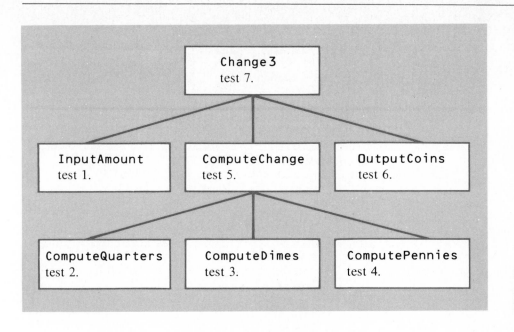

Figure 4.6
One order for
bottom-up testing.

For example, suppose that in the procedure `ComputeDimes`, we had mistakenly written

`AmountLeft := AmountLeft ` *div* ` 10`

instead of

`AmountLeft := AmountLeft ` *mod* ` 10`

In other words, suppose we had mistakenly written *div* in place of *mod* in the procedure `ComputeDimes`. Then our program would output the correct number of quarters and dimes, but would usually give the wrong number of pennies. The natural inference is that the problem is in the procedure `ComputePennies`. This might result in our wasting hours looking for the mistake in that procedure, when in fact the mistake is in the procedure `ComputeDimes`. By testing each procedure separately, we would immediately detect that the mistake is in the procedure `OutputDimes`.

Testing each procedure separately may sound like a very time-consuming process. However, if you follow this strategy, you will find that the time saved by quickly locating bugs will allow you to write the final program faster than if you wrote and tested the program as a single undivided unit.

Top-Down and Bottom-Up Strategies

The bottom-up testing strategy, presented in the last section, is a reasonable strategy for testing a small program or small portions of a larger program. However, when testing a large program, the bottom-up strategy does not always

top-down
testing

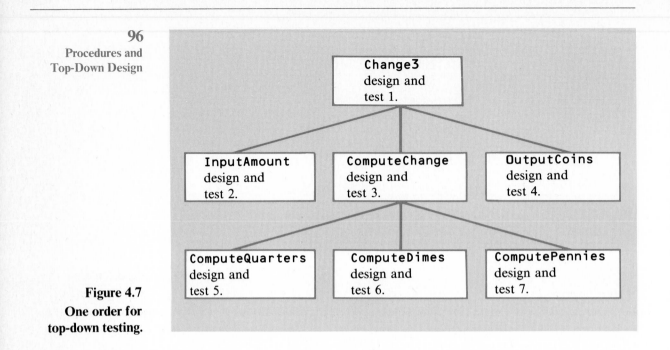

**Figure 4.7
One order for
top-down testing.**

make sense. The best way to design a program is top-down. First, break the task down into subtasks. Then write procedures for the subtasks. These procedures will contain calls to yet other procedures to perform smaller subtasks. In order to test the basic design strategy, it frequently is a good idea to test each procedure before going on to design the procedures it uses. This method of testing is called *top-down testing*. For example, a possible top-down order for testing the procedures in our change program is given in Figure 4.7.

How can you test a procedure or program, such as **Change3**, before writing the procedures it uses? The answer is to write simple versions of the missing procedures and to use these simplified versions to test the calling program (or procedure). The simple version will not do what the final procedure is supposed to do, but it will behave like the procedure is supposed to behave on the test cases it is run on. For example, the following will do as a temporary version of **ComputeChange**:

```
procedure ComputeChange;
{Sets the values of Quarters, Dimes and Pennies
so that those numbers of coins total to Amount.
THIS IS ONLY A TEMPORARY VERSION TO USE IN TESTING}
  begin{ComputeChange}
    writeln('Enter numbers of quarters, dimes and');
    writeln('pennies that total to $ ', Amount);
    readln(Quarters, Dimes, Pennies)
  end; {ComputeChange}
```

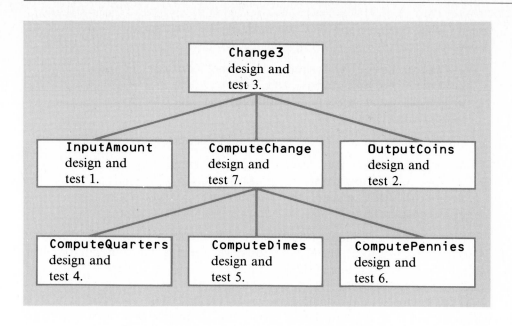

Figure 4.8
One order for a
mixed strategy.

You can also write temporary versions of **ComputeDimes** and **Compute-** *stub*
Pennies. You can then use these temporary versions to test the program *programs*
Change3. Early versions of the program with simplified versions of some
procedures are frequently called *stub* programs.

The advantages of bottom-up testing are obvious. Each procedure is tested
with fully debugged, final versions of the procedures it uses. The advantage of
top-down testing is that it allows you to test your basic design strategy before you
get too far along in the design process. It allows you to test whether or not a
particular breakdown of tasks into subtasks will work as desired. If it will not,
there is no need to solve the subtasks. In that case, you need to back up and
rethink the way you divided the task into subtasks.

Sometimes it is best to test bottom-up, sometimes it is best to test top-down
and sometimes it is best to mix the two strategies, testing some procedures
bottom-up and some top-down. Figure 4.8 gives a mixed strategy that we could
have used to design and test our change program. If the procedures are designed
in the order given there, then the above simplified version of **ComputeChange**
can be used until the final version is written.

Variable Parameters

Suppose we want to design a program to help our cashier total the cash on hand
at the end of a work day. The cashier counts the number of each coin and enters
the number of each coin; the program then computes the dollar value of the
coins. To avoid input errors, each input statement is prefaced by a warning of

exactly what to input and how to input it. The program might start out as follows:

```
writeln('Enter the number of half dollar coins.');
writeln('Do not total the amount.');
writeln('Just enter the number of coins.');
readln(HalfDollars)
```

The program might next request the number of quarters, as follows:

```
writeln('Enter the number of quarters.');
writeln('Do not total the amount.');
writeln('Just enter the number of coins.');
readln(Quarters)
```

Since the last three lines of these two pieces of code are essentially the same, it makes sense to declare them as a procedure. There is, however, one problem with this idea. The last line is slightly different in these two pieces of code. One time we use the variable **HalfDollars** and one time we use the variable **Quarters**. One solution would be to make the procedure only two lines long and omit the last of the three lines from the procedure, just as we are choosing to omit the first of these lines. That will work, but it is not a very good solution. What we really want is a procedure that has a blank for the variable and can have this blank filled in with **HalfDollars** in the first procedure call, filled in with **Quarters** in the second call and filled in with **Dimes**, **Nickels** and **Pennies** later on. Pascal allows us to do just that.

*formal
variable
parameters*

The object which acts as a blank to be filled is called a *formal variable parameter*, and while it looks exactly like a variable, it is not a variable. It is a labeled blank that must be filled in with a variable when the procedure is called. A formal variable parameter may be any identifier other than a reserved word. A procedure called **GetNumber**, which uses a formal variable parameter called **Number** and performs the task we desire, is given in the program in Figure 4.9. In order to use the procedure with the particular variable **HalfDollars** substituted for the formal variable parameter **Number**, use a procedure call that looks like the following:

GetNumber(HalfDollars)

*actual
variable
parameters*

The variable in the procedure call, in this case **HalfDollars**, is called an *actual variable parameter*. When the procedure is called, *every occurrence* of the formal variable parameter within the body of the procedure declaration is replaced by the actual variable parameter and then the statements in the procedure body are executed. This process is sometimes called *parameter passing*. As that program illustrates, a procedure may be called more than once using different actual parameters each time.

Notice that a formal variable parameter has a type that must be stated in the procedure heading and that the formal and actual parameters must agree in type. The type specification for a formal variable parameter looks very much like a variable declaration and is given in the procedure heading in parentheses after the

Program

```pascal
program TotalChange(input, output);
{Reads in the number of each coin and outputs their total value.}

const MoneyLength = 7; {Field length for total amount}
var HalfDollars, Quarters, Dimes,
    Nickels, Pennies: integer;
    Total: real;

procedure GetNumber(var Number: integer);
{Writes instructions to the user, and then reads a number
of coins from the keyboard and stores that number in Number.}
   begin{GetNumber}
     writeln('Do not total the amount.');
     writeln('Just enter the number of coins.');
     readln(Number)
   end; {GetNumber}

begin{Program}
   writeln('Enter the number of half dollar coins.');
   GetNumber(HalfDollars);

   writeln('Enter the number of quarters.');
   GetNumber(Quarters);

   writeln('Enter the number of dimes.');
   GetNumber(Dimes);

   writeln('Enter the number of nickels.');
   GetNumber(Nickels);

   writeln('Enter the number of pennies.');
   GetNumber(Pennies);

   Total := 0.50*HalfDollars +
            0.25*Quarters +
            0.10*Dimes +
            0.05*Nickels +
            0.01*Pennies;

   writeln(HalfDollars, ' half dollars ',
                        Quarters,' quarters,');
   writeln(Dimes, ' dimes,', Nickels,' nickels and');
   writeln(Pennies, ' pennies');
   writeln('Total to: $', Total :MoneyLength:2)
end. {Program}
```

Figure 4.9

**Program with
parameterized
procedures.**

Sample Dialogue

Enter the number of half dollar coins.
Do not total the amount.
Just enter the number of coins.
12
Enter the number of quarters.
Do not total the amount.
Just enter the number of coins.
325
Enter the number of dimes.
Do not total the amount.
Just enter the number of coins.
103
Enter the number of nickels.
Do not total the amount.
Just enter the number of coins.
107
Enter the number of pennies.
Do not total the amount.
Just enter the number of coins.
57
    12 half dollars,   325 quarters,
    103 dimes,   107 nickels
and 57 pennies
Total to: $ 103.47

Figure 4.9 (cont'd)

procedure name. Since the type of the parameter is given in the procedure heading, it need not be given anyplace else. In particular, it should not be declared in the variable declarations of the program. After all, it is not a variable.

Parameter Lists

*formal
parameter
list*

A procedure can have any number of formal variable parameters. They are simply all listed in parentheses after the variable name in the procedure heading and are separated by semicolons. For example, one procedure heading might be:

```
procedure ComputeTax(var P1: integer;
                     var P2: real; var P3: real);
```

When two or more formal variable parameters are of the same type and occur one after the other in the list of parameters, then they may be combined so that their type need only be written once. In that case, the combined parameters are separated by commas. For example, the following procedure heading is equivalent to the one just given:

```
procedure ComputeTax(var P1: integer;
                     var P2, P3: real);
```

Notice that there is a **var** for each group of formal variable parameters.

When the procedure is called, the actual variable parameters are given in parentheses after the procedure name and their types must correspond exactly to that of the formal parameters. The substitution follows the ordering: the first actual parameter is substituted for the first formal parameter, the second actual parameter is substituted for the second formal parameter and so forth. Hence in the following sample procedure call:

```
ComputeTax(Number, Cost, Tax)
```

the actual variable parameter **Number** must be a variable of type **integer**; the actual variable parameters **Cost** and **Tax** must be variables of type **real**. **Number** is substituted for *all* occurrences of **P1** in the procedure declaration, **Cost** is substituted for *all* occurrences of **P2** and **Tax** is substituted for *all* occurrences of **P3**.

As indicated by this example, one minor syntactic difference between formal and actual parameters is that the actual parameters are separated by commas rather than semicolons. The list of parameters, either formal in the procedure heading or actual in the call, is referred to as a *parameter list*, which means that at least one term dealing with parameters is easy to remember.

The order of substituting actual for formal parameters is illustrated in Figure 4.10. Figure 4.11 shows our example embedded in a complete program and illustrates one way to visualize the complete procedure-call process. First, the actual parameters are substituted for the formal parameters. Second, the body of the procedure declaration is substituted for the procedure call. Finally, the actions prescribed by the resulting code are executed. This sample program computes the amount of sales tax due on a specified number of items, such as two sweaters at $100.00 each.

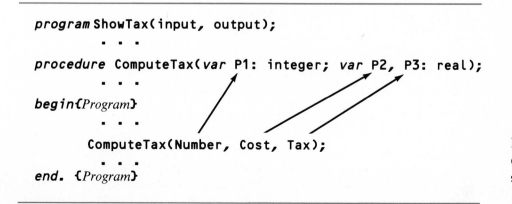

Figure 4.10
Order of parameter
substitutions.

Program

```
program ShowTax(input, output);

const Rate = 0.06;
      TaxLength = 6; {Field length for Tax.}
var Cost, Tax: real;
    Number: integer;

procedure ComputeTax(var P1: integer; var P2, P3: real);
{Computes tax on P1 items which cost P2 each
and sets the value of P3 to the amount of tax.}
    begin{ComputeTax}
      P3 := Rate * P2 * P1
    end; {ComputeTax}

begin{Program}
  writeln('Enter cost of one item,');
  writeln('and the number of items:');
  readln(Cost, Number);
  ComputeTax(Number, Cost, Tax);
  writeln('Tax is $', Tax:TaxLength:2)
end. {Program}
```

1. Substitute formal parameters for actual parameters
to obtain the meaning of the procedure body:

```
begin{ComputeTax}
  Tax := Rate * Cost * Number
end; {ComputeTax}
```

2. Substitute the procedure body for the procedure call:

```
begin{Program}
  writeln('Enter cost of one item,');
  writeln('and the number of items:');
  readln(Cost, Number);
  Tax := Rate * Cost * Number;
  writeln('Tax is $', Tax:TaxLength:2)
end. {Program}
```

3. Execute the resulting code:

Sample Dialogue

Enter cost of one item,
and the number of items:
100.00   2
Tax is $ 12.00

Figure 4.11
How variable
parameters work.

Choosing Parameter Names

Sometimes it is convenient to have formal and actual parameters of the same name. This is perfectly legitimate. Figure 4.12 shows a rewritten version of the program in Figure 4.11. In the rewritten version, the formal and actual parameters are given identical names. Technically speaking, the formal parameter **Number** and the actual parameter **Number** are two different objects that just happen to have the same name. The compiler will even substitute the actual parameter **Number** for the formal parameter **Number** in the program in Figure 4.12. However, when thinking about the program you need not do a mental substitution in this case. Although this can be a good memory aid when a human being reads the program, the compiler does not rely on any such memory tricks. It simply substitutes the first actual parameter for the first formal parameter, the second actual parameter for the second formal parameter and so forth. So, you must be certain that the parameter names are listed in the same orders in the formal and in the actual parameter lists; parameters "differently arranged have a different meaning, and meanings differently arranged have different effects."

The idea of having formal and actual parameters with the same name may seem pointless at first; the same effect can be obtained by completely omitting parameters as we did in Figure 4.3. However, if you use parameters, you make the

```
program ShowTax(input, output);

const Rate = 0.06;
      TaxLength = 6;{Field length for Tax.}
var Cost, Tax: real;
    Number: integer;

procedure ComputeTax(var Number: integer;
                     var Cost, Tax: real);
{Computes tax on Number items which cost Cost each
and sets the value of Tax to the amount of tax.}
    begin{ComputeTax}
      Tax := Rate * Cost * Number
    end; {ComputeTax}

begin{Program}
  writeln('Enter cost of one item,');
  writeln('and the number of items:');
  readln(Cost, Number);
  ComputeTax(Number, Cost, Tax);
  writeln('Tax is $', Tax:TaxLength:2)
end. {Program}
```

actual parameter

formal parameter

Figure 4.12
Procedure call with formal and actual parameters of the same name.

effects of the procedure easier to see. The procedure call gives an indication of what variables it might change. For this reason, you should follow the style shown in Figure 4.12 rather than that in Figure 4.3.

Summary of Problem Solving and Programming Techniques

When designing programs by the top-down method, the subtasks are implemented as procedures. Each procedure should be tested separately in a program that includes no procedures except itself and possibly some other procedures that have already been completely tested and debugged.

You can test a procedure or program before all the procedures it uses have been written. To do so, use simplified versions of the missing procedures.

◇

Little strokes fell great oaks.
Benjamin Franklin, Poor Richard's Almanac

◇

Summary of Pascal Constructs

procedure declaration

Syntax:

> *procedure* ⟨procedure name⟩**(**⟨formal parameter list⟩**);**
> > *begin*
> > > ⟨statement⟩**;**
> > > ⟨statement⟩**;**
> > > ⋮
> > > ⟨statement⟩
> > *end;*

Example:

> *procedure* GetInfo(*var* X, Y: integer; *var* Z: char);
> > *begin*
> > > writeln('Enter two integers and a letter');
> > > readln(X, Y, Z)
> > *end;*

The statements may be any Pascal statements and may contain the formal parameters. (See the next two entries in this summary.)

procedure heading

Syntax:

> *procedure* ⟨procedure name⟩**(**⟨formal parameter list⟩**);**

Examples:

```
procedure GetInfo(var X: integer; var Y: integer;
                                   var Z: char);
procedure GetInfo(var X, Y :integer; var Z: char);
```

The procedure heading is the first thing in a procedure declaration. The ⟨procedure name⟩ can be any identifier other than a reserved word. The ⟨formal parameter list⟩ is a list of identifiers that will serve as formal variable parameters. Each formal variable parameter is prefaced by **var** and is followed by both a colon and its type. The parameters are separated by semicolons. Formal variable parameters of the same type may (optionally) be grouped together and separated by commas. The above two examples are equivalent.

procedure call
Syntax:

⟨procedure name⟩**(**⟨actual parameter list⟩**)**

Example:

```
GetInfo(A, B, C)
```

The ⟨actual parameter list⟩ contains the actual parameters separated by commas. There must be exactly as many actual variable parameters as there are formal variable parameters. The actual variable parameters are substituted into the statements in the body of the procedure and the procedure statements are executed. The first actual variable parameter is substituted for the first formal variable parameter, the second actual variable parameter is substituted for the second formal variable parameter and so forth. Formal and actual parameters must agree in type.

formal variable parameter A formal variable parameter is a labeled blank in a procedure declaration. It may be any identifier other than a reserved word. It is given a type in the formal parameter list of the procedure heading. When the procedure is called, it is replaced by a variable of that type. The variable that replaces it is called an actual variable parameter.

actual variable parameter An actual variable parameter is a variable that replaces a formal variable parameter when a procedure is called. The actual variable parameters are given in the actual parameter list of the procedure call.

Exercises

Self-Test and Interactive Exercises

1. What is the output of the following program?

```
program Exercise1(input, output);
  procedure Friendly;
    begin{Friendly}
      writeln('Hello')
    end; {Friendly}
  procedure Shy;
    begin{Shy}
      writeln('Goodbye')
    end; {Shy}
  begin{Program}
    writeln('Begin Conversation');
    Shy; Friendly;
    writeln('One more time:');
    Friendly; Shy;
    writeln('End Conversation')
  end. {Program}
```

2. What is the output of the following program?

```
program Exercise2(input, output);
  procedure Proced1;
    begin{Proced1}
      write('One ')
    end; {Proced1}
  procedure Proced2;
    begin{Proced2}
      Proced1;
      write('Two ')
    end; {Proced2}
  procedure Proced3;
    begin{Proced3}
      Proced2;
      writeln('Three ')
    end; {Proced3}
  begin{Program}
    Proced1; writeln;
    Proced2; writeln;
    Proced3; writeln
  end. {Program}
```

3. What is the output of the following program?

```
program Exercise3(input, output);
  var X, Y: integer;
  procedure Tricky(var Y, X: integer);
    begin{Tricky}
      writeln(X, Y)
    end; {Tricky}
begin{Program}
  X := 1; Y := 2;
  Tricky(Y, X);
  Tricky(Y, Y);
  Tricky(X, Y)
end. {Program}
```

4. Type up and run the program in Figure 4.12. Then interchange the order of the formal parameters **Cost** and **Tax** and run the program again.

5. Write a procedure with two formal variable parameters **X** and **Y** of type **integer**. The procedure will write the values of **X** and **Y** to the screen, then set the value of **X** equal to the value of **Y**, and then again write the values of **X** and **Y** to the screen. Embed the procedure in a program that sets the value of two integer variables **A** and **B**, and then uses the two variables as actual variable parameters in a procedure call.

6. Rewrite the program from the previous exercise only this time use the same identifiers, **X** and **Y**, for both the formal and the actual variable parameters. Run the modified program.

7. Write a procedure that asks the user to type in a real number, then asks the user to type an integer for the number of decimal places desired and finally echos the real number with exactly as many decimal places as were requested. Embed it in a program and test it.

8. (UCSD Pascal users only) Write a procedure with one parameter of type **string**. The procedure should output appropriate instructions and then fill the **string** variable with the user's name. Embed it in a program and test it.

Regular Exercises

9. Rewrite the program in Figure 4.3 so that each procedure has formal variable parameters for each variable in the body of the procedure declaration. Also add a heading comment to each procedure. Next, enhance your program so that it accepts as input an amount of dollars and cents as a value of type **real** and then outputs the bills as well as the coins that equal that amount. Use bill denominations of $20, $10 and $5. Also include nickels as a possible coin in this version. Use procedures as in the first version.

10. Write a procedure that has two formal parameters, one for the radius of a circle and one for the circumference. The procedure computes the circumference of a circle with the given radius and stores the answer in the parameter for the circumference. Embed this in a program to compute the circumference of a circle. Use two additional procedures, one for input and one for output.

11. Write a procedure that computes the average and standard deviation of four scores. The standard deviation is defined to be the square root of the average of the four values: $(s_i - a)^2$, where a is the average of the four scores s_1, s_2, s_3 and s_4. The procedure will have six parameters and will call two other procedures. Embed the procedure in a program to test it.

12. Write a program that asks the user to type in his/her height, weight and age, and then computes clothes sizes according to the formulas: hat size = weight in pounds divided by height in inches and all that multiplied by 2.9; sweater size (chest in inches) = height times weight divided by 301 and then adjusted by adding 1/8th of an inch for each 10 years of age; waist in inches = weight divided by 5.7 and then adjusted by adding 1/10th of an inch for each 2 years of age. Use procedures for each calculation.

13. You have a choice of two different auto repair mechanics with different rate structures. One charges a flat fee of $20 plus $5 for each quarter hour. The other charges $18 for the first quarter hour and then $5.75 for each quarter hour after that. Write a program that will compute the two rates and display them when the number of hours is input. You can assume that all repairs take at least a quarter hour. Use four or more procedures.

14. Write a program that is a major improvement on the program **Cashier** in Figure 2.4. This improved version asks for the amount tendered by the customer as well as the price of the item. It responds with the price, tax, total price, amount tendered and the change due. It then goes on to tell the cashier exactly what combination of bills and coins will equal the amount of change. Use procedures for subtasks. The program **Change3** in Figure 4.3 can be used as a model for the last part, except that you should use parameters instead of global variables in the procedure declarations.

15. Redo (or do for the first time) Exercise 26 from Chapter 2. Use three procedures, one for input, one for output and one to perform the calculation.

16. Redo (or do for the first time) Exercise 27 from Chapter 2. Use three procedures, one for input, one for output and one to perform the calculation.

17. Redo (or do for the first time) Exercise 30 from Chapter 2. Use at least three procedures, one for input, one for output and one to perform the calculation.

18. Redo (or do for the first time) Exercise 31 from Chapter 2. Use procedures.

19. Redo (or do for the first time) Exercise 16 from Chapter 3. Use at least four procedures.

20. Redo (or do for the first time) Exercise 17 from Chapter 3. Use three procedures, one for input, one for output and one to perform the calculation.

21. Redo (or do for the first time) Exercise 18 from Chapter 3. Use at least four procedures.

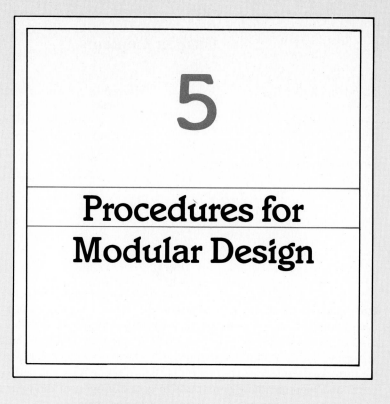

5

Procedures for Modular Design

"My memory is so bad, that many times
I forget my own name!"
Miguel de Cervantes, Don Quixote

Chapter Contents

P rocedures separate a program into smaller, and hence more manageable, pieces. In order to get the full benefit of this decomposition, the procedures must be self-contained units that are meaningful outside the context of the program. A program that is built out of such self-contained procedures is often said to have a *modular* design. In this chapter we introduce some Pascal constructs that allow us to write self-contained procedures and then use these constructs to give examples of modular design. As part of this topic we continue our discussion of parameters.

Local and Global Variables

In order to introduce the notions of local and global variables, we will consider a simple but frequently occurring task and design a procedure to accomplish this task.

Suppose we wish to write a procedure to interchange the value of two variables of type **integer**. The procedure heading will be:

```
procedure Exchange(var X, Y: integer);
```

The body of the procedure presents more of a problem. An obvious but incorrect thing to try is:

```
X := Y; Y := X
```

This sets the new value of **X** to the old value of **Y**, but it sets the new value of **Y** to the *new* value of **X** and so leaves **Y** unchanged. (If this seems unclear, plug in some values and see what happens.) What we need to do is to save the original value of **X** before we change the value of **X**. We can then use that saved value to set the value of **Y**. What we need is another variable to temporarily hold this saved value. Let us call this extra variable **TEMP**. The correct procedure now reads:

```
procedure Exchange(var X, Y: integer);
{Interchanges the values of X and Y.}
  begin{Exchange}
    TEMP := X;
    X := Y;
    Y := TEMP
  end; {Exchange}
```

That will work nicely except for one annoying detail. Since the procedure **Exchange** changes the value of **TEMP**, we must remember not to use the variable **TEMP** for anything else. This is most unfortunate. The whole idea of stepwise refinement and procedures was to break big tasks into smaller tasks. We make no headway in this direction if when designing a procedure, we need to remember the details of how all the other procedures work. Once we get a procedure to work, we should only need to remember what it does and not how it does it. The procedure heading and one explanatory comment are all we should need to remember. In this case, the following two lines should be all we need to know to use the procedure safely and effectively:

```
procedure Exchange(var X, Y: integer);
{Interchanges the values of X and Y.}
```

Clearly, these two lines are not all we need to remember. We must also remember that the variable **TEMP** has its value changed.

Ideally, we should not have to remember anything about **TEMP**, not even that it was used. What we need is a special version of the variable **TEMP** that exists only for the duration of the procedure call. Fortunately, Pascal and many other programming languages allow such variables. They are called "local variables."

Program

```
program Sample(input, output);

var A, B, TEMP: integer;

procedure Exchange(var X, Y: integer);
{Interchanges the values of X and Y.}
    var TEMP: integer;
begin{Exchange}
  TEMP := X;
  X := Y;
  Y := TEMP;
  writeln(A, B, TEMP)
  {This writeln is here to illustrate the concept of a
  local variable. It would not normally be included.}
end; {Exchange}

begin{Program}
  A := 1;
  B := 2;
  TEMP := 3;
  Exchange(A, B);
  writeln(A, B, TEMP)
end. {Program}
```

Output

2 1 1
2 1 3

Figure 5.1
Procedure with a
local variable.

local variables

global variables

A *local variable* is a variable that is declared within a procedure. Variables that are declared for the entire program are called *global variables*. All the variables we have used up until now are global variables. Local variables are declared just like global variables except that the declaration is placed inside the procedure declaration between the procedure heading and the **begin** that marks the start of the procedure body. A local variable is only meaningful inside the procedure. No statement outside the procedure body may reference the local variable.

The program in Figure 5.1 includes the procedure **Exchange** with **TEMP** declared as a local variable. A **writeln** has been added to the procedure in order to show the value of the local variable. Although the procedure has numerous useful applications, this particular program does not have any applications. It is just an example to illustrate how global and local variables work.

interpreting local variables

The program in Figure 5.1 has two variables called **TEMP**: one global variable declared for the entire program and one local variable declared for the procedure **Exchange**. What is the relationship between these two different variables called

TEMP? They share the same name, but otherwise, there is no relationship between them. They are two totally different variables. The computer does manage to keep track of these two different variables even though they have but one name between them. It is as if the computer acted in the following way: When a procedure is called, the computer checks to see if there are any local variables. If there are, such as **TEMP** in the procedure **Exchange**, it looks to see if there are also any global program variables called by the same name as one of these local variables; in this case there is one such variable. The computer then gives the global variable a temporary name that is not a Pascal identifier, but otherwise behaves like a variable name. It then executes the procedure call using the Pascal identifier as the name of the local variable. During the execution of the procedure, the global variable has no Pascal name. Up until the time the procedure call is completed, the shared name always applies to the local variable. When the procedure call is completed, the Pascal name is restored to the global variable, and from that point on there is no way to refer to the local variable.

In the procedure declaration in Figure 5.1, the identifier **TEMP** on the left-hand side of the assignment operator names the local variable, not the global variable. Hence, the global variable is not changed. That is why the second output line is *2 1 3* as shown. If **TEMP** were not declared as a local variable, that is, if the following line were omitted from the procedure declaration:

example

    var TEMP: integer;

then the output would instead be:

    2 1 1
    2 1 1

The notion of a local variable can be confusing at first and so it will not hurt to have another equivalent characterization. Local variables behave as if the computer did the following: When the compiler is given the Pascal program, it first manufactures some extra identifiers that do not occur anyplace in the program. It then looks at each procedure to see if the procedure contains any local variables. If a procedure contains a local variable, it replaces all the occurrences of that local variable (all of which are inside the procedure declaration) by some one of these extra identifiers. The global variables are left alone. After doing this to all the local variables, it then translates the program into machine code.

Because the computer handles local variables in this way, we can design procedures using local variables and not even bother to remember which identifiers we used for the local variables. If, outside the procedure, we reuse those identifiers to mean something else, the computer will know we mean something else.

Other Local Identifiers

Identifiers other than variable names may be local to a procedure. Any kind of declaration allowed in a Pascal program is also allowed in a Pascal procedure. A procedure may have local constants and local procedures of its own as well as

*local
declarations*

Program

```pascal
program Talk2(input, output);
const OpeningLine = 'Hello, my name is Ronald Gollum.';
      Compliment = 'You''re a wonderful person.';
      Farewell = 'I hope we meet again.';

procedure BreakIce;

  const OpeningLine = 'Haven''t we met somewhere before?';
  var FirstI, LastI: char;
  procedure Compliment;
    begin{Compliment}
      writeln('A lovely name.');
      writeln('I really like that name.')
    end; {Compliment}

begin{BreakIce}
  writeln(OpeningLine);
  readln;
  writeln('What is your first name?');
  readln(FirstI);
  Compliment;
  writeln('What is your last name?');
  readln(LastI);
  Compliment;
  writeln('Pleased to meet you ', FirstI,'.',LastI,'.')
end; {BreakIce}

begin{Program}
  writeln(OpeningLine);
  BreakIce;
  writeln(Compliment);
  writeln(Farewell)
end. {Program}
```

Figure 5.2
Local identifiers.

Hello, my name is Ronald Gollum.
Haven't we met somewhere before?
I don't think so.
What is your first name?
Jane
A lovely name.
I really like that name.
What is your last name?
Doe
A lovely name.
I really like that name.
Pleased to meet you J.D.
You're a wonderful person.
I hope we meet again.

Figure 5.2 (cont'd)

local variables. The situation with respect to these local declarations is the same as that of local variables. The local constant or local procedure exists only while the procedure in which it is declared is executing. Outside of the procedure, you can reuse a local identifier to name something else. The ordering of local declarations in a procedure is the same as the ordering of declarations within a program.

local
constants

Figure 5.2 shows a procedure that has a local constant and a local procedure, in addition to local variables. There are two string constants called **Opening-Line**, one global and one local to the procedure **BreakIce**. The identifier **Compliment** is defined globally to be a string constant. However, within the procedure declaration **BreakIce**, it is also declared to be the name of a local procedure. Within the procedure **BreakIce**, the identifier **Compliment** names a procedure. Outside the procedure **BreakIce** it names a string constant.

local
procedures

An advantage of local procedures is that they make the calling procedure a self-contained unit. Hence, if they are short and not used outside of the calling procedure, it makes sense to use local procedures. However, large procedures are seldom made local to other procedures. The inclusion of numerous long local procedures can separate a procedure heading from the main part of the procedure and so make the calling procedure awkward to read.

Scope of a Local Identifier

In a simple program with one procedure, every variable or other identifier is either local to the procedure or global to the whole program. However, if the program includes procedures that call other procedures, then the notion of global

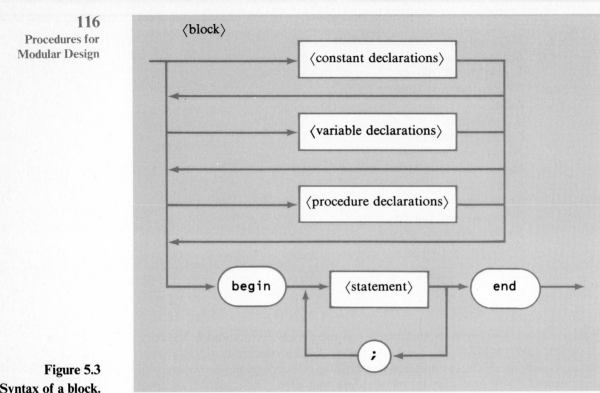

Figure 5.3
Syntax of a block.

and local are not absolute but relative. In such cases, the explanation of local identifiers is a bit more complicated.

block

A set of declarations together with the list of statements it applies to is called a *block*. (The syntax is summarized in Figure 5.3.) This term is used to refer to a procedure and also to an entire program. All the identifiers declared at the start of

scope

a block are said to be *local to that block* or, equivalently, to have that block as their *scope*. The meaning given to the identifier by that declaration applies only within that block. Moreover, if the identifier is declared in two blocks, one within the other, then in the inner block its meaning is the one determined by the declaration in the inner block. A possible arrangement of blocks and local identifiers is illustrated in Figure 5.4.

Value Parameters

A procedure can use variable parameters to give and to receive information from the rest of the program. There is another class of parameters called *value parameters*. Value parameters are "one-way" parameters; they can be used to supply information to a procedure, but they can not be used to get information out of a procedure. On the positive side, value parameters allow us to use more

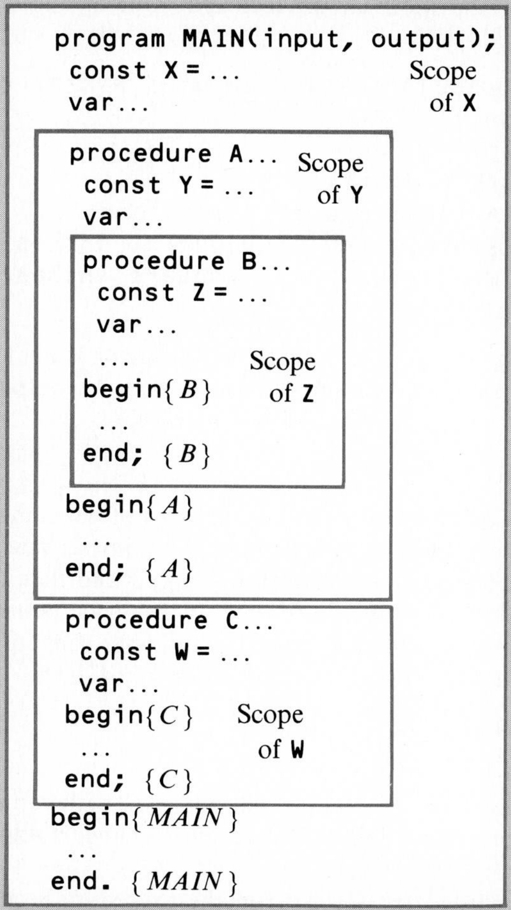

```
program MAIN(input, output);
  const X = ...              Scope
  var...                     of X
    procedure A...  Scope
      const Y = ...    of Y
    var...
      procedure B...
        const Z = ...
      var...
      ...              Scope
      begin{B}          of Z
      ...
      end;  {B}
    begin{A}
    ...
    end;  {A}
    procedure C...
      const W = ...
    var...
    begin{C}    Scope
    ...            of W
    end;  {C}
  begin{MAIN}
  ...
  end.  {MAIN}
```

Figure 5.4
Scope of identifiers.

complicated expressions as the actual parameters in a procedure call. The notion is best introduced by means of an example.

Suppose we want to write a procedure that will output the area of a rectangle to the screen. In this case, the procedure will have two parameters, one for the length and one for the width of the rectangle. Our first attempt at writing the procedure might be as follows:

```
procedure OutputArea1(var Length, Width: real);
  var A: real;
begin{OutputArea1}
  A := Length * Width;
  writeln('A rectangle of dimensions:');
  writeln(Length, ' by ', Width, ' inches');
  writeln('Has area ', A, ' square inches')
end; {OutputArea1}
```

This will work, but in some situations it is inconvenient. If the length and width are stored in variables, say **X** and **Y**, then to output the area of the rectangle, the following procedure call will do nicely:

OutputArea1(X, Y)

Suppose, however, that we wish to output the area of a rectangle four inches long by three inches wide. Since an actual variable parameter must be a variable, we will have to first set two variables equal to **4** and **3** and then use the variables as the actual parameters. That is unfortunate. It would be better if we could write the following expression and then have the computer substitute **4** for the formal parameter **Length** and **3** for the formal parameter **Width**.

OutputArea1(4, 3)
{*Will not work with a variable parameter***}**

As the comment indicates, this simply will not work with variable parameters. To make the above procedure call work, we must change **Length** and **Width** to value parameters.

syntax for
formal
value
parameters

Formal value parameters are listed in the procedure heading along with the formal variable parameters. However, a formal value parameter is not preceded by the word **var**. To make **Length** and **Width** value parameters in our sample procedure, we use the following procedure heading:

procedure OutputArea2(Length, Width: real);

The rest of the procedure is unchanged. The complete procedure using formal value parameters is shown in the first program in Figure 5.5. The second program is equivalent to the first and is given to help explain the meaning of the value parameters in the first program.

actual
value
parameters

When a procedure with formal value parameters is called, it must be supplied with one *actual value parameter* to correspond to each formal value parameter. The value of the actual parameter is used to set the corresponding formal value parameter. Formal value parameters are special kinds of local variables. They are

Program

```
program Value(input, output);

procedure OutputArea2(Length, Width: real);
  var A: real;
begin{OutputArea2}
  A := Length * Width;
  writeln('A rectangle of dimensions:');
  writeln(Length, ' by ', Width, ' inches');
  writeln('has area ', A, ' square inches.')
end; {OutputArea2}

begin{Program}
  OutputArea2(4, 3)
end. {Program}
```

Equivalent (But Not Very Well Written) Program

```
program LikeValue(input, output);
procedure OutputArea3;
  var A, Length, Width: real;
begin{OutputArea3}
  Length := 4;
  Width := 3;
  A := Length * Width;
  writeln('A rectangle of dimensions:');
  writeln(Length, ' by ', Width, ' inches');
  writeln('has area ', A, ' square' inches.')
end; {OutputArea3}

begin{Program}
  OutputArea3
end. {Program}
```

Output (Same for Both Programs)

A rectangle of dimensions:
*   4.00000E00 by   3.00000E00 inches*
has area   1.20000E + 01 square inches.

Figure 5.5
**Procedure with
value parameters.**

just like any other local variables except that they have one additional property. When the procedure is called, the value of each formal value parameter is initialized to the value of the corresponding actual parameter.

The relationship between formal and actual *value* parameters is similar to that between formal and actual *variable* parameters. However, unlike an actual *variable* parameter, an actual *value* parameter is not simply "plugged in as is." It is first evaluated and its *value* is then plugged in for the *value* of the formal parameter. For example, if the actual value parameter is a variable **X** whose value is **3**, then it is the **3** that is used rather than the **X**. After the value of the formal value parameters have been set, the statements in the procedure declaration are executed.

*expressions
as
parameters*

Since only the value of an actual value parameter is used, the actual value parameter can be any expression that evaluates to the specified type. That means the actual value parameter can be a variable, but it might instead be a constant or arithmetic expression or anything which evaluates to a value of the correct type. Hence with **OutputArea2**, all of the following sample procedure calls are allowed (**X** and **Y** are variables of type **real**):

```
OutputArea2(X, Y);
OutputArea2(5.2, 3.71E-12);
OutputArea2(X + 7.1, sqrt(2.0))
```

*formal value
parameters
as local
variables*

Since a formal value parameter is a local variable, you can use it just like any other local variable. Figure 5.6 illustrates a value parameter being used as a local variable. The formal value parameter **Minutes** in the procedure **OutputTime** is a local variable that is changed by the procedure. Only the value of the actual parameter **TimeWorked** is used and so that variable is not changed by the procedure call:

```
OutputTime(TimeWorked)
```

Program

```
program Payroll(input, output);
```
{*Input is the number of minutes worked.
Output is the time worked in hours and minutes
as well as the pay due at a rate of Rate cents per minute.*}

```
const Rate = 10;{Cents per minute}
      MoneyLength = 7;{Field width for PayDue}
var TimeWorked: integer;
    PayDue: real;
```

Figure 5.6

**A value parameter
used as a local
variable.**

```
procedure OutputTime(Minutes: integer);
```
{*Outputs Minutes number of minutes as hours and minutes.
The value of the actual parameter corresponding to Minutes
is unchanged.*}

```
      var Hours: integer;
      begin{OutputTime}
        Hours := Minutes div 60;
        Minutes := Minutes mod 60;
        writeln(Hours, ' hours and ', Minutes, ' minutes')
      end; {OutputTime}

procedure ComputePay(Minutes: integer; var Pay: real);
{Minutes is the time worked in minutes. Rate is a global
constant equal to the pay rate expressed as pennies per
minute. Pay is set to the pay due expressed in dollars.}
      var PennyPay: integer;
      begin{ComputePay}
        PennyPay := Rate * Minutes;
        Pay := PennyPay/100
      end; {ComputePay}

begin{Program}
  writeln('Enter the number of minutes you worked');
  readln(TimeWorked);
  write('You worked: ');
  OutputTime(TimeWorked);
  ComputePay(TimeWorked, PayDue);
  writeln('At ', Rate, ' cents per minute,');
  writeln('you earned: $', PayDue:MoneyLength:2)
end. {Program}
```

Output

Enter the number of minutes you worked
62
You worked: 1 hours and   2 minutes
At   10 cents per minute,
you earned: $ 6.20

Figure 5.6 (cont'd)

Mixed Parameter Lists

You may use any number of parameters in a procedure and they may be any combination of variable and value parameters. You simply list them all in the procedure heading. For example, one procedure heading might be:

procedure Sample(W: real; var X: real; Y, Z: char);

Each formal parameter has a type associated with it. Those that are variable parameters are preceded by the word **var**. Formal value parameters are indicated by the absence of the **var**. In the sample heading, **X** is a variable parameter; **W**, **Y** and **Z** are value parameters. The various formal parameters are separated by semicolons. When two consecutive parameters are of the same type and are either both value or both variable parameters, then you can combine their type specification in the way illustrated by **Y** and **Z** in the sample heading. The details are summarized by the syntax diagram in Figure 5.7.

In the procedure call, the actual parameters are given in parentheses after the procedure name and they must correspond in type to the formal parameters. For example, in the procedure call

Sample(2.5, A, 'B', C)

the actual value parameter **2.5** is substituted for the value of **W**, the actual variable parameter **A** is literally substituted for formal parameter **X**, the actual value parameter **'B'** is substituted for the value of **Y** and the value of the actual value parameter **C** is substituted for the value of **Z**. The variable **A** must have been declared to be of type **real** and the variable **C** must have been declared to be of type **char**.

*summary
of the
kinds of
parameters*

There are four kinds of parameters: formal variable parameters, actual variable parameters, formal value parameters and actual value parameters. The long names convey meaning about how the parameters are used. The way to think of parameters is in a two-step process: first, the parameter is either *formal* or *actual*; second, it is either *variable* or *value*. These two two-way distinctions yield the four possible kinds of parameters. A formal parameter appears in a procedure declaration and is changed when the procedure is called. The actual parameter governs the change and that change is always some sort of substitution of the actual parameter for the formal parameter. A formal parameter and its corresponding actual parameter are either both called variable parameters or both called value parameters. The distinction between value and variable parameters refers to the manner in which the substitution is performed. In the case of variable parameters, the actual parameter is literally substituted for the formal parameter. In the case of value parameters, the value of the actual parameter is used to initialize ("is substituted for") the value of the formal parameter.

Most programming languages have a distinction similar to value versus variable parameters. All programming languages with facilities for parameters employ the distinction between formal and actual parameters.

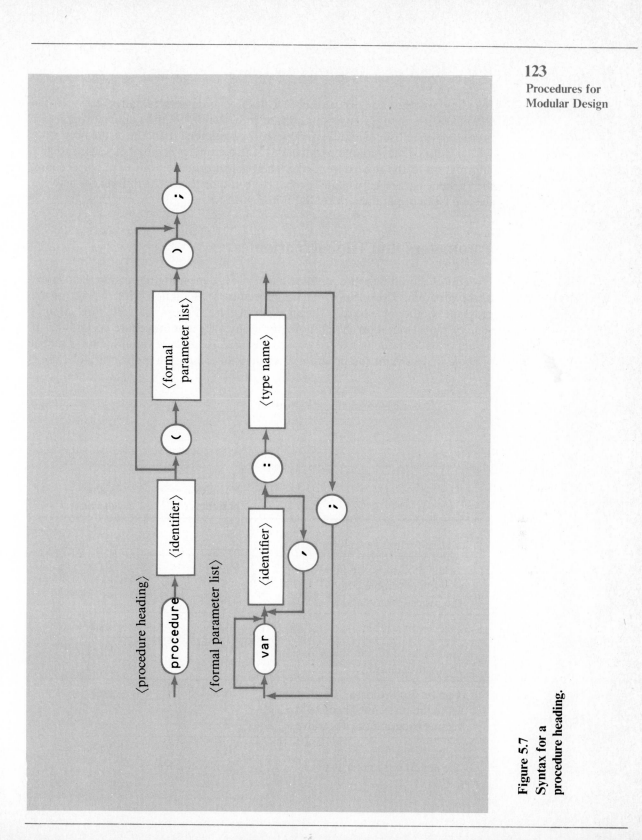

Figure 5.7
Syntax for a
procedure heading.

What Kind of Parameter to Use

Deciding whether to use variable or value parameters is fairly easy. If the procedure is supposed to communicate information to the calling program or procedure, then use a variable parameter (or parameters) and have the procedure set the value of the variable parameter. If the parameter is only being used to give information to the procedure, rather than get information out of the procedure, then a value parameter can and probably should be used. The differences between the two types of parameters are listed in Figure 5.8.

Parameters and Global Variables

*the problem
with global
variables*

Procedures should be self-contained units that are meaningful outside the context of the program. This means that the procedure's interaction with the rest of the program should be entirely through parameters. Except in very rare circumstances, global variables should not appear anyplace in a procedure declaration. If a temporary variable is needed in a procedure, use a local variable, not a global variable. If you want the program to change the value of a global variable, use a

**Figure 5.8
Differences
between variable
and value
parameters.**

	Variable parameter	Value parameter
var in formal parameter list	YES	NO
Is just a blank to be filled in with a variable when the procedure is called	YES	NO
Is a local variable	NO	YES
Can be used to pass information to the procedure	YES	YES
Can be used to pass information from the procedure back to the calling program or procedure	YES	NO
Expressions allowed in the actual parameter list	NO (just variables)	YES

formal parameter in the procedure declaration, and then use the global variable as the actual parameter in a procedure call.

Self-Documenting Procedures

Our previous programs dealing with money treated amounts of money as **real** numbers representing an amount like $45.98 as the **real** number **45.9800**. Frequently it makes more sense to treat amounts of money as data of type **integer**. For example, in this other method $45.98 is represented as the **integer** value **4598** , which can be thought of as that many pennies. The reason for doing this is that **integer** values are represented as exact quantities while **real** values are represented only as approximate quantities. Accountants do not generally deal in approximate quantities, and the approximate representation of **real** values can sometimes cause even a simple calculation to deviate a penny or so from the correct answer. The extra accuracy obtained by using integers instead of reals does make our programming task more complicated in numerous ways. Dealing with these complications will give us an opportunity to illustrate the value of procedures and to explain an important point about how to write understandable procedures.

Working in this way with amounts expressed as pennies, we will from time to time need to include output statements to display amounts of money on the screen. To be concrete, let's say that **Cost** is a variable of type **integer**, containing the cost of something in cents, and suppose we wish to display this cost on the screen. One possibility is:

```
write('The cost is: ');
write(Cost, ' cents')
```

This will work but it can give very unusual looking output such as:

The cost is: 12598 cents

The output should look like the following:

The cost is: $ 125.98

The number of dollars is **Cost** *div* **100**, in other words, the number of pennies divided by **100** with the remainder discarded. The remainder, **Cost** *mod* **100**, is the amount of cents. Thus, one way to get output in the desired format is:

```
write('The cost is: $');
write((Cost div 100):4, '.', (Cost mod 100):2)
```

The parentheses around the dollar and cent amounts are not needed but they do make it easier to see what the field width specifications apply to.

If we need to output these sorts of amounts frequently in a program, we do not want to rewrite all that detail for each amount output. We should instead design a procedure containing one formal parameter, call it **Pennies**, that will later be filled in with actual parameters such as **Cost** and that will output the amount in a nice format. The following procedure does what is desired:

```
procedure MoneyWrite(Pennies: integer);
{Outputs Pennies cents to screen in dollars and cents format.}
begin
    write('$', (Pennies div 100):4,
                    '.', (Pennies mod 100):2)
end;
```

Even though this procedure contains only one statement, it does free us from worrying about small details so that we can concentrate on the central tasks of the program, such as computing the cost.

The above procedure has a well-chosen name and is explained by a comment. It will be very easy to use. However, it is not all that easy to read the procedure itself. If you leave it and come back to it in a week or month or if somebody else reads it, its meaning is certainly not transparently clear. What is the significance of **Cost** *div* **100** and of **Cost** *mod* **100**? What is that funny little speck in quotes? We can rewrite our procedure **MoneyWrite** to be more readable by using two local variables and a constant as shown in Figure 5.9. By choosing suitably suggestive names for the local variables and constants, we can get the effect of comments such as:

> {*Pennies div 100 is the number of dollars in Pennies cents.*}
> {*Pennies mod 100 is the number of cents left in Pennies cents*
> *after deleting as many dollars as possible.*}
> {*Outputs dollars and cents with a decimal point.*}

By carefully choosing variable names, we can pack in all the information that such comments would provide, but we do not need to clutter the procedure declaration with such long wordy comments.

By carefully laying out programs, carefully choosing substeps and choosing meaningful identifiers, we can write easy to understand programs that do not

Figure 5.9
Procedure with
self-documenting
local variables.

```
procedure MoneyWrite(Pennies: integer);
{Outputs Pennies cents to screen in dollars and cents format.}
    const DollarLength = 4;
          DecimalPoint = '.';
    var Dollars, Cents: integer;

begin{MoneyWrite}
    Dollars := Pennies div 100;
    Cents := Pennies mod 100;
    write('$', Dollars:DollarLength,
                DecimalPoint, Cents:2)
end; {MoneyWrite}
```

need many comments. Such procedures and programs that explain themselves, so to speak, are said to be *self-documenting*. Since it saves space and is usually clearer than wordy comments, you should use self-documenting techniques whenever possible.

Designing a Sample Procedure

In this section we will design a procedure to write "HI" on the screen in large block letters.

There is an obvious decomposition of this task into two subtasks: Write an "H" and then write an "I." In order to decompose these tasks into subtasks, we observe that most letters, including these two, can be formed out of combinations of horizontal and vertical bars as follows:

This is similar to the way that digits are formed on a digital watch display except that, unlike a digital watch display, we will allow our procedure to move the various bars to the left or to the right.

We next design procedures for the subtasks of drawing vertical and horizontal bars. The amount of indentation will be a value parameter to the procedures. For example, our procedure for drawing a vertical bar is as follows:

```
procedure VertBar(Indent: integer);
{Draws a vertical bar. Skips Indent spaces on the left.}
begin{VertBar}
  writeln('*':Indent + 1);
  writeln('*':Indent + 1)
end; {VertBar}
```

This procedure draws a bar of height two spaces. The reason for the extra space in the field width is that this procedure is supposed to leave **Indent** blanks and then write a vertical bar of width one space.

When we start to use this procedure to draw an "H" we immediately observe a problem. Pascal does not allow a program to "back up" and rewrite a line of output. Hence, this procedure will not allow us to draw two vertical lines side by side. Since that is what we need in order to form an "H," we must write a separate procedure to draw two vertical bars. Our procedure for two vertical bars is:

```
procedure TwoVertBars(Indent: integer);
begin{TwoVertBars}
  writeln('*':Indent + 1, '*':LetterWidth - 1);
  writeln('*':Indent + 1, '*':LetterWidth - 1)
end; {TwoVertBars}
```

In the above procedure, `LetterWidth` is the width of a single letter. Since this same constant will be used by more than one procedure and since we may want to change it, `LetterWidth` is declared as a constant. We must be able to place the vertical bar of the letter "I" in the center of that field. Hence, this constant must be an odd number. To ensure that any future changes to this

---

Program

```
program HI(input, output);
{Writes 'HI' in block letters.}

    const LetterWidth = 5; {Should be an odd number}
          LetterBar = '*****'; {Letter Width*'s}
          Indent = 10; {Number of spaces on left side of 'HI.'}

procedure VertBar(Indent: integer);
{Draws a vertical bar. Skips Indent spaces on the left.}
begin{VertBar}
  writeln('*':Indent+1);
  writeln('*':Indent+1)
end; {VertBar}

procedure TwoVertBars(Indent: integer);
{Draws two vertical bars so as to fill a field of
width LetterWidth; skips Indent spaces on left.}
begin{TwoVertBars}
  writeln('*':Indent+1, '*':LetterWidth-1);
  writeln('*':Indent+1, '*':LetterWidth-1)
end; {TwoVertBars}

procedure HorizBar(Indent: integer);
{Draws a horizontal bar of width LetterWidth;
skips Indent spaces on left.}
begin{HorizBar}
  writeln(LetterBar:Indent+LetterWidth)
end; {HorizBar}

procedure BigH(Indent: integer);
{Draws a large 'H'. Skips Indent spaces on the left.}
begin{BigH}
  TwoVertBars(Indent);
  HorizBar(Indent);
  TwoVertBars(Indent)
end; {BigH}
```

Figure 5.10
Procedure BigHI
in a program.

```
procedure BigI(Indent: integer);
{Draws a large 'I'. Skips Indent spaces on the left
and then centers the I in a field of length LetterWidth.}
    var HalfWidth: integer;
begin{BigI}
  HalfWidth := LetterWidth div 2;
  HorizBar(Indent);
  VertBar(Indent + HalfWidth);
  VertBar(Indent + HalfWidth);
  HorizBar(Indent)
end; {BigI}

procedure BigHI(Indent: integer);
{Draws a big 'HI'. Skips Indent spaces on the left.}
    const OffSet = 5;
begin{BigHI}
  BigH(Indent);
  BigI(Indent + OffSet)
end; {BigHI}

begin{Program}
  writeln('This is a test HI.');
  BigHI(Indent);
  writeln('Had this been a real application,');
  writeln('more program would follow.')
end. {Program}
```

Output

This is a test HI.
```
        *       *
        *       *
        * * * * *
        *       *
        *       *
              * * * * *
                  *
                  *
                  *
              * * * * *
```

Had this been a real application,
more program would follow.

Figure 5.10 (cont'd)

constant honor that constraint, we add it as a comment appended to the constant declaration.

The procedure to write a horizontal bar is straightforward and is displayed in the final program in Figure 5.10. Rather than analyze it and all the other procedures, we will only discuss two of the most interesting procedures, the one to draw an "I" and the one to write out the "HI."

The procedure to write a big "I" is:

```
procedure BigI(Indent: integer);
  var HalfWidth: integer;
  begin{BigI}
    HalfWidth := LetterWidth div 2;
    HorizBar(Indent);
    VertBar(Indent + HalfWidth);
    VertBar(Indent + HalfWidth);
    HorizBar(Indent)
  end; {BigI}
```

The additional indentation needed to center the vertical bars in the letter field is computed from **LetterWidth** and stored in a local variable called **HalfWidth**. These sorts of calculations require careful analysis and some testing to be sure they are not off by one. It is a good exercise to figure out and explain why the actual parameter to **VertBar** is not one more or one less than the expression shown.

The procedure to write "HI" is shown in Figure 5.10. Notice that it contains a local constant called **Offset**. This constant gives the amount that the second letter "I" is offset to the right of the "H." The reason for the offset is purely aesthetic.

Summary of Problem Solving and Programming Techniques

Procedures should be written in such a way that they can be used safely and effectively by a programmer who only reads the procedure heading and the explanatory comment that follows the heading. The interaction of a procedure and the rest of the program should be via parameters. Global variables normally should not appear in a procedure declaration. Parameters and local variables should be used instead.

◇

Good things come in small packages.
Proverb

◇

Summary of Pascal Constructs

procedure declaration
Syntax:

> *procedure* ⟨procedure name⟩**(**⟨formal parameter list⟩**);**
>   ⟨local constant declarations⟩
>   ⟨local variable declarations⟩
>   ⟨local procedure declarations⟩
> *begin*
>   ⟨statement 1⟩**;**
>   ⟨statement 2⟩**;**
>   :
>   ⟨statement *n*⟩
> *end;*

The statements may be any Pascal statements. See the following entries for details on declarations.

local variable   A local variable is one that is declared within a procedure declaration. A local variable exists only for the duration of a procedure call. The identifier used to name a local variable can also be used to name another variable (or constant or other object) outside the procedure declaration.

local identifier   A local identifier is one that is declared within a procedure. The thing it names exists only for the duration of the procedure call. A local identifier can also be used outside the procedure declaration to name something else. Local variable names, local constant names and local procedure names are examples of local identifiers.

global variable   A variable that is declared for the entire program; i.e., one whose scope is the block of the entire program.

block   A set of declarations followed by the statements they apply to. For example, if you remove the heading and final semicolon from a procedure declaration, then what is left is a block.

scope of an identifier   The block in which an identifier is declared is called its *scope*. If an identifier is declared in two blocks, one inside the other, then in the inner block its meaning is the one declared in the inner block.

procedure heading
Syntax:

> *procedure* ⟨procedure name⟩**(**⟨formal parameter list⟩**);**

Examples:

```
procedure Sample(var X: real; var Y: real;
                          A: char; B: char);
procedure Sample(var X, Y: real; A, B: char);
```

The procedure heading is the first thing in a procedure declaration. The ⟨procedure name⟩ can be any identifier other than a reserved word. The ⟨formal parameter list⟩ is a list of identifiers that will serve as formal parameters. Each formal parameter is followed by a colon and its type. The formal variable parameters are prefaced by **var**. The formal value parameters are not. The parameters are separated by semicolons. Formal parameters of the same kind (i.e., same type and all value or all variable parameters) may (optionally) be grouped together and separated by commas. The above two samples are equivalent.

formal parameter   A formal parameter appears in a procedure declaration and is changed when the procedure is called. The change is a simple substitution in the case of formal variable parameters and a change in value in the case of formal value parameters. The formal parameters for a procedure are listed in the procedure heading.

procedure call

Syntax:

⟨procedure name⟩**(**⟨actual parameter list⟩**)**

Example:

```
Sample(R1, R2, 'A', L)
```

The ⟨actual parameter list⟩ contains the actual parameters separated by commas. There must be exactly as many actual parameters as there are formal parameters. The first actual parameter corresponds to the first formal parameter, the second actual parameter corresponds to the second formal parameter and so forth. Corresponding formal and actual parameters must agree in type. If a formal parameter is a variable parameter (i.e., prefaced by **var**), then the corresponding actual parameter must be a variable. If a formal parameter is a value parameter (i.e., not prefaced by **var**), then the corresponding actual parameter may be anything that evaluates to the type of the formal parameter. When a procedure is called, some kind of substitution of actual parameters for the corresponding formal parameters is made and then the procedure statements are executed. (See *variable parameter* and *value parameter*.)

actual parameter   The thing used to change a formal parameter when a procedure is called. The actual parameters are listed in a procedure call in the way shown in the previous entry.

variable parameter   Formal and actual parameters come in pairs. The pair is either a pair of value parameters or a pair of variable parameters. If the pair is a pair of variable parameters, then a **var** is written in front of the formal parameter in the formal parameter list of the procedure heading. If the pair is a pair of variable parameters, the actual parameter must be a variable. A formal variable parameter is a labeled blank. When the procedure is called, the actual variable parameter is substituted for the corresponding formal variable parameter.

value parameters   Formal and actual parameters come in pairs. The pair is either a pair of value parameters or a pair of variable parameters. If the formal parameter is not prefaced by **var** in the formal parameter list of the procedure heading, then the pair is a pair of value parameters. If the pair is a pair of value parameters, the actual parameter may be anything that evaluates to the type of the corresponding formal parameter. A formal value parameter is a local variable. When the procedure is called, the value of the formal value parameter is initialized to the value of the corresponding actual value parameter.

Exercises

Self-Test and Interactive Exercises

1. Predict the output of the following program:

```
program Exercise1(input, output);
  var A, B, C: integer;
procedure Funny(var X, Y: integer);
    var C: integer;
    begin{Funny}
      X := 4; Y := 5; C := 6;
      writeln(X, Y, C)
    end; {Funny}
begin {Program}
  A := 1; B := 2; C := 3;
  Funny(A, B);
  writeln(A, B, C)
end. {Program}
```

2. What will be the output of the program in Exercise 1 if the procedure heading is changed to the following? (The **var** is left out.)

```
procedure Funny(X, Y: integer);
```

3. What will be the output of the program in Exercise 1 (not Exercise 2) if the procedure call is changed to:

```
Funny(B, A)
```

4. What will be the output of the program in Exercise 1 (not Exercise 2) if the procedure call is changed to:

```
Funny(A, A)
```

5. What will be the output of the program in Exercise 1 (not Exercise 2) if the procedure call is changed to:

```
Funny(A, C)
```

6. What is the output of the following program?

```
program Exercise6(input, output);
  var X, Y: char;
procedure Mixed(X: char; var Y: char);
  begin{Mixed}
    X := 'A'; Y := 'B';
    writeln(X, Y)
  end; {Mixed}
```

```
begin{Program}
  X := 'X'; Y := 'Y';
  Mixed(X, Y);
  writeln(X, Y)
end. {Program}
```

7. Run the program in Figure 5.1 twice, once as shown and once omitting local variable declaration:

var TEMP: integer;

8. Run the program in Figure 5.1 again, but this time use **A** and **B** for both the formal and actual parameters. The procedure heading should read:

procedure Exchange(**var A,** B: integer);

The other **X**'s and **Y**'s in the procedure declaration should also be changed to **A**'s and **B**'s. The procedure call should not be changed. This should make no difference in how the program behaves.

9. Write a procedure to find the area of a rectangle and store the answer in a variable parameter called **A**. This procedure will have two value parameters, as in **OutputArea2** (Figure 5.5), plus the variable parameter **A** for a total of three formal parameters. Embed this in a program and run the program.

10. (UCSD Pascal only) Rewrite the program **Talk2** in Figure 5.2 so that it uses variables of type **string** to hold complete names instead of using variables of type **char** to hold initials.

Regular Exercises

11. Write a program that writes your first, middle and last initials to the screen. Use Figure 5.10 as a model. If you have no middle initial, follow your two initials with an exclamation sign, "!". Allow the user to enter the amount of indentation from the keyboard. In order to get your initials, you may need to develop procedures for more building blocks than just horizontal and vertical bars.

12. Write a program that writes "HELLO" to the screen one letter at a time. Each letter should be about the size of those produced by the program in Figure 5.10. To get the next letter, the user presses the return key.

13. Write a procedure with three parameters, one value parameter of type **real** and two variable parameters of type **integer**. One variable parameter is set to the whole number part of the real value; the other is set to the value of the first digit after the decimal point.

14. Write a program that will read in a real number (representing that many inches) and then output the area of a square with sides of that length and the area of a circle with diameter that length. Use two procedures to compute the two areas.

15. Write a program that will read in a length in feet and inches and will then output the equivalent length in meters and centimeters. Use at least three procedures: one for input, one or more for calculating and one for output. There are 0.3048 meters in a foot and 100 centimeters in a meter.

16. Write a program to read in an amount in Mexican pesos as well as the peso-to-dollar exchange rate. The program then outputs the equivalent amount in dollars and cents. Use

at least three procedures, one for input, one for output and one or more procedures to do the actual calculation.

17. Write a single procedure to replace the three procedures **ComputeQuarters**, **ComputeDimes** and **ComputePennies** used in Figure 4.3. Your procedure should have three parameters: One called **AmountLeft** will be a variable parameter; one called **CoinValue** will be a value parameter of type **integer** and will be used with the values **25**, **10** and **1** to get the three versions of the procedure that are needed. Rewrite the program in Figure 4.3 using your procedure. It will be necessary to start the program by setting the initial value of **AmountLeft** equal to **Amount**.

18. Redo Exercise 17 but also include all the embellishments described in Exercise 9 in Chapter 4. Include a general-purpose procedure for bills similar to the one for coins.

19. Write a program for the discount installment loan algorithm described in Exercise 11 of Chapter 1. Implement subtasks as procedures.

20. Redo (or do for the first time) Exercise 21 from Chapter 3. Use three procedures, one for input, one for output and one to perform the calculation.

21. Redo (or do for the first time) Exercise 22 from Chapter 3. Use three procedures, one for input, one for output and one to perform the calculation.

22. Redo (or do for the first time) Exercise 23 from Chapter 3. Use at least three procedures.

23. Redo (or do for the first time) Exercise 25 from Chapter 3. Use at least four procedures.

6

Designing Programs That Make Choices

"If you think we're wax-works," he said, "you ought to pay, you know. Wax-works weren't made to be looked at for nothing. Nohow!"

"Contrariwise," added the one marked "DEE," "if you think we're alive, you ought to speak."

Lewis Carroll,
Through the Looking-Glass

138

Designing Programs
That Make Choices

Chapter Contents

The programs we have seen thus far were structurally very simple. They consisted of a list of statements to be executed in order, one after the other. We used procedures to group related statements together, but our programs were all equivalent to simple lists of statements. Our programs never made a choice between two or more alternatives. However, many common algorithms do require a choice between alternative actions. For example, an automated banking program might allow the user to decide between processing deposits or withdrawals. A program for an airline reservation system will do different things depending on whether a requested flight is fully booked or has an opening. A program to play chess will need to perform different actions depending on what its opponent does. Any programming construct that chooses one out of a number of alternative actions is called a *branching* mechanism. In this chapter we introduce the branching mechanisms available in the Pascal language. We then go on to discuss techniques for using branching mechanisms in designing algorithms and programs.

The Case Statement

The most straightforward Pascal branching mechanism is the *case* statement. The *case* statement is a complex statement made up from other simpler statements. When the *case* statement is executed, one (and only one) of the simpler statements is selected and executed. As usual, an example is likely to be more enlightening than an abstract discussion.

Consider the program shown in Figure 6.1. The five lines starting with the identifier *case* and ending with *end* contain a *case* statement (followed by a semicolon and a comment). The *case* statement contains three substatements: one labeled by the pair `'A'`, `'B'`, one labeled by the constant `'C'` and one labeled by the pair `'D'`, `'F'`. When the *case* statement is executed, exactly one of these three substatements will be executed; which one is executed depends on the value of the variable `Grade`. When the *case* statement is executed, the value

example

Program

```
program CaseSample(input, output);
  var Grade: char;
  begin{Program}
    writeln('What grade did you receive?');
    readln(Grade);
    case Grade of
      'A', 'B': writeln('Very Good!');
      'C': writeln('Passing.');
      'D', 'F': writeln('Too bad.')
    end; {case}
    writeln('I have to go study. Goodbye.')
  end. {Program}
```

Sample Dialogue 1

What grade did you receive?
A
Very Good!
I have to go study. Goodbye.

Sample Dialogue 2

What grade did you receive?
F
Too bad.
I have to go study. Goodbye.

Figure 6.1

Program with a *case* statement.

syntax

*label
list*

*type of
controlling
expression*

*leap year
example*

of **Grade** is checked and then the substatement labeled by that value is executed. Hence, if the value of **Grade** is either ´**A**´ or ´**B**´, then the **writeln** following that pair will be executed. If instead the value of **Grade** is ´**C**´, then the **writeln** following the ´**C**´ will instead be executed. If the value of **Grade** is either ´**D**´ or ´**F**´, then the third **writeln** is executed.

The syntax of a *case* statement is given in Figure 6.2 and the meaning of a *case* mechanism is given in Figure 6.3. A *case* statement may have any number of alternatives to choose between. Each alternative consists of exactly one statement. Each alternative statement must be prefaced by a list of one or more constants, separated by commas and followed by a colon. The list of constants is called a *label list*. The same constant may not appear in two label lists, since that would produce an ambiguous instruction. The alternatives in the list are separated by semicolons and the entire *case* statement is terminated with the identifier *end*. There is no matching *begin* for this final *end*. Instead it is matched to the reserved word *case*.

The expression that follows the word *case* need not be a variable. You can use any expression of type **integer** or **char** to control a *case* statement. However, you cannot use the types **real** or **string** to control a *case* statement. When the *case* statement is executed, the expression is evaluated and then the alternative labeled by that value is executed. Hence, the constants which label the alternative substatements must match this expression in type.

Figure 6.4 includes a *case* statement with a more complicated controlling expression. The program in that figure calculates leap years using the rule: Leap years are those years which are evenly divisible by four. This rule works for all years except century years like 1900 or 2000.

You will quickly realize that using just one simple statement for each alternative is rather weak and that it is desirable to have each alternative consist of a list of statements. This is in fact possible. In order to have more than one statement associated with a *case* label list, simply separate the statements in the list by semicolons and enclose the list between the identifiers *begin* and *end*. An example of this is shown in Figure 6.5.

You must ensure that the expression in a *case* statement evaluates to something that labels one of the alternatives. If it does not, then, in standard Pascal, that is considered an error, and almost anything might happen. In UCSD Pascal, the statement is ignored when this happens and the program goes on to the next statement. Whatever your system does, it is safest to always make sure the expression evaluates to something that labels one of the alternative substatements. For example, the program in Figure 6.5 includes lower-case as well as upper-case letters in the label lists. This helps to ensure that the value of **Grade** will always label some alternative.

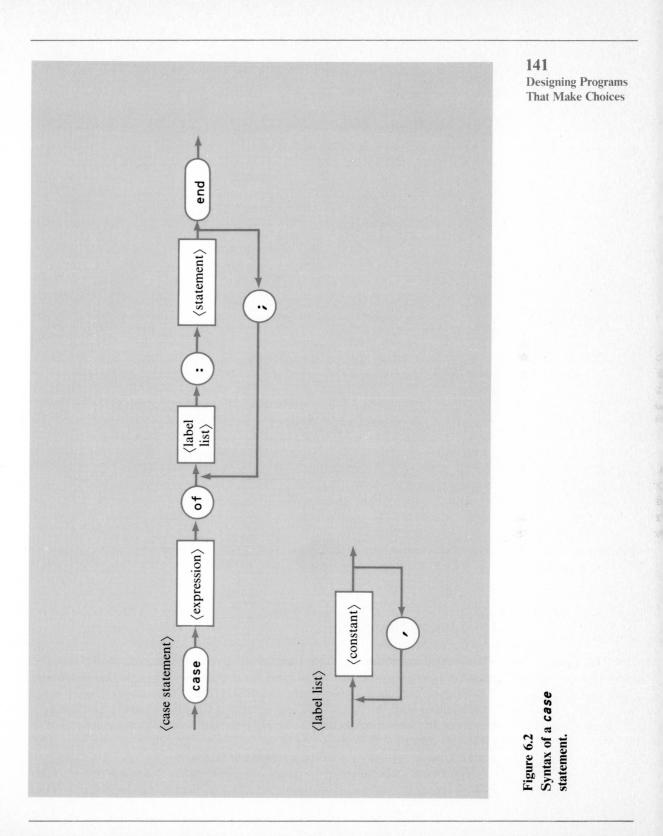

Figure 6.2
Syntax of a *case* statement.

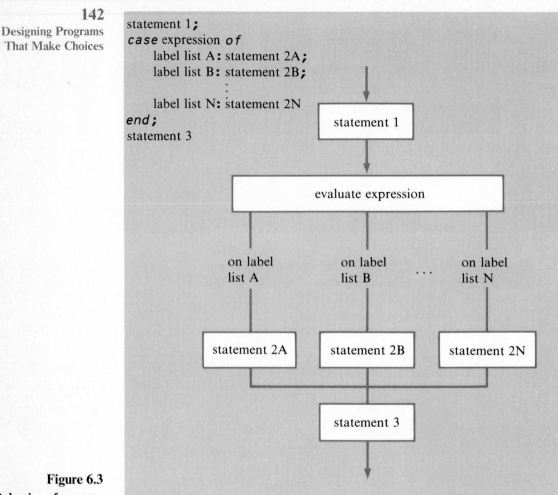

```
statement 1;
case expression of
     label list A: statement 2A;
     label list B: statement 2B;
                   :
     label list N: statement 2N
end;
statement 3
```

Figure 6.3
Behavior of a *case*
statement.

Compound Statements

The syntax diagram for the *case* statement is given in Figure 6.2. Notice that the syntax diagram says that after each label list there must be exactly one statement. Yet we just had an example where we used a list of statements. There is no contradiction here. In Pascal you can convert a list of statements into a single statement by separating them with semicolons and enclosing them between the identifiers *begin* and *end*, just as in the body of a procedure or program. The resulting larger statement is called a *compound statement*.

The Pascal mechanism for forming compound statements is analogous to the English language mechanism of joining several sentences by means of semicolons.

Program

```
program LeapYear(input, output);
{Determines if the current or the next year is a leap year.
Only works for years which are not divisible by 100.}

  var Year: integer;

begin{Program}
  writeln('Enter a year.');
  readln(Year);

  case (Year mod 4) of
    0: writeln('That year is a leap year.');
    3: writeln('The following year is a leap year.');
    1, 2: writeln('That year is not a leap year.')
  end {case}
end. {Program}
```

Sample Dialogue 1

Enter a year.
1964
That year is a leap year.

Sample Dialogue 2

Enter a year.
2001
That year is not a leap year.

Figure 6.4
case **statement
with an expression.**

Pascal and English are alike in this regard; the only difference is that English does not use the ***begin/end*** pair.

Nested Statements

Since ***case*** statements and compound statements are statements, they can occur anyplace a statement is allowed. So a ***case*** statement can occur inside a compound statement, and that compound statement can occur inside another ***case*** statement, and so on. Any pattern of nesting statements inside statements is permitted, so long as it is consistent with the syntax diagrams. As we proceed we will describe other types of statements, any one of which can occur inside a

Program

```
program CaseSample2(input, output);
  var Grade: char;
begin{Program}
  writeln('What grade did you receive?');
  readln(Grade);

  case Grade of

    'A', 'a', 'B', 'b':
        begin{A, B}
          writeln(Grade, ' is very good!');
          writeln('I wish I could do as well.')
        end; {A, B}

    'C', 'c': writeln('Passing.');

    'D', 'd', 'F', 'f':
        begin{D, F}
          writeln('Too bad.');
          writeln(Grade, ' is not very good.')
        end {D, F}

  end; {case}

  writeln('I have to go study. Goodbye.')
end. {Program}
```

Sample Dialogue

What grade did you receive?
A
A is very good!
I wish I could do as well.
I have to go study. Goodbye.

Figure 6.5
Sample use of a
***case* statement.**

compound or ***case*** statement and which may itself contain other statements, including compound or ***case*** statements.

This nesting of statements inside statements points out one peculiarity in the definitions of compound and ***case*** statements. When we defined each of these statements, we said that they could contain any sort of statement, including one of the same kind. This may seem circular. That is because it is. Circular

recursive
(circular)
definitions

definitions and even circular program instructions are common in computer science. In computer science, circular definitions and instructions are usually referred to by the word *recursive* rather than the word *circular*.

It is not always wrong or even undesirable to give a circular definition. The same thing happens in English grammar but there we seldom notice that it is circular. We have already mentioned the possibility of making two English sentences into one by joining them with a semicolon. That grammar rule for English sentences refers to sentences and so is recursive (i.e., circular). There are many other instances in English of sentences nested inside sentences. As another example, a sentence may be formed out of two smaller sentences by joining them with the word *and*. The grammar rules for each of these types of sentences involve a circular reference because they include the word *sentence*. Consider the English sentence "That English allows circular definitions is interesting." Or the sentence "That John was home surprised Sue." In both these English sentences the subject of the sentence is itself a sentence. The subject of the first sentence is the sentence "English allows circular definitions." The subject of the second sentence is "John was home." In order to use an English sentence as the subject of another English sentence, you need merely preface it by the word *that*. Moreover, you can iterate these English grammar principles to get complicated nested sentences such as:

That John was home surprised Sue and she ran out of the room.

*how to
formulate
recursive
definitions*

Recursive (circular) definitions do require a bit of care in how they are formulated, though. In order for such a definition to be meaningful, it should contain some clauses that are not circular. In a grammar for English sentences, some types of sentences are defined without referring, directly or indirectly, to sentences. For example, the long English sentence displayed above is obtained by combining two sentences using the word *and*. The second of these two component sentences does not contain any subparts that are themselves sentences and so the circularity ends for that part; it satisfies a condition for sentencehood that does not refer to sentences. The first of the two main component sentences contains a subpart that is a sentence, namely: "That John was home surprised Sue," and that sentence contains a subpart that is itself a sentence, namely: "John was home." However, this sentence does not contain any other sentence but satisfies some rules of grammar that do not mention sentences.

The general pattern is that some sentence may qualify for sentencehood because some subpart (or subparts) is itself a sentence and that subsentence may similarly contain a subpart that is a sentence and so forth, but eventually this chain of subsentence, sub-subsentences and so forth must bottom out with a sentence that does not contain a sentence.

*recursive
syntax
diagrams*

Just as the nesting of English sentences within other English sentences must bottom out with simple sentences, so too must the nesting of Pascal statements bottom out with simple Pascal statements. This is exhibited by the syntax diagrams shown in Figures 6.2 and 6.6. For example, consider the **case** statement in Figure 6.5. In order to see that it is a valid **case** statement, consult the syntax diagrams. The diagram for the **case** statement says start with the identifier **case**; followed by an expression, in this example the simple expression

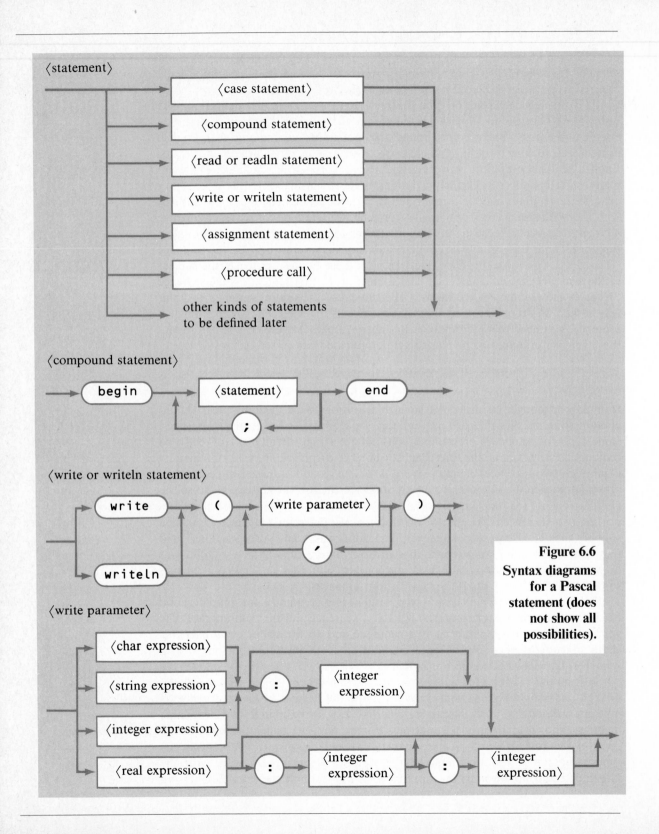

Figure 6.6
Syntax diagrams
for a Pascal
statement (does
not show all
possibilities).

Grade; followed by a list of constants, in this example ´**A**´, ´**a**´, ´**B**´, ´**b**´; followed by a colon; followed by a statement. At this point, the syntax diagrams become a nontrivial maze.

We must somehow decide what kind of statement comes next and check that one of these statements does indeed follow the colon. If we decide to check for a compound statement, we will be lucky because the program piece between the next *begin* and its matching *end* does satisfy the syntax diagram for a compound statement. As we manipulate this compound statement through the syntax diagrams, we find that each of the smaller statements in the list is a **writeln** statement and so their syntax diagram definition does not use the concept of a statement. So this process finally does bottom out with a syntax diagram path that is not circular. A similar thing happens with the other compound statement.

If-Then-Else Statements

if – then – else statements choose between exactly two alternatives. The choice depends on whether a particular controlling expression is true or false. For example, consider the following sample statement:

```
if Profit > 0
   then writeln('Give the manager a raise!')
   else writeln('Fire the manager!')
```

If the value of **Profit** is positive, then the first **writeln** will be executed. If it is zero or negative, then the second **writeln** will be executed.

An expression that is either true or false is called a *boolean expression*. We will explain boolean expressions shortly. Until then, we will only use a few simple boolean expressions whose meanings should be obvious.

*boolean
expressions*

As the basis for another example, consider the program for checking leap years given in Figure 6.5. This program does not work for years that are divisible by 100, that is, for turn-of-the-century years. Years that are divisible by 100 are not leap years unless they are also divisible by 400. So 1900 was not a leap year because it is not divisible by 400, even though it is divisible by four. On the other hand, the year 2000 is a leap year, because it is divisible by 400. By using *if – then – else* statements, we can write a program that also works for century years. The program is shown in Figure 6.7. It uses an *if – then – else* statement to choose one of two procedures depending on the boolean expression below:

```
(Year mod 100) = 0
```

This expression is true when (and only when) **Year** is divisible by **100**.

Program

```
program BetterLeapYear(input, output);
{Determines if the current or the next year is a leap year.}

  var Year: integer;

procedure RegularCalc(Year: integer);
{Determines if Year or the next year is a leap year.
Does not work for years that are divisible by 100.}
  begin{RegularCalc}
    case (Year mod 4) of
      0: writeln('That year is a leap year.');
      3: writeln('The following year is a leap year.');
      1, 2: writeln('That year is not a leap year.')
    end {case}
  end; {RegularCalc}

procedure CenturyCalc(Year: integer);
{Determines if Year is a leap year. Only works for years
which are divisible by 100. Such years are never
followed by a leap year.}

  begin{CenturyCalc}
    if (Year mod 400) = 0
      then writeln('That year is a leap year.')
      else writeln('Not even close to a leap year.')
  end; {CenturyCalc}

begin{Program}
  writeln('Enter a year.');
  readln(Year);
  if (Year mod 100) = 0
    then CenturyCalc(Year)
    else RegularCalc(Year)
end. {Program}
```

Sample Dialogue 1

Enter a year
1900
Not even close to a leap year.

Sample Dialogue 2

Enter a year.
2003
The following year is a leap year.

Figure 6.7
Program with
if - then - else
statements.

If-Then Statements

A variant of the *if - then - else* statement is the simple *if - then* statement.
An *if - then* statement is like an *if - then - else* statement, except that it
has no *else* part. If the boolean expression evaluates to true, then the statement
following the *then* is executed. If it evaluates to false, no action is taken and the
program proceeds to the next instruction. The sample program in Figure 6.8
includes two simple *if - then* statements. The boolean expressions in that
program use the symbol pair **> =**, which is the way that you write the greater-
than-or-equal sign in Pascal. In mathematics this sign is usually written as $\geq$. So,
the Pascal expression

```
Age >= 18
```

is true if the value of **Age** is **18** or more; otherwise, it is false.
The syntax of both *if - then* and *if - then - else* statements is summarized in Figure 6.9; their behavior is summarized in Figure 6.10.

Program

```
program AgeTalk(input, output);
  var Age: integer;
begin{Program}
  writeln('Please enter your age.');
  readln(Age);
  if Age >= 18
    then writeln('You are old enough to join the army.');
  if Age >= 21
    then writeln('You are old enough to drink.');
  writeln('Good luck!')
end. {Program}
```

Sample Dialogue

Please enter your age.
19
You are old enough to join the army.
Good luck!

Figure 6.8
**Program with *if -
then* statements.**

Figure 6.9
Syntax of *if - then* and *if - then - else* statements.

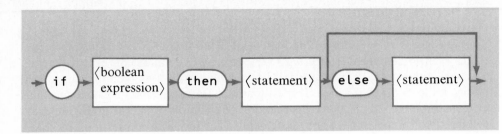

Simple Boolean Expressions

relational operators

The simplest type of boolean expression consists of a comparison of two values. We have already seen comparisons using the relations **=** , **>** and **>=** . A list of some of the most common *relational operators* is given in Figure 6.11. Some of the operators have unusual spellings as two symbols because most keyboards do not have symbols such as ≠ and ≤ . These symbol pairs are considered to be single items and so you should not insert any spaces between the two symbols.

In a simple boolean expression, the two things being compared can be any expressions so long as they yield values of the same type. We will eventually encounter other types for these expressions, but for now they must be both **integer**, both **real** or both **char**. The usual exception concerning numbers applies here, namely, that it is possible to mix values of type **real** and type **integer**.

reals and equality

The approximate nature of **real** values can cause special problems when used in some boolean expressions. In particular, values of type **real** should never be used with the equality operator, since the comparison is, for all practical purposes, meaningless. It does not make sense to test two approximate quantities to see if they are *exactly* equal.

ordering of characters

When relational operators such as **<** and **<=** are applied to items of type **char**, they check for alphabetic order. Hence, **'A' < 'B'** is true and **'Z' < 'H'** is false. However, there is no uniformity in how Pascal treats the interaction of upper-case and lower-case letters. On some systems **'a' < 'Z'** evaluates to true and on others it evaluates to false. The result is guaranteed to check for alphabetic order only if both letters are upper-case or both letters are lower-case.

Below are three examples of simple boolean expressions:

```
(A mod 25) <> 0

round(X) <= (trunc(Y) + 2)

Answer = 'Y'
```

The parentheses around **trunc(Y) + 2** are not required, but they do make the expression easier to read. The values of these boolean expressions depend on the values of the variables involved. For example, if **A** has value **25**, then the first

statement 1;
if boolean expression *then* statement 2';
statement 3

statement 1;
if boolean expression
    then statement 2A
    else statement 2B;
statement 3

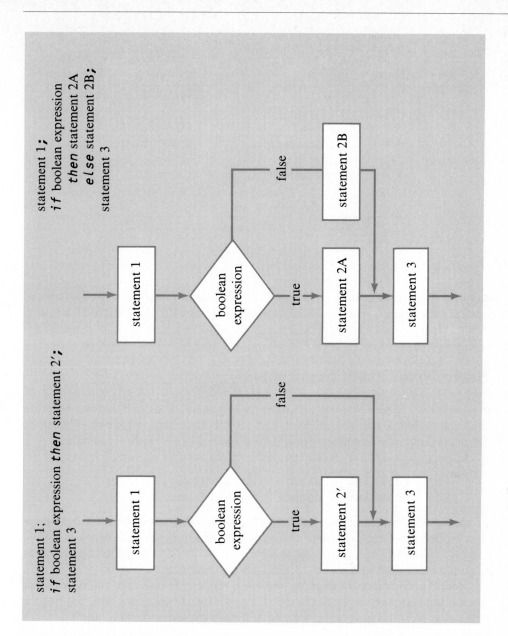

**Figure 6.10
Behavior of
if – then and
if – then – else
statements.**

Figure 6.11
List of relational
operators.

Math	Pascal	English	Pascal Sample	Math Equivalent
=	=	equals	Ans = 'N'	Ans = 'N'
≠	<>	not equal	X <> Y	$X \neq Y$
<	<	less than	X < 2	$X < 2$
≤	<=	less than or equal	X <= 1	$X \leq 1$
>	>	greater than	Y > 0	$Y > 0$
≥	>=	greater than or equal	Y >= 1	$Y \geq 1$

boolean expression is false; if **X** has value **2.3** and **Y** has value **6.5**, then the second expression is true; the third expression is true only if the value of **Answer** is **'Y'**.

Some Notes about Semicolons

As we have stated a number of times before, semicolons are used to separate statements, but a semicolon is not part of the statement it follows. This is of particular importance when writing *if - then - else* statements, such as:

```
if Ans = 'Y'
  then writeln('I assume you said yes.')
  else writeln('I assume you said no.')
```

If you place a semicolon after the first **writeln**, then your program will produce a compiler error message. The compiler will assume that you wrote a simple *if - then* statement followed by another statement starting with *else*. Since no statement can start with *else*, it issues an error message.

empty statement Since a semicolon is used to separate statements, the last statement in a compound statement or in the body of a procedure or program does not need a semicolon after it. However, as we said before, it causes no harm to add this extra semicolon. This seems to violate the syntax diagram for a compound statement as shown in Figure 6.6. That diagram states that every compound statement has a statement, not a semicolon, just before the final *end*. In order to allow an extra semicolon, and for other reasons, Pascal includes a special construct called the *empty statement*. The empty statement is indicated by writing down nothing, and when it is executed, nothing happens. For example, the following compound statement does satisfy the syntax diagram for a compound statement:

```
begin
  writeln('statement 1');           ┌──────── The empty statement
  writeln('statement 2');  ▼        is here.
end
```

The empty statement is a formal trick that has the effect of making that final semicolon optional. However, this trick only works in certain limited situations, such as compound statements. It does not allow you to insert semicolons in other places, such as before an *else*.

More on Indenting

With nested statements we can have complicated statements, such as compound statements, inside even more complex statements, which in turn are inside yet more complex statements. This multilevel structuring requires multiple levels of indenting in order to make the structure apparent to anybody who reads the program.

For example, look at the program in Figure 6.5. The statements in the main body of the program are indented to one level. The compound statements within the *case* statement are indented more. The statements inside the compound statements are indented still more. The indenting and spacing of a program should make the structure of nested statements clearly visible. One way to accomplish this is to indent things that are at the same level of nesting by the same amount.

Nesting If-Then and If-Then-Else Statements

if - then statements and *if - then - else* statements may be nested within one another. In such cases there is a potential for the meaning of the nested statement to be ambiguous. To illustrate the problem, consider the following scenario. The variable **P** contains an integer amount representing some number of pennies. We want to design a statement that will output nothing if the value of **P** is zero and will output the value of **P**, correctly annotated with the word **'penny'** or **'pennies'**, if the value of **P** is one or more. The following is one way to accomplish this goal:

```
if P > 0 then
        if P = 1 then writeln('one penny')
                else writeln(P, ' pennies')
```

By properly indenting the statements we have masked the problem. To see the problem write it as follows; the spacing is irrelevant to the compiler and this rewriting should not affect the meaning:

```
if P > 0 then
if P = 1 then writeln('one penny')
        else writeln(P, ' pennies')
```

Written like this it is not apparent which of the two *then*'s is supposed to be paired with the single *else*.

rules for
pairing
else
with then

Pascal clarifies such ambiguities by specifying that an *else* always is paired with the closest preceding *then*. So the meaning of our output statement is equivalent to that of statement (2) in Figure 6.12, which is what we intended it to be. Without such an explicit rule the meaning could just as well have been that of (3) in Figure 6.12. This can be a bit confusing at first. To see that there is a difference between statements (2) and (3), notice that when **P** has value zero, statement (2) outputs nothing. On the other hand, if **P** has value zero and statement (3) is executed, there will be some output to the screen saying there are zero pennies.

extra
begin / end

Notice that in (2) and (3) the pair *begin/end* is being used to force an association of the *else* with a particular *then*. This is analogous to the use of parentheses in arithmetic expressions, and just as extra parentheses can aid

---

(1) The statement:

```
if P > 0 then
if P = 1 then writeln('one penny')
        else writeln(P, ' pennies')
```

(2) Correct meaning [(1) and (2) mean the same]:

```
if P > 0 then
        begin{outer then}
          if P = 1 then writeln('one penny')
                  else writeln(P, ' pennies')
        end {outer then}
```

(3) Different meaning [(1) and (3) do not mean the same]:

```
if P > 0 then
        begin{outer then}
          if P = 1 then writeln('one penny')
        end {outer then}
      else writeln(P, ' pennies')
```

Figure 6.12
Which *then* does
the *else* go with?

readability, so too can an extra **begin/end** pair aid readability. The **begin/end** pair in (2) is not required, but it does help to clarify the meaning of that statement.

UCSD Pascal—string Comparisons

In UCSD Pascal the relational operators listed in Figure 6.11 may be applied to two expressions of type **string**. In this case the order is the so-called *lexicographic* order, which is, roughly speaking, alphabetical order. The ordering is unpredictable with respect to upper-case and lower-case letters and it is difficult to correctly compare strings of different lengths. Hence, it is dangerous to use **<** to test for alphabetic order except between two strings of equal length which both consist of all upper-case or all lower-case letters.

Guarded Commands—One Method for Designing Branches

The **case** statement chooses one of several statements to execute but is rather restricted in its use. The choice of which statement to execute must be made on the basis of a single value. There is a more versatile way to think about multiple branching situations, and there is a way to translate that reasoning into Pascal code.

When designing an algorithm, we often encounter a situation that is handled most naturally by branching to one of a large number of actions. Different conditions require different program actions. Moreover, the list of conditions and actions may be large and varied. One good way to proceed is to simply list all the conditions and the action that needs to take place under each condition. Keep listing conditions and actions until the list of conditions covers all possibilities. There is no single Pascal statement that corresponds to this sort of branching, although the **case** statement does come close. Nonetheless, this kind of branch is perfectly sensible. Moreover, we can design algorithms using it and still translate the algorithms into Pascal. This sort of algorithm branch is called a *guarded command*.

By way of example, suppose you are designing a game-playing program in which the user must guess the value of some number. The number can be named **Number** and the guess can be called **Guess**. If you wish to give a hint after each guess, you might design the following subalgorithm:

```
writeln('Too high.') provided Guess > Number
writeln('Too low.') provided Guess < Number
writeln('Correct!') provided Guess = Number
```

To write a guarded command in pseudocode, simply list all the conditions together with their corresponding action. The conditions are called *guards*, since

pseudocode

*Pascal
code*

they intuitively "guard" the actions and determine when they will be executed. We choose to use the format of listing each action followed by the word *provided* followed by its guard. There are no rigid syntax rules for writing pseudocode, and so you need not follow this exact syntax.

Once you have written the pseudocode for a guarded command, it is easy to translate it into Pascal code by using a nested *if – then – else* statement. For example, the above guarded command translates to:

```
if Guess > Number then writeln('Too high.')
else if Guess < Number then writeln('Too low.')
else if Guess = Number then writeln('Correct!')
```

The above nested Pascal statement needs a bit of explanation. It certainly produces the desired effect, but it may seem like a peculiar way to accomplish that effect. First of all, the last *if* is superfluous. The preceding version is equivalent to the following simpler version:

```
if Guess > Number then writeln('Too high.')
else if Guess < Number then writeln('Too low.')
else writeln('Correct!')
```

*the last
guard*

The third condition need not be checked. If the first two guards fail, then in this case, we know the third one must hold. Moreover, if we omit the last *if*, the program has less to do and so should run a little bit faster. On the other hand, by placing the third guard in the program, we make the program reflect our reasoning and so make the program easier to read. There is a third possibility that combines both these advantages. We can include the third guard but place it in a comment. In Figure 6.13, we have embedded this guarded command statement in

Figure 6.13
**Procedure including
a guarded
command.**

```
procedure Game(Number: integer);
  var Guess: integer;
begin {Game}
  writeln('I am thinking of a number.');
  writeln('Try to guess it and enter your guess.');
  readln(Guess);

  if Guess > Number then writeln('Too high.')
  else if Guess < Number then writeln('Too low.')
  else {Guess = Number} writeln('Correct!');

  writeln('The number was ', Number)
end; {Game}
```

a procedure and have done just that. In these cases we usually omit the words *if* and *then* from the comment.

Another thing that may look strange about the Pascal version of this guarded command is that it violates our general guidelines on indenting. If we followed our indenting rules, we would produce something like the following:

```
if Guess > Number
   then writeln('Too high.')
   else if Guess < Number
           then writeln('Too low.')
           else writeln('Correct!')
```

This is one of those rare cases when our general guidelines for indenting of nested statements should not be followed. The reason is that by lining up all the **else**'s, as shown in Figure 6.13, we also line up all the guards and so make the layout of the program reflect our reasoning.

Assertions

If a program contains branches, then it might perform different actions when run on different data. This makes the program more difficult to understand. One way to add clarity to a program is to add comments at strategic places in the program. One very useful kind of comment is called an *assertion*. Assertions are neither very new nor very complicated. An assertion is simply a comment that states what the programmer expects to be true when the program execution reaches the assertion. If the program is correct, then each assertion will be true whenever the program execution reaches the comment. An example will help to explain things.

Below we have reproduced some Pascal code together with two simple examples of assertions:

```
{X > = 0 and Y > = 0}
if X < Y then M := sqrt(X)
         else M := sqrt(Y)
{M is equal to the square root of the minimum of X and Y.}
```

The first assertion says that when (and if) the program execution gets to that point, the values of **X** and **Y** will be nonnegative. If this assertion is not true, then the code that follows is not guaranteed to work. For example, if the values are negative, the program will attempt to take a negative square root and produce an error. An assertion that states what should be true before some statement or statements are executed is called a *precondition*. If the programmer wrote the rest of the program correctly, then at this point the precondition will be true. Of course, simply writing in an assertion does not make it true. If the rest of the program was not correctly written, then **X** or **Y** may be negative. However, the precondition will explain the programmer's intent and will thus make the program easier to test and, if need be, to change.

precondition

The second assertion states what the programmer expects to be true after the piece of code is executed. Assertions of this sort are called *postconditions*. If the precondition is true and the piece of code is correct, then the postcondition will also be true.

In a situation like the one we just described, the two assertions are not labels with the words *precondition* and *postcondition*. The notions of precondition and postcondition are relative. The precondition for this piece of code was also the postcondition of whatever came before it and the postcondition for this piece of code is the precondition of whatever comes after it. Both comments are assertions, but whether an assertion is a precondition or postcondition depends on what part of the program you are checking.

*commenting
procedures*

There is one situation where it makes sense to label an assertion as being a precondition or a postcondition, namely, in the comment which accompanies a procedure heading. One way to explain a procedure is by stating the precondition that the procedure expects to hold and the postcondition that will then hold after the procedure terminates. For example, a good comment for the procedure **RegularCalc** in Figure 6.7 is shown below. (Prior to 1582 a different calendar was used and so the algorithm does not apply to those years.)

> **procedure RegularCalc(Year: integer);**
> {*Precondition: Year > 1582 and Year is not divisible by 100.*
> *Postcondition: One of the following messages is written on the screen: If Year or Year + 1 is a leap year, then the message says so; otherwise, the message says Year is not a leap year.*}

If only a postcondition is given, the procedure should work for any parameters of the appropriate type. For example, a procedure that only handles input will often have only a postcondition.

It is not always necessary to use the words *precondition* and *postcondition* in the comment, but you should always think in those terms when you formulate your description of the procedure.

Designing a Sample Program

*blackjack
example*

In this section we will design a program to score a blackjack hand. Blackjack is a card game in which the players attempt to get as close to a value of 21 as possible, without going over that value. Numeric cards are counted at face value, the jacks, queens and kings count as 10 and aces are counted as either 1 or 11, whichever is better for the player. If the total exceeds 21, the player is said to be "busted." A busted player never wins. Initially, the player is given two cards. In the usual version, a player can have as many additional cards as he/she wants. For purposes of this example, we will assume that a player can have at most one additional card. We assume that the cards have already been dealt when the program is run.

We divide the task into three main subtasks:

1. **GetCards**: Have the user input two or three card values. Allow the user to use words such as *ace,* as well as numbers.
2. **ChangeToNumber**: Convert the cards to a numeric value between 2 and 11; somehow mark aces for special consideration.
3. **OutputTotal**: Output the total plus a message if the user is "busted."

subtasks

The three subtasks are accomplished by three procedures, named as indicated.

Since we are letting the user enter input as strings, such as `'King'`, we must read the input as some number of characters stored in variables of type **char**. Fortunately, each possible input is determined by its first character: `'Q'` for `'Queen'`, `'2'` for `'2'`, `'1'` for `'10'` and so forth. It is important to note that the numbers such as 2 are read in as the character `'2'` and not as a numeric value. That is because we have decided that the variables to receive the input are to be of type **char** some of the time, and hence, must be of that type all the time. Also notice that, since we only use one character, the number ten is represented by `'1'`.

unifying cases

If we can somehow interpret the case of two cards as if it were three cards, then we will be able to have a more uniform and hence simpler algorithm. One way to do this is to treat the two-card case as if it had one card with the value zero.

The complete program is shown in Figure 6.14. The first procedure, **GetCards**, is straightforward. The second procedure, **ChangeToNumber**, is a simple *case* statement. Notice that we have allowed the user to use either upper-case or lower-case letters by listing both upper-case and lower-case letters in the label list. To save space, we have placed several of the case alternatives on a single line. Aces are always given the value **11**. Later on, the program will change some or all of them to **1** if that is to the advantage of the player.

The third procedure, **OutputTotal**, is divided into two cases. The easy case is when, counting aces as **11**, the total of the three cards is **21** or less. The hard case is when the total exceeds **21**. The hard case is made into a separate procedure called **AcesAsOne**. This procedure computes the number of aces. A guarded command is used to treat the cases of zero, one, two or three aces separately. If an ace was found, then the procedure tries decreasing the total by **10** for each ace that might help the player to get a score of under **21**. The decrease of **10** is equivalent to replacing the ace value of **11** with the alternative value **1**. Once a player's score is **21** or less, all the remaining aces are left at the value of **11**.

Program

```pascal
program Scorer(input, output);
{Scores a 2 or 3 card blackjack hand.}

var Card1, Card2, Card3: char;
    Value1, Value2, Value3: integer;

procedure GetCards(var Card1, Card2, Card3: char);
{Reads two or three cards as a CHARACTER code: "2"-"9" for 2-9; "1"
for 10; "A" for Ace, etc.; if there are only two cards, then Card3 is set to "0"}

  var NumberOfCards: integer;

begin{GetCards}
    writeln('How many cards do you have, 2 or 3?');
    readln(NumberOfCards);
    writeln('Enter cards as either 2 through 10,');
    writeln('Jack, Queen, King or Ace.');
    writeln('Enter your first card:');
    readln(Card1);
    writeln('Enter your second card:');
    readln(Card2);
    if NumberOfCards = 2
        then Card3 := '0'
        else begin{input third card}
                writeln('Enter your third card:');
                readln(Card3)
             end {input third card}
end; {GetCards}

procedure ChangeToNumber(Card: char; var Value:integer);
{Precondition: The value of Card is one of: "0" through "9", "J", "Q", "K",
"A"(or their lower-case version). Postcondition:Value is equal to the numeric
equivalent of Card; "1" is valued at 10; "A" at 11; "J", "Q", "K" at 10.}

begin{ChangeToNumber}
    case Card of
      '2': Value := 2; '3': Value := 3;
      '4': Value := 4; '5': Value := 5;
      '6': Value := 6; '7': Value := 7;
      '8': Value := 8; '9': Value := 9;
      '1', 'J', 'j', 'Q', 'q', 'K', 'k':
                                  Value := 10;
      'A', 'a': Value := 11;
      '0': Value := 0
    end
end; {ChangeToNumber}
```

Figure 6.14
**Program using
branching.**

```
procedure AcesAsOne(Value1, Value2, Value3,
                                    Total: integer);
```
{*Precondition: Total = Value1 + Value2 + Value3 and Total > 21. All the
conditions for the procedure OutputTotal also apply to this procedure.*}

```
  var AceCount: integer;

begin{AcesAsOne}
  AceCount := 0;
  if Value1 = 11 then AceCount := AceCount + 1;
  if Value2 = 11 then AceCount := AceCount + 1;
  if Value3 = 11 then AceCount := AceCount + 1;
```
  {*AceCount is the number of aces in the hand; Total is
  the total score counting aces as 11; Total > 21.*}

```
  if AceCount = 0 then
    writeln('Sorry busted: you went over 21.')
  else if AceCount = 1 then
    if Total - 10 <= 21
      then writeln('Your score is ', (Total - 10):2)
      else writeln('Sorry busted: you went over 21.')
  else if AceCount = 2 then
    begin{AceCount = 2}
      if Total - 10 <= 21 then
        writeln('Your score is ', (Total - 10):2)
      else if Total - 20 <= 21 then
        writeln('Your score is ', (Total - 20):2)
      else writeln('Sorry busted: you went over 21.')
    end {AceCount = 2}
  else {AceCount = 3} writeln('Your score is 13')
end; {AcesAsOne}

  procedure OutputTotal(Value1, Value2, Value3: integer);
```

{*Precondition: Parameters are the numeric values of cards; Ace has value 11,
face cards have value 10. Postcondition: The score is output to the screen; Aces
are counted as 1 if that is needed to bring the score below 21.*}

```
  var Total: integer;

begin{OutputTotal}
  Total := Value1 + Value2 + Value3;
```
  {*Total contains the hand score counting all aces as 11.*}
```
  if Total <= 21
    then writeln('Your score is ', Total:2)
    else AcesAsOne(Value1, Value2, Value3, Total)
end; {OutputTotal}
```

**Figure 6.14
continues on next
page**

```
begin{Program}
   writeln('This program scores a two or three card');
   writeln('blackjack hand.');
   writeln('Jack, Queen, King count as 10.');
   writeln('Ace counts as either 1 or 11.');
   writeln('If you exceed 21 you are ``busted.''');
   GetCards(Card1, Card2, Card3);
   ChangeToNumber(Card1, Value1);
   ChangeToNumber(Card2, Value2);
   ChangeToNumber(Card3, Value3);
   OutputTotal(Value1, Value2, Value3)
end. {Program}
```

Sample Dialogue

This program scores a two or three card
blackjack hand.
Jack, Queen, King count as 10.
Ace counts as either 1 or 11.
If you exceed 21 you are "busted."
How many cards do you have, 2 or 3?
3
Enter cards as either 2 through 10,
Jack, Queen, King or Ace.
Enter your first card:
Ace
Enter your second card:
5
Enter your third card:
ace
Your score is 17

Figure 6.14 (cont'd)

Summary of Problem Solving and Programming Techniques

One approach to solving a task or subtask is to write down conditions and the corresponding actions that need to take place under those conditions. This produces pseudocode for an instruction known as a guarded command. That pseudocode can be translated into Pascal as a series of nested *if – then – else* statements.

One way to document a program and to help clarify your thinking is to insert assertions into your programs. An assertion is a comment that states something you expect to be true when the program execution reaches that comment.

$$\diamond$$

"Contrariwise," continued Tweedledee, "if it was so, it might be; and if it were so, it would be; but as it isn't, it ain't. That's logic."

Lewis Carroll, Through the Looking-Glass

$$\diamond$$

Summary of Pascal Constructs

case statement

Syntax:

```
case ⟨expression⟩ of
  ⟨label list 1⟩: ⟨statement 1⟩;
  ⟨label list 2⟩: ⟨statement 2⟩;
         :
  ⟨label list n⟩: ⟨statement n⟩
end
```

Example:

```
case N of
  2: writeln('Value of N is 2');
  7,9,4: writeln('Value of N is 7, 9 or 4')
end
```

⟨expression⟩ must evaluate to something of type **integer** or type **char**. (Later we will discover other allowable types.) It can not be of type **real** or of type **string**. The label lists must be lists of values of the same type as that of ⟨expression⟩ and all these values must be different. The statements may be any Pascal statements. When the **case** statement is executed, ⟨expression⟩ is evaluated and the statement with that value on its label list is executed.

compound statement

Syntax:

```
begin
  ⟨statement 1⟩;
  ⟨statement 2⟩;
        ⋮
  ⟨statement n⟩
end
```

Example:

```
begin
  writeln('This is done first.');
  writeln('This is done second.');
  writeln('This is done last.')
end
```

The statements may be any Pascal statements. The effect of this statement is the same as that of executing the list of statements in order.

simple boolean expression

Syntax:

⟨expression 1⟩ ⟨relational operator⟩ ⟨expression 2⟩

Examples:

```
X <= 0
Ans = 'Y'
```

Form of a simple boolean expression. A boolean expression is an expression whose value is either true or false.

if-then-else statement

Syntax:

```
if ⟨boolean expression⟩
    then ⟨statement 1⟩
    else ⟨statement 2⟩
```

Example:

```
if X > 0
  then writeln('Value of X is greater than zero')
  else writeln('Value of X is zero or negative')
```

⟨statement 1⟩ and ⟨statement 2⟩ may be any Pascal statements. ⟨boolean expression⟩ may be any boolean expression. If the value of ⟨boolean expression⟩ is true, then ⟨statement 1⟩ is executed. If the value of ⟨boolean expression⟩ is false, then ⟨statement 2⟩ is executed.

if-then-else statement

Syntax:

```
if ⟨boolean expression⟩ then ⟨statement⟩
```

Example:

```
if X > 0
    then writeln('value of X is greater than zero')
```

The ⟨statement⟩ may be any Pascal statement. ⟨boolean expression⟩ may be any boolean expression. If the ⟨boolean expression⟩ evaluates to true, then ⟨statement⟩ is executed. If the value of ⟨boolean expression⟩ is false, then no action is taken.

Exercises

Self-Test and Interactive Exercises

1. Write a program whose input is a month entered as a number from 1 to 12 and whose output is the number of days in that month.

2. Write a program whose input is a one-digit number and whose output is that number written as a word. For example, an input of **5** should produce an output of *five*.

3. Write a program that will read in two **integer** values and write them back in numeric order.

4. Write a program that will read in an upper-case letter and output a message telling whether or not that letter follows '**M**' in the alphabet.

5. Which of the following evaluate to true and which evaluate to false?

```
(24 mod 12) <> 0          'y' = 'Y'
'H' <= 'J'              -12 <= maxint
```

6. Convert the following mathematical and English expressions into Pascal boolean expressions:

$$\sqrt{x} \le y + 1$$

Z is positive, **W** is not zero, **X** is evenly divisible by 12.

7. What output will be produced by the following code when embedded in a complete program?

```
writeln('Start');
if 2 <= 3 then
    if 0 <> 1 then writeln('First writeln')
             else writeln('Second writeln');
writeln('Next');
if 2 > 3 then
    if 0 = 1 then writeln('Third writeln')
             else writeln('Fourth writeln');
writeln('Enough')
```

8. Embed the following code in a complete program and run it several times using different input values each time:

```
writeln('Type in two integers:');
readln(X, Y);
```

```
if X > 0 then
    if Y > 0 then writeln('first writeln')
             else writeln('second writeln')
```

Predict the outputs before you run the program.

9. Embed the following code in a complete program and run it several times using different input values each time:

```
writeln('Type in three integers:');
readln(X, Y, Z);

if X > 0 then writeln('X is greater than zero')
else if Y > 0 then writeln('Y is greater than zero')
else if Z > 0 then writeln('Z is greater than zero')
else writeln('They are all zero or negative')
```

Predict the outputs before you run the program.

Regular Exercises

10. Write a program that reads in the radius of a circle and then outputs one of the following depending on what the user requests: circumference of the circle, area of the circle or diameter of the circle.

11. Equations of the form $ax^2 + bx + c = 0$ can be solved by the formula:

$$x = \frac{-b \pm \sqrt{b^2 - 4ac}}{2a}$$

Write a program to compute the roots of such an equation when the values a, b and c are input. Be sure to test for negative square roots and to tell the user that there are no (real) roots in that case.

12. Write a program that accepts dates written as three numbers separated by spaces and then outputs the date written in the usual American English manner. For example, the input:

2 15 52

should produce the output:

February 15, 1952

13. Write a program that accepts a three-digit integer and outputs the value in words. For example, the input 235 should produce the output:

two hundred thirty-five

14. Write a program whose input is a number from 1 to 10 written as an English word and whose output is the numeral for that number. For example, an input of *five* should produce an output of *5*.

15. Write a program to determine grades in a course with three quizzes each scored on a basis of five points. Grades are determined according to the rule: A is an average of 4.0 or better; B is an average of 3.0 or better (up to 4.0); C is an average of 2.0 or better; D is an average of 1.0 or better; less than 1.0 is an F.

16. A bicycle salesperson is offered a choice of wage plans: (a) a straight salary of $300 per week; (b) $3.50 per hour for 40 hours plus a 10% commission on sales; (c) a straight

15% commission on sales with no other salary. Write a program that will take as input the salesperson's expected weekly sales and will output the expected wages paid under each plan as well as announcing the best-paying plan.

17. Write a program that takes the name of a month as input and outputs the number of days in that month. The month is to be input as a name such as *January* and not as a number. If the month is February, the program also asks the year in order to determine whether it is a leap year. The program should allow the month to be spelled with any combination of capital and lowercase letters. It should accept misspelled months as long as the first three letters are correct.

18. Write a program to compute state income tax according to the algorithm developed in Chapter 1. Use procedures for subtasks. Define gross income as the amount on the taxpayer's W-2 form plus interest plus dividends plus two-thirds of short-term capital gains plus half of long-term capital gains. (You do not need to know what long- and short-term capital gains are to write this program.) Define adjustments to income as medical expenses plus charitable contributions plus a $1,000 deduction for each dependent.

19. Write a program that computes the cost of postage on a first-class letter according to the following rate scale: 20 cents for the first ounce or fraction of an ounce, 7 cents for each additional half ounce, plus a 5-dollar service charge if the customer desires special delivery.

20. Write a program to compute the interest due, total amount due and the minimum payment for a revolving credit account. The program accepts the account balance as input, then adds on the interest to get the total amount due. The rate schedules are the following: The interest is 1.5% on the first $1,000 and 1% on any amount over that. The minimum payment is 10% of the total amount due, provided that amount is $10 or more; otherwise, it is the entire amount due or $10, whichever is smaller.

21. Write a program that will read in a time of day in 24-hour notation and output it in 12-hour notation. For example, if the input is 13:45, then the output should be:

1:45 PM

The program should instruct the user to always type in exactly five characters. So, nine o'clock should be input as:

09:00

7

Programming with Boolean Expressions

He who would distinguish the true from
the false must have an adequate idea of
what is true and false.

Benedict Spinoza, Ethics

Chapter Contents

Boolean expressions determine the outcome of branches such as *if - then - else* branches. They are also used in other programming constructs still to be introduced. It is almost impossible to write a complex Pascal program that does not contain a boolean expression. They are the primary mechanism for controlling the order in which program actions are carried out. In this chapter we describe this important class of expressions more completely and illustrate how they can be used effectively in designing programs.

The Type boolean

Expressions such as **X > 0** are evaluated and have a value, namely, they are either true or false. The type of such values is called **boolean**, after the nineteenth-century English mathematician George Boole who developed the foundations for a formal calculus of such expressions. The Pascal type **boolean** is quite simple. It has exactly two values, the value **true** and the value **false**. Although it has only two values, the type **boolean** has all the same machinery as the other types do. In particular, a program can have variables and constants of type **boolean**, as well as boolean expressions. Before discussing them, however, let us finish the description of boolean expressions that we began in Chapter 6.

Complex Boolean Expressions

In Chapter 6 we introduced some simple boolean expressions. You can form more complicated boolean expressions out of simpler ones by combining boolean expressions using the operators *and*, *or* and *not*. These operators work very much as they do in English, combining simpler boolean expressions to yield a new complex boolean expression.

    A boolean expression formed from two smaller boolean expressions by joining them with an *and* evaluates to **true** provided that both subexpressions evaluate to **true**; otherwise, it evaluates to **false**. For example, *and*

    (X < Y) and (Y < Z)

evaluates to **true** if both the value of **X** is less than the value of **Y** and the value of **Y** is less than the value of **Z** ; otherwise, its value is **false**. In mathematics, pairs of inequalities are usually expressed as follows:

    $x < y < z$

Expressions with such chains of interlocking comparisons are not allowed in Pascal. Instead you must break them into parts and connect these parts with *and*'s. It is natural to think that the parentheses in the above Pascal boolean expression are optional. Unfortunately, they are not and their omission will cause problems.

    The syntax for expressions involving *or* is similar to what we described for *and*. For example:

    (X < Y) or (Y < Z)

This expression is **true** provided the value of **X** is less than the value of **Y** or *or* the value of **Y** is less than the value of **Z** *or both*. This is the so-called "inclusive" meaning of "or". It is the meaning that is always used in mathematics, but it is not always used in ordinary conversation. Ordinary conversational English has trouble coping with situations where two true statements are joined by the word "or". Pascal and mathematical disciplines in general have no such problems. In

Program

```
program FindScorpios(input, output);
{Determines if user is a Scorpio: birthday
between October 24th and November 22nd, inclusive.}

  var Month, Day: integer;

begin{Program}
  writeln('Enter your month and day');
  writeln('of birth, as two numbers.');
  readln(Month, Day);

  if (Month = 10) and (Day >= 24)
      then writeln('You''re an October Scorpio.')
  else if (Month = 11) and (Day <= 22)
          then writeln('You''re a November Scorpio.')
  else writeln('You''re not a Scorpio.');

  writeln('I knew it!')
end. {Program}
```

Sample Dialogue 1	**Sample Dialogue 2**
Enter your month and day	*Enter your month and day*
of birth, as two numbers.	*of birth, as two numbers.*
10 26	**2 21**
You're an October Scorpio.	*You're not a Scorpio.*
I knew it!	*I knew it!*

Figure 7.1
Use of complex
boolean
expressions.

Pascal, if two things are connected by an **or**, then the resulting expression is **true** provided one or both subexpressions are **true**; otherwise, it is **false**.

not

The boolean operator **not** reverses truth values, much as the word *not* does in English. However, the Pascal syntax for **not** is quite different from English. In Pascal the **not** always is placed in front of the expression being negated. The expression being negated is usually written in parentheses. So the syntax is the same as what it would be if **not** were a function. In fact, **not** is a function, but that is not the way we usually think of it. As examples, consider the following boolean expressions:

```
not('A' = 'Z')
not(2 < 3)
```

Since **not** changes **true** to **false** and **false** to **true**, the first of these two boolean expressions evaluates to **true** and the second to **false**.

These complex boolean expressions are used in the same way as the simple boolean expressions we used in the last chapter. For example, the program in

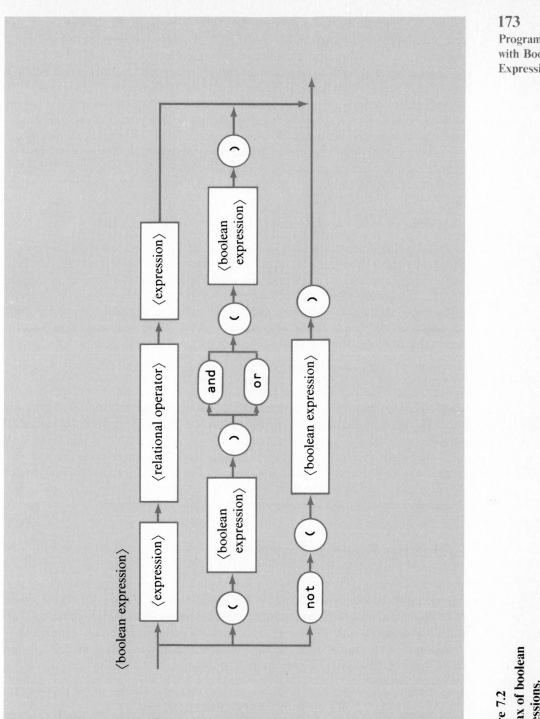

Figure 7.2
Syntax of boolean expressions.

nested
expressions

Figure 7.1 determines if the user's zodiac sign is Scorpio. For purposes of this program, a Scorpio is anybody whose birthday falls between October 24 and November 22, including the starting and ending dates.

The rules for forming boolean expressions are yet another example of a recursive (circular) definition. Some kinds of boolean expressions, such as **X < 5**, are defined by simple rules that do not refer to boolean expressions, but others, such as **not(X < Y)**, arise from rules that define complex boolean expressions in terms of other boolean expressions. The situation is completely analogous to that of the Pascal definition of statements and just as we can iterate the definition of statement in order to get nested statements, we also can iterate the definition of boolean expression to obtain complicated nested boolean expressions; for example:

(Time < 60) and (not((Ans = 'N') or (Ans = 'n')))

parentheses

Our syntax diagrams, shown in Figure 7.2, assumes that you want expressions to be fully parenthesized. This is not always required. The default precedence if you omit parentheses is: **not** first, then **and** and then **or**. However, it is good practice to include most parentheses in order to make the expression easier to understand. One place where parentheses can safely be omitted is a simple string of **and**'s or **or**'s, but not a mixture of the two. The following expression is acceptable in terms of both the Pascal compiler and readability:

(X < 100) and (Ans <> 'N') and (Ans <> 'n')

When they are included in more complicated expressions, the parentheses around simple boolean expressions, such as **(X < 100)**, are never optional. If they are omitted, the compiler will either give an error statement or produce unwanted results.

Most high level programming languages have boolean expressions that are formed and used in pretty much the same way as they are in Pascal. Such minor details as the placement of parentheses will vary from language to language but the general ideas are the same for most programming languages.

Evaluating Boolean Expressions

Boolean expressions are evaluated by first evaluating the subexpressions and then combining those values according to the tables shown in Figure 7.3. This method of evaluation gives rise to one subtle pitfall. As we stated the evaluation rule, *all* the subexpressions are evaluated, and *then* the value of the full expression is determined. This means that all the subexpressions must be well defined and capable of being evaluated. As an example, consider the following reasonable looking statement:

if (Kids <> 0) and (Pieces div Kids >= 2)
    then writeln('Each child may have two pieces!')

Expression	Value	Expression	Value
true and true	true	true or true	true
true and false	false	true or false	true
false and true	false	false or true	true
false and false	false	false or false	false
not(true)	false	not(false)	true

Figure 7.3
Truth Tables

undefined
subexpressions

If the value of **Kids** is not zero, this statement performs fine. However, suppose the value of **Kids** is zero. Then we might expect the boolean expression to evaluate to **false**. After all, using an *and* to combine **false** with any other value will yield a value of **false**. Unfortunately, the computer will try to evaluate *both* subexpressions *before* it evaluates the *and*; this will produce an error, since *div* is being asked to divide by zero.

One way to avoid this problem is to use the following:

```
if Kids <> 0 then
  if Pieces div Kids >= 2 then
    writeln('Each child may have two pieces!')
```

In this version, the second boolean expression is not evaluated when the value of **Kids** is zero.

The compilers for some other programming languages and even some Pascal compilers are smart enough to cope successfully with either of the above two statements. However, the first one should not be used, since it cannot be guaranteed to work.

The odd Function

The type **boolean** arises in more kinds of situations than you might at first expect. There is a standard function, **odd**, which returns a value of type **boolean**. The function takes an argument of type **integer** and returns the value **true** if the integer is odd, for example, **1, 3, 5, -1, -3, -5** and so forth; it returns **false** if the integer is even (i.e., not odd), for example, **2, -2, 4** and so forth. The expression **odd(7)** thus returns **true**, whereas the expression **odd(4)** returns **false**. The function **odd** can be used inside Pascal boolean expressions in the same way as simple relational boolean expressions such as **X < 5**. For example, the following will write a message to the screen, provided the value of **N** is a positive odd number, like **1**, **3**, **5** and so forth:

```
if (N > 0) and odd(N)
  then writeln(N, ' is a positive odd number')
```

Introduction to Sets

We often want a program to check whether a value is on some list. For example, the program might ask the user to type in the letter **'Y'** or **'N'** for "yes" or "no" and then read the answer into the variable **Ans**. The user might get confused and type in something else, such as *OK*. In this situation you want the program to make sure the value of **Ans** is either **'Y'** or **'N'** before going on.

in

There is a type of boolean expression that can test to see if the value of an expression is on a specified list of values. The procedure in Figure 7.4 uses such a boolean expression, namely:

```
Ans in ['Y', 'N']
```

This boolean expression means just what you naturally expect it to mean. It evaluates to **true** if the value of **Ans** is equal to **'Y'** or **'N'**. In other words it is exactly equivalent to the boolean expression:

```
(Ans = 'Y') or (Ans = 'N')
```

When the list consists of just two or three values, you can just as well use an expression with **or**, like the above, but when the list of values is four or more, this new kind of boolean expression is very handy.

sets

The list of values is called a *set*. A set consists of a list of constants, separated by commas and enclosed in square brackets. Only square brackets can be used. In

Figure 7.4
A boolean
expression
using *in*.

```
procedure GetAnswer(var Ans: char);
{Instructs the user to type in Y or N for yes or no. Checks
the user's response and asks again if anything else is typed in.}

begin{GetAnswer}
  writeln('Type in Y for Yes or N for No');
  readln(Ans);
  if not( Ans in ['Y', 'N'] ) then
    begin{then}
      writeln('You typed in ', Ans);
      writeln('Please type in upper case N');
      writeln('or upper case Y, nothing else.');
      readln(Ans)
    end {then}
end; {GetAnswer}
```

Pascal the different kinds of brackets, '**)**', '**}**' and '**]**', have different uses and you can not interchange them.

To form a boolean expression involving a set, you write an expression followed by the reserved word *in* followed by a set. For example:

```
(X + Y) in [8, 34, -30]
```

The type of the expression in front of the *in* may be **integer** or **char**; it can not be either **real** or **string**. All the constants in the list must be of the same type as the expression. The entire boolean expression evaluates to **true** if the value of the expression, such as **(X + Y)**, is on the list; otherwise, it evaluates to **false**.

Since these expressions involving *in* are boolean expressions, they may be used as subparts of other more complex boolean expressions containing **and**, **or** or **not**. Figure 7.4 shows an example of one such boolean expression involving both **not** and **in**. Be sure to notice the syntax of how **not** and **in** are combined. The following is not allowed as a Pascal boolean expression:

```
Ans not in ['Y', 'N']
{NOT ALLOWED IN PASCAL}
```

Boolean expressions using *in* are particularly useful for making **case** statements safer. In a standard Pascal **case** statement, it is an error if the expression that controls the branch evaluates to something not on any label list. For example, if the value of **Aces** is **0** or **5** when the following is executed, then the effect is unpredictable:

*making
case statements
safer*

```
case Aces of
  1: writeln('Big deal.');
  2: writeln('A high pair.');
  3: writeln('Very good.');
  4: writeln('Wow!')
end
```

```
if Aces in [1, 2, 3, 4]
    then
      case Aces of
        1: writeln('Big deal.');
        2: writeln('A high pair.');
        3: writeln('Very good.');
        4: writeln('Wow!')
      end
    else writeln('ERROR: illegal case value!')
```

Figure 7.5
**A safer *case*
statement.**

There is a way to guard against this error and to produce an error message should the value of **Aces** be other than what is expected. The trick is to use a boolean expression involving *in*. The version of the *case* statement in Figure 7.5 always gives a meaningful output.

Some Pascal systems, such as UCSD Pascal, do allow the controlling expression of a *case* statement to evaluate to something that is on no *case* label list. On those systems, if the value is on no case label list, then the program performs no action but merely proceeds to the next statement. Of course, making use of this nonstandard property will cause your programs to be less portable.

Programming with Boolean Variables

Variable and named constants of type **boolean** are declared in the same place and in the same way as other types of variables and constants. A hypothetical program might start out:

```
program Sample(input, output);
  const Winter = false;
        AnnualRainFall = 30;
  var Ans: char;
      Raining: boolean;
```

A boolean variable (one of type **boolean**) can be given a value in most of the same ways that other types of variables are given a value, that is, by an assignment operator or by being an actual variable parameter to a procedure. For example, the following assignment statement sets the value of the variable **Raining**:

```
Raining := Ans in ['y', 'Y']
```

At first, such assignment statements look strange, but you quickly adjust to them. The rules are the same as they are for variables of other types: the expression on the right-hand side of the assignment operator is evaluated (since it is a boolean expression, this value will be either **true** or **false**); after that, the value of the boolean variable is set equal to this value of **true** or **false**. In the preceding example, if the value of **Ans** is either 'Y' or 'y', then **Raining** gets the value **true**; otherwise, it is set to **false**. Hence, this assignment statement is equivalent to the following longer and somewhat inefficient statement:

```
if Ans in ['y', 'Y']
     then Raining := true
     else Raining := false
```

The longer statement, which was given only to help explain the assignment statement, is poor programming style.

Boolean variables can be used to remember a condition that may change later or that will not be easy to check later on. An equally important use of boolean variables is to make the meaning of a program more apparent. In the program fragment below, the boolean variable **Raining** frees the programmer from having to remember the exact wording of the question **'Is it raining?'** The question might have been **'Has it stopped raining?'** and the programmer who forgets the exact wording of the question can easily misinterpret the meaning of **Ans**, even if the value of **Ans** does not change.

```
writeln('Is it raining?');
readln(Ans);
Raining := Ans in ['y', 'Y'];
if Raining
    then writeln('Too bad.')
    else writeln('Would you like to go for a walk?')
```

Many other common programming languages do not have boolean variables. In these languages, programmers frequently simulate boolean variables by some trick, such as pretending that the integer 1 means true and that 0 means false.

A Longer Example

The program in Figure 7.6 illustrates almost all the Pascal features and means of documenting a program that we have seen so far. It is based on the program in Figure 2.5. Like that program, the task of this one is to carry on a conversation with the user.

Boolean Input and Output

Reading in a value of type **boolean** cannot be done directly. Instead, some other type of input such as a character must be read in and used to set the boolean variable. The following program fragment sets the value of the variable **BV** of type **boolean** using the variable **Ans** of type **char**.

```
writeln('Type T for True or F for False');
readln(Ans);
BV := Ans in ['T', 't']
```

In many versions of standard Pascal, boolean values can be written as output; in UCSD Pascal, they can not. In any version of Pascal, the following will serve to output the value of the boolean variable **BV**:

```
if BV then write('true')
    else write('false')
```

Program

```pascal
program Talk2(input, output);

const Period = '.';
var FirstI, LastI: char;
    Raining, Kids: boolean;

procedure Introduction(var FirstI, LastI: char);
{Postcondition: The values of FirstI and LastI are the
initials of the names the user typed in.}

begin {Introduction}
  writeln('Good day. My name is Ronald Gollum,');
  writeln('but you can call me R.G.');
  writeln('First things first, as they say.');
  writeln('So, please tell me your first name.');
  readln(FirstI);
  writeln('A very nice name, indeed!');
  writeln('And what is your last name?');
  readln(LastI);
  if (FirstI = 'R') and (LastI = 'G')
    then writeln('We have the same initials!')
    else writeln('Pleased to meet you ',
                 FirstI, Period, LastI, Period)

end; {Introduction}

procedure RainTalk(var Raining: boolean);
{Postcondition: Raining is true if user
claimed it was raining; otherwise, it is false.}
    var Ans: char;
begin {RainTalk}
  writeln('Say, is it raining out now?');
  readln(Ans);
  Raining := Ans in ['Y', 'y'];
  if not Raining
    then writeln('Good. I don''t care for rain.')
    else
    begin {outer else}
      writeln('Do you think it will rain tomorrow?');
      readln(Ans);
      if Ans in ['N', 'n']
        then writeln('Good. I don''t care for rain.')
        else writeln('Hmmm.')
    end {outer else}
end; {RainTalk}
```

Figure 7.6
Enhancement of
the program in
Figure 2.5.

```
procedure ChildrenTalk(var Kids: boolean);
```
{*Postcondition: Kids is true if the user said he / she
has children and is false otherwise.*}
```
  var NumKids: integer;
      Ans: char;
begin{ChildrenTalk}
  writeln('Do you have any children?');
  readln(Ans);
  Kids := Ans in ['Y', 'y'];
  if not( Kids )
    then writeln('Neither do I.')
    else
    begin{Kids}
      writeln('How many children do you have?');
      readln(NumKids);

      if NumKids = 1 then
        writeln('An only child. I was also an only child.')
      else if NumKids = 2 then
        begin{NumKids = 2}
          writeln('Are they twins?');
          readln(Ans);
          if Ans in ['Y', 'y']
            then writeln('I knew it!')
            else writeln('I didn''t think so.')
        end {NumKids = 2}
      else if NumKids > 3 then
        writeln('That''s a pretty big family')
      else {if NumKids < = 0 then}
        writeln('Your answers do not make sense.')
    end {Kids}
end; {ChildrenTalk}

procedure EndTalk(FirstI, LastI: char;
                  Raining , Kids: boolean);
```
{*Precondition: FirstI and LastI contain the user's initials. Raining
is true if the user said it was raining; otherwise, it is false.
Kids is true if the user said he / she has kids; otherwise, it is false.*}
```
begin {EndTalk}
  writeln('Oh my! I seem to have lost track of time.');
  writeln('I really must go.');
  writeln('Goodbye ', FirstI, Period, LastI, Period);
  writeln('I enjoyed talking with you.');
```

**Figure 7.6 continues
on next page**

```
if Raining then
  writeln('You brightened up this rainy day.');
if Kids then
  writeln('Give my regards to your children.')
end; {EndTalk}

begin{Program}
  Introduction(FirstI, LastI);
  RainTalk(Raining);
  writeln('Let''s talk about something else.');
  ChildrenTalk(Kids);
  EndTalk(FirstI, LastI, Raining, Kids)
end. {Program}
```

Sample Dialogue

Good day. My name is Ronald Gollum,
but you can call me R.G.
First things first, as they say.
So, please tell me your first name.
Killer
A very nice name, indeed!
And what is your last name?
Granawich
Pleased to meet you K.G.
Say, is it raining out now?
yes
Do you think it will rain tomorrow?
yes
Hmmm.
Let's talk about something else.
Do you have any children?
no
Neither do I.
Oh my! I seem to have lost track of time.
I really must go.
Goodbye K.G.
I enjoyed talking with you.
You brightened up this rainy day.

Figure 7.6 (cont'd)

A Design Example

In Chapter 4 we designed a program to determine the number of coins needed to give an amount of change from 1 to 99 cents. That program produced outputs such as the following:

```
27 cents can be given as:
 1 quarters
 0 dimes and
 2 pennies
```

This sort of output is frequently acceptable, but it would be nicer to have output that is grammatically correct and that does not contain pointless information. Ideally, the output should look like:

```
27 cents can be given as:
one quarter and 2 pennies
```

In this section we will design a procedure to produce this sort of output.

When you stop to think of all the grammatical details we do automatically when writing phrases such as the desired sample output, you quickly realize that designing output can be a complicated task. The program must somehow ignore coin amounts of zero, it needs to decide between singular and plural forms, it needs to place the `'and'` correctly and it needs to insert a comma if all three types of coins are used, as in:

```
37 cents can be given as:
one quarter, one dime and 2 pennies
```

We will assume that the total amount and the count of each coin are given by the value parameters **TotalAmount**, **Quarters**, **Dimes** and **Pennies**. We will also assume, as in the original progamming task, that **TotalAmount** is between 1 and 99 (cents) and that the coin counts are correct for that amount. We will use a very straightforward decomposition of this task into subtasks: write the heading, write the number of quarters, write the number of dimes inserting a comma or `'and'` if necessary and finally write the number of pennies, inserting an `'and'` if necessary.

In order to determine whether it should output a comma or `'and'`, the *flag* program needs some way to test if there were any previous coins output. This could be done by checking to see if certain parameters are equal to zero. However, we will use a more straightforward method. We will use a boolean variable **PreviousCoins**. This variable will be initialized to **false** and will have its value changed to **true** as soon as a nonzero number of coins are output. A variable, such as **PreviousCoins**, that changes value to indicate that some event has taken place is often called a *flag*. In this sample, "when the flag goes up," it is time to insert a comma or the connective `'and'`. The complete procedure, embedded in a test program, is given in Figure 7.7.

Program

```
program Test(input, output);

var TotalAmount, Quarters, Dimes, Pennies: integer;

procedure OutputCoins(TotalAmount,
                          Quarters, Dimes, Pennies: integer);
```
{*Outputs a collection of coins that total to TotalAmount cents.*
Precondition: 0 < TotalAmount < = 99 and the coins total to TotalAmount.}
```
   const CommaSpace = ', ';
   var PreviousCoins: boolean;{Set to true
   after the first output of a number of coins.}
begin{OutputCoins}
   writeln(TotalAmount:2, ' cents can be given as:');
   PreviousCoins := false;

   if Quarters > 0 then
     begin{Quarters > 0}
       if Quarters = 1 then write('one quarter')
                       else write(Quarters:1,'quarters');
       PreviousCoins := true
     end; {Quarters > 0}

   if Dimes > 0 then
     begin{Dimes > 0}
       if PreviousCoins then
         if Pennies <> 0 then write(CommaSpace)
                         else write(' and ');
       if Dimes = 1 then write('one dime')
                    else write(Dimes:1,'dimes');
       PreviousCoins := true
     end; {Dimes > 0}

   if Pennies > 0 then
     begin{Pennies > 0}
       if PreviousCoins then write(' and ');
       if Pennies = 1 then write('one penny')
                      else write(Pennies:2, 'pennies')
     end; {Pennies > 0}

   writeln
end; {OutputCoins}
```

Figure 7.7
Enhanced procedure
to output coins.

```
begin{TestProgram}
  writeln('Enter: Quarters, Dimes, Pennies:');
  readln(Quarters, Dimes, Pennies);
  TotalAmount := 25*Quarters + 10*Dimes + Pennies;
  OutputCoins(TotalAmount, Quarters, Dimes, Pennies)
end. {TestProgram}
```

Sample Dialogue

Enter: Quarters, Dimes, Pennies:
1 2 0
45 cents can be given as:
one quarter and 2 dimes

Figure 7.7
(cont'd)

Iterative Enhancement

One way to design a program is to simplify the design goals so as to make the programming task easier and to then design the simpler version of the program. After that, features can be added. For example, the program for making change that we designed in Chapter 4 (Figure 4.3) worked acceptably. However, we can enhance its performance by using the procedure **OutputCoins** from Figure 7.7. We can enhance it more by adding still other features, such as including nickels or including bills. This process is sometimes referred to as *iterative enhancement*. The early simplified versions of the program are sometimes called *stub programs*, because many parts of the program have been abbreviated.

Do not confuse iterative enhancement with trial-and-error programming. It definitely is not that. Each version of the program is well specified and well thought out. It just does not have as many features as the final program will have.

There are a number of reasons for programming in this way. It produces a full working program more quickly. It allows a thorough early test of the general design strategy. It also means that, if you fail to achieve the final programming goal by some deadline, you will at least have a working program and not just a collection of disconnected pieces of code. Iterative enhancement can also be a way of implementing a divide-and-conquer strategy. If a program can be made to run without one of the desired subtasks, then the rest of the program can be designed and tested before that subtask is tackled.

stub
programs

The Throwaway Program

The program in Figure 7.6 was obtained by starting with the program in Figure 2.5 and embellishing it using the constructs and techniques we have learned. It is a good model of how branching and boolean variables can be used. It also illustrates another technique for designing programs.

The ideal way to design a program is to first define the task to be accomplished, then divide that task into subtasks, keep dividing subtasks into smaller tasks until you have manageable size tasks, design algorithms for those small subtasks and translate them into Pascal code and finally put the procedures together into a complete program, testing them one at a time.

This is a great method. But what do you do if you can not accomplish the first step? What do you do if the task is not clearly defined? What do you do if you can not think of any natural subtasks? Writing a program that makes conversation is one such task. The specifications are very vague. Moreover, which kinds of subtasks are useful and amenable to computer implementation is not clear. In short, it is difficult to get started. One method to get over this stumbling block is to just charge ahead and write a program to do something that approximates what is desired. Unlike iterative enhancement, this really is trial-and-error programming. After you have some sort of program, say the one in Figure 2.5, you will have learned something about the problem and possible solution methods. You can then enhance your solution by inserting additions and by improving parts. These improvements may get you from a program like the one in Figure 2.5 to one like that in Figure 7.6.

Now suppose you want to write a program to carry on long interesting conversations. The temptation is to try to continue to improve the program you have. It may seem that if you just keep refining it you will eventually get the program you want. That is a reasonable point of view. Unfortunately, it is almost always a disastrous way to proceed. This first unsystematically arrived at program will undoubtedly be far worse than what you can write in a systematic way now that you understand the problem better. Experience indicates that if you throw out the program and start from scratch in a systematic way, you will get a program that is easier to understand, contains fewer bugs and performs better. What may not be so obvious is that you will probably find that writing a new program from scratch is faster and less painful than trying to save the old program. It is difficult to throw away the results of hard work, but it is frequently a very wise move.

The technique of throwing away a program and starting over is frequently useful even if you work in a completely systematic way. Ideally, you should think the problem through completely before you start, and if you do so, you should produce a nice clean correct program. That *should* always happen if you follow the rules we outlined for systematically designing a program. However, human beings make mistakes and learn from their mistakes. You will sometimes find that, despite your careful design efforts, your program is not clear or just does not perform well. In that case throw it out and start over again. The effort expended on the discarded program is not wasted. You learned from it and what you learned will help you to design the new program. One last bit of advice: when you write the next version of your program, do not cut corners but apply all the design rules we have suggested.

Summary of Problem Solving and Programming Techniques

One way to design a program is to design a simplified version and then add enhancements. When a program performs very poorly or is very poorly written, it is best to throw it out and start over.

You can use a boolean expression with *in* to test whether the controlling expression in a *case* statement evaluates to something on one of the label lists. You can use a boolean variable as a flag in a program. A flag records whether or not some event has taken place.

◇

"Care is no cure, but rather corrosive,
For things that are not to be remedied."
William Shakespeare, King Henry VI, Part I

Plan to throw one away; you will, anyhow.
F. P. Brooks, Jr., The Mythical Man-Month
◇

Summary of Pascal Constructs

the type boolean
Syntax:

```
boolean
```

Example:

```
var Raining: boolean;
```

A Pascal type. There are exactly two values of this type, namely, **true** and **false**. A Pascal program can have variables, constants, expressions and/or functions of this type.

use of and
Syntax:

(⟨boolean expression 1⟩) *and* (⟨boolean expression 2⟩)

Example:

```
(X < 1) and (X <> Y)
(Ans in ['Y', 'y']) and (X > 0)
```

One way to make a larger boolean expression out of two smaller boolean expressions. If both ⟨boolean expression 1⟩ and ⟨boolean expression 2⟩ evaluate to **true**, then the entire expression evaluates to **true**. If at least one of ⟨boolean expression 1⟩ and ⟨boolean expression 2⟩ evaluates to **false**, then the entire expression evaluates to **false**.

use of or

Syntax:

(⟨boolean expression 1⟩) *or* (⟨boolean expression 2⟩)

Example:

(Ans = 'Y') *or* (Number = 7)

One way to make a larger boolean expression out of two smaller boolean expressions. If at least one of ⟨boolean expression 1⟩ and ⟨boolean expression 2⟩ evaluate to **true**, then the entire expression evaluates to **true**. If both ⟨boolean expression 1⟩ and ⟨boolean expression 2⟩ evaluate to **false**, then the entire expression evaluates to **false**.

use of not

Syntax:

not(⟨boolean expression⟩)

Examples:

not(X < 0)
not(Ans *in* ['Y', 'y'])

One way to make a larger boolean expression out of a smaller one. *not* reverses boolean values. If ⟨boolean expression⟩ evaluates to **true**, then the expression with the *not* evaluates to **false**. If ⟨boolean expression⟩ evaluates to **false**, then the expression with the *not* evaluates to **true**.

use of in

Syntax:

⟨expression⟩ *in* ⟨set⟩

Examples:

X + Y *in* [3, 4, -7]
Ans *in* ['Y', 'y', 'N', 'n']

A kind of boolean expression. ⟨expression⟩ can be an expression of type **integer**, **char** or **boolean**. ⟨set⟩ is a list of constants separated by commas and all of the same type as ⟨expression⟩. This boolean expression evaluates to **true** if the value of ⟨expression⟩ is equal to the value of one of the constants on the list.

Exercises

Self-Test and Interactive Exercises

1. Classify each of the following as incorrectly formed, evaluating to **true** or evaluating to **false**:

```
(0 = 1) and (2 < 3)        (0 = 1) or (2 < 3)
(7 not in [1, 3, 5])        7 not in [1, 3, 5]
('Y' = 'y') and (maxint = 65535)
not(true and (6*2 <= 13))
not( (31 mod 15) in [1, 2, 3] )
```

2. Translate the following English and mathematics expressions into Pascal boolean expressions: two plus two equals four, **X** plus seven is more than one hundred, 'Z' is not one of the first three letters of the alphabet,

$$x \leq y + 2 \leq z$$

3. Write the Pascal statement for a guarded command that classifies an integer **X** into one of the following categories and writes out an appropriate message:

$$X < 0 \text{ or } 0 \leq X \leq 100 \text{ or } X > 100$$

4. Write a program that will read in three numbers and will output a message telling whether or not the numbers are in numeric order.

5. The following four boolean expressions divide into two groups with two equivalent expressions in each group. What are the two groups?

```
not(Footloose) and not(FancyFree)
not(Footloose) or not(FancyFree)
not(Footloose and FancyFree)
not(Footloose or FancyFree)
```

6. Write a program that will read in three integers and output a message telling whether exactly two of them are greater than 10. There is no need to be fancy. It is perfectly all right to use a long boolean expression that tests all possible pairs of variables.

7. The expression **A or B** evaluates to **true** provided that the value of either *or both* of the variables is **true**. Design a boolean expression that evaluates to **true** provided that the value of *exactly one* of the two variables is **true**.

8. Write a procedure that sets a variable parameter **Ans** equal to 'Y' or 'N' depending on whether the user types in 'Yes' or 'No'. The procedure should correct for lower-case letters. For example, if the user types in 'yes', then **Ans** is set to 'Y', rather than 'y'. If the user types in a response that does not start with one of these letters, then the procedure issues a message and asks for the answer again. Figure 7.4 can be used as a guide.

9. Write a program to carry on a conversation.

10. Write a program that computes state income tax according to the following formula: Net income is gross income minus deductions (both given as input); tax is:

3% on each dollar of net income up to $7,999 plus
5% on each dollar of net income from $8,000 to 14,999 plus
8% on each dollar of net income over $15,000.

11. Write a program to give a student's final grade in a course with the following grading scheme: three quizzes worth 10 points each, a midterm worth 100 points and a final worth 100 points. The grade is based on the following weights: 50% on the final exam, 25% on the midterm and 25% on the quiz average. (Be sure to normalize the quiz average to 100 by multiplying by 10.) The grade is determined from the weighted average in the traditional way: 90 or over is an A, below 90 down to 80 is a B, below 80 to 70 is a C, below 70 to 60 is a D, below 60 is an F.

12. Write a program that accepts dates written in the usual way and then outputs them as three numbers. For example, the input:

February 15, 1952

should produce the output:

2-15-52

13. Write a program that accepts a "three digit" number written in words and then outputs it as a value of type **integer**. For example, the input:

two hundred thirty-five

should produce the output:

235

14. Write a program that accepts years written in Roman numerals and outputs the year written in arabic (ordinary) numerals.

15. Write a program that guesses the user's height. The program makes a first guess and then asks the user if it is too high or too low. The program continues to guess and ask the user until the user says the guess is correct or for three tries, whichever comes first.

16. Write a program to score the "paper-rock-scissors" game. Each of two users types in either ´P´, ´R´ or ´S´ and the program announces the winner as well as the basis for determining the winner: "paper covers rock," "rock breaks scissors," "scissors cut paper," or "nobody wins." Be sure to allow the users to use lowercase as well as uppercase letters (if they are available on your machine).

17. Write an astrology program. The user types in his or her birthday and the program responds with the user's sign and horoscope. The month may be entered as a number from 1 to 12. Use a newspaper horoscope section for the horoscopes and dates of each sign. Then enhance your program so that if the user is only one or two days away from an adjacent sign, then the program announces that the user is on a "cusp" and also outputs the horoscope for that nearest adjacent sign. For a nicer but harder program, let the user type in the month as a word rather than as a number.

18. Redo (or do for the first time) Exercise 17 from Chapter 6.

19. Write a program that will read in two initials and will then echo them back in large block letters. See Figure 5.10 for a hint.

20. Enhance the blackjack program in Figure 6.14 to add the following features: the user may enter up to five cards per hand; the program scores two hands and announces the winner as well as the two scores; if both players have 21 and one player used five cards while the other used four or less, then the hand with five cards wins. ("Five cards under 21" is a hard hand to get and hence given more value.)

8

Looping Mechanisms

It is not true that life is one damn thing after another—It's one damn thing over and over.

Edna St. Vincent Millay

Chapter Contents

A very common sort of algorithm is one that repeats an action a number of times. For example, in order to find the average of 100 numbers, a program might initialize a variable **Sum** to zero and then repeat the following 100 times:

```
begin
  writeln('Enter a number');
  readln(Number);
  Sum := Sum + Number
end
```

body of a loop

After that the average can be computed as **Sum** divided by 100. Any programming construct that tells the computer to repeat an action is called a *looping mechanism* or, more simply, a *loop*. The program code that gets repeated is called the *body of the loop*. In the preceding averaging example, the displayed compound statement is the body of the loop.

In this chapter we will introduce the looping mechanisms available in the Pascal language. We will also describe a number of techniques for designing algorithms and programs that use loops.

Repeat Statements

One common kind of loop is one that repeats an action until the user signals the program to stop. Our first Pascal looping mechanism is perfectly suited to this sort of task. The *repeat statement* tells the computer to repeat a list of statements again and again until the value of a controlling boolean expression becomes **true**. As an example, suppose we want the following statement repeated until the user signals the computer to stop:

```
writeln('Hi there.')
```

The following Pascal construct will do what we want, provided the variable **Ans** is declared to be of type **char**:

```
repeat
  writeln('Hi there.');
  writeln('Do you want me to do this again?');
  writeln('Type Y for Yes or N for No.');
  readln(Ans)
until Ans = 'N'
```

This will cause the three **writeln** statements to be executed. The user must then type in a character that is read into the variable **Ans**. If the value of **Ans** is anything except **'N'**, then the whole process is repeated. If the second time around the user again types in something other than **'N'**, then the process is repeated again. The four statements will be repeated again and again until the value of the boolean expression at the end is **true**, that is, until the value of **Ans** is **'N'**.

This sort of looping mechanism is defined to be a particular type of Pascal statement called a *repeat statement*. It is another instance of a complex statement that is made up of other simpler statements. The syntax for the **repeat** statement is given in Figure 8.1. The list of statements separated by semicolons forms the *body* of the **repeat** loop.

syntax

When the **repeat** statement is executed, the first action is like that of a compound statement. First the list of statements in the body is executed in order. Next the boolean expression is evaluated. If it evaluates to **true**, then the

behavior of repeat loop

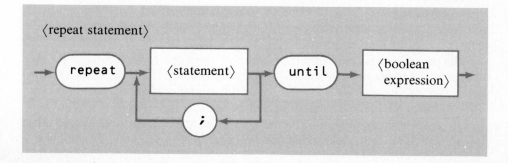

⟨repeat statement⟩

Figure 8.1
Syntax of a repeat statement.

repeat statement ends and the program goes on to the next instruction. If the boolean expression evaluates to **false**, then the statements in the body are executed again. This process of executing the body of the loop and then evaluating the boolean expression is repeated until the boolean expression evaluates to **true**.

Needless to say, you normally want one of the statements in the body of the loop to change something in the controlling boolean expression. Otherwise, the value of the boolean expression will never change and the *repeat* statement might never end.

Example—Testing a Procedure

We have advocated testing procedures separately by writing a small test program for each procedure. To add to our confidence in the correctness of the procedure, we need to test it with a number of different parameter values. A *repeat* loop in the test program will allow us to test the procedure as often as we wish without having to rerun the test program.

For example, in Chapter 7 we wrote a program to test a procedure named **OutputCoins**. That program tested one set of parameter values and then terminated. If we add a *repeat* loop, as shown in Figure 8.2, then we can test the input on several different sets of parameter values without having to rerun the program.

When reading Figure 8.2, there is no need to look back at the previous chapter to see the body of the procedure. The procedure heading and the comment are all you need in order to understand the loop. The sample dialogue is short due to space limitations. This procedure should be tested on many more than the three sets of values shown.

Unrolling a Loop

averaging example

The *repeat* statement has other uses besides repeating a new calculation until the user signals it to stop. A loop can frequently be a necessary part of a single unified calculation. By way of example, suppose we wish to write a program to average a list of nonnegative integers. For example, the list might be a list of quiz scores or a list of bowling scores.

The program must read in a list of numbers and compute their average. The number of numbers to be averaged is not known when the program is written, and so this will necessitate a loop to read in the numbers and add them up. The heart of the loop is clear. The program should keep a running sum of the numbers read in so far and should count the number of numbers read in. It should look something like the following, where **Sum** will end up with the sum of the numbers

Program

```
program Test(input, output);

var Ans: char;
    TotalAmount, Quarters, Dimes, Pennies: integer;

procedure OutputCoins(TotalAmount,
                      Quarters, Dimes, Pennies: integer);
```
{*Outputs a collection of coins that total to TotalAmount cents.*
Precondition: 0 < TotalAmount < = 99 and the coins total to TotalAmount.}
⟨⟨⟨⟨⟨The rest of the procedure is shown in Figure 7.7⟩⟩⟩⟩⟩

```
begin{TestProgram}
  repeat
    writeln('Enter: Quarters, Dimes, Pennies:');
    readln(Quarters, Dimes, Pennies);
    TotalAmount := 25*Quarters + 10*Dimes + Pennies;
    OutputCoins(TotalAmount, Quarters, Dimes, Pennies);
    writeln('Do you want to test again?');
    readln(Ans)
  until (Ans = 'N') or (Ans = 'n');
  writeln('End of test program.')
end. {TestProgram}
```

Sample Dialogue

Enter: Quarters, Dimes, Pennies:
1 2 0
45 cents can be given as:
one quarter and 2 dimes
Do you want to test again?
Yes
Enter: Quarters, Dimes, Pennies:
2 1 5
65 cents can be given as:
2 quarters, one dime and 5 pennies
Do you want to test again?
yes
Enter: Quarters, Dimes, Pennies:
2 0 0
50 cents can be given as:
2 quarters
Do you want to test again?
no
End of test program.

Figure 8.2

Testing a procedure using a *repeat* loop.

and `Count` will count the number of numbers read in:

```
repeat
  read(Next);
  Count := Count + 1;
  Sum := Sum + Next
until ⟨boolean expression⟩
```

Although this loop body may not be exactly the loop body we end up with, we can be certain that the correct loop body will contain the three statements shown.

We still need to determine the ⟨boolean expression⟩. It should be equivalent to: "All the numbers have been read in." But how can the program know when all the numbers have been read in? The user will tell it when it has read in all the numbers. One solution would be to read in a number and then ask the user if there are more numbers to read in and to do this on every repetition of the loop, rather like the examples we have already seen. Although that will work, it is not a good idea. The user will get tired of being asked if there are more numbers, especially if the list of numbers is long. It is preferable for the user to type in all the numbers and then type in a signal that indicates that the list has ended. One natural way to mark the end of the list is with a negative number. It is known that a negative number cannot be a member of the list. So this is a way to unambiguously mark the end of the list. Moreover, a negative number can be read into the variable `Next` and the value of `Next` can be tested to see if it is negative and thus at the end of the list. The ⟨boolean expression⟩ in the *repeat* loop should be something like: `Next < 0`. So, our next attempt at the loop is:

```
repeat
  read(Next);
  Count := Count + 1;
  Sum := Sum + Next
until Next < 0
```

*starting
and ending
problems*

Now the problems inherent in writing a loop rear their ugly heads. The preceding loop almost works but does not quite do what it is supposed to. The loop will add up and count the nonnegative numbers, and when it encounters a negative number, the loop will end. Unfortunately the negative number will also be added into `Sum`, and the variable `Count` will include an extra increment for that negative number. This sort of problem is frequently encountered when writing a loop. It is relatively easy to design a loop that does the right thing most of the time, but inevitably there is some peculiarity about the first or last time through the loop. Moreover, at least one of these peculiarities typically presents a problem. In this example, it is the last time through the loop that presents a problem. The problem is that in the last iteration of the loop body, we do not want the following two statements executed:

```
Count := Count + 1;
Sum := Sum + Next
```

In other words, we want to stop the loop before all the statements in the body of the loop have been executed. One way to achieve this is to rearrange the order of the statements so that they end with the one we want. In this case we want the loop to end with the **read** statement. The statements in the body of a loop can be thought of as being in a circle. If we take one statement from the beginning of the loop body and move it to the end of the loop body, we preserve the circle. We can do this repeatedly until we get the loop to end with the statement we want. In this case we need move only one statement from the beginning to the end of the list. That produces the following, which does end with the statement we want:

```
repeat
  Count := Count + 1;
  Sum := Sum + Next;
  read(Next)
until Next < 0
```

When we "rotate" a loop in this way, we get the correct last statement, but we may cause the loop to start with the wrong statement. It sounds like we are just exchanging one problem for another, but things are not really that bad. In this case we want the loop to start with the **read** statement; otherwise, the variable **Next** will be uninitialized. So all we need to do is to insert an extra **read** statement just before the loop, as illustrated in Figure 8.3, which shows the loop embedded in a program to compute averages.

This technique for designing a loop is sometimes called *unrolling the loop*. We can imagine the list of statements written on a ribbon. The list of statements is repeated a number of times and the ribbon is coiled around a spool. Each revolution of the spool contains one complete loop body. So the loop body starts and ends at the place where the loose end of the ribbon leaves the spool. In order to change the order of the statements in the loop body, we unroll the spool of ribbon. The process is diagramed in Figure 8.4. When we unroll one or more statements, in this case the **read** statement, they are moved off the spool, which represents the loop body, but they are still in the program. In the program, they are placed before the loop.

unrolling

This technique is one way to design loops that we want to start and stop at different places. We first design the loop to start where we want. Then we unroll it until the loop body ends where we want it to. In the program, the extra statements that are unrolled get placed before the loop. Hence, the effect of the loop plus these extra statements is equivalent to that of starting and stopping the loop at different places in the loop body.

There is one problem that can arise when we design a loop by unrolling it. In our example, we made the tacit assumption that the list contained at least one number plus the end marker. In this case that was a reasonable assumption. In other cases it might not be. For example, suppose the loop is being used to calculate the total number of people in an office who smoke and the total number of cigarettes they smoke per day. The list will probably not be empty, but it might be. If the list might be empty, then we need to add some additional check such as

*check
the first
iteration*

Program

```
program OneAverage(input, output);

var Sum, Count: integer;
    Average: real;

procedure ComputeAverage(var Sum, Count: integer;
                                  var Average: real);
```
{*Reads in a list of integers. Sets the parameters to*
the total, the number of integers and the average, respectively.}
```
  var Next: integer;
begin{ComputeAverage}
  writeln('Enter a list of nonnegative integers.');
  writeln('Terminate the list with a negative integer.');

  Sum := 0;
  Count := 0;

  read(Next);
  repeat
    Count := Count + 1;
    Sum := Sum + Next;
    read(Next)
  until Next < 0;

  Average := Sum / Count
end; {ComputeAverage}

begin{Program}
  writeln('This program will average');
  writeln('a list of nonnegative integers.');
  ComputeAverage(Sum, Count, Average);
  writeln(Count, ' numbers totaled to ', Sum);
  writeln('for an average of ', Average)
end. {Program}
```

Sample Dialogue

This program will average
a list of nonnegative integers.
Enter a list of nonnegative integers.
Terminate the list with a negative integer.
5 10 8 -1
  3 numbers totaled to 23
for an average of   7.66666666666667E + 00

Figure 8.3
Procedure with a
repeat
statement.

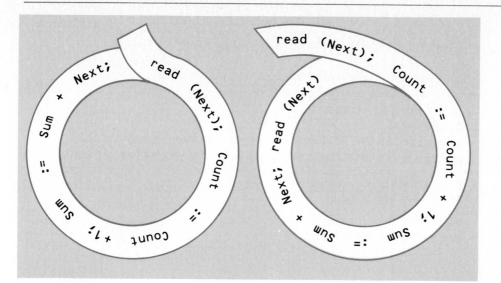

Figure 8.4
Unrolling a loop.

the following:

```
read(Next);
if Next >= 0 then
  repeat
    Count := Count + 1;
    Sum := Sum + Next;
    read(Next)
  until Next < 0
```

(If the program performs an averaging calculation as in Figure 8.3, then a test for division by zero will also be needed.)

Whenever you unroll a **repeat** loop, you must either be certain that you want the program to execute the new **repeat** loop at least once or else you should embed the loop in an **if - then** statement. With any sort of loop, you should always check to see that the loop body is not repeated one too many or one too few times.

While Statements

The **while** statement is a slight variant of the **repeat** statement. For example, the **repeat** statement in Figure 8.3 can be rewritten as the following, almost equivalent, **while** statement:

```
while Next >= 0 do
  begin{while}
    Count := Count + 1;
    Sum := Sum + Next;
    read(Next)
  end {while}
```

```
procedure ComputeAverage(var Sum, Count: integer;
                                    var Average: real);
```
{*Reads in a list of nonnegative integers. Sets the parameters to
the total, the number of numbers and the average,respectively.*}
```
    var Next: integer;
begin{ComputeAverage}
  writeln('Enter a list of nonnegative integers.');
  writeln('Terminate the list with a negative integer.');

  Sum := 0;
  Count := 0;

  read(Next);
  while Next >= 0 do
    begin{while}
      Count := Count + 1;
      Sum := Sum + Next;
      read(Next)
    end; {while}

  Average := Sum / Count
end; {ComputeAverage}
```

Figure 8.5

**Figure 8.3 rewritten
using a *while*
loop.**

The complete rewritten procedure is shown in Figure 8.5. If this version of the procedure is used in the program in Figure 8.3, then the dialogue will be the same as that shown in Figure 8.3.

syntax
The body of a *while* statement must always be a single statement. That is why the above *while* loop contains a *begin/end* pair. They convert a list of statements to a single compound statement. The body can be any sort of statement. It need not be a compound statement. For example, the following is a valid *while* statement provided **SomeProcedure** is a procedure with one parameter of the appropriate type:

while X > 0 do SomeProcedure(X)

*differences
between
while and
repeat*
One difference between a *while* and a *repeat* loop is that a *while* loop ends when its boolean expression is **false**, in contrast to a *repeat* loop, which ends when its boolean expression is **true**. The procedure call in the preceding *while* loop will be executed as long as the value of **X** is positive. That is not a major difference. However, there is one important difference between these two kinds of loops. With a *while* loop the boolean condition is checked first and if it evaluates to **false**, the body of the loop is never executed; in a *repeat* loop, the body of the loop is always executed at least once. The behaviors of the two loop statements are diagramed in Figure 8.6.

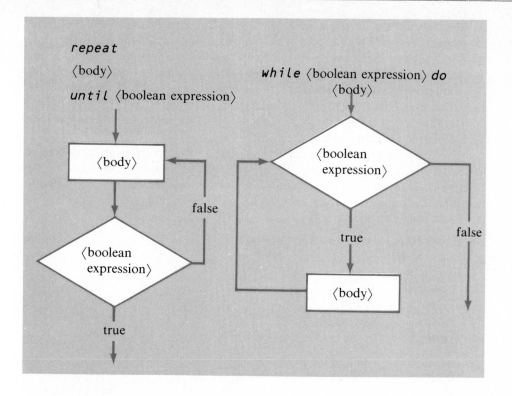

Figure 8.6
Behavior of
***repeat* and**
***while* statements.**

Infinite Loops

Some loops are not required to end—for example, those loops which repeat a task again and again until the user says he or she is through. The user need not ever be through. Other loops perform one specific task once and should end. For example, a loop to add the numbers from 1 to 100 should eventually end. A loop that repeats forever is called an *infinite loop*. If the loop is supposed to end and provide a result, then you must make sure it is not an infinite loop. If the loop is a ***repeat*** loop, you should check to be certain that the controlling boolean expression does eventually become **true**. If the loop is a ***while*** loop, you should check to be certain that the controlling boolean expression does eventually become **false**.

Invariant Assertions and Variant Expressions
(Optional)

A program with loops can be more complicated and more difficult to understand than the simple programs we examined prior to this chapter. Consequently, you need to document the loops in your programs carefully. In this section we will describe some widely used methods for commenting loops.

invariants

Recall that an assertion is a comment that states something which the programmer expects to be true whenever the program execution reaches the assertion. If the program is correct, then the assertion will be true. The only sort of assertions we have had any significant contact with are preconditions and postconditions. As with other programming constructs, loops of any complexity should be documented with preconditions and postconditions. The precondition asserts what is true before the loop is executed and the postcondition asserts what should be true after the loop is executed.

There is one other kind of assertion that is frequently used to document loops. This type of assertion is called a *loop invariant* or simply an *invariant*. An invariant is an assertion that is true before the loop is executed and that remains true after each iteration of the loop. As a simple example of a loop, consider the following piece of code:

```
N := 10;
Sum := 10;
while N >1 do
  begin{while}
    N := N - 1;
    Sum := Sum + N
  end {while}
```

Since an invariant is an assertion that is true before the loop is executed, it must be true just before the program execution gets to the word **while**. It must also be true after each iteration of the loop; hence, it must be true just before the word **end**. This implies that it is true each time the program gets to that point. It also implies that it will be true after the **while** loop has ended. One invariant of this loop is the assertion:

*N ≥ 1 and the value of Sum is the sum of
all the integers x such that N ≤ x ≤ 10.*

The assertion is true before the loop is ever executed because then the values of **Sum** and **N** are both **10**. Each iteration of the loop decreases **N** by one and then increases the value of **Sum** by this new value of **N**. Hence, after each iteration, the value of **Sum** is the sum of the integers from the new value of **N** up to **10**. The loop is not iterated unless **N** has value greater than one. Hence, after each iteration, we know that **N** ≥ **1** as stated in the invariant assertion. The values of **N** and **Sum** are changed but they are changed in such a way that the assertion is true after each loop iteration. That is why it is called an "invariant"; its truth does not vary as the loop progresses.

A correct invariant for a correct loop will be true after each iteration of the loop. However, it may become false at some time during the execution of the loop. In fact, any useful invariant will become false at some time during the execution of the loop. The loop shown in Figure 8.7 has been annotated to indicate when the invariant is true and when it is false. (The comment that starts out *The variant expression...* will be explained shortly; for the moment you can safely ignore it.)

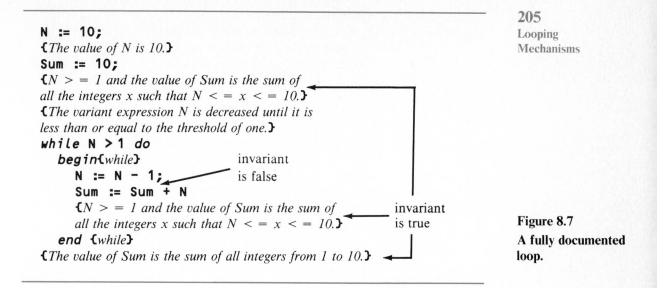

Figure 8.7
**A fully documented
loop.**

There is always more than one invariant for a loop. For example, *Sum ≥ 10 and N ≥ 0* is also an invariant for the loop in Figure 8.7, but a much less informative one. The invariant chosen for documenting the loop should say something informative about what you want the loop to do. An invariant is a sort of bridge between the precondition and the postcondition. It says something about how the precondition gets transformed into the postcondition.

As we have described invariants, it sounds as if the precondition must imply the invariant. This is not quite true. Most loops require that some variables or other things be initialized before the loop is executed. These initialization statements may come from unrolling the loop or from other considerations. In any event, these initialization statements are conceptually attached to the loop. Hence, the precondition goes before these initialization statements. The invariant goes after any initialization statements. For this reason, the invariant need not follow from the precondition alone.

One way to see that a loop will eventually end is to find some quantity that is changed each time through the loop until it reaches or passes some given value. An expression for a quantity that changes each time the loop is executed is called a *variant expression*. The value the variant expression must reach or pass is called a *threshold*. There are two important properties that the variant expression and threshold must have:

variant expression

1. The value of the variant expression must decrease by some fixed amount each time the body of the loop is executed.
2. Whenever the value of the variant expression is less than or equal to the threshold, the loop must terminate.

Any loop that has a variant expression and threshold with these properties will eventually terminate. If the value of the expression is below the threshold, it

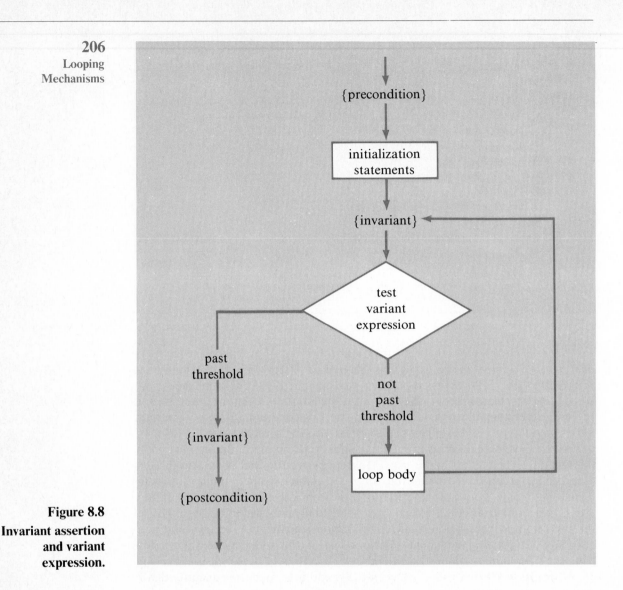

Figure 8.8
Invariant assertion
and variant
expression.

terminates right away. In the more typical case where the initial value of the variant expression is greater than the threshold, we know that the value will be decreased each time through and so will eventually fall below the threshold. When that happens we know the loop will terminate. The process is shown diagrammatically in Figure 8.8.

A variant expression for our sample **while** loop is the simple expression **N**. It is decreased by one on each iteration, and once it is less than or equal to the threshold of one, the loop must terminate.

We chose to state variant expressions and thresholds in terms of a decreasing quantity. It is also possible to think in terms of an increasing quantity. In that case, the loop terminates when the variant expression is greater than the threshold.

Invariant assertions and variant expressions complement each other very well. One tells what remains constant and the other what changes in a loop. If they are chosen carefully, the postcondition will follow from the invariant assertion and the fact that the variant expression has passed the threshold. This means that if these items are chosen carefully, they can be used to conclusively demonstrate that a loop behaves as the programmer claims it does.

*demonstrating
a postcondition*

For example, consider the loop shown in Figure 8.7. The invariant assertion says that the following will be true after each iteration of the loop:

> {*N > = 1 and the value of Sum is the sum of
> all the integers x such that N < = x < = 10.*}

Since it is true after each loop iteration, it must be true when the loop ends. When the loop ends, the variant expression **N** is less than or equal to one. That means that the value of **N** is one, and hence the postcondition must hold:

> *The value of Sum is the sum of all integers from 1 to 10.*

It may seem that all this documentation is overdoing things a bit. Indeed, the simple loop in Figure 8.7 is buried in comments, some of which can just as well be omitted. Normally, it is sufficient to include the invariant assertion only once, typically at the end of the loop. The precondition stating that the value of **N** is **10** is obvious and should not be included. We only included it in order to have a complete and simple example. You should have a variant expression and threshold in mind when writing a loop. However, if they are obvious enough, then you need not include them in a comment. For complicated loops all this documentation should be included. For very simple loops, omitting some details can actually aid readability.

For Statements

The *while* and *repeat* statements are all the loop mechanisms that you absolutely need. In fact, the *while* statement alone is enough. However, there is one sort of loop that is so common that Pascal includes a special "tailor-made" loop statement for it. In performing numeric calculations, it is common to do a calculation with the number 1, then with 2, then with 3 and so forth until some last value is reached. For example, to write out the "2 times table," we want the computer to perform the following:

```
writeln('2 times ', I, ' is ', 2*I)
```

first with **I** equal to **1**, then with **I** equal to **2** and so forth up to, say, **10**. One way to do this is with a *while* statement such as:

```
I := 1;
while I <= 10 do
  begin
    writeln('2 times ', I, ' is ', 2*I);
    I := I + 1
  end
```

Although a **while** loop will do here, this sort of situation is just what the *for statement* (also called a *for loop*) was designed for. The above piece of code will produce the same output as the following **for** statement:

```
for I := 1 to 10 do
    writeln('2 times ', I, ' is ', 2*I)
```

for statements come in two very similar varieties. The above example is of the first variety whose general form is:

```
for ⟨control variable⟩ := ⟨initial exp⟩ to ⟨final exp⟩ do
                        ⟨body⟩
```

The ⟨body⟩ may be any single Pascal statement. In particular, it can be a compound statement. For now we will insist that the *control variable* be a variable of type **integer**. Hence, the loop control variable must be declared to be of type **integer**. Eventually we will see how to use other types for the control variable, but the idea is clearest in the case of **integer** variables. ⟨initial exp⟩ and ⟨final exp⟩ are expressions that must evaluate to something of type **integer**. Their values are called the *initial value* and *final value* of the loop control variable. Typically we want the initial value to be less than the final value, but that is not required. Typically ⟨body⟩ includes some reference to the ⟨control variable⟩, but that also is not required.

When the **for** loop is executed, the expressions ⟨initial exp⟩ and ⟨final exp⟩ are evaluated to obtain the initial and final values for the loop control variable. After that, ⟨body⟩ is executed with ⟨control variable⟩ equal to this initial value, then with ⟨control variable⟩ equal to the initial value plus one, then with ⟨control variable⟩ equal to the initial value plus two and so on, increasing the value of ⟨control variable⟩ by one each time. The last time through the loop, ⟨body⟩ is executed with ⟨control variable⟩ equal to that final value that was obtained from the expression ⟨final exp⟩. This behavior is diagramed in Figure 8.9.

A **for** loop need not start with one. For example, the following will give the "2 times table" for all values from −10 up to +10:

```
for I := -10 to 10 do
    writeln('2 times ', I, ' is ', 2*I)
```

The loop control variable is automatically increased by one each time through. There is no need to include anything like the following in the body of the loop:

```
I := I + 1
```

In fact, it is an error to do so. The body of a **for** loop is not allowed to change the loop control variable in any way. If it does, the effect of the **for** loop is unpredictable. The body can use the value of the control variable, but it can not change it.

A loop control variable is intended to be used to control the **for** loop and nothing else. The value it has before the **for** loop is executed is irrelevant to the **for** loop, and its value is undefined after the **for** loop has ended. Hence, it is natural to make it a local variable. Moreover, in Pascal it is required to be a local

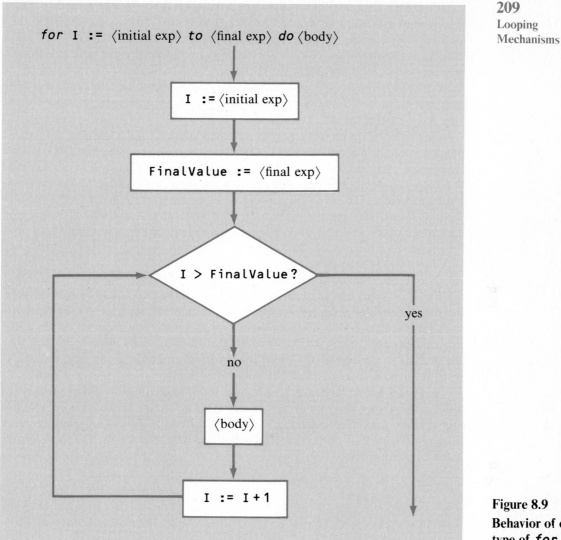

for I := ⟨initial exp⟩ to ⟨final exp⟩ do ⟨body⟩

I := ⟨initial exp⟩

FinalValue := ⟨final exp⟩

I > FinalValue?

yes

no

⟨body⟩

I := I + 1

Figure 8.9
Behavior of one
type of for loop.

variable. If a **for** loop appears in a procedure, then the loop control variable must be declared in that procedure.

It is natural to wonder what happens when the value of ⟨initial exp⟩ is greater than that of ⟨final exp⟩. When this happens in Pascal, this kind of **for** loop is equivalent to the empty statement; that is, the loop body is not executed and the program goes on to the next thing. That means that in Pascal it is impossible to write a **for** loop that is an infinite loop.

There are some technical points about the control variable that you should be aware of. When the **for** statement is completed, the value of the loop control variable is undefined, which means its value is completely unpredictable. So it should not be reused unless it is first reinitialized; the exception to this is that it can be reused as the loop control variable of another *for* loop. Reusing it as a loop control variable requires no extra initialization, since the *for* loop itself includes an initialization. Also it is dangerous to include the loop control variable in ⟨final exp⟩. The technical explanation of what happens in that case is as follows: both ⟨initial exp⟩ and ⟨final exp⟩ are evaluated once at the start of the loop and those two values are used to control the loop. Hence the body of the loop has no effect on the stopping of the loop.

One cultural point that is of some significance to the design of readable programs has to do with names of *for* loop control variables. Most of our *for* loops use **I** and **J** as loop control variables. It has become custom to use **I**, **J** and **K** as loop control variables. The reasons are historical. Those letters carry no mnemonic value. However, the custom is so well ingrained that it is pointless to fight it. When you see these letters in programs they will very likely be loop control variables, and this convention can be a slight aid in reading the programs. Of course, if you can come up with good mnemonic names of *for* loop control variables, that is even better.

downto

The second version of the *for* statement is very similar to the first. The only difference in syntax is that **to** is replaced by **downto**. The difference in what happens when it is executed is that, with the **downto** version, the loop control variable is decreased by one each time through. In this case, the value of ⟨initial exp⟩ is typically greater than or equal to that of ⟨final exp⟩, and if it is not, then the body is not executed at all and the program proceeds to the next thing. The word **downto** is a single identifier and should not be written as two words.

other increment sizes

In Pascal a *for* loop control variable is always changed by either plus one or minus one. Other programming languages allow it to change by any specified amount. At first this looks like a real limitation in Pascal, but it is easy to program around this limitation. To output the even numbers 0, 2, 4, 6, 8, 10, the following trick works:

```
for I := 0 to 5 do
   write(2*I)
```

This same sort of trick can be used to get something equivalent to increments of fractional size as well. To see the effect of small changes in interest rates one might use a *for* loop such as the following:

```
for J := 1 to 200 do
      begin
        Rate := 0.001*J;
        Interest := Amount * Rate;
        writeln('a rate of ', Rate*100, ' percent,');
        writeln('yields ', Interest, 'in interest')
      end
```

nested for loops

Loops may be nested inside loops. This is quite common with *for* loops. Since the body of a *for* loop may be any Pascal statement, it may, in particular, be another *for* loop. For example, the following nested *for* statement writes out a complete set of times tables:

```
for I := 1 to 10 do
    for J := 1 to 10 do
        writeln(I,' times ', J, ' equals ', I*J)
```

Example—Summing a Series

Figure 8.10 contains a complete program that includes a *for* loop. The program computes the average number of times you need to flip a coin in order to get the coin to come up heads. The program uses the following formula to approximate the average:

$$\frac{1}{2} + \frac{2}{2^2} + \frac{3}{2^3} + \cdots + \frac{N}{2^N}$$

As N is chosen larger and larger, we get better and better approximations to the true value of this average. N equal to 100 is more than large enough to give as much accuracy as most computers are capable of delivering, and so the program uses the formula with N set equal to 100.

```
program CoinToss(input, output);
   const NumberOfTerms = 100;
   var I: integer;
       Sum, Power: real;
begin{CoinToss}
   Sum := 0;
   Power := 1;
   for I := 1 to NumberOfTerms do
      begin{for}
         Power := Power * 2;
         Sum := Sum + I/Power
         {Sum is the sum of all numbers of the form:
         x/(2 to the power x) where 1 < = x < = I.
         Power is 2 to the power I.}
      end; {for}
   writeln('On the average it will take ', Sum);
   writeln('tosses of a balanced coin');
   writeln('to get heads the first time.')
end. {CoinToss}
```

Figure 8.10
Summing a series.

Notice that **Sum** is initialized to zero, while **Power** is initialized to one. This is because **Sum** will contain a sum of numbers, while **Power** will contain a product of numbers. Zero plus the first number added yields that first number, which is why **Sum** is initialized to zero. Since **Power** is a product of numbers it must be initialized differently. Zero times the first in a sequence of numbers to be multiplied will yield the incorrect result of zero. On the other hand, one times the first of the numbers to be multiplied will yield that first number, which explains why **Power** is initialized to one. By checking the assertion inside the *for* loop you can easily check to see if things have been initialized correctly; just see whether the assertion is true after one iteration of the *for* loop.

Also notice that **Power** is declared to be of type **real**, even though its value is conceptually an integer. The reason for this is that the value of **Power** gets very large, and on most systems would produce an integer overflow; that is, its value becomes larger than **maxint**. Since computers can store much larger **real** values than they can **integer** values, the change to type **real** overcomes this problem. When doing numeric calculations with *for* loops, this can be a common problem. We will have more to say about this problem in Chapter 15.

Invariant Assertions and For Loops
(Optional)

for loops do not lend to documentation with invariants as easily as *repeat* and *while* loops do. This is because the natural statement of an invariant for a *for* loop usually includes a reference to the loop control variable. This presents a problem since the loop control variable of a *for* loop is frequently undefined or irrelevant before the loop is executed and it is always undefined after the loop is executed. The problem is more of a notational one than a conceptual one. When designing a *for* loop it makes sense to think in terms of invariants. However, when actually writing the *for* loop comments, it is usually easier and clearer to use some close approximation to an invariant. If the *for* loop body is a compound statement, then one possible solution is to include an assertion within that compound statement. Since the loop control variable is well defined within the body, that assertion can refer to the loop control variable in a clearly meaningful way.

There is no need to design variant expressions and thresholds for *for* loops. That is because a *for* loop already has a built-in variant expression and a built-in threshold. The variant expression is the loop control variable and the threshold is its final value.

What Kind of Loop to Use

When designing a loop the choice of which type of Pascal statement to use is best postponed to the end of the design process. First design the loop using pseudo-

Program

```pascal
program GamblingAdvice(input, output);
  const Width = 6;{Field width for money amounts}
  var Wagers, Winnings, Next, NetWinnings: real;
begin{Program}
  writeln('How much did you bet at the race track?');
  writeln('Spare me the dollar sign.');
  writeln('Just enter the number.');
  readln(Wagers);
  writeln('Enter the payoff of each winning ticket.');
  writeln('Spare me the dollar signs.');
  writeln('Just enter the numbers.');
  writeln('Terminate your list with a minus number.');
  writeln('If you never won, just enter a minus number.');

  Winnings := 0;
  read(Next);
  while Next > 0 do
    begin{while}
      Winnings := Winnings + Next;
      read(Next)
    end; {while}

  NetWinnings := Winnings - Wagers;

  if NetWinnings > 0
    then writeln('Congratulations! You won $',
                                   NetWinnings:Width:2)
    else writeln('Give it up. You lost $',
                          -NetWinnings:Width:2)
end. {Program}
```

Sample Dialogue

How much did you bet at the race track?
Spare me the dollar sign.
Just enter the number.
86
Enter the payoff of each winning ticket.
Spare me the dollar signs.
Just enter the numbers.
Terminate your list with a minus number.
If you never won, just enter a minus number.
−1
Give it up. You lost $ 86.00

Figure 8.11
A *repeat* loop
will not work here.

code, and then translate the pseudocode into Pascal code. At that point it is easy to decide what type of Pascal loop statement to use. If the loop involves a numeric calculation that is repeated a fixed number of times using a value that is changed by equal amounts each time through the loop, then use a *for* loop. In fact, anytime you have a loop for a numeric calculation, you should consider using a *for* loop. It will not always be possible, but in many cases of numeric calculations it is the clearest and easiest loop to use. In all other cases, you must use a *repeat* or *while* loop. It is fairly easy to decide whether to use a *while* or a *repeat* loop. If you want to insist that the loop body will be executed at least once, then use a *repeat* loop. If there are circumstances for which the loop body should not be executed at all, then you can not use a *repeat* loop and so must use a *while* loop. A common situation that demands a *while* loop is when there is a possibility of no data at all. An example of this is the program shown in Figure 8.11. In that program, if the user wins no bets, then the compound statement in the *while* loop is never executed.

Example—Calendar Program

Our last sample program (Figure 8.12) outputs the traditional display of a calendar month. The user enters the number of days in the month and the day of the week that the month starts on. The program then outputs the display. The number of days in the month is stored in the variable **NumberOfDays** and the day of the week is stored in the variable **FirstDay**. The day of the week is coded as a number: **1** for Sunday, **2** for Monday and so forth. After receiving these two numbers, the program writes out a heading that names the days of the week. It then calls the procedure **DisplayMonth** to fill in the day numbers in the appropriate columns.

In the procedure **DisplayMonth**, the first *for* loop, writes out the appropriate number of blank fields. For example, if the month starts on Wednesday, it will write out three blank fields under the headings *Sun, Mon, Tue*.

The other *for* loop increments the variable **DayCount** from one up to the number of days in the month and it writes out the numbers one per field width. A field width of **Width** (equal to four) is used for each column of the calendar. Another variable called **WeekDay** is used to keep track of the days of the week. The only difference between **WeekDay** and **DayCount** is that **WeekDay** counts Sunday as **1** whether or not the month starts on Sunday. Hence the boolean expression

```
(WeekDay mod 7) = 0
```

can be used to check for the end of a 7 day week. After each 7 days, a **writeln** is inserted to start a new line for the next week.

Debugging Loops

No matter how carefully a program is designed, mistakes will still sometimes occur. In the case of loops, there is a pattern to the kinds of mistakes most often made. Most loop errors involve the first or last iteration of the loop. If you find that your loop does not perform as expected, check to see if the loop is iterated one too many or one too few times. Be sure that you are not confusing less-than with less-than-or-equal. Be sure that you have initialized the loop correctly. Check the possibility that the loop may sometimes need to be iterated zero times and check that your loop handles that possibility correctly. Remember that numbers of type **real** are stored as approximate values. Hence testing two **real** values for equality yields almost no information. Controlling a loop with a boolean expression that tests two **real** values for equality is virtually guaranteed to end the loop too soon or not at all. Always arrange to test **real** values for an inequality of some sort.

If you check and recheck your loop and can find no error, but the program still misbehaves, then you will need to do some more sophisticated testing. First of all, make sure that the mistake is indeed in the loop. Just because the program is performing incorrectly does not mean the bug is where you think it is. If your program was designed to be modular and contains lots of procedures, then it should be easy to locate the approximate location of the bug or bugs. Once you have decided that the bug is in a particular loop, you should watch that loop as it performs its calculations. This can be done using a technique called "tracing."

Tracing a program, or portion of a program, consists of adding some extra **write** statements to output intermediate results so that you can watch the program working. For example, consider the following piece of code:

```
N := 10;
Sum := 10;
repeat
  Sum := Sum + N;
  N := N - 1
  {The value of Sum is the sum of all the integers y
  such that: N < = y < = 10.}
until N < = 1
{ The value of Sum is the sum of all integers from 1 to 10.}
```

The last comment explains what the value of **Sum** is supposed to be. If you run this code, you will find that it does not set **Sum** to that value. The value of **Sum** will be larger than it is supposed to be. The loop can be tested by tracing the

Program

```pascal
program Calendar(input, output);
{Displays a calendar layout of any month.}

var FirstDay, NumberOfDays: integer;
    Ans: char;

procedure DisplayMonth(NumberOfDays, FirstDay: integer);
{Displays the usual layout for a month with NumberOfDays days in it.
FirstDay codes the first day of the month: 1 for Sunday, 2 for Monday, etc.}
  const Width = 4; {Field width for one day of the calendar}
        Blank = ' ';
  var WeekDay, DayCount: integer;
begin{DisplayMonth}
  writeln('Sun':Width, 'Mon':Width, 'Tue':Width,
      'Wed':Width, 'Thu':Width, 'Fri':Width, 'Sat':Width);
  for WeekDay := 1 to FirstDay - 1 do
      write(Blank:Width);
  WeekDay := FirstDay;
  for DayCount := 1 to NumberOfDays do
    begin{for}
      {WeekDay is the day of the week
      for day number DayCount.}
      write(DayCount:Width);
      if (WeekDay mod 7) = 0 then writeln;
      WeekDay := WeekDay + 1
    end; {for}
  writeln
end; {DisplayMonth}

begin{Program}
  writeln('I will display a calendar of a month.');
  repeat
    writeln('Enter the number of days in the month:');
    readln(NumberOfDays);
    writeln('Enter the first day of month, 1 for Sunday,');
    writeln('2 for Monday, 3 for Tuesday and so on.');
    readln(FirstDay);
    DisplayMonth(NumberOfDays, FirstDay);
    writeln('Do you want to see another month?');
    writeln('(yes or no):');
    readln(Ans)
  until (Ans = 'N') or (Ans = 'n');
  writeln('Have a good month!')
end. {Program}
```

Figure 8.12
Calendar program.

I will display a calendar of a month.
Enter the number of days in the month:
31
Enter the first day of month, 1 for Sunday,
2 for Monday, 3 for Tuesday and so on.
3

Sun	Mon	Tue	Wed	Thu	Fri	Sat
		1	2	3	4	5
6	7	8	9	10	11	12
13	14	15	16	17	18	19
20	21	22	23	24	25	26
27	28	29	30	31		

Do you want to see another month?
(yes or no):
no
Have a good month!

Figure 8.12 (cont'd)

variable **Sum**; that is, by writing out its value after each iteration of the loop. Suitable **writeln** statements to do the job are shown in Figure 8.13.

If the loop with the trace statement is embedded in a program and run, then the source of the error will immediately become apparent. The first two values of **Sum** will be **10** and **20**, but the value of **Sum** after one iteration of the loop should be **10 + 9** or **19**, rather than **20**. Thus we can immediately see that the value of **N** is the source of the problem. After we discover this, it is easy to see that **N** should be added into **Sum** after it is decremented, rather than before. In

```
   N := 10;
   Sum := 10;
{TEMP}; writeln('N = ', N, ' Sum = ', Sum);
{TEMP}; writeln('Before loop');
   repeat
     Sum := Sum + N;
     N := N - 1
     {The value of Sum is the sum of all the integers y
     such that: N <= y <= 10.}
{TEMP}; writeln('N = ', N, ' Sum = ', Sum);
   until N <= 1
{TEMP}; writeln('After loop');
{TEMP}; writeln('N = ', N, ' Sum = ', Sum);
   {The value of Sum is the sum of all integers from 1 to 10.}
```

Figure 8.13
Tracing a loop.

other words, the correct order for the statements in the loop body is:

```
N := N - 1;
Sum := Sum + N
```

Before leaving this example, we should comment on some peculiarities of the trace statements in Figure 8.13. First of all they violate our guidelines on indenting. This was intentional. Trace statements are temporary statements that will not appear in the final program. Hence, we want them to be easy to find and delete. One way to accomplish this is with comments such as those shown in the figure.

The trace statements in the figure also seem to have semicolons in strange places. That was not necessary, but is a good idea. If we precede each trace statement by a semicolon, then we know that it will be separated from the previous statement by a semicolon. In this case two of the three semicolons in front of the **writeln** statements were actually needed. The third extra semicolon does no harm. This saves us from the worry of fixing up semicolons. It looks strange, but remember that the trace statements are only temporary statements. They and the extra semicolons will not appear in the final program.

Finally, it may seem that the trace statements that precede and follow the loop are not needed. In this case they were not, but remember that you are using trace statements because you do not know where the error is. It is dangerous to leave any possibility unchecked. A good practice is to place one trace statement before the loop, one after the loop and one or more inside the body of the loop, even if some of these traces are "clearly" redundant.

*long
loops*

The above idea of tracing the loop through each iteration will work fine on a loop that is iterated 10 times, but if the loop is iterated 1000 times, it is likely to produce too much information to digest. For example, the following will produce nothing but a blur of light on a video display screen:

```
for K := 0 to 1000 do
    begin
       Sum := Sum + K
{TEMP}; writeln(K, Sum);
    end
```

A better approach is to take a smaller sample, for example, by doing the following:

```
for K := 0 to 1000 do
    begin
       Sum := Sum + K
{TEMP}; if (K mod 100) = 0 then writeln(K, Sum);
    end
```

This will output a trace statement every time **K** is a multiple of **100**. There is a possibility that such a uniform sampling technique will fail to detect certain kinds of periodic problems. If a trace like the above yields no insights, then try a different sampling technique such as using

```
(K mod 100) = 1
```

This will sample every one hundredth iteration, but the value of **K** will not be a "round number". If that fails change **100** to some other number.

Designing a Loop Using Invariants
(Optional)

strategy

Invariant assertions and variant expressions can be useful in designing a loop as well as being good ways to document a loop. They and the loop itself are ideally designed together. Frequently it is a good idea to design the invariant before you design the loop. Although there is no set of rules that is guaranteed to guide you to a well-designed loop, the following plan of attack will give you one systematic way to go about designing a loop:

1. First be sure the preconditions and postconditions are clear.
2. Look for an invariant that resembles the postcondition and has something, such as a variable, that can be changed by the loop. Do not be very concerned with the precondition at this point. It is the postcondition more than the precondition that determines a good invariant.
3. Check that there are some simple initialization statements that can make the invariant true, assuming that the precondition is true before they are executed. This takes care of the precondition.
4. Look at the invariant and try to find something that can be changed in such a way as to preserve the truth of the invariant but that intuitively brings things closer to the postcondition. Once you have found such a thing, the loop body is likely to be obvious. If a simple loop body is not obvious, then use the guarded command strategy we described in Chapter 6.
5. Next verify that the loop does eventually terminate by finding a variant expression and a threshold. (If the loop is not supposed to terminate, you of course omit this step.)
6. Finally, go back and check that the invariant assertion, variant expressions and threshold have the properties they are supposed to have.

If at any point the process breaks down, go back and redo the previous step. If need be, back up several steps. A simple example will help to illustrate the process.

Suppose we wish to design a piece of code that starts with four variables $X0$, $X1$, $X2$ and $X3$, assumed to contain integers, and that rearranges their values so as to make the following true:

*sorting
example*

$$X0 \leq X1 \leq X2 \leq X3$$

The numbers remain the same, but they are rearranged to put them in order. Since the final correct order can be obtained by repeatedly exchanging the values of variables, a loop seems likely.

First be sure we have the precondition and postcondition precisely formulated. Since the four numbers will remain the same but the values of the variables will change, it will help to have names for the initial values of the numbers. We will use $x0$, $x1$, $x2$ and $x3$ to denote the initial values of the variables **X0** through **X3**. Now that we have some notation, the precondition is obvious:

X0 $= x0$, **X1** $= x1$, **X2** $= x2$ and **X3** $= x3$.

The postcondition is a little harder to write. A first try might be:

X0 $\leq$ **X1** $\leq$ **X2** $\leq$ **X3**

This is easy to attain. All we need do is set all the variables equal to zero. Clearly that will not do. We are also tacitly assuming that the four initial values are preserved. The postcondition should make all, or almost all, conditions explicit. So a reformulated version of the postcondition is:

X0 $\leq$ **X1** $\leq$ **X2** $\leq$ **X3** *and the values of* **X0**, **X1**, **X2** *and* **X3** *are*
x0, x1, x2 and x3 in some order.

invariant
Next we look for an invariant that looks like it has something to do with the postcondition. We want to preserve the four values as the loop progresses. Hence a likely invariant is:

The values of **X0**, **X1**, **X2** *and* **X3** *are*
x0, x1, x2 and x3, in some order.

In this example step 3 is easy. Since the invariant follows from the precondition, no initialization is needed. Next we go to step 4 and look for something to change that will move the program closer to the goal of the postcondition. One way to do this is to interchange the values of some variables. We have already defined a procedure to do that. Recall that in Chapter 5 we defined a procedure to interchange the values of its two parameters. For reference, the procedure heading is reproduced below:

```
procedure Exchange(var X, Y: integer);
     {Interchanges the values of X and Y.}
```

There is no need to recall how this procedure performs the interchange. All we need to know is that it does accomplish the interchange.

designing
the body
Now which variables should the program interchange? It is hard to think of an interchange that will help no matter what the values of the variables are. However, it is easy to make up conditions under which we would want to interchange the values of some specific variables. In this situation, it pays to use the guarded command strategy we developed in Chapter 6. When we do that, we start writing out conditions such as:

Exchange(X0, X1) provided **X0** > **X1**

Eventually we get a list of guards that cover all cases except the case where we have the variable values in the desired order. The complete guarded command, written in pseudocode, will look like:

Do one of the following:
```
    Exchange(X0, X1)  provided X0 > X1
    Exchange(X1, X2)  provided X1 > X2
    Exchange(X2, X3)  provided X2 > X3
```

To see that no case has been overlooked, note that if all the guards are false, then

$$X0 \le X1 \le X2 \le X3$$

and in that case the loop has accomplished its goal. This also suggests a test to terminate the loop. We terminate the loop as soon as the values of the variables are in the correct order, that is, as soon as the above boolean expression is **true**. If we use a **while** loop, that means we want to perform the loop while the above expression is **false**. If we convert all this to Pascal code, we get:

```
while (X0 > X1) or (X1 > X2) or (X2 > X3) do
  begin{while}
    if X0 > X1 then Exchange(X0, X1)
    else if X1 > X2 then Exchange(X1, X2)
    else if X2 > X3 then Exchange(X2, X3)
    {The values of X0, X1, X2 and X3 are
    x0, x1, x2 and x3, in some order.}
  end {while}
```

So far we have accomplished quite a bit. The invariant is true before the loop is executed. Every time the loop is executed the truth of the invariant is preserved. We can even see that if the loop terminates, then the postcondition will hold. But how can we be certain that the loop will eventually terminate? For that we need a variant expression and so we go on to step 5.

*variant
expression*

The variant expression should be "how much the current order differs from the correct order," in some sense of the phrase "differs from the correct order." Although we do not yet know the variant expression, it is becoming pretty clear that it is not a simple Pascal expression. That is no problem, though. The variant expression is placed in a comment and so need not satisfy the Pascal rules of syntax. Now, each iteration of the loop should decrease "the amount by which the current order differs from the correct order" until "the amount by which it is out of order" becomes zero. So the threshold will undoubtedly be zero. But in order to come up with the variant expression, we still need some way to count the amount by which the current order differs from the correct order.

Before we present an expression that works, let us first dispose of a tempting but incorrect candidate for the variant expression. It is tempting to use *the number of adjacent pairs that are out of order* as the variant expression. Each iteration of the loop does put an adjacent pair in order. Unfortunately, it may also put some other adjacent pair, or pairs, out of order. Try the values 3, 4, 2, 5 in that order.

One iteration of the loop will change them to 3, 2, 4, 5. In both lists there is one adjacent pair which is out of order. The loop put one adjacent pair in order, but caused another adjacent pair to become out of order.

As it turns out, the thing to count is the total number of pairs which are out of order, including *nonadjacent* pairs like the first and third values. The total number of pairs out of order is always decreased. In the example that number decreases from two (the first and third values and also the second and third values) to one. So the desired bounding expression is:

The number of pairs (i, j) such that $0 \leq i < j \leq 3$ and $Xi > Xj$.

To establish that the variant expression is decreased by at least one on each iteration, we will show that each interchange of values decreases the variant expression by one. Since each iteration of the loop produces at least one interchange, each iteration will thus cause the variant expression to decrease by at least one.

To see that the interchange of values between Xi and Xj will decrease the variant expression, we reason as follows. Before the interchange, the values for the pair *(i, j)* were out of order, and after the interchange, they are in order. That represents a decrease of one. Furthermore, the number of other pairs having out of order values is not changed; the exact pairs that are out of order may change, but the total number of them does not. Hence, the other changes have no net effect on the variant expression, and so the variant expression is seen to decrease by one.

We still need to show that the total number of pairs which are out of order, not counting *(i, j)*, is not altered by the interchange of Xi and Xj. We obviously need only consider pairs that involve one of the indices *i* and *j*. Consider a value *k* such that:

$k < i < j$

If Xk is less than both Xi and Xj before the interchange of Xi and Xj, then it is less than both after the interchange. Similarly, if it is greater than both before, then it will be greater than both after. If Xk is greater than one and less than the other before the interchange, then it will be greater than one and less than one afterwards; which one it is greater than and which one it is less than will change, but it will still be greater than one and less than one. In any event the number of pairs that involve *k*, as well as one of *i* or *j*, and that contribute to the variant expression will remain constant. A similar reasoning holds if *k* is greater than both *i* and *j*. That accounts for all pairs in question.

Finding the variant expression required a bit of inspiration. That is typical. Nontrivial computer programs require a bit of inspiration. These are only guidelines to help the inspiration along.

It was a lot of work to obtain the variant expression and after we found it we did not change the code for the loop. So what was accomplished by the variant expression? It was a way to see that the loop does always terminate. Before we found it, we knew that if the loop terminated, then it terminated with the postcondition true. However, it took the variant expression to establish that the loop does eventually terminate.

At this point it pays to see if we can clean up the Pascal code produced. If we study the code, we will see that there is no harm in executing more than one of the guarded commands and so a simple list of *if – then* statements will do. Hence, we can rewrite the code to the following:

```
while (X0 > X1) or (X1 > X2) or (X2 > X3) do
  begin{while}
    if X0 > X1 then Exchange(X0, X1);
    if X1 > X2 then Exchange(X1, X2);
    if X2 > X3 then Exchange(X2, X3)
  end {while}
```

Some programmers will contend that this version is more efficient or clearer. Actually, neither version is clearly superior. So use the one that appeals to you the most.

There is one last step, namely 6, checking that all the desired relationships between assertions, the variant expression and the threshold do hold. A list of things to check is:

Check that the invariant holds after the precondition is changed by any initialization statements.

Check that the invariant is true after each iteration of the loop.

Check that the loop stops when the value of the variant expression passes the threshold.

Check that the postcondition follows from the invariant and the fact that the value of the variant expression has passed the threshold.

If you go back and check the loop we just designed, you will see that all these points check out properly.

Summary of Problem Solving and Programming Techniques

Many problems with loops have to do with the first or last iteration of the loop. Always check to see if there is a possibility that, under some circumstances, the loop should not be iterated even once. If that is the case, a *repeat* loop can not be used. You must instead use a *while* or possibly a *for* loop. In order to design a loop that has the effect of stopping and starting at different places in the loop body, you can use the technique of unrolling a loop. When debugging loops, always check to see if the loop is iterated one too many or one too few times. When you can not discover what is wrong with a loop, insert some temporary

writeln statements to trace the values of variables as the loop computes on some test data.

Summary of Pascal Constructs

repeat statement
    Syntax:

```
repeat
    ⟨statement 1⟩;
    ⟨statement 2⟩;
         ⋮
    ⟨statement n⟩
    until ⟨boolean expression⟩
```

Example:

```
repeat
  Sum := Sum + Next;
  read(Next)
  until Next <= 0
```

When the **repeat** statement is executed, the statements are executed in order and then the ⟨boolean expression⟩ is evaluated. If it evaluates to **true**, the **repeat** statement is over and the program goes on to the next thing. If the ⟨boolean expression⟩ evaluates to **false**, then the statements are repeated again. The list of statements is repeated again and again until the ⟨boolean expression⟩ evaluates to **true**. At that point the **repeat** statement is complete and the program goes on to the next thing.

while statement
    Syntax:

```
while ⟨boolean expression⟩ do
        ⟨body⟩
```

Example:

```
while X <> 3
  begin
    write(X);
    X := X + 1
  end
```

The ⟨body⟩ can be any Pascal statement. When the **while** statement is executed the ⟨boolean expression⟩ is first evaluated. If it evaluates to **true**, then the ⟨body⟩ is executed. If the ⟨boolean expression⟩ instead evaluates to **false**, then nothing more happens. The ⟨boolean expression⟩ is evaluated again and again. Each time it evaluates to **true** the ⟨body⟩ is executed. The first time it evaluates to **false** the **while** statement terminates and the program goes on to the next thing.

Syntax:

```
for ⟨control variable⟩ := ⟨initial exp⟩ to ⟨final exp⟩ do
                    ⟨body⟩
```

Example:

```
for J := 20 to 500 do
   begin
     Sum := Sum + J;
     writeln(Sum)
   end
```

⟨control variable⟩ must be a variable of type **integer** (other types are possible and will be discussed in Chapter 10.) Both ⟨initial exp⟩ and ⟨final exp⟩ must be expressions that evaluate to the same type as the ⟨control variable⟩. The ⟨body⟩ may be any Pascal statement. When the **for** statement is executed, ⟨initial exp⟩ and ⟨final exp⟩ are first evaluated. If the value of ⟨final exp⟩ is less than that of ⟨initial exp⟩, then the **for** statement terminates without doing anything else. If the value of ⟨initial exp⟩ is less than or equal to the value of ⟨final exp⟩, then the ⟨body⟩ is executed with the value of ⟨control variable⟩ set equal to the value of ⟨initial exp⟩, then executed with the value of ⟨control variable⟩ increased by one, then by one more and so forth. The last time ⟨body⟩ is executed the value of ⟨control variable⟩ is equal to the value obtained when ⟨final exp⟩ was evaluated. The ⟨control variable⟩ may not be changed by the ⟨body⟩; if it is, the effect is unpredictable.

Syntax:

```
for ⟨control variable⟩ := ⟨initial exp⟩ downto ⟨final exp⟩ do
                    ⟨body⟩
```

Example:

```
for J := 500 downto 20 do
   begin
     Sum := Sum + J;
     writeln(Sum)
   end
```

Similar to the previous kind of **for** statement except that with this kind the ⟨control variable⟩ is decreased by one on each iteration of the loop. If the value of ⟨final exp⟩ is greater than that of ⟨initial exp⟩, then the **for** statement terminates without doing anything.

Exercises

Self-Test and Interactive Exercises

1. Choose any of the programs from previous exercises that do a simple calculation and that you have written. Add a loop so that the calculation can be repeated again and again with new input as long as the user desires. Do it once with a **repeat** loop. Do it again with a **while** loop, and this time allow the user to change his/her mind and not do the calculation even once.

2. What is the output of the following (when embedded in a correct program with **X** declared to be of type **integer**.):

```
X := 10;
while X > 0 do
   X := X - 3
writeln(X)
```

3. What is the biggest difference between a **repeat** and a **while** loop?

4. Write a program that outputs all the even numbers between **1** and **25**.

5. What is the output of the following program fragment:

```
Limit := 3;
for I := 1 to Limit do
      begin
        writeln(I, Limit);
        Limit := 2
      end
```

6. Predict the output of the following nested **for** loop. Then embed it in a program, run the program and check your prediction:

```
for J := 10 downto 1 do
  for I := 1 to 10 do
     writeln(I, ' times ', J, ' equals ', I*J)
```

7. Show that any **while** statement can be replaced by a statement consisting of an **if-then** statement that contains a **repeat** statement as a subpart. Show that any **repeat** statement can be replaced by a compound statement and a **while** statement.

Regular Exercises

8. Write a program to determine the largest value of n such that your computer can compute $n!$ without integer overflow. $n!$ is the product of all positive numbers less than or equal to n. For example, $3! = 1 \times 2 \times 3 = 6$. By convention $0!$ is set equal to 1.

9. Write a program that takes one **real** value as input and computes the first integer n such that 2^n is greater than or equal to the input value. The program should output both n and 2^n.

10. Write a program that will read in a number *n* and then output the sum of the squares of the numbers from 1 to *n*. So if the input is 3, the output should be 14, because:

$$1^2 + 2^2 + 3^2 = 1 + 4 + 9 = 14$$

The program should allow the user to repeat this calculation as often as desired.

11. Write a program to list the numbers from 0 to 25, their squares, square roots, fourth power and fourth root. The output should be in a neat five-column format.

12. Write a program to read in a **real** number *x* and output the integer *n* closest to the cube root of *x*; that is, output the integer *n* such that:

$$n^3 \leq x < (n + 1)^3$$

Assume that *x* is always nonnegative.

13. A *perfect number* is a positive integer that is equal to the sum of all those positive integers (excluding itself) which divide it evenly. The first perfect number is 6, because its divisors (excluding itself) are 1, 2, 3, and because 6 = 1 + 2 + 3. Write a program to find the first three perfect numbers (including 6 as one of the three).

14. The *Fibonacci numbers* F_n are defined as follows. F_0 is 1, F_1 is 1 and $F_{i+2} = F_i + F_{i+1}$, for $i = 0, 1, 2, \ldots$. In other words, each number is the sum of the previous two numbers. The first few Fibonacci numbers are 1, 1, 2, 3, 5, 8. One place where these numbers occur is as certain population growth rates. If a population has no deaths, then the series shows the size of the population after each generation. A generation is the time it takes a member to reach reproducing age. The formula applies most straightforwardly to asexual reproduction at a rate of one offspring per generation. In any event, the "green crud" population grows at that rate and produces one generation every five days. Write a program that takes the initial size of the green crud population and outputs the size of the population after 1 month, 6 months and 1 year.

15. Write a program to find all integer solutions to the equation

$$4x + 3y - 9z = 5$$

for values of *x*, *y*, and *z* between 0 and 100.

16. Write a program that outputs the balance of an account after each succeeding year. The input is the initial balance, the interest rate, the first year and the last year. Assume the deposit is made on January first. Next modify the program so that it shows three different balances for three different ways of calculating the interest: simple interest, calculated semiannually and calculated quarterly.

17. Modify the program in the previous exercise (or do it from scratch) so that interest is compounded monthly (and not any other way such as semiannually) and so that the output shows the interest at the end of each month. You should insert a **readln** with no arguments to stop the output at the end of each year. When the user hits the return key, the figures for the following year are displayed. If this were not done, the user would not have time to read the output. After that enhance the program so that the calculation can be made as often as desired with different inputs.

18. Write a program to read in a list of test scores and output the highest score, the lowest score and the average score.

19. Write a program that will read in and evaluate expressions such as:

$$+15 + 90 - 100 - 7 + 36\,end$$

The expression is a sequence of integers each preceded by a sign. The expression is terminated with the word *end*. There are no blanks in the expression.

20. The value e^x can be approximated by the sum:

$$1 + x + x^2/2! + x^3/3! + \cdots + x^n/n!$$

Write a program that takes a value x as input and outputs this sum for n taken to be each of the values **1** to **100**. The program should also output e^x calculated using the standard function **exp**. The program should repeat the calculation for new values of x until the user says he/she is through. Use variables of type **real** to store the factorials or you are likely to produce integer overflow.

21. Modify the calendar program so that it takes a month and year as input (for example *2 1995* for February, 1995) and then outputs the calendar for that month, including a heading with the name of the month. The program in Figure 6.7 can provide the code for calculating leap years.

22. Write a program to draw a stick figure of a house with a pitched roof, a door and two windows.

References for Further Reading

The following books give more detailed discussions of loop invariants (optional section) and related topics.

S. Alagic and M. A. Arbib, *The Design of Well-Structured and Correct Programs*, 1978, Springer-Verlag, New York.

D. Gries, *The Science of Programming*, 1981, Springer-Verlag, New York. The chapter sections on loop invariants were, in large part, based on portions of this book.

9

Functions

The White Rabbit put on his spectacles. "Where shall I begin, please your Majesty?" he asked.

"Begin at the beginning," the King said, very gravely, "and go on till you come to the end: then stop."

Lewis Carroll, Alice in Wonderland

Chapter Contents

We have already encountered a number of predefined standard functions, such as **sqrt**, **trunc** and **round**. They are automatically provided in the Pascal language. You can also define new functions within a Pascal program. In this chapter we describe how these new functions are defined and used.

Use of Functions

These programmer-defined functions are called in exactly the same way as the standard functions we have been using. To *call* any function in Pascal, the program provides the function with one or more arguments and the function returns a single value. For example, in the statement

call

```
X := round(2.9)
```

the function **round** returns the value **3**. A function call is a particular kind of expression, and like all other expressions, it has a value. That value is called the value *returned* by the function.

value
returned

In Pascal, a function is very much like a procedure, but it normally plays a much more limited role than most procedures do. Functions are designed for one specific kind of task: taking a list of values (called *arguments*) and returning a single value. You declare a function in much the same way as you declare a procedure except that there is an additional provision for specifying the value to be returned. The function declarations and procedure declarations appear in the same place in a program, possibly even intermixed. To get the feel of these function declarations, we will start with a simple example.

A Sample Function Declaration

Figure 9.1 shows a program with a function declaration for a function called **Cube**. This function takes one argument of type **integer** and returns a value of type **integer**; more specifically it returns the cube of its argument. Function

parameter
list

Program

```
program Sample1(input, output);

var N: integer;

function Cube(X: integer): integer;
{Returns X cubed.}
begin{Cube}
  Cube := X*X*X
end; {Cube}

begin{Program}
  N := Cube(2);
  writeln('2 cubed is ', N)
end. {Program}
```

Output

2 cubed is   8

Figure 9.1
A simple function declaration.

arguments

*function
declarations*

declarations have formal parameter lists that have the same syntax as procedure parameter lists. The sample function has one formal value parameter whose value is set equal to the value of the function argument when the function is called. Function arguments are nothing more or less than parameters. For functions they are traditionally called *arguments* but that is just another name for parameters.

Although a function declaration greatly resembles a procedure declaration, it does differ in some ways from a procedure declaration. First of all, it starts with the word ***function*** rather than the word ***procedure***; but that is very reasonable since it is a function, and the compiler should be told it is a function and not a procedure. The two significant differences are concerned with specifying the value to be returned. The first significant difference is that the function is given a type in the function declaration heading. In Figure 9.1, the second instance of **integer** (the one at the end before the semicolon) tells the compiler that the function **Cube** is of type **integer**. That means that the value returned will be of type **integer** and, hence, the function can only be used in places where it is appropriate to use a value of type **integer**. The complete syntax for a function heading is given in Figure 9.2.

*assignment to
function name*

The second major difference is that somewhere within the body of the function declaration, the function name must appear on the left-hand side of an assignment statement. This is the way the function declaration specifies the value to be returned. Although it looks like a simple assignment of a value to a variable, the statement

```
Cube := X*X*X
```

*value
returned*

in Figure 9.1 is something very different. The function name, in this example **Cube**, is not a variable, and the assignment statement does not mean what an assignment statement usually means. The only reason it is written in this fashion is that this is a convenient and traditional way to write it. The meaning of one of these special assignment statements (with the function name on the left-hand side) is that it specifies the value that is returned by the function call. In this example, the above assignment statement means: return **X** times **X** times **X** as the value of **Cube**. When the function **Cube** is called in the program statement

```
N := Cube(2)
```

the value of the argument, in this case **2**, is used to set the value of **X** and the expression **X*X*X** is evaluated. The statement

```
Cube := X*X*X
```

says to return this value, namely **8**, as the value of the function. In the sample program, the value of **Cube(2)**, and hence the new value of **N**, is **8**. There is no variable named **Cube** that gets set to **8** or to any other value. The identifier **Cube** is not the name of a variable. It is the name of a function.

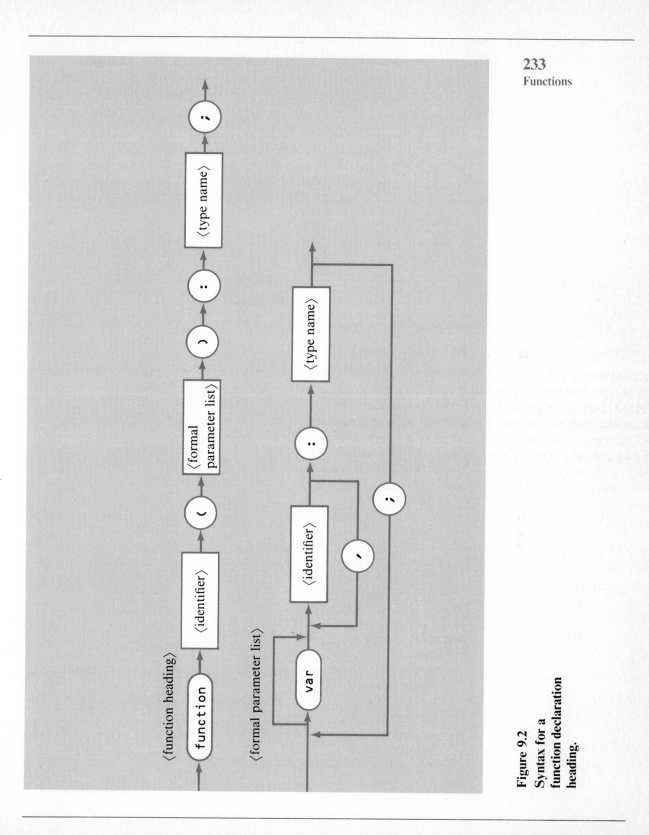

Figure 9.2
Syntax for a
function declaration
heading.

Computing Powers—A More Complicated Example

As a second example, Figure 9.3 shows a function that computes powers of the form

$$x^n$$

where x is of type **real** and n is some nonnegative whole number.

*local
identifiers*

Notice that a function can have more than one argument and that a function declaration may have local variables, just like a procedure declaration. Functions may also have local constants. They may even have local procedures and local

---

Program

```pascal
program Test(input, output);

var Arg1: real;
    Arg2: integer;
    Ans: char;

function Power(X: real; N: integer): real;
{Returns X to the power N; Returns 1 when N equals 0.
      Precondition: N > = 0.}
  var I: integer;
      Product: real;
begin{Power}
  Product := 1;
  for I := 1 to N do
    begin
      Product := Product*X
      {Product is X to the Power I.}
    end;
  Power := Product
end; {Power}

begin{Program}
  repeat
    writeln('Enter a real and a nonnegative integer.');
    readln(Arg1, Arg2);
    writeln(Arg1, ' to the power ', Arg2);
    writeln(' is ', Power(Arg1, Arg2));
    writeln('Another test? Yes or No');
    readln(Ans)
  until (Ans = 'N') or (Ans = 'n')
end. {Program}
```

**Figure 9.3
Function
declaration in a
test program.**

Sample Dialogue

Enter a real and a nonnegative integer.
2.0   3
   2.00000000E + 00 to the power   3
is   8.00000000000E + 00
Another test? Yes or No
yes
Enter a real and a nonnegative integer.
0.12   2
   1.20000000E − 01 to the power   2
is   1.44000000000E − 02
Another test? Yes or No
no

Figure 9.3 (cont'd)

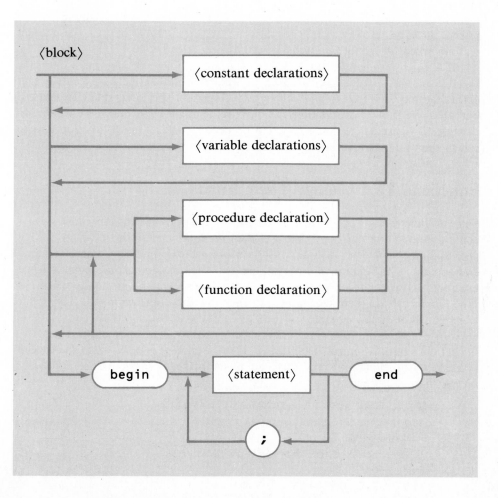

Figure 9.4
Syntax for a block.

functions. These local variables, constants and so forth are declared and used just as they are in procedures. As with procedures, the local declarations plus the list of statements in a function declaration are referred to as a *block*. Figure 9.4 summarizes the order of declarations within a block. This ordering applies to the main block of a program and the block of a procedure declaration, as well as the block of a function declaration.

Side Effects

what a function can do

The purpose of a function is to take the values of some arguments and return a single value. However, a Pascal function can actually do much more. In Pascal, a function is a procedure with the added feature of returning a value. Hence, a function can do anything that a procedure can do. All our examples used value parameters as arguments. This is typical, but a function is allowed to have variable parameters as well as value parameters as its arguments. A function can change the value of a global variable, write a message to the screen, read a value from the keyboard, or do anything else that a procedure can do, so long as it also returns a value. However, it is usually a bad idea to use any of these other features when designing functions.

what a function should not do

If a function changes the value of a global variable or sets the value of a variable parameter or causes a **read** or **write** statement to be executed, that extra feature is referred to as a *side effect*. Generally speaking, side effects are a bad idea. We think of a function as simply returning a value and if we want it to do more it is usually clearer to write a procedure rather than a function and to return the value via a variable parameter.

Functions That Change Their Minds

Since a function always returns a value, a function declaration must always contain at least one statement that uses the function name on the left-hand side of an assignment operator. A function can contain more than one such statement, and sometimes a function call may cause two such assignment statements to be executed. If two or more assignments to the function name are made when the function is called, then the value returned by the function is the last value assigned to the function name.

example

For example, the following function returns zero if its argument is a negative integer or is zero. It returns its argument if the argument is positive. In the case of positive **X**, the function name **NonNeg** is set twice. It is the value of the last setting that is returned.

```
function NonNeg(X: integer): integer;
   begin
     NonNeg := 0;
     if X > 0 then NonNeg := X
   end;
```

Although the identifier **NonNeg** in this example is assigned a value twice, it still is not a variable and can not be used as a variable. In particular, the name of a function can not be used on the right-hand side of an assignment statement (except in a function call).

Boolean Valued Functions

Boolean valued functions are defined in the same way as other functions and, technically speaking, are even used in the same way. However, their usage is different in one important respect: they can be used to control an *if - then* statement or any other statement whose behavior depends on a boolean expression. Using them in this way can help to make a program easier to read. By means of a function declaration, we can associate a complex boolean expression with a meaningful name and use that name as the boolean expression in an *if - then*, *if - then - else*, *repeat* or *while* statement. The result can often make a program read rather like English. For example, the statement

```
if ((Rate >= 10) and (Rate < 20)) or (Rate = 0)
        then begin{then}
            . . .
        end{then}
```

can be made to read

```
if Appropriate(Rate) then
        begin{then}
            . . .
        end{then}
```

provided the following boolean function has already been defined:

```
function Appropriate(Rate: integer): boolean;
  begin{Appropriate}
    Appropriate :=
      ((Rate >= 10) and (Rate < 20)) or (Rate = 0)
  end; {Appropriate}
```

Example—Testing for Primes

Figure 9.5 gives another example of a boolean valued function. The function **Prime** returns **true** if its argument is a prime number. A *prime* number is an integer greater than one which has no divisors other than itself and 1. In other words, the prime numbers are the positive integers (other then 1) that cannot be factored. For example, 12 can be factored into 2 times 6 and so is not prime. The first few primes are 2, 3, 5, 7, 11 and 13.

primes

The procedure uses the following algorithm to test if **N** is a prime:

1. If **N** is **1** then **N** is not a prime.
2. If **N** is **2** then **N** is a prime.
3. If **N** > **2** then do the following:
   for each **I** such that **1** < **I** < **N**,
   test if **I** is a divisor of **N**;
   if it is, then **N** is not a prime.

Program

```
program TestPrimes(input, output);

var N: integer;

function Prime(N: integer): boolean;
{Returns true if N is a prime; otherwise, returns false.
Precondition: N > 0.}
  var I: integer;
begin{Prime}
  if N = 1 then Prime := false
  else if N = 2 then Prime := true
  else
    begin{N > 2}
      Prime := true; {tentatively}
      for I := 2 to N-1 do
        if (N mod I = 0) then Prime := false
    end {N > 2}
end; {Prime}

begin{Program}
  writeln('Enter a positive integer and');
  writeln('I will tell you if it is prime.');
  writeln('Enter a zero to quit.');

  writeln('Enter an integer:');
  readln(N);
  while N > 0 do
  begin{while}
    if Prime(N) then writeln(N, ' is a prime.')
                else writeln(N, ' is not a prime.');
    writeln('Enter an integer:');
    readln(N)
  end; {while}

  writeln('End of program.')
end. {Program}
```

Figure 9.5

A boolean function
that tests for
primes.

Enter a positive integer and
I will tell you if it is prime.
Enter a zero to quit.
Enter an integer:
15
    15 is not a prime.
Enter an integer:
17
    17 is a prime.
Enter an integer:
0
End of Program

Figure 9.5 (cont'd)

The following boolean expression is **true** if **I** is a divisor of **N** and is **false** otherwise:

```
N mod I = 0
```

So step 3 can be rewritten to:

```
Prime := true;
for I := 2 to N - 1 do
  if (N mod I = 0) then Prime := false
```

Prime is the name of the function. It is tentatively set equal to **true**. If a divisor is not found, then the value **true** is returned. If a divisor is found, then the function changes its mind and returns **false**.

Some More Standard Functions
(Optional)

Figure 9.6 is a list of some more standard functions. If you have occasion to use trigonometric functions or logarithmic functions, you should use these instead of defining your own versions. Be sure to note that the standard trigonometric functions must have their arguments expressed in radians rather than in degrees. There are 2π radians in a complete circle of 360 degrees. The exponential function **exp** and the logarithm function **ln** use the number e as their base. So **exp(3)** has e cubed as its value. The number e is approximately equal to 2.71828.

Name	Description	Type of Argument	Type of Result	Example	Value of Example
`arctan`	arctangent	`real` or `integer`	`real`	`arctan( 1.0 )`	0.785 (radians)
`cos`	cosine	`real` or `integer`	`real`	`cos( 0.78 )` (argument in radians)	0.71091
`sin`	sine	`real` or `integer`	`real`	`sin( 1.57 )` (argument in radians)	1.00
`exp`	exponential	`real` or `integer`	`real`	`exp( 2 )`	e^2 (not Pascal notation)
`ln`	natural logarithm	`real` or `integer`	`real`	`ln(2.71828)` (*e* is approx. 2.71828)	1.000

Figure 9.6 (Optional) Some more predefined Pascal functions.

UCSD Pascal— More String Functions and Procedures

It is natural to assume that in UCSD Pascal you can have programmer-defined functions that return values of type **string**. Although it is natural to assume this, unfortunately it is false. In UCSD Pascal the possible types returned are the same as they are for standard Pascal. However, UCSD Pascal does provide a number of predefined functions that return values of type **string**. In Chapter 3 we introduced the functions **concat** and **length**. In this section we will describe one additional UCSD Pascal function and two procedures for string manipulation. These functions and procedures are not available in standard Pascal. Hence, programs written using them are not completely portable.

Frequently, one wants to search for a string and replace one particular word (or other substring) with another. In UCSD Pascal this is particularly easy. The function **pos** can be used to locate the word which is to be replaced. For example, suppose that **Line** is a variable of type **string** that contains a line of text. Suppose that we want some Pascal code that will replace the word `´hard´` in that line with the word `´easy´`.

We first must locate the word `´hard´`. The following assignment statement does just that:

```
N := pos('hard', Line)
```

This function **pos** returns an **integer** value that gives the position of the first letter of the string `'hard'`. If `'hard'` is the first word, it returns **1**, setting the value of the **integer** variable **N** equal to **1**. If the first letter of `'hard'` is the tenth character in the line, it returns **10**. If `'hard'` does not occur at all in the line, then it returns **0**.

In general, the function **pos** takes two arguments, both of type **string**. So a call to **pos** is of the form: *pos*

pos(⟨pattern⟩**,** ⟨source⟩**)**

The value returned is the location of the start of the first occurrence of ⟨pattern⟩ in the string ⟨source⟩. If ⟨pattern⟩ does not occur at all in ⟨source⟩, it returns **0**.

Now suppose things are as we have outlined and a program contains

N := pos('hard', Line)

where **N** is of type **integer** and **Line** contains the string

`'It is hard to do text editing.'`

The value of **N** will then be set to **7**. Note that the blank is counted as a symbol.

The word `'hard'` can be removed using the procedure **delete**. The general form of a procedure call to **delete** is: *delete*

delete(⟨string⟩**,** ⟨start⟩**,** ⟨number⟩**)**

⟨string⟩ is a variable parameter of type **string**; ⟨start⟩ and ⟨number⟩ are both value parameters of type **integer**. This call will delete ⟨number⟩ characters from the string ⟨string⟩, starting at position ⟨start⟩. For example, to delete the word `'hard'` from the string in the variable **Line** of our example, the following will work:

delete(Line, N, 4)

To complete this example, we use the UCSD Pascal procedure **insert**. The general form of a call to this procedure is: *insert*

insert(⟨new piece⟩**,** ⟨string⟩**,** ⟨start⟩**)**

⟨new piece⟩ is a value parameter of type **string**; ⟨string⟩ is a variable parameter of type **string** and ⟨start⟩ is a value parameter of type **integer**. This procedure call will insert the string ⟨new piece⟩ into the string ⟨string⟩ starting at position ⟨start⟩. To complete our example, the following will change the value of **Line** to what we want:

insert('easy', Line, N)

After this procedure call, the value of **Line** will be:

`'It is easy to do text editing.'`

Another useful string-editing function is **copy**. It can be used to "copy out" a substring of a given string. A call to **copy** is of the form: *copy*

copy(⟨string⟩**,** ⟨start⟩**,** ⟨length⟩**)**

where ⟨string⟩ is an expression of type **string** and the remaining two arguments are expressions of type **integer**. The value returned is the substring of ⟨string⟩ starting with symbol number ⟨start⟩ and continuing for ⟨length⟩ symbols. For example, if **Line** has the string value given at the end of the previous paragraph, then

```
copy(Line, 7, 10)
```

returns the string

```
'easy to do'
```

Random Number Generators

Suppose you flip a coin, write down 0 if it comes up heads and write down 1 if it comes up tails. You have just made a *random* choice between 0 and 1. If you roll a single die and count the number of dots on the top face, you will get a random number between 1 and 6. These are two ways of generating random numbers. There are numerous occasions when a computer program needs, or at least can profitably use, a source of random numbers. Perhaps the most obvious example is that of game-playing programs. Random numbers are also used in simulation programs. A program to model the performance of a proposed new highway interchange would typically use a random number generator to model the arrival times of vehicles. A program to write poetry might use a random number generator to guide the choice of words. These are just a few of the numerous uses for random number generators.

pseudorandom numbers

An exact definition of what constitutes a *true random number generator* is a matter of significant philosophical debate. However, the examples of the coin flip and the die provide an adequate feel for the concept. Computer programs typically do not use true random number generators. Instead they use procedures or functions that generate sequences of numbers that appear to be random. Since these sequences are generated by procedures or functions, they are not "truly random." Hence these generators are referred to as *pseudorandom number generators.*

For most applications, these pseudorandom number generators are a close enough approximation to a true random number generator. In fact, they are usually preferable to a true random number generator. A pseudorandom number generator has one important advantage over a true random number generator. The sequence of numbers it produces is repeatable. If run twice with the same initial conditions a pseudorandom number generator will always produce exactly the same sequence of numbers. This can be very handy for a number of purposes. It is very useful for debugging. When an error is discovered, the proposed program changes can be tested with the *same* sequence of pseudorandom numbers that exposed the error. Similarly, a particularly interesting run of a simulation program may be reproduced, provided a pseudorandom number generator was used. With a true random number generator every run of the program is likely to be different.

The most common method of generating pseudorandom numbers is the *linear congruence method*. This method starts out with a number called the *seed*. For each individual run of the program, the seed is usually chosen by the user. It completely determines the sequence of numbers produced. There are three other numbers called the **Multiplier**, the **Increment** and the **Modulus**, which are fixed constants. The formula for generating hopefully random looking numbers is quite simple:

The first number is:

(Multiplier*Seed + Increment) *mod* **Modulus**

The $n + 1$st number is:

(Multiplier*(the *n*-th number) **+ Increment)** *mod* **Modulus**

For example, suppose we take the **Multiplier** to be **2**, the **Increment** to be **3** and the **Modulus** to be **5**. With a seed value of **1**, that produces the following sequence of numbers:

(2*1 + 3) *mod* **5** or **0**, **(2*0 + 3)** *mod* **5** or **3**,
(2*3 + 3) *mod* **5** or **4**, **(2*4 + 3)** *mod* **5** or **1**,
(2*1 + 3) *mod* **5** or **0**,...

The pattern of numbers produced is thus **0, 3, 4, 1, 0, 3, 4, 1, 0, 3, 4, 1,**.....

Something is not right. This formula should produce a sequence that looks like a sequence of randomly chosen integers between zero and one less than the modulus. In this example, the numbers should range from **0** to **4**. But the above pattern is a repeating pattern and does not contain **2**. So the value **2** will never be produced. Changing the seed will not help much. If we use **2** as the seed, we obtain the sequence: **2, 2, 2, 2, 2,**..... That produces the value **2** all right, but generates no other numbers. The problem is in the choice of the other constants and not in the choice of the seed.

Any choice of values for the constants in our pseudorandom number generator will produce a sequence that ultimately falls into a repeating pattern. However, if the constants are chosen carefully, the pattern will be large and will appear to be random. The values given in Figure 9.7 should work reasonably well on any implementation whose value of **maxint** is **32761** or larger. With those constants, the random number generator will produce 729 numbers before repeating a number.

Notice that the function **Random** has a variable parameter for the seed and that it changes the value of this parameter, which violates our guideline that functions should not have side effects. This is one of those rare occasions when it is acceptable to violate the guideline. In this case, a variable parameter or something like it is necessary. The generator must somehow remember the last value it produced, since that determines the next value it will produce.

Figure 9.7

A pseudorandom
number generator.

```
function Random(var Seed: integer): integer;
{Returns a pseudorandom number between 0 and (Modulus − 1).
Seed is changed to a value in this range with each call of the function.
Precondition: The value of Seed is between 0 and (Modulus − 1).}
   const Modulus = 729;
         Multiplier = 40;
         Increment = 3641;
begin {Random}
   Seed :=
      (Multiplier*Seed + Increment) mod Modulus;
   Random := Seed
end; {Random}
```

Using Pseudorandom Numbers

*changing
the range*

Very few programs require an integer chosen at random from the range **0** to **728** (the value of **Modulus-1**). Usually it is a different and typically smaller range. For example, a program might need a pseudorandom integer between **0** and **10**. One possibility is to use the following formula:

Random(Seed) *mod* **11**

The procedure **ZeroToTen** in Figure 9.8 uses this formula. The program shown there uses the pseudorandom numbers to produce random looking output.

Random numbers can be scaled by additive constants. One way to get a pseudorandom number in the range **1** to **10** is to add one to an expression that yields numbers in the range **0** to **9**. The following is one such expression:

1 + (Random(Seed) *mod* **10)**

*pseudorandom
reals*

The function **Random** shown in Figure 9.7 will produce a pseudorandom number in the range **0** to **728**. But what if you want a **real** value in the range **0** to **1**? Simply divide by the largest value that our random number generator produces. The function **RandomReal** shown in Figure 9.9 uses this technique to return a pseudorandom value between **0** and **1**. To get a **real** value in any other range, multiply by an appropriate factor, and if need be, add an appropriate constant.

Designing good pseudorandom number generators is not an easy task. They frequently need some sort of "tuning" to keep them from producing a sequence of numbers that looks blatantly nonrandom. The pseudorandom number generators in this section will work reasonably well on virtually any system. However,

Program

```pascal
program RatingGame(input, output);

const Width = 2; {field width for numbers 1 to 10}
var Seed, Rating: integer;
    Ans: char;

function Random(var Seed: integer): integer;
{Returns a pseudorandom number between 0 and (Modulus - 1).
Seed is changed to a value in this range with each call of the function.
Precondition: The value of Seed is between 0 and (Modulus - 1).}
```

■   ■   ■

⟨The rest of the declaration is given in Figure 9.7.⟩

■   ■   ■

```pascal
function ZeroToTen(var Seed: integer): integer;
{Returns a pseudorandom number between 0 and 10.}
    begin{ZeroToTen}
      ZeroToTen := Random(Seed) mod 11
    end; {ZeroToTen}

begin{Program}
  writeln('Hi, my name is Gollum.');
  writeln('I''m a perfect 10. What are you?');
  writeln('Answer with a number between 0 and 10.');
  readln(Seed);
  if Seed >7 then writeln('Not bad.')
             else writeln('Oh well.');
  writeln('Now let''s rate some other people.');

  repeat
    writeln('You name somebody and I''ll give a rating.');
    readln;
    Rating := ZeroToTen(Seed);
    writeln('That individual is a ', Rating:Width);
    writeln('Want to rate somebody else? (Yes or No)');
    readln(Ans)
  until Ans in ['N', 'n'];

  writeln('Before I leave, let me rate you.');
  Rating := ZeroToTen(Seed);
  writeln('I''d say you were a ', Rating:Width)
end. {Program}
```

Figure 9.8
Program using a pseudorandom number generator (cont'd on next page).

Sample Dialogue

Hi, my name is Gollum.
I'm a perfect 10. What are you?
Answer with a number between 0 and 10.
10
Not bad.
Now let's rate some other people.
You name somebody and I'll give a rating.
Joseph Cool
That individual is a 0
Want to rate somebody else? (Yes or No)
yes
You name somebody and I'll give a rating.
Mary Jekubovich
That individual is a 10
Want to rate somebody else? (Yes or No)
yes
You name somebody and I'll give a rating.
Flaco Freddy
That individual is a 4
Want to rate somebody else? (Yes or No)
no
Before I leave, let me rate you.
Figure 9.8 (cont'd)   *I'd say you were a 4*

```
function RandomReal(var Seed: integer): real;
{Returns a pseudorandom real value between zero and one.
Calls the function Random given in Figure 9.7.
Precondition: The value of Seed is between 0 and Max (see const declaration).
The function changes the value of Seed to another value in this range.}

  const Max = 728;
          {The largest value returned by Random.}

begin{RandomReal}
  RandomReal := Random(Seed)/Max
end; {RandomReal}
```

Figure 9.9

A random number generator for *real* values between 0 and 1.

some systems have been extended to include a predefined generator that has been carefully tuned to run efficiently and to produce the most "random looking" sequences possible, given the limitations of the particular computer system. If your system includes such a predefined function, it makes sense to use it rather than the one given in Figure 9.7.

A Better Method for Scaling Random Numbers
(Optional)

Sequences of pseudorandom numbers produced by the linear congruence method do have at least one undesirable property. They frequently have a pattern that can become apparent when the numbers are scaled in certain innocent looking ways. For example, one way to obtain a pseudorandom number chosen from the three values **0**, **1** and **2** is to use the following formula:

Random(Seed) *mod* **3**

If this formula is used with a seed value of **100**, the resulting sequence will be: **0**, **2**, **1**, **0**, **2**, **1**, **0**, **2**, **1**,... The sequence repeats after just three numbers.

One solution is to adjust the constants in the function **Random** for each individual application. However, it is not always clear when or how they should be changed. Moreover, if you are using a predefined pseudorandom number generator this is not even a possibility. However, there is one general purpose trick that can be used to avoid many of these problems. Patterns like this frequently depend heavily on the last digits of the numbers. So one way to break the pattern is to discard the last digit. The following formula yields pseudorandom numbers produced by the generator **Random** but with the last digit discarded:

Random(Seed) *div* **10**

For example, a seed value of **100** produces a value of **114** before applying the *div* operator and **11** after applying the *div* operator.

If we combine the two tricks of discarding the last digit and then scaling by applying a *mod* **3**, we get the following formula for producing pseudorandom numbers in the range **0** to **2**:

(Random(Seed) *div* **10)** *mod* **3**

Again starting with a seed value of **100**, this more complicated formula produces a more random looking sequence which starts out: **2**, **0**, **1**, **2**, **0**, **2**, **2**, **2**, **0**, **1**,...

The techniques presented here will work well for most simple applications. More sophisticated generating and scaling techniques are discussed in the references.

Standard Pascal—Functions and Procedures as Parameters
(Optional)

Many versions of standard Pascal allow functions and procedure names to be parameters to other functions and/or procedures. Unfortunately, not all implementations allow this and, moreover, the details vary somewhat from system to system. (It is not allowed at all in UCSD Pascal.) We will describe the most common way of doing this, as well as one common variation in syntax.

A procedure or function parameter is neither a value nor a variable parameter. *Function parameters* and *procedure parameters* are two additional kinds of parameters. In the formal parameter list, function parameters and procedure parameters are listed by giving a function or procedure heading. Since they are formal parameters which will be replaced by other identifiers when the procedure is called, the identifiers may be any nonreserved word identifiers. For example, the following is a sample procedure heading:

```
procedure Sample(var X:real;
    function F(N:integer):real; procedure Pro(Y:char));
```

This procedure has three formal parameters: **X** is a variable parameter of type **real**, **F** is a function parameter and **Pro** is a procedure parameter. Such long procedure headings seldom fit comfortably on one line. Hence, you should be certain to indent the second line so that the identifiers *procedure* and *function* in the formal parameter lists are not misinterpreted as the start of a new declaration. A sample procedure call corresponding to this heading is:

```
Sample(Z, G, ActualPro)
```

The actual parameter **Z** must be a variable of type **real**. The actual parameter **G** must be the name of a function which has one argument of type **integer** and returns a value of type **real**. The actual parameter **ActualPro** must be a procedure with one value parameter of type **char**.

The exact syntax for listing the formal function parameters and procedure parameters varies a little from system to system. On some systems, the parameters to the function and procedure parameters are not listed in the formal parameter lists. On these systems the sample procedure heading would instead be:

```
procedure Sample(var X:real;
    function F:real: procedure Pro);
```

A complete example using a function parameter is given in Figure 9.10. The function **SumValue** in that program has a function parameter.

There are restrictions on what kinds of functions and procedures may be used as parameters. Specifically, a function or procedure parameter may itself have only value parameters. So a procedure parameter may not have either variable, function or procedure parameters.

```
program StandardPascal(input, output);
{Outputs the sum 1 / 1 + 1 / 2 + 1 / 3 + 1 / 4 + 1 / 5.}

function Reciprocal(Int: integer): real;
{Precondition: The value of Int is not zero.}
   begin {Reciprocal}
      Reciprocal := 1 / Int
   end; {Reciprocal}

function SumValue( function F(X: integer): real;
                                     N: integer): real;
{F is a formal function argument.
SumValue returns the value F(1) + F(2) + ... + F(N).}
   var I: integer;
       Sum: real;
begin{SumValue}
   Sum := 0;
   for I := 1 to N do
       Sum := Sum + F(I);
   SumValue := Sum
end; {SumValue}

begin{Program}
   writeln('The sum of the reciprocals of');
   writeln('1 through 5 is:');
   writeln(SumValue(Reciprocal, 5))
end. {Program}
```

**Figure 9.10
(Optional)
Function with
another function
as an argument.**

Summary of Problem Solving and Programming Techniques

When designing a program, it is very common for one or more subtasks to be the computation of a single value. In those cases the subtasks should be implemented as functions. When designing functions it is usually a bad idea to allow side effects such as changing a global variable or using a variable parameter. If such things are needed it is usually clearer to use a procedure rather than a function.

◇

Chance is a word void of sense; nothing can exist without a cause.

Voltaire, A Philosophical Dictionary

◇

Summary of Pascal Constructs

function declaration heading

Syntax:

function ⟨function name⟩**(**⟨formal parameter list⟩**):** ⟨type returned⟩**;**

Example:

function `Area(Length, Width: real): real;`

The ⟨formal parameter list⟩ can be anything which is allowed as a procedure formal parameter list. ⟨type returned⟩ may be any of the types `integer`, `real`, `char` or `boolean`.

function declaration   The syntax for a function declaration is the same as that for a procedure declaration except for two points: the heading of a function declaration is as described above and the body of the declaration must contain an assignment statement with the function name on the left-hand side of the assignment operator.

call of a function

Syntax:

⟨function name⟩**(**⟨argument list⟩**)**

Example:

`X := Area(3.79, 8.9)`

A function call can appear in exactly the same places that a constant of the type returned by the function can appear. It is an expression and evaluates to a value of the type specified in the function declaration. This value is called the value returned. The value returned is equal to the last value assigned to the function name when the statements given in the function declaration are executed. The ⟨argument list⟩ is the same thing as an actual parameter list and is handled in exactly the same way as an actual parameter list for a procedure.

Exercises

Self-Test and Interactive Exercises

1. Write a function declaration for a function, called **Half**, that has one argument of type **integer** and that returns a value of type **real** equal to one half its argument. For example, the value of **Half(5)** is **2.5**.

2. List all the types that are allowed as the type of the value returned by a function in Pascal.

3. Write a function that has two arguments for the length and width of a rectangle and which returns the area of a rectangle with those dimensions. The sample function heading in the Pascal summary can be used as the function heading.

4. What is wrong with the following function declaration?

```
function TwoPower(N: integer): integer;
{Returns 2 to the power N. Precondition N > = 0.}
    var I: integer;
begin{TwoPower}
  TwoPower := 1;
  for I := 1 to N do
    TwoPower := TwoPower*2
end; {TwoPower}
```

5. Write a boolean function of two **integer** arguments that returns **true** if the first argument evenly divides the second and returns **false** otherwise.

6. Write a boolean function declaration for a function **InOrder** that has three integer arguments and returns **true** if the three integer arguments are in ascending order. So, **InOrder(1, 2, 3)** should return **true** and **InOrder(1, 3, 2)** should return **false**.

7. Write a function declaration for a function called **Grader** that takes a numeric score and returns a letter grade. So, **Grader** has one argument of type **integer** and returns a value of type **char**. Use the rule 90 to 100 is an A, 80 to 89 is a B, 70 to 79 is a C and less than 70 is an F.

8. Write a program that requests a seed value and then outputs twenty random numbers generated by the function **Random** in Figure 9.7.

9. Do the same as in the previous exercise but this time use the function **RandomReal** from Figure 9.9.

10. Write a function that returns a pseudorandom number chosen from the even numbers between 2 and 20. Use the random number generator developed in this chapter.

11. (This exercise uses the optional section "Some More Standard Functions".) For positive values of x, the value x^y can be computed as:

exp(y*ln(x))

The advantage of this formula over the function **Power** in Figure 9.3 is that this formula allows fractional exponents. Write a program that reads in decimal numbers x and y and outputs x^y.

Regular Exercises

12. (This exercise makes sense only if you have both upper-case and lower-case letters on your keyboard.) Write a function declaration for a function called **CapYN** which has one argument of type **char** and returns a value of type **char**. This function will check to make sure that its argument is one of the values 'y', 'Y', 'n' or 'N'. If its argument is not one of these four values, it should write an error message to the screen. The function then changes 'y' and 'n' to upper-case letters. So **CapYN('y')** returns 'Y' and **CapYN('Y')** returns 'Y'. Similarly, **CapYN('n')** and **CapYN('N')** both return 'N'. It does not matter what **CapYN** returns with other arguments.

13. The perimeter P of an n-sided polygon circumscribing a circle of radius r is given by:

$$P = 2\,n\,r \times tan(\,\pi\,/\,n\,)$$

Write a function declaration that will return the perimeter of such a polygon given the values of n and r as arguments. Embed the function in a program as a test of the function declaration.

14. Write a program that gives the user the choice of computing any of the following: the area of a circle, a square, a rectangle or a triangle. The program should include a loop to allow the user to do as many calculations as desired. Use a function for each of the different kinds of calculations.

15. In order to discourage excess consumption, an electric company charges its customers a lower rate for the first 8 kilowatt-hours, namely $4.78 for the first 8 kilowatt hours, and a higher rate of $5.26 for each additional kilowatt-hour. In addition, a 10% surtax is added to the final bill. Write a program to calculate electric bills given the number of kilowatt-hours consumed as input. Use two function declarations, one to compute the amount due without the surtax and one to compute the total due. The declaration for the second function should include a call to the first function.

16. The function **Prime** in Figure 9.5 can be made more efficient in a number of ways. First, there is no reason to continue to loop through more checks once a divisor of **N** is found. At that point you know that **N** is not prime. For example, once you know that **1000** is divisible by **2** you know it is not a prime and need not test to see if it is divisible by **3**, **4** and so forth. Replace the **for** loop by a **repeat** or **while** loop that will terminate the loop as soon as it is discovered that an argument is not a prime. Also, there is no need to test all numbers up to **N − 1**. Determine and use a smaller limit on the maximum number of loop iterations.

17. The greatest common divisor of two positive integers is the largest integer that divides them both. For example, the greatest common divisor of 9 and 6 is 3. Write a function declaration for a function with two integer arguments that returns their greatest common divisor.

18. Write a program that outputs random but grammatically correct sentences. The sentences can be simple sentences of the form: a noun, followed by a verb, followed by a noun. Use a pseudorandom number generator to choose a noun from a list of 10 nouns and a verb from a list of 10 verbs.

19. (This exercise is for UCSD Pascal users.) Redo the previous exercise so that the user types in a person's name and the program responds with a sentence that mentions that person by name.

20. Write a program that will simulate a roll of two dice to produce a value between **2** and **12**. If your system has a predefined pseudorandom number generator, use it; otherwise, use the function **Random** described in the text.

21. The game of *Nim* is played as follows. There are three piles of sticks. Two players take turn making moves. A move consists of picking up as many sticks as the player desires subject to the following constraints: all the sticks must be picked up from the same pile and a player must pick up at least one stick. The player who picks up the last stick loses. Write a program to play Nim with the user. Use a pseudorandom number generator to choose the size of the three piles subject to the constraint that the three piles must be of different sizes and must contain at least two and at most 10 sticks. The computer can use a pseudorandom number generator to decide on moves or it can use any other strategy that is reasonable.

22. Write a function declaration for a function called **Deal** that returns a card chosen at random from a standard 52 card deck. Code the value of the card (2 to 10, jack, queen, king or ace) as a value of type **char**. So the function will return a value of type **char**. You can ignore suits (diamonds, clubs and so forth).

23. Write a program that plays blackjack with the user. Use the function from the previous exercise. The program in Figure 6.14 may be of some help.

24. One way to estimate the area of a figure is to enclose it in a figure whose area you know and to then choose points at random within the figure of known area. The ratio of points in the figure of unknown area to points in the enclosing figure of known area is the same as the ratio of the unknown area to the known area. (Remember to count the total number of points as the points in the figure of known area. Those that are in the figure of unknown area are also in the larger figure.) Use this technique with a circle enclosed in a square to estimate the area of a circle with radius one. Then use the formula

$$Area = \pi r^2$$

with that estimate of *Area* and solve for π to get an estimate of π. Do this all with a program that uses a pseudorandom number generator to choose points.

25. (This exercise uses the optional section "Some More Standard Functions".) Write a function declaration for a function called **SineDeg**. This function differs from the standard function **sine** in that its argument is in degrees rather than radians. Use a local function that converts from degrees to radians and use a call to **sine**. Write a similar function declaration for **cos** and **tan**. Embed these in a program that takes as input an angular measure in degrees and will then output the sine, cosine and tangent of that angle.

References for Further Reading

D. E. Knuth, *The Art of Computer Programming, Volume 2 / Seminumerical Algorithms*, second edition, 1981, Addison-Wesley, Reading, Mass. More advanced material on random number generators. Does not use Pascal, but the text can be read without reading the programs.

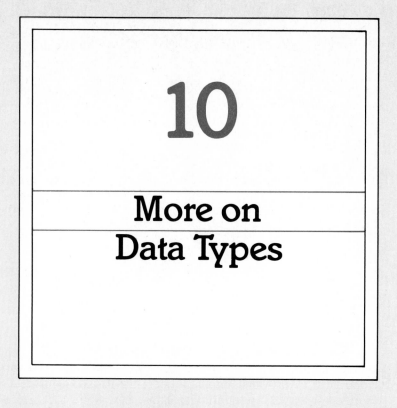

10

More on
Data Types

Memory is necessary for all
the operations of reason.

Blaise Pascal

Chapter Contents

We have already had some experience with data types. The types **integer**, **real**, **char** and **boolean** are all data types. They are provided automatically in the Pascal language. As we shall see shortly, you can define additional data types within a Pascal program. The word ''data'' in its most general meaning refers to anything that can be manipulated by a computer program. A *data type* is a particular type or kind of data together with some rules for how these data items can be manipulated.

Another way to think of a data type is as a description of the values that a variable of that type can have. A data type is specified by specifying the values of that type and by specifying the operations that are allowed on those values. For example, the values of the Pascal type **integer** are all the positive integers less than or equal to **maxint**, all the negative integers greater than or equal to the smallest negative integer the computer can handle (approximately −**maxint**) and the integer zero. The operations that are provided include addition, subtraction, multiplication, *div* and *mod*. The type **boolean** consists of the two values, **true** and **false**, together with the operations on those values. The operations consist of *and*, *or*, *not*, and a few order-testing operations explained below.

You may be used to thinking of **and, or** and **not** as combining boolean expressions rather than the values **true** and **false**, but that is not the point of view that we will take. By way of illustration, consider the following boolean expression:

(1 < 2) *or* (5 > 7)

The point of view we will take is that the subexpression

(1 < 2)

evaluates to **true** and that the subexpression

(5 > 7)

evaluates to **false** and that *or* combines these two values of type **boolean**. So the above boolean expression is equivalent to:

true *or* false

That in turn evaluates to **true**. The situation is completely analogous to how we usually think about integers. The operation **+** combines integers. So, in the expression

(5*2) + (6 - 4)

we do not think of the operation **+** as combining the two subexpressions. We instead think of the operation **+** as combining two integers. In this case it combines the integers **10** and **2** to produce the integer **12**.

The expression **(1 < 2)** illustrates one other characteristic of data types. They are not completely independent of each other. Sometimes an operation that is applied to values of one data type can yield a value of another data type. For example, the operation greater-than can combine two integers and yield a boolean value.

In this chapter we reexam the data types already introduced. We then go on to describe how new data types are defined and used.

Ordinal Types

The most straightforward way to specify the values of a data type is to list them. In the case of the type **boolean**, that is easy to do. There are just two values: **false** and **true**. In the case of the type **char** the list is much longer: **A, B, C,...** . In the case of the type **integer** the list is so long that it would be unrealistic to write it out, but in principle the values could all be listed. In Pascal, a type whose values are specified by a list is called an *ordinal type*. The types **integer, boolean** and **char** are all ordinal types.

Since the items of any list are ordered, the values of an ordinal type have an order determined by their order in the list. The operation **<** can be used to test this ordering. It is an operation defined on all Pascal ordinal types, and it always yields a boolean value. The most obvious case of this is the ordinal type

integer

boolean

char

integer. In that case the order is the usual less-than ordering on the integers. For example, **1 < 2** and **-5 < -3** both evaluate to **true**. In the case of the type **boolean**, **false** is considered to be less than **true**. There is not much intuitive meaning to that ordering. It really is arbitrary. Nonetheless, it is the prescribed ordering and so **false < true** evaluates to **true**.

The ordering on the type **char** is more or less the obvious one. Letters are ordered alphabetically. So **'A' < 'B'** and **'A' < 'Z'** both evaluate to **true**, while **'Z' < 'X'** evaluates to **false**. The digits are ordered as you would expect. For example, **'1' < '2'** and **'0' < '9'** both evaluate to **true**, while **'3' < '2'** evaluates to **false**. The ordering of the digits reflects the ordering of the numbers they stand for. What about the character pairs which do not have a traditional ordering? Is the semicolon less than the comma or greater than the comma? Is upper-case **'A'** less than or greater than lower-case **'a'**? Pascal does not say. It does specify that the capital letters are ordered alphabetically among themselves, the lower-case letters are ordered alphabetically among themselves and the digits are ordered in the obvious way. Moreover, it says that the digits are contiguous; that is, there is no character between two intuitively adjacent digits such as **'4'** and **'5'**. Within those constraints, the compiler can be implemented in any way the designer finds convenient. So on one system you may find that **'a' < 'A'** evaluates to **true**, while on another system it evaluates to **false**. The moral is clear: you should avoid using any ordering properties that can change from system to system.

The type **char** is a good example of a type that is only partially determined by the definition of the language. This is quite common. The usual thing to do is to require a data type to have the properties that programmers normally expect and need but to let the compiler writer do whatever is convenient with the unspecified properties. Although it may be incomplete, the definition of a data type should not be vague. Pascal specifies that the order of the digits is exactly: **'0'**, **'1'**, **'2'**, **'3'**, **'4'**, **'5'**, **'6'**, **'7'**, **'8'**, **'9'**. Similarly, the ordering of any two upper-case letters is rigidly specified and so forth. Whatever is specified is precisely specified.

The ordering properties of ordinal types can be used in a program. For example, it is sometimes useful to test two letters to determine if they are in alphabetic order. An obvious example of this would be in a program that alphabetizes a list of words. We have already seen that there are numerous reasons why a program might compare two integer values.

When comparing two values of an ordinal type, the variations on the **<** operation, namely **<=**, **>** and **>=** are all available and have the obvious interpretation.

real

Of all the simple types we have seen, only the type **real** is not an ordinal type. This is a consequence of the abstract model of the real numbers which is used in mathematics. In that model the real numbers can not be listed. Computers can represent only a finite number of **real** constants, and so the **real** values for any particular implementation can, in principle, be listed. However, the definition of Pascal does not specify the list; moreover, we do not normally think of the **real** values as being on a list. For these reasons the type **real** is not considered to be an ordinal type. As we have seen, the comparison operators, like **<**, can be applied to values of type **real**, in the same fashion as they can be applied to values of ordinal types.

In many ways, but not all ways, the type **real** is like an ordinal type. The unifying term *simple type* is used to mean any type which is either the type **real** or is an ordinal type. The type **real** is both important and troublesome. All of Chapter 15 is devoted to discussing this type.

UCSD Pascal—The Type string

The type **string** in UCSD Pascal is not an ordinal type, although values of type string are ordered. The ordering of string values was discussed in Chapter 6.

Subrange Types

The simplest kind of type that can be defined within a Pascal program is a *subrange type*. A subrange type is obtained from an ordinal type by specifying two constants of that type. The type from which the two constants are chosen is called the *host type*. The values of the subrange type are all the values of the host type that fall between the two specified constants. A subrange type is an ordinal type and the values are ordered in the same way as they are in the host type. A subrange type definition is a declaration and so goes in the declaration part of a program. For example, a program might start as follows:

*host
type*

```
program Sample(input, output);
  const PI = 3.14159;
  type SmallInteger = -10..10;
  var Big: integer;
      Little: SmallInteger;
      X, Y: real;
```

The third line is called a *type declaration*. The type **SmallInteger** is defined to be all **integer** values between **-10** and **10**, including the end points. The variable **Little** is defined to be of type **SmallInteger**, and so it can take on values from **-10** to **+10**. Hence, the following is a Pascal statement that might legitimately appear in this program:

*type
declaration*

```
Little := 4
```

However, the following should produce an error message when the program is run:

```
Little := 11{Not allowed}
```

Subrange type declarations, as well as the other type declarations which we will introduce later, go in the heading of a program between the constant and variable declarations. The general form of a subrange type declaration follows the model of the sample we just discussed: the identifier *type*, followed by an identifier to serve as the name of the type, followed by an equal sign and then the definition of the type. The definition consists of two constants from the host type, separated by two periods. As you might expect, the first constant must be less than or equal to the second.

It is usually possible to use a subrange type definition directly in a variable declaration, rather than first defining a type name. For example, the following declares the variable **I** to be of type **1..10**:

> *var* I: **1..10**;

In most cases, it is, however, preferable to declare a type name.

type
compatibility

Subrange types and their host types are compatible in the sense that any value of a subrange type is also considered to be of the host type. For example, using the preceding program heading, any value of type **SmallInteger** is also of type **integer**. So in this program, the following is a legitimate statement:

> **Big := Little**

The following program code is also legitimate:

> **readln(Big);**
> **Little := Big**

However, if the **readln** statement sets the value of **Big** to a value outside the range of the subrange type **SmallInteger**, then the assignment statement should precipitate an error message.

The subrange type inherits all the operations of its host type. For example, a program with types declared as above could add or subtract two things of type **SmallInteger**.

error
checking

One important use of subrange types is as a device to detect certain programming errors. If you expect a variable to always take on values within a certain range, then that variable should be declared as having a subrange type. That way, if an error does cause it to take on a value outside the specified range, then an error message will be produced. Otherwise, the error might go undetected. For example, if a variable **X** is expected to hold only positive integers, then the following declarations will serve to declare **X** in such a way that nonpositive values will produce an error message:

> *type* PositiveInt = **1..maxint**;
> *var* X: PositiveInt;

As another example, suppose **Final** is supposed to hold a letter grade in a classroom grading program. Suppose furthermore that the possible grades are A, B, C, D and F. Then **Final** should be declared as follows:

> *type* Grade = **'A'..'F'**;
> *var* Final: Grade;

With the variable **Final** declared to be of a subrange type as shown, the computer should give an error message if for some reason the value of **Final** is set to, say, ´**G**´. There is a limit to how much of this type checking can be handled by subrange types. Subrange types consist of *all* the values between the two limits. Hence, the above declaration does not provide for an error message in the event that the value of **Grade** is set to ´**E**´.

Extra care must be taken when using a subrange type as the type of a variable parameter in a procedure. The rules for matching parameters say that the formal and actual parameters must be of the same type. This can sometimes cause subtle problems. As an example, recall the procedure **Exchange** defined in Chapter 5. All the information we need about the procedure is given in the procedure heading. This as well as some other declarations that might appear in a program are:

```
type Rating = 0..10;
var A, B: Rating;
procedure Exchange(var X, Y: integer);
{Interchanges the values of X and Y.}
```

In a program with these declarations it seems perfectly natural to include a procedure call such as:

```
Exchange(A, B)
```

Although it seems natural, it will produce an error message and prevent the program from running to completion. The reason is that the formal and actual parameter types do not match. The formal parameters are of type **integer**, whereas the actual parameters are of type **Rating**. Sometimes this problem can make the use of a subrange type impractical.

The same rule for matching parameters applies to value parameters as well, but in that case it is less of a problem. A value of a subrange type is also considered to be a value of the host type, and so type conflicts are not as likely to occur. For example, consider the following procedure:

```
procedure WriteResult(X: integer);
   begin
     writeln(´The result is ´, X)
   end;
```

With **A** declared to be of type **Rating**, the following procedure call is perfectly valid:

```
WriteResult(A)
```

There is no type conflict in this case because it is the *value* of the actual parameter **A** that must agree in type with the formal parameter **X**. Although **A** is of type **Rating**, the *value* of **A** is considered to be of type **integer**, as well as being of type **Rating**.

The For and Case Statements Revisited

Ordinal types are like the integers in the sense that they can be listed. Given two bounds, we can proceed from the lower bound to the next value in the ordered list, then the next and so forth until we reach the upper bound. This is the only property of the type **integer** that the *for* statement uses. It thus seems natural to allow the loop control variable in a *for* statement to be of any ordinal type. Pascal does just that. Of course, the expressions that give the initial and final values of the loop control variable must be of the same ordinal type as the variable. For example, the following is a perfectly legitimate Pascal statement:

```
for I := 'A' to 'Z' do
        write(I)
```

Provided that **I** is declared to be of type **char** or an appropriate subrange type, this will output the alphabet. (In some implementations, there may be other characters interspersed as well. This is because the specification of the type **char** does not demand that there be nothing between, for example, **'A'** and **'B'**.)

Since a loop control variable assumes values between two bounds, it is natural to declare it to be of a subrange type. This is a good idea since it serves as one additional check on the program.

Now that we have defined the ordinal types, we can define the *case* statement more completely and compactly. The expression that governs a *case* statement may be of any ordinal type. The label lists must, of course, consist of constants of that ordinal type.

The Functions ord, chr, pred and succ
(Optional)

pred

succ

Since the values of an ordinal type are ordered in a list, a programmer may find it useful to refer to the value preceding a given value, or to the value following a given value in this list. Pascal provides two functions, **pred** and **succ**, for exactly those purposes. Given a value of some ordinal type as an argument, such as **18**, the function **pred** returns the preceding value of that type and the function **succ** returns the next value in the ordering of that type. For example, **pred(18)** returns **17** and **succ(18)** returns **19**. Similarly, **succ('B')** usually returns **'C'** and **pred('B')** usually returns **'A'**. Since the exact ordering of the characters may vary from system to system, the values returned by **pred** and **succ** may vary somewhat from system to system.

ord

Since the values of an ordinal type are listed in some order, we can meaningfully ask where a specified value is located on the list. The Pascal function **ord** provides a way of doing this. However, the ordinal types are usually numbered starting with 0 rather than 1. So **ord** applied to the first value of an ordinal type returns **0**; when applied to the second value it returns **1** and so forth. The type **integer** is the sole exception to this general numbering scheme. The function **ord** applied to any value of type **integer** simply returns that value. For example, **ord(-5)** returns **-5**.

Since it is the type **char** that is ultimately used when a program communicates with the outside world, it is a special type in a number of ways. One of its special features is a standard function that is the inverse of **ord**. Given a nonnegative integer value, the function **chr** returns the character value in that position on the list of values of type **char**. So **chr(0)** returns the first value of type **char**, **chr(1)** returns the next value **chr(2)** returns the next value and so forth. For numbers that do not correspond to any character value, **chr** is undefined.

These various functions, which depend on the ordering of ordinal types, are occasionally useful but are neither essential nor even very widely used. Only a few specialized uses are very common. One use involves text processing. Although it is not part of the definition of Pascal, most systems list the letters with the upper-case letters contiguous (nothing between `'A'` and `'B'`, for example) and the lower-case letters contiguous. On these systems, there is some number x such that the upper-case and lower-case versions of a letter are always exactly x places apart. So, for example, **chr(ord('A') + x)** returns `'a'`, and **chr(ord('P') + x)** returns `'p'`. Similarly, a program can compute upper-case letters from lower-case letters using minus x. The number x can be computed using the relation:

$$x = \text{ord('a')} - \text{ord('A')}$$

Another use for the **chr** function has to do with nonprintable characters. A computer frequently has the ability to send messages to the video screen output device which mean things like "clear the screen," "ring the bell" or some other manipulation of the output device other than simply writing a letter on the screen. These signals are usually considered to be values of type **char**. So, for example, if the "character" that rings the bell happens to be numbered **29** on some system, then the following will ring the bell on the output device of that system:

```
write(chr(29))
```

These sample uses of **chr** and **ord** are highly implementation-dependent. Different systems will order the values of type character differently. Even the list of available characters will differ from system to system. Some systems do not have a bell to ring. Some do not have curly brackets `'{'`and`'}'`. Some do not have lower-case letters. Hence, any program written using these techniques will definitely not be portable. These sorts of manipulations should always be isolated into clearly documented procedures, so that they can be easily changed. For example, suppose that the "character" to clear the screen on your system is numbered **56**. The following is a reasonable procedure to clear the screen:

```
procedure ClearScreen;
{Implementation-dependent procedure to clear screen. The
"clear screen" signal on system XYZ is character number 56.}
    begin{ClearScreen}
      write(chr(56))
    end; {ClearScreen}
```

In Pascal, a few tasks such as the above can only be done in implementation-dependent ways. However, if care is taken to isolate the implementation-dependent details, then the program can still be quite portable. For example, to change the above procedure to work on another system, all that normally need be done is to change the constant **56** in the procedure **ClearScreen**.

Enumerated Types
(Optional)

There is one other kind of ordinal type. Types of this other kind are called *enumerated types*. An enumerated type is just a list of values named by identifiers. The values of an enumerated type have no properties other than their order and their names. Despite their simple nature, enumerated types can be useful. By choosing the identifiers to be meaningful names they can sometimes be used to make a program easier to read. For example, the following type declaration declares the names of four kinds of vehicles to be an enumerated type:

type Vehicle = (Motorcycle, Car, Bus, Truck);

This type has four values named by the four identifiers in the list.

declaration

The general form of an enumerated type declaration follows this example: The identifier *type* is followed by a type name chosen by the programmer, then the equal sign and then a list of identifiers enclosed in parentheses and separated by commas. The list of identifiers contains the names of the constants of that type, and they are ordered as in the list.

variables

Just like other types, there can be variables of an enumerated type. For example, the following declares **Class** to be of type **Vehicle**:

var Class: Vehicle;

Variables of an enumerated type and their values behave much like those of any other type. For example, the following makes **Bus** the value of the variable **Class**:

Class := Bus

uses of enumerated types

One common use of enumerated types is in *case* statements, such as:

```
case Class of
  Motorcycle: Toll := 0.25;
  Car: Toll := 0.50;
  Truck, Bus: Toll := 1.00
end
```

The enumerated type serves two purposes here: it makes the program meaning clearer and it guarantees that the *case* statement is almost always defined. The variable **Class** can not take on a value that is not on some statement label list. The only way the *case* statement can be undefined is if the variable **Class** was never initialized. Of course, a similar thing can sometimes be done with a

Program

```
program Payroll(input, output);
{Computes an hourly employee's weekly pay.}
    const Width = 8; {Field width for total wages}
            SatAdjustment = 1.5; {Time and one half}
            SunAdjustment = 2.0; {Double time}
  [ type WeekDay = (Mon, Tue, Wed, Thur, Fri, Sat, Sun);
    var BaseRate, Rate, Wages: real;
        Day: WeekDay;
        Hours: 0..24;
begin{Program}
    writeln('Enter the basic hourly wage rate:');
    readln(BaseRate);
    Wages := 0.0;
    writeln('Enter the hours worked');
    writeln('for Monday through Sunday:');

    for Day := Mon to Sun do
      begin{for}
        read(Hours);

        case Day of
          Mon, Tue, Wed, Thur, Fri: Rate := BaseRate;
          Sat: Rate := SatAdjustment*BaseRate;
          Sun: Rate := SunAdjustment*BaseRate
        end; {case}

        Wages := Wages + Hours*Rate
      end; {for}
    readln;

    writeln('Wages for the week total: $', Wages:Width:2)
end. {Program}
```

Sample Dialogue

Enter the basic hourly wage rate:
10.00
Enter the hours worked
for Monday through Sunday:
8 8 8 8 8 0 2
Wages for the week total: $ 440.00

Figure 10.1
**Program using an
enumerated type.**

subrange type, but an enumerated type allows more flexibility in choosing label names.

It is important to note that the elements of an enumerated type are not strings and can not be either read in or written out by a program. In a program with the above declarations, the following will usually produce no output other than an error message:

write(Truck) {*Not Allowed*}

Figure 10.1 shows a program that uses an enumerated type for the days of the week.

Arrays—An Introduction to Structured Types

structured types

Simple types, whether provided by Pascal or defined by the programmer, have values that intuitively are indivisible units. The character ´**A**´ can not be meaningfully decomposed into parts. The real number **2.34** intuitively could be decomposed in a few different ways, but we usually think of it as a single item and the Pascal language treats it as a single item. The same holds for the other simple types. In addition to these simple types, Pascal and most other programming languages allow the programmer to define more complicated types whose values are compound items composed of a number of values of some simpler types. These sorts of compound types are called *structured types* because, unlike the simple types, they have a structure that can be meaningfully decomposed by operations provided within the programming language. It is easier to understand this notion in the concrete setting of some specific structured data types. The first structured types we will see are the array types.

why arrays

The array types allow you to have a single uniform way to name a number of related values of the same type. For example, suppose we wish to write a program that reads in five test scores and performs some manipulations on these scores. For instance, the program might compute the highest test score and then output the amount by which each score falls short of the highest score. Since all five scores must be retained in storage until after the highest score is computed, we will need something like five variables of type **integer** to hold the five scores. However, five variables are hard to keep track of. We could make the program more readable by giving the variables related names such as **Score1**, **Score2** and so forth, but this solution becomes absurd if the number of scores is very large. Imagine doing the same thing for 100 scores.

The solution to this dilemma is to use an *array*. An array is rather like a list of variables, but there is one important difference. In an array the individual variable names can themselves contain variables and even expressions. For example, we can declare an array called **Score** to hold the five test scores. The type and variable declarations can be:

```
type SmallArray = array[1..5] of integer;
var Score: SmallArray;
```

The type, such as **integer** in the above declaration, is called the *component type*. This declaration is like declaring the following five variables to all be of type **integer**:

```
Score[1], Score[2], Score[3], Score[4], Score[5]
```

The above items are not valid Pascal identifiers and so may not look like variables. However, they have all the properties of variables and a few additional properties as well. To keep from confusing them with the simple variables we have used up until now, we will call these new sort of variables *indexed variables*. The number inside the square brackets is called the *index expression* or, more simply, the *index*. The indexes are truly **integer** values. Any integer expression that evaluates to a value of the subrange type **1..5** can be placed inside the square brackets. This provides the program with a way to manipulate the names of the variables. For example, the following code sets the value of **Score[2]** to **99** and outputs it to the screen twice:

```
X := 2;
Score[X] := 99;
writeln(Score[X]);
writeln(Score[2])
```

The variable **X** may be of type **1..5** or of type **integer**.

Two things should be observed in the preceding piece of code. First, the array index can be a variable. This allows the program to say things equivalent to "do the following to the **X**th array element." The values of the indexed variables are usually called *elements*. Second, the identity of an indexed variable, such as **Score[X]**, is determined by the value of its index (and, of course, the array name like **Score**). In the above example **Score[2]** and **Score[X]** are the exact same indexed variable because the value of **X** is **2**.

For another example, suppose the value of **X** is **2**, and **Pro** is a procedure with one variable parameter of type **integer**. Then the procedure call

```
Pro(A[X])
```

is equivalent to:

```
Pro(A[2])
```

Hence, when an indexed variable is an actual variable parameter, the index expression is always evaluated before the indexed variable is plugged in for the formal parameter.

The form of an array type declaration is given by the syntax diagram in Figure 10.2. In the above example the ⟨array type name⟩ was **SmallArray**. Any identifier, except a reserved word, can be used as the ⟨array type name⟩. In the above example we used **1..5** as a ⟨subrange type definition⟩. Any subrange type definition or any previously declared name of a subrange type can be used

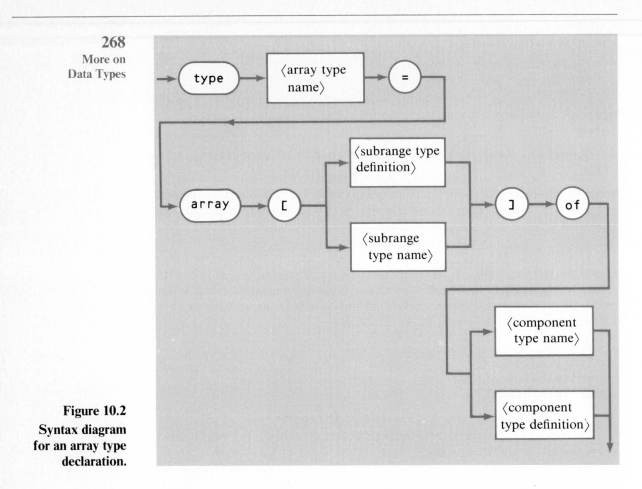

**Figure 10.2
Syntax diagram
for an array type
declaration.**

instead. The component type can be any of the types we have seen. In fact, the component type can be almost any Pascal type, including most of the types we will introduce in later chapters. The reserved word **type** is used only once in the type declaration section, even if more than one type is defined. The following is an example of a program type declaration section that defines four different array types:

```
type BigArray = array[-1000..1000] of real;
     Line = array[1..80] of char;
     Count = array['A'..'Z'] of 0..80;
     Checks = array[0..79] of boolean;
```

Once an array type has been declared, a particular array is declared just like a variable. Given the above type declarations, the following are all valid array declarations:

```
var A, B: BigArray;
    Title: Line;
    Counter: Count;
    Present: Checks;
```

Notice that neither the square brackets nor the index expression is included in the declaration of an array.

An array is declared like a variable and can be used like a variable. For example, suppose **A** and **B** are declared as shown; then the following is a valid assignment statement:

```
A := B
```

arrays in assignment statements

The meaning of this assignment statement is that all the values of all the indexed variables of **B** are copied to those of **A**. In other words, the above assignment statement is equivalent to the following:

```
for J := -1000 to 1000 do
      A[J] := B[J]
```

input output

A complete program using an array is shown in Figure 10.3. Notice that when reading into an array or writing out an array, the elements of the array are read or

Program

```
program ArraySample(input, output);
   type ThreeLetters = array[1..3] of char;
   var Abbrev: ThreeLetters;
       I: 1..3;

begin{Program}
   writeln('What day of the week is it?');
   for I := 1 to 3 do
     read(Abbrev[I]);
   readln;
   case Abbrev[1] of
     'M', 'm': writeln('I hate Mondays.');
     'F', 'f', 'S', 's': writeln('I like weekends.');
     'T', 't', 'W', 'w':
       begin{Tue through Thu}
         for I := 1 to 3 do
           write(Abbrev[I]);
         writeln('. is a very ordinary day.')
       end {Tue through Thu}
   end {case}
end. {Program}
```

Sample Dialogue

What day of the week is it?
Thurs.
Thu. is a very ordinary day.

Figure 10.3
Program with an array.

written separately. There is no way to read in a whole array by a statement such as:

read(Abbrev) {*NOT ALLOWED if Abbrev is an array*}

Similarly, there is no way to write a whole array by a statement like:

write(Abbrev) {*NOT ALLOWED if Abbrev is an array*}

*array
values
as a list*

One way to think of an array is as a collection of variables of the component type and this is the point of view we normally take. However, another way to view an array is as a single variable of a complicated type. The values of the array types are lists of values of the component type. The list is indexed by the subrange type specified in the array type declaration. For example, suppose **C** and **D** are declared as follows:

```
type SmallArray = array[0..4] of integer;
var C, D: SmallArray;
```

A value for the array **C** can be thought of as a list of **integer** values such as:

10, 56, 99, 0, 87

The indexed variable expression **C[0]** names the first value in the list, in this example **10**. The second member of the subrange type **0..4** indexes the second value on the list, so **C[1]** names **56**, and so forth.

This second point of view explains why an array type is called a structured type. It is a type because it can be specified by specifying the values which variables of that kind can have. The values are the lists. The arrays are the variables. Each complete array, such as **C**, is a single variable in this point of view. An array type is said to be structured because these values have a structure, namely, that of an indexed list. This point of view helps to explain why arrays are frequently referred to by their array names without any index. When referred to in this way, an array is being thought of as a single variable whose value is a list of values of the component type. For example, if the array **D** is of the same type as **C** and the value of **C** is the previously displayed list, then the following sets the value of **D** equal to this same list:

D := C

*array
parameters*

An array is also treated as a single variable with a structured value when it is a parameter to a procedure. When used as a formal parameter in a procedure heading or as an actual parameter in a procedure call, an array is always specified by giving the array name without square brackets or indexes. For example, if the array type **SmallArray** is declared as above, then the following is a legitimate procedure declaration:

```
procedure Double(X: SmallArray; var Y: SmallArray);
{Sets each indexed variable of Y equal to twice
the value of the corresponding indexed variable of X}
    var I: 0..4;
  begin{Double}
    for I := 0 to 4 do
      Y[I] := 2*X[I]
  end; {Double}
```

If **C** and **D** are declared to be of type **SmallArray** and the value of **C** is the above list of five integers, then the following is a valid procedure call:

Double(C, D)

The effect of this procedure call is to change the value of **D** to

20, 112, 198, 0, 174

In other words, the value of **D[0]** becomes **20**, that of **D[1]** becomes **112** and so forth.

Viewing an array as a single value naturally leads to the conclusion that a function can return an array as a value. This conclusion is, however, wrong for the Pascal language. In Pascal, the value returned by a function can not be an array type. There is no compelling conceptual reason for this. This is done purely in order to make the compiler's job easier.

Type Declarations—A Summary

All type declarations are given together. Figure 10.4 gives the syntax for the declaration section of a block (program or procedure).

Types may be defined in terms of other constants and in terms of other types. In fact, it can aid readability to do so. For example, a program might open as follows:

```
program Sample(input, output);
    const Low = 0;
          High = 100;
    type Index = Low..High;
         List = array[Index] of real;
    var X, Y: real;
        I: Index;
        A, B: List;
```

Notice that the type declarations come after the constant declarations and before the variable declarations. Also notice that no type name is used before it is defined.

local types

Just like the other kinds of declarations, type declarations may be local to a procedure. The order of local declarations in a procedure is the same as that for a program.

It is usually possible to use a type definition directly instead of first defining a type name. Hence, the following program opening is equivalent to the preceding one:

```
program Sample(input, output);
    const Low = 0;
          High = 100;
    var X, Y: real;
        I: Low..High;
        A, B: array[Low..High] of real;
```

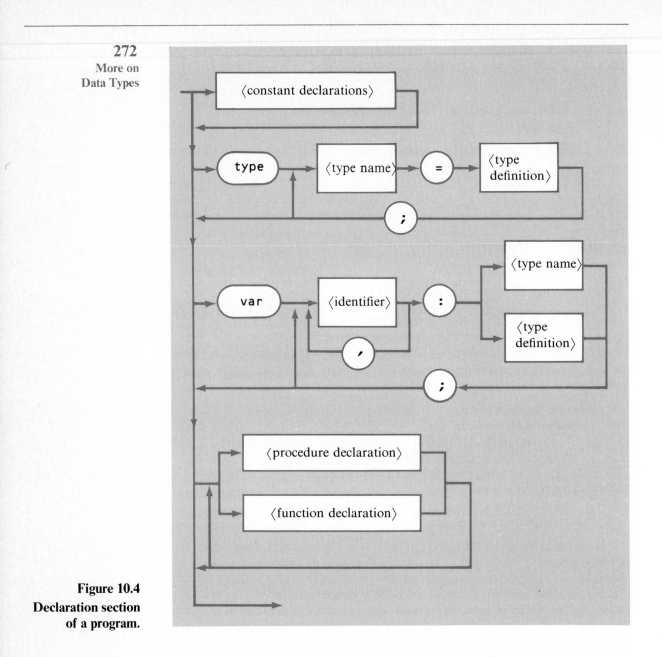

Figure 10.4
Declaration section
of a program.

parameter
types

However, it is better to declare a name for complicated types and to refer to the type by its defined name. In some cases it is absolutely necessary to use a type name. One such case is that of the formal parameter list of a procedure or function heading. The type of a formal parameter must be given by a type name rather than a type definition. For example, the following is not allowed:

```
procedure Sort(var A: array[Low..High] of integer);
                    {NOT ALLOWED}
```

Instead, it is necessary to define a type name such as the type **List** defined in the first sample program heading of this section; the type name is then used in the procedure heading as follows:

```
procedure Sort(var A: List);
```

Type Equivalence

In Pascal, two types are not the same unless they have the same name. For example, consider the type declarations below:

```
type FirstName = array[1..10] of integer;
     SecondName = array[1..10] of integer;
```

In Pascal, the two types **FirstName** and **SecondName** are considered to be *different* types. Hence, among other things, an actual parameter of type **First-Name** can not be substituted for a formal parameter of type **SecondName** in a procedure call. Another instance of this, which is more likely to arise in practice, is the following set of declarations:

```
type FirstName = array[1..10] of integer;
var A: array[1..10] of integer;
```

With these declarations, the array **A** cannot be used as an actual parameter of type **FirstName**. The way to avoid all these problems is obvious: always declare a unique name for an array type and always refer to it by that name. This lesson applies to all defined types and not just to arrays.

Example—Sorting an Array

Figure 10.5 shows a procedure for sorting an array **A** as well as enough of the rest of the program to understand the procedure. In Figure 10.5, and in future programs as well, omitted portions of the program are indicated by dots. This procedure uses a simple algorithm called *bubble sort*. The **for** loop checks each pair of adjacent values to see if they are in the correct order. If they are not, the two values are interchanged. This **for** loop is embedded in a **repeat** loop that performs the complete **for** loop again and again until the array is sorted. Figure 10.6 shows the changes in an array **A** after each iteration of the **repeat** loop.

bubble sort

Notice that in the procedure **BubbleSort** the final value of the **for** loop control variable is:

```
High - 1
```

It is not **High**. This is because the loop body considers index

```
I + 1
```

If the final value for **I** were taken to be **High**, then the program would try to find

off by one errors

```
program UsesSorting(input, output);

const Low = 1;
      High = 10;
type Index = Low..High;
     List = array[Index] of integer;
var . . .
         . . .

procedure Exchange(var X, Y: integer);
{Interchanges the values of X and Y.}
   var TEMP: integer;
begin{Exchange}
   TEMP := X;
   X := Y;
   Y := TEMP
end; {Exchange}

procedure BubbleSort(var A: List);
{Sorts the array A into increasing order.
Postcondition: The array elements have been rearranged
so that A[Low] < A[Low + 1] < ... < A[High]}
   var I: Index;
       InOrder: boolean;
begin{BubbleSort}
   repeat
     InOrder := true; {Tentatively}
     for I := Low to High - 1 do
       if A[I] > A[I+1] then
         begin{then}
           Exchange(A[I], A[I+1]);
           InOrder := false
         end {then}
       {InOrder is true if the last pass through the
       for loop made no interchanges. Hence, if InOrder is
       true, then the array is in order.}
   until InOrder
end; {BubbleSort}
   . . .
```

Figure 10.5
Procedure to sort
an array.

A[1]	A[2]	A[3]	A[4]	A[5]	A[6]	A[7]	A[8]	A[9]	A[10]	Comment
11	10	13	12	16	15	14	17	19	18	I = 1
10	11	13	12	16	15	14	17	19	18	I = 3
10	11	12	13	16	15	14	17	19	18	I = 5
10	11	12	13	15	16	14	17	19	18	I = 6
10	11	12	13	15	14	16	17	19	18	I = 9
10	11	12	13	15	14	16	17	18	19	second time through repeat loop with I = 5
10	11	12	13	14	15	16	17	18	19	

Figure 10.6
Array being sorted by procedure BubbleSort.

the array element numbered

High + 1

However, there is no such index for the array **A**. Hence, this would produce an error message when the program is run. The programmer must ensure that all index values stay within the subrange bounds declared for the array.

To test if the array is sorted, a boolean variable **InOrder** is used as a "flag." That boolean variable is set to **true** before the **for** loop and is only set to **false** if a pair of adjacent values are found to be out of order. Hence, if the boolean variable has value **true** at the end of the **for** loop, then the array is sorted; otherwise the entire **for** loop is repeated.

Example—Partially Filled Array

The required size of an array may not be known at the time a program is written. Sometimes the required size will differ from one run of the program to another. Many programming languages allow the size of an array to be determined by some sort of input at the time that the program is run. Pascal has no such facility. In Pascal, if you do not know how large an array is needed, you must declare the array to be of the largest size the program could possibly need. Then the program is free to use as much or as little of the array as it needs. This does require some care. The program must keep track of how much of the array is used and not reference any indexed variable which is not used. For example, to write the array out to the screen it will not suffice to write out the entire array. Those indexed variables that are not used have undefined values. The program must only write out those elements that are defined. Figure 10.7 displays a program that illustrates this as well as a number of other techniques for manipulating arrays.

Program

```pascal
program InspectGrades(input, output);
{Reads in a list of grades; displays the grades in the order
lowest to highest; shows the amount that each differs from the
median. Assumes that grades are nonnegative integers.}

const Max = 50; {Maximum number of scores}
      MaxPlus = 51; {Max + 1}
type Index = 1..Max;
     IndexPlus = 1..MaxPlus;
     List = array[Index] of integer;
var A: List;
    Last: Index;

procedure ReadList(var A: List; var Last: Index);
{Prompts user; then reads scores into positions 1 through
Last of array A. Last is set to last index of A which is used.}
     var I: IndexPlus;
         Buffer: integer;
begin{ReadList}
   writeln('Enter the list of scores.');
   writeln('Terminate the list with a negative integer.');

   I := 1;
   read(Buffer);

   while (Buffer >= 0) and (I <= Max) do
     begin{while}
       A[I] := Buffer;
       I := I+1;
       read(Buffer)
     end; {while}
   readln;

   Last := I-1;

   if Buffer >= 0 then {Last = Max and there are more scores.}
     begin{then}
       writeln('Could not read in all the data.');
       writeln('Last value stored is ', A[Last])
     end {then}
end; {ReadList}

procedure Exchange(var X, Y: integer);
{Interchanges the values of X and Y.}
   . . .
```

Figure 10.7
Program using a partially filled array.

```
procedure Sort(var A: List; Last: Index);
{Sorts elements 1 to Last of the array A into increasing order.
Precondition: A[1] through A[Last] all have a value; Postcondition:
Array elements rearranged so that A[1] < A[2] < ... < A[Last]}
      var I: Index;
          InOrder: boolean;
begin{Sort}
   repeat
      InOrder := true; {Tentatively}
      for I := 1 to Last - 1 do
        if A[I] > A[I + 1] then
          begin{then}
            Exchange(A[I], A[I + 1]);
            InOrder := false
            {InOrder is true if elements 1 through I + 1
            are in order and is false otherwise.}
          end {then}
   until InOrder
end; {Sort}

function Median(A: List; Last: Index): real;
{Returns the median of those elements of A which are
indexed by 1 through Last. Assumes that A is already sorted.}
      var SmallerHalf: integer;
begin{Median}
   SmallerHalf := Last div 2;
   if Last mod 2 = 1 {i.e., if Last is odd}
     then Median := A[SmallerHalf + 1]
     else Median := (A[SmallerHalf] + A[SmallerHalf + 1]) / 2
end; {Median}

procedure Display(A: List; Last: Index; Median: real);
{Assumes that Median is the median of the values in positions 1 through
Last of array A. Displays the elements in position 1 through Last
of array A and shows the amount that each differs from the median.}
      const Column1 = 5; {spaces in first column of output}
            Column2 = 22; {spaces in second column of output}
      var I: Index;
begin{Display}
   writeln('Median is ', Median:Column1:1);
   writeln('Score':Column1, 'Distance from median':Column2);
   for I := 1 to Last do
     writeln(A[I]:Column1, abs(A[I] - Median):Column2:1)
end; {Display}
```

Figure 10.7
(continues on
p. 278)

```
begin{Program}
    writeln('This program displays sorted scores');
    writeln('and distances from the median.');
    ReadList(A, Last);
    Sort(A, Last);
    Display(A, Last, Median(A, Last))
end. {Program}
```

Sample Dialogue

This program displays sorted scores
and distances from the median.
Enter the list of scores.
Terminate the list with a negative integer.
40 60 0 100 −1
Median is 50.0

Score	Distance from median
0	*50.0*
40	*10.0*
60	*10.0*
100	*50.0*

Figure 10.7 (cont'd)

---

algorithm
design

The program in Figure 10.7 was designed to help instructors see the grade distribution of their classes, perhaps to help decide what scores get an A, B and so forth. The program displays the scores in order and also shows the amount that each differs from the median. Recall that the median is the midpoint score; if there is no exact midpoint, it is the average of the two scores in the middle. The first analysis of the problem might break it down into subtasks as follows:

1. Read in the scores.
2. Sort the scores.
3. Compute the median.
4. Write out the median, the scores and the amount each score differs from the median.

Each of these subtasks is performed by a procedure or function in the program. We will not trace the complete development of the program, but will only discuss some key issues.

The scores are to be read into an array, called **A** in the program. Since the instructor has several classes, we can not specify the exact size of the array. The largest class contains 50 students and so we set the array index to be the range **1..50**. To make it easy to change the program should class sizes change, we declare the upper bound of 50 as the constant **Max**. The variable **Last** is used to hold the index of the last indexed variable used. So the array elements actually used are the elements one through **Last**. The task of reading the scores into the array **A** is performed by the procedure **ReadList**, which is discussed in the next paragraph.

The scores are assumed to be nonnegative. This allows us to use a negative integer to mark the end of the input list. The variable **Buffer** in procedure **ReadList** is used to hold a value read in until it is determined whether it is nonnegative and so whether it should be placed in the array. Anything that holds data that is on its way from one location to another is called a *buffer*. That explains the choice of name for that variable. Alternatively, the program could have read things directly into the array. That would eliminate the need for the buffer variable and possibly be a bit more efficient. However, the buffer variable does seem to make the reasoning clearer.

The variable **Last** is set equal to the last array index used to index a score. Be sure to notice that the counter **I** ends up with a value one more than that desired for **Last**. That explains why it is declared to be of type **IndexPlus**, rather than of type **Index**. The type of **I** depends on the constant **Max**. To avoid any confusion should the program be changed, that dependency is made apparent by using another constant **MaxPlus** whose relation to **Max** is clearly explained at the start of the program.

Notice that the procedure **ReadList** checks to see if the array capacity has been exhausted. If the user attempts to input more than **Max** scores, the array will not be able to hold them all. The test for **I** being less than **Max** prevents the error situation that would result from trying to index a nonexisting array element. The final *if* statement ensures that the user will be warned if not all the data can be read in.

The procedure **Sort** is essentially the same as the procedure **BubbleSort** which we have already designed. However, since only part of the array is used, the procedure **Sort** needs one additional parameter to tell it the index of the last array element that is to be used.

The procedure **Sort** makes a call to the procedure **Exchange**. As usual, we only display the procedure heading for **Exchange**. The complete program would, of course, include a complete procedure declaration there. If it is known that the scores will range from zero to 100, one might be tempted to declare the type **List** as follows:

> *type* List = *array*[Index] *of* 0..100;

However, this will produce a type conflict in the following statement, which occurs in the procedure **Sort**:

> Exchange(A[I], A[I + 1])

The problem is that **Exchange** expects arguments of type **integer**. If we declare the type **List** as above, then the indexed variables are of a subrange type and are not of type **integer**. This is exactly the problem we discussed in the section on subrange types. An alternative approach is to use this other type declaration for the array type and to also change the type **integer** in the procedure heading of **Exchange** to the type **0..100**. This will also work, but to see that it does we must go back and check the details of the procedure **Exchange**.

If the computation of the median is not clear, simply try it on two sample lists, one of size four and one of size five. That should clarify the algorithm.

Array Example with Noninteger Indexes

As we already noted, the index type of an array need not be a subrange of the integers; it can be a subrange type of any ordinal type. The program in Figure 10.8 illustrates the use of the subrange type **'a'..'z'** both as an array index type and as the type of a **for** loop control variable. That program reads in a sentence and then uses an array indexed by **'a'..'z'** to count the number of occurrences of **'a'**, **'b'** and so forth in the sentence. The program assumes that the lower-case letters are contiguous (no symbols between any two alphabetically consecutive lower-case letters). This assumption holds for most, though not all, systems.

Storage Efficiency

If you do not know exactly how large an array a program will need, you might be tempted to declare the array type as follows:

```
type List = array[1..maxint] of integer;
{THIS WILL NOT WORK}
```

Program

```
program CountLetters(input, output);
{Counts the number of occurrences of each letter in a
sentence. Assumes the lower-case letters are contiguous.}

const Period = '.';
      Blank = ' ';
      Comma = ',';
      Semicolon = ';';
 type Letter = 'a'..'z';
      LetterCounter = array[Letter] of integer;
var Count: LetterCounter;

procedure ReadSentence(var Count: LetterCounter);
{Sets Count['a'] equal to the number of 'a'-s
in an input sentence, Count['b'] equal to the number
of 'b'-s and so forth down to Count['z'].}
   var Symbol: char;
```

Figure 10.8
Program using the ordinal type 'a'..'z'.

```
begin{ReadSentence}
    for Symbol := 'a' to 'z' do
      Count[Symbol] := 0;

    read(Symbol);
    repeat
      if not(Symbol in [Blank, Comma, Semicolon]) then
        Count[Symbol] := Count[Symbol] + 1;
      read(Symbol)
    until Symbol in [Period, '!', '?'];
    readln
end; {ReadSentence}

procedure DisplayCount(Count: LetterCounter);
{Outputs the nonzero elements of the array Count.}
    var Symbol: Letter;
begin{DisplayCount}
    for Symbol := 'a' to 'z' do
      if Count[Symbol] <> 0 then
        writeln(Count[Symbol], Blank, Symbol)
end; {DisplayCount}

begin{Program}
    writeln('Enter a sentence.');
    writeln('All lower-case letters please.');
    writeln('End it with a ! or ? or period.');
    ReadSentence(Count);
    writeln('Your sentence contains:');
    DisplayCount(Count)
end. {Program}
```

Sample Dialogue

Enter a sentence.
All lower - case letters please.
End it with a ! or ? or period.
hi, how are you?
Your sentence contains:
        1 a
        1 e
        2 h
        1 i
        2 o
        1 r
        1 u
        1 w
        1 y

Figure 10.8 (cont'd)

This would ensure that the array is about as large as possible. However, as the comment indicates, this will not work. The compiler typically allows one storage location for each indexed variable and the computer may not have enough storage to hold even one such array. Even in less dramatic cases storage can be a consideration. On small computers a program can easily run out of storage. On a large computer excessive use of storage can cause a program to run more slowly.

Ordinarily there is no reason to be obsessed with saving storage, but it is a good idea to avoid blatantly wasteful practices. Arrays use large amounts of storage and you can use several techniques to avoid excessive use of storage for arrays. The most obvious technique is to not declare arrays to be any larger than necessary. Another technique for saving storage has to do with procedures.

efficiency
of variable
parameters

Variable parameters typically consume less storage than value parameters. The reason is that a value parameter is a local variable that is set to the value of the actual parameter. So if **X** is a formal value parameter of an array type and **A** is the corresponding actual parameter, then when the procedure is called, two arrays are in storage, the global array **A** and the local array **X**. If, on the other hand, **X** is a variable parameter, then it is just a formal blank, which gets filled in with **A**; in that case there is only one array in storage. Hence, even if a procedure does not change an array, it may make sense to declare it as a variable parameter in order to save storage.

Packed Arrays
(Optional)

There is a special class of arrays in Pascal that are supposed to be implemented so as to save storage. These are the *packed* arrays. They are not absolutely needed but can sometimes save storage.

The Pascal language does not specify exactly how an array must be implemented. However, the language does specify that there will be two different implementations of arrays. One implementation is supposed to make the program run faster but may use more storage. That form of array consists of the basic array types that we have been discussing. The other implementation is supposed to save storage, but may make the program run much slower.

These storage-efficient arrays are called *packed arrays* and are declared just like ordinary arrays, except that they have the identifier **packed** inserted before the word **array**. For example:

```
PackedList = packed array[0..100] of integer;
```

The word **packed** instructs the compiler to use memory more efficiently. A typical scenario is as follows. Without the word **packed** the compiler will reserve one memory location for each indexed variable. When the word **packed** is included, the compiler will instruct the computer to place ("pack") as many array elements as possible into one memory location.

Packed arrays are used in basically the same way as ordinary arrays. For example, if a packed array **A** is declared by:

var **A: PackedList;**

then it can be used in the same way as an ordinary array of characters except for the few special cases discussed below.

Packed arrays save storage, and so, all other things being equal, it should be preferable to use packed arrays rather than ordinary arrays. However, "all other things" are usually far from equal. There are a number of disadvantages to packed arrays. Hence, they are usually used only when storage efficiency is a major issue. One disadvantage of packed arrays is that they tend to make the program run slower.

One of the biggest disadvantages of packed arrays has to do with using them as parameters to procedures. An indexed variable of a packed array cannot be a variable parameter to a procedure. If a procedure heading is

*restrictions
on packed
arrays*

procedure **Exchange(***var* **X, Y: integer);**

and **A** is declared as above, then the following procedure call is not allowed:

Exchange(A[1], A[2])

This has repercussions beyond user defined procedures. The same prohibition applies to the standard procedures **read**, **readln**, **write** and **writeln**. In order to read values into a packed array, the program must first read them into an ordinary array and then transfer them to the packed array.

Other problems with packed arrays arise from the fact that packed arrays are considered to be a different type than the corresponding ordinary array type. Given the declarations

type **L:** *packed array*[1..80] *of* **char;**
       PL: *array*[1..80] *of* **char;**

the assignment **L := PL** produces a type conflict and is not allowed. Similarly, if a packed array is to be the actual parameter to a procedure, the formal parameter must also be a packed type.

Standard Pascal—Packed Arrays of Characters
(Optional)

There are occasions when storage efficiency is very important. Hence, despite all their disadvantages, packed arrays can occasionally be very useful. The storage savings resulting from using packed arrays is particularly large in the case of arrays of characters. Usually several characters can be packed into one memory location. Since packed arrays of characters behave very much like the type

*assignment
of strings*

string, packed arrays of characters are frequently called *string types* and the identifier **String** is frequently used as the type name for a packed array of characters.

A few special features apply to packed arrays of characters. It is possible to fill a packed array of characters using an assignment operator and a string constant. Packed arrays of characters are also allowed as arguments to **write** and **writeln**. For example, suppose a program contains the following declarations:

```
type String = packed array[1..24] of char;
var S: String;
```

The following code is then allowable:

```
S := 'It sure is tight in here';
writeln(S)
```

The output produced by these two lines is:

It sure is tight in here

Some systems allow the use of a packed array of characters in a **read** or **readln** statement as a way of reading a string constant into the array. However, many other systems do not allow the **read** and **readln** statements to be used in this way.

Packed arrays of characters may be compared using the less-than relation **<**. The ordering is approximately alphabetic ordering. However, the exact result of a comparison will vary from one implementation to another.

When filling a packed array with a string constant, remember that the length of the array is important and any constant assigned to it must have exactly the same number of letters as the array has elements. To place the constant **'Lots of room to fill'** into the array **S** declared above, you must pad it with four spaces like so:

```
S := 'Lots of room to fill    '
```

Summary of Problem Solving and Programming Techniques

Declaring variables to be of a subrange type, or other type with a small number of values, is a good way to get the computer to do some error checking for you. If you expect the values of some variable to be in the range, say, **0..10**, then declare the variable to be of this subrange type rather than of the type **integer**.

An array type can be used to produce a unified naming scheme for a collection of related values. A big advantage of array types is that by manipulating the array index a program can actually compute the name of a (indexed) variable.

Arrays do present some special problems. When using arrays and *for* loops, a common mistake is to try to index one element more than the declared size of the array. If the program attempts to find an array element with an index outside the declared range for the array, an error results and the program usually is terminated immediately. In Pascal, the size of an array must be declared at the time the program is written. Hence, if the desired size will vary from one run of the program to another, then the array must be declared to be of the largest size possible. In that case, the program must keep track of which indexed variables are actually used, since the values of unused indexed variables are undefined.

◇

It would produce a dreadful mess if we were to do anything together. You see, we're different types.

Overheard at a cocktail party

◇

Summary of Pascal Constructs

type declaration

Syntax:

> *type* ⟨type name 1⟩ = ⟨type definition 1⟩;
> ⟨type name 2⟩ = ⟨type definition 2⟩;
> . . .
> ⟨type name *n*⟩ = ⟨type definition *n*⟩;

Example:

```
type Index = 0..100;
     List = array[Index] of char;
```

The type names are identifiers chosen by the programmer. The type definitions can be any type definitions described in this chapter or in following chapters. The type declaration section of a block comes after the constant declarations and before the variable declarations. The identifier *type* is used only once, even if there is more than one type definition.

subrange type

Syntax:

> ⟨lower limit⟩..⟨upper limit⟩

Example:

```
1..100
```

Form of a subrange type definition. ⟨lower limit⟩ and ⟨upper limit⟩ must be constants of the same ordinal type. ⟨lower limit⟩ must be less than or equal to ⟨upper limit⟩.

array types
Syntax:

> ***array*[**⟨index type⟩**]** *of* ⟨component type⟩

Examples:

> ***array*[0..100]** *of* integer

> ***array*[Index]** *of* char

Form of an array type definition. ⟨index type⟩ must be either the definition of a subrange type or the name of a subrange type. The ⟨component type⟩ may be any type we have seen so far. (To be precise, it can be any type which does not involve files, a class of types discussed in Chapters 13 and 16.)

array declaration
Syntax:

> ***var*** ⟨array variable name⟩**:** ⟨array type name⟩**;**

Example:

> ***var*** A: List;

The way to declare an array variable. It is just like declaring a variable of any other type. Note that the array variable is declared without appending any square brackets or indexes. The sample array type List is defined in the first entry of this summary.

indexed variable
Syntax:

> ⟨array name⟩**[**⟨index expression⟩**]**

Example:

> A[I + 1]

An indexed variable of the array ⟨array name⟩. The ⟨index expression⟩ may be any expression that evaluates to a value in the index type of the array.

Exercises

Self-Test and Interactive Exercises

1. Determine the ordering of the letters on your system. Do lower-case letters come before upper-case letters or after them, or are they intermixed? Are there any special characters mixed in with the letters? For example, is there any character between ´A´ and ´B´?

2. Write a program that will read six letters into an array and will then output them in reverse order.

3. Which of the following are legal type definitions:

```
type SmallNegInteger = -100..-1;
     Alias = real;
     GradePoint = 0.0..4.0;
     NeedList = array['a'..'z'] of SmallNegInteger;
     Count = array[0.0..4.0] of integer;
```

4. Give suitable type declarations for data of each of the following kinds: exam scores in the range zero to 100; the nonnegative integers; a list of 10 scores, each in the range zero to 100.

5. The following piece of code is supposed to test an array of elements to see if they are in order. It contains a bug. What is it?

```
var InOrder: boolean;
    I: integer;
    A: array[First..Last] of integer;
    . . .
      . . .
InOrder := true;
for I := First to Last do
   if A[I] > A[I + 1] then InOrder := false
```

6. The following piece of code is supposed to add all the elements in an array **A** with 100 elements. It does not work. What is wrong with it and how should it be fixed?

```
Sum := 0;
for Element := A[1] to A[100] do
  Sum := Sum + Element
```

7. Write a program that will allow the user to type in up to 10 positive numbers and will then echo back the numbers typed in. Have the user terminate the list with a negative number.

8. Insert the trace statements shown below inside the **for** loop of the procedure **BubbleSort** in Figure 10.5. Redefine the constant **High** to be **10**, embed the procedure in a program, run the program and observe how the array elements are moved by the bubble sort algorithm.

```
{Output the whole array}
for J := Low to High do
      write(A[J]);
writeln;
```

You will need to add suitable **begin/end** pairs and to declare the variable **J**.

9. (Uses the optional section "The Functions **ord, chr, pred** and **succ**.") Determine the "clear screen" character number for your system. Feel free to use a **for** loop to find it by looking at all possible characters. Feel free to look it up in a manual or to ask a friend.

10. (Uses the optional section "Enumerated Types.") Can a program read in a value of an enumerated type from the keyboard? Can it write one to the screen?

11. Write a program that will read in a person's name in the format:

First name ⟨Middle name or initial or nothing⟩ Last name!

The program should then output the name in the format:

Last name, First name Middle initial.

If the person input no middle name or initial, then the output should of course omit the middle initial. The program should work the same whether or not the user places a period after the middle initial.

12. A queue is a list that is used in a restricted way. Items are always added to the end of the list. For example, when X is added to A, B, C the result is A, B, C, X. Items can only be removed from the front of the list. In order to remove C from the list, A and B must first be removed. Write a set of procedures for treating an array of characters as a queue. There should be procedures for insertion and deletion. The limits of the array index should be defined constants of type **integer**. Allow the possibility that the number of elements in the queue is less than the size of the array.

13. Modify the program in Figure 10.7 in four ways: The scores are listed in the order highest to lowest rather than lowest to highest. The average as well as the median is computed. The distance of each score from the average is shown. The value of **Max** is changed to **10**.

14. Two related arrays with the same indices are often called *parallel arrays*. They can be used to keep track of more than one value for each index. Use parallel arrays in a program that reads in five playing cards and then displays the hand sorted for poker; i.e., cards of the same value are grouped together and the groups are sorted by value. Each card has a value (2 to 10, ace, king etc.) and a suit (clubs, diamonds, spades or hearts).

15. Write a program that will read in a sentence and then output the sentence with letters corrected for capitalization. In other words, the output sentence should start with an upper-case letter but contain no other upper-case letters. Do not worry about proper names. The input sentence should be terminated with a period, question mark or exclamation mark. For example, the input

the Answer IS 42!

should produce the output:

The answer is 42!

(This program can be written more cleanly using material in the optional section "The Functions **ord**, **chr**, **pred** and **succ**.")

16. Write a program to read in four letters and then output all 24 permutations of these letters. Use an array to hold the four letters. Do not cut corners in designing this one; it can be confusing.

17. (Uses the optional section "Enumerated Types.") Write two procedures that perform the equivalent of reading and writing the type **WeekDay** defined in Figure 10.1. For example, the procedure for writing might be called **DayWrite** and then the statement

```
DayWrite(Fri)
```

should cause the word *Fri* to be written to the screen. Embed the procedures in a test program.

18. Write a program that will read in two lists of 10, or fewer, numbers each into one of two arrays. The input is assumed to be in numeric order. The program will then output a list of all the (up to 20) numbers in numeric order. This is called *merging* the lists.

19. Bubble sort is only one of many known sorting algorithms. Another simple sorting algorithm is *selection sorting*. In selection sorting the algorithm first finds the smallest element in the array and exchanges it with the first array element. At that point the correct element is in the first position. It then finds the smallest element in the rest of the array (i.e., in all but the first position) and exchanges that element with the second element. It then positions the third smallest etc., until the entire array is sorted. Write a procedure that sorts the same type of arrays as **BubbleSort** (Figure 10.5) but uses the selection sort algorithm.

20. Compare the procedure from the previous section to the procedure **BubbleSort**. Add extra code to each procedure to count the number of comparisons and the number of interchanges. Run both algorithms on arrays of the following sorts: one that starts out already sorted, one that is sorted backwards (largest to smallest) and at least three that are in random order.

21. Write a program to play *Nim* using five piles of sticks. Use an array to store the size of the piles. The game is explained in Exercise 21 of Chapter 9.

22. Write a procedure declaration for a procedure called **Deal** that sets the value of a variable parameter to a value that represents a card chosen at random from a standard 52-card deck. The function should also keep track of the cards already dealt out, so that it does not deal a card twice. Use an array parameter to keep track of the cards already dealt out. There is no need to keep track of suits (clubs, hearts etc.).

23. Write a program to play blackjack which uses the procedure **Deal** from the previous exercise. The program deals two cards to the user and two cards to itself (all cards are shown to the user). The user can then request more cards until he/she is busted or wants to stop. The program then deals additional cards to itself until its score exceeds 16. Allow the user to play additional hands until the user wants to stop or until the entire deck is used. The program in Figure 6.14 may be of some help.

24. Since phone dials have letters as well as numbers, some phone numbers spell words. For example 452-4357 is also 452-HELP. Write a program to help people find words for phone numbers. The program should read in the last four digits of a phone number and then output all possible letter versions of that number. For example, 4357 can be HELP. It can also be GDJP. It can also be other letter combinations. Use three arrays indexed by **0..9** to hold the three letters that correspond to each number. There are no letters for **0** or **1**. Do something graceful with those digits. If you prefer, you can use **1..9** or **2..9** as the array index type.

11

Program Design Methodology

The Analytical Engine has no pretensions whatever to *originate* anything. It can do whatever we *know how to order it* to perform. It can *follow* analysis; but it has no power of *anticipating* any analytical relations or truths. Its province is to assist us in making *available* what we are already acquainted with.

Ada Augusta, Countess of Lovelace

Chapter Contents

The writing of a program can be divided into three stages: the problem solving stage, including problem definition and algorithm design; the code writing stage; and, finally, testing and debugging. Throughout this book we have described a number of techniques to apply at each of the three stages. In this chapter we summarize these techniques and then go on to discuss a few other issues connected with the design and maintenance of computer programs.

Some Guidelines for Problem Solving

The first computer similar in character to today's machines was designed by Charles Babbage, an English mathematician and physical scientist. The project began sometime before 1822, consumed the rest of his life and, despite the fact that he never completed the construction of the machine, the design was a conceptual milestone in the history of computing. His colleague, Ada Augusta, was an interesting figure in a number of ways. She was the daughter of the poet Byron. Later she became Countess of Lovelace. It is primarily through her writings that the work of Babbage has been made available to the world. Indeed, she is frequently given the title of the first computer programmer. Her comments, quoted in the chapter opening, still apply to the process of solving problems on a computer. Computers are not magic and do not, at least as yet, have the ability to formulate sophisticated solutions to all the problems we encounter. Computers simply do what the programmer *orders* them to do. The solutions to problems are carried out by the computer, but the solutions are formulated by the programmer. Hence, in order to solve problems on a computer, you must know how to design algorithms.

If we could provide you with a method that is guaranteed to lead you to a correct algorithm for any problem you might encounter, then programming would be a very simple task. However, neither this nor any other book can provide such a method. There is no algorithm for writing algorithms. Designing algorithms is a creative process. There are, however, some guidelines that can sometimes help in your search for algorithms. These guidelines have some similarity to an algorithm for writing algorithms. They do, however, fall short of being an algorithm for producing algorithms in two ways: the steps are not precisely defined and they are not guaranteed to produce a correct algorithm. The guidelines are listed in Figure 11.1.

The algorithm may be produced at any point after step 1. The earlier the better. For example, if you are asked to write a program for computing the square root of a number, you could design an algorithm from scratch. However, if you simply take an existing algorithm that has stood the test of time, it is likely to be more efficient and less likely to contain any subtle errors. In this extreme case there is even a predefined Pascal function to do the task. In other cases, such as sorting a list, there is no predefined Pascal procedure for the task, but there are a number of well-known algorithms for the problem, such as the bubble sort algorithm discussed in Chapter 10. You may wish to solve these problems on your own as a training exercise, but in a "real world" situation, where it is the performance of the program which counts, you should always see what algorithms others have produced. *use known algorithms*

Step 3 requires that you cultivate a "bag of tricks," or do a search of the literature, or both. A number of tricks are well known to experienced programmers. Often they have to do with choosing and manipulating a data representation. An example of one such trick is the use of a temporary variable. That trick was used in designing the procedure **Exchange** (Figure 5.1), which we discussed in Chapter 5. Other examples were discussed in Chapter 10 when we *standard tricks*

1. Formulate a precise statement of the problem to be solved by the algorithm.
2. See if somebody has already formulated an algorithm to solve the problem.
3. See if any standard techniques ("tricks") can be used to solve the problem.
4. See if the problem is a slight variation of a problem for which somebody has already formulated an algorithm. If so, try to adapt that known algorithm to the new problem.
5. Break the problem into subproblems and apply this method to each of the subproblems.
6. If all else fails, simplify the problem, and apply this method to the simplified problem. When you obtain a solution to the simplified problem try to adapt the algorithm to fit the real problem. If that fails or if the algorithm produced is unclear, incorrect or inappropriate to the real problem, then discard this first attempt and start the process all over again at step 1. (You should then have a better feel for the problem and a better chance of success.)

Figure 11.1
Some guidelines
for algorithm
design.

---

discussed filling arrays with data read in from the keyboard. The use of a buffer variable and the use of a variable to remember how much of the array is filled are two techniques we presented there. (Figure 10.7 shows a sample program and the accompanying text explains the "tricks.") A number of other and more powerful standard techniques are discussed in other chapters of this book, particularly Chapters 14, 15 and 17. Frequently these so-called "tricks" are rare and brilliant insights that are easy to understand and use, but difficult to discover on your own.

adapting
another
algorithm

As a simple example of step 4, consider the following code for computing the sum of the numbers stored in an array **A**:

```
Sum := 0;
for I := First to Last do
    Sum := Sum + A[I]
```

If we instead wish to compute the product of all the numbers in the array, we can adapt the algorithm by substituting multiplication for addition and by substituting **1** for **0**. If we also rename the variable **Sum** to **Product**, that yields:

```
Product := 1;
for I := First to Last do
    Product := Product * A[I]
```

top-down
design

Step 5 is the top-down design strategy that we have been using and advocating throughout this book. The subproblems are attacked by these same guidelines, starting with step 1. Eventually the subproblems become so small that their solutions are obvious or one of the other steps applies, such as when there is a well-known solution to the subproblem.

Sometimes step 6 can be a variation on step 5. First design an algorithm with some features missing, then design embellishments for the missing features. The change making program we designed earlier in this book is an example of this technique. In Chapter 4 we designed the basic program for calculating change. In Chapter 7 we showed how to enhance it to have much neater and clearer output. Step 6 is also the step to use when you are completely stumped by a problem and need a way to overcome a mental block. If you cannot solve the problem at hand, solve a related and simpler problem as a practice exercise. That should give you some new insights. Then throw out the practice algorithm and start over. Do not be reluctant to throw out an algorithm or program. It is usually faster and easier to design an algorithm from scratch than to salvage a poor design. (If the idea of step 6 is less than clear, it may help to review the two sections of Chapter 7 entitled "Iterative Enhancement" and "The Throwaway Program".)

These are all just guidelines. You should always consider them, but you need not adhere to them rigidly. In particular, the order of steps (especially the order of steps 3, 4 and 5) is certainly not rigid. Moreover, they are certainly not a complete list of known techniques. They are merely a general plan of attack that can and should be augmented with other design techniques. In Chapter 8 (particularly in the optional sections) we discussed some additional techniques that apply to the design of loops. Those techniques can be used in conjunction with the plan of attack given in Figure 11.1.

Writing Code

When a program is divided into subtasks, the algorithms for the subtasks can and should be coded and tested separately. Even when simply coding somebody else's algorithm, divide the algorithm into subparts and code the subparts separately. That way they can be tested and debugged separately. It is relatively easy to find a mistake in a small procedure. It is nearly impossible to find all the mistakes in a large untested program that was coded and tested as a single large unit, rather than as a collection of well-defined modules. The rules we have been advocating for indenting and documentation all apply to the task of writing code. In fact, they apply even earlier. Pseudocode should have an indenting pattern and a collection of comments that will carry over with only minor changes to the final Pascal code.

Testing and Debugging

The three-stage division consisting of problem solving, coding and finally testing and debugging is a very neat conceptual division. However, the division is not, or at least should not be, very rigid. Some coding and debugging for some tasks can be done before the complete algorithm is derived. When a task is broken into subtasks, some simple testing can and usually should be done immediately. If the tasks are well defined and fit together simply enough, then a pencil-and-paper simulation of the algorithm can be used to test this reformulation of the problem. If the test cannot be carried out with pencil and paper, then a skeleton of a program can be written to see if the pieces will fit together. If the pieces do not fit together, then there is no point in proceeding to derive algorithms for the subtasks.

For example, consider the following task. Suppose we wish to gather statistics on how much time student programmers spend at the terminal during any one session. Perhaps this will be used to help redesign the chairs so that students will be more comfortable while coding up their homework assignments. To get a good profile of usage, we want a program that will compute the average time per session for each individual student, as well as the average session length averaged over all sessions used by all students. The input is to consist of a list of students, with each student's name followed by a list of the times that student spent in each individual session. Dividing this task into subtasks might produce the following pseudocode:

1. Compute each student's average time per session.

2. Output the averages.

3. Compute the average of the student averages obtained in 1 and output that as the overall average.

The presence of a logical flaw in this algorithm can be discovered by testing, even before algorithms for the subtasks are designed. Consider the following sample data:

Joseph Cool:
    10 min., 10 min.

Sally Workhard:
    60 min., 60 min., 60 min., 60 min.,
    60 min., 60 min., 60 min., 60 min.

We do not need a computer to simulate the pseudocode on this simple data. The two student averages are trivially seen to be 10 and 60 min. Now step 2 of the pseudocode says to average these two numbers, which yields:

$$(10 + 60)/2 = 35 \text{ min.}$$

The algorithm's computation of the average session length is wrong. A little bit of pencil-and-paper or mental arithmetic or a hand calculator will show that the average length of a session is really:

$$(2*10 + 8*60)/10 = 50 \text{ min.}$$

As it turns out, the average length of a session is not the average of the individual student averages.

All programs should be divided into procedures and the procedures, as well as the interaction between procedures, should be tested separately. This general technique was described in more detail in the section of Chapter 4 entitled

"Top-Down and Bottom-Up Strategies." Below, we give some hints on how to test and debug the individual procedures.

Programming errors can be divided into three classes: syntax errors, run-time errors and logical errors. A *syntax error* occurs when a portion of the program violates the syntax rules of the programming language, for example, omitting a required semicolon or an **end**. These are usually easy to find. The compiler will discover them and produce an error message. The error message may not accurately describe the nature or location of the error, but it definitely does indicate an error and the location given is very likely to be the approximate location of the error.

*syntax
errors*

Run-time errors are also errors that result from the program violating the rules of the language, in our case Pascal. However, they are not syntax errors and so are not discovered by the compiler. As illustrated in Figure 11.2, the two types of errors are discovered at different stages of program processing. A run-time error is only detected when the program is run. For example, the statement below will produce a run-time error if the value of **N** is zero:

*run-time
errors*

```
X := 1 / N
```

Whether or not it is an error depends on running the program to see if **N** does receive the value zero. Run-time errors also produce an error message that gives some hint of the location and nature of the error. They are harder to find than syntax errors but still have the advantage that they are likely to produce an error message, although they are not guaranteed to do so. That is because they may only occur for certain inputs and not for others. For example, the above line of code will not produce a run-time error on those inputs that cause **N** to take on any value other than zero. (Additional discussion of both syntax errors and run-time errors can be found in the section of Chapter 3 entitled "Testing and Debugging.")

The third type of error is the hardest to locate. *Logical errors* are errors in the algorithm or in the translation of the algorithm from pseudocode to Pascal. They are difficult to find because the computer does not give any error message. They occur when the program is a perfectly valid Pascal program that performs a perfectly valid computation and gives out an answer. The only problem is that the answer is sometimes wrong. For example, the following piece of code is supposed to output the average of the elements in the array **A** of type *array*[0..10] *of* **integer**:

*logical
errors*

example

```
Sum := 0;
for I := 0 to 10 do
    Sum := Sum + A[I];
writeln(Sum / 10)
```

This is a perfectly valid piece of Pascal code and will run with no problems or error messages. For most values of the array elements the answers will even look "about right." However, there is a logical error. Since the array bounds go from **0** to **10**, there are 11 elements and not 10 elements. Hence the last line should be:

```
writeln(Sum / 11)
```

**Figure 11.2
Syntax and
run-time errors.**

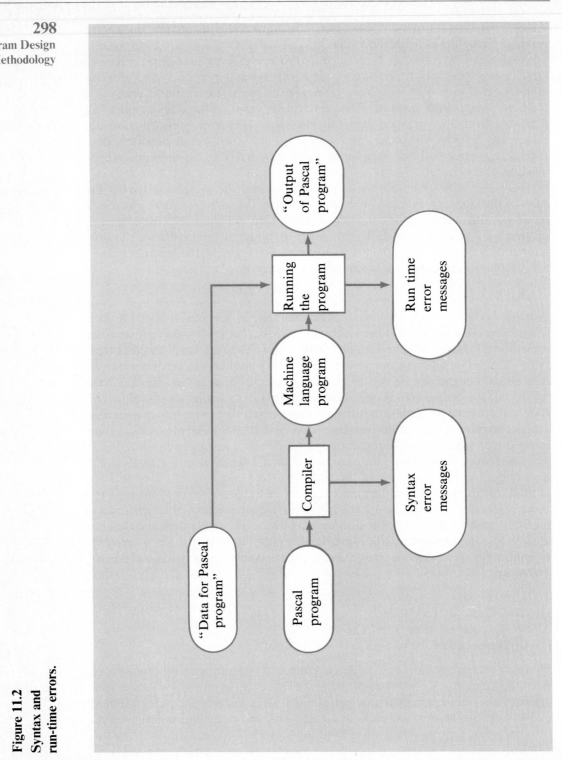

When a logical error is discovered, it is usually not too difficult to fix. The problem is finding the logical errors. Since the computer produces no error messages, it is difficult to be certain that a program contains no logical errors.

Correcting run-time and logical errors is a three-stage process. The first stage is error avoidance. If a program is carefully designed along the lines we have suggested in this book, then the number of such errors should be few. The second stage is testing. In the testing stage, the program is checked to see if it contains any mistakes. By testing procedures separately, this will also serve to tell which procedure(s) contains the mistake(s). The last stage is debugging. In that stage the exact nature of the error is determined and the error is corrected.

*choosing
test data*

When testing a procedure, you want to find some input values or parameter values that will expose possible errors. One way to catch an error is to find input values for which you know the correct output—perhaps by doing the calculation in some other way or by looking the answer up. Then you can run the procedure or program on those values. If the procedure's answer differs from the correct answer, then you know there is a mistake in the procedure. However, always remember that just because a procedure or program works correctly on 10 or even 100 test cases, this is not a guarantee that it does not contain an error. It might make a mistake on the next new input that is tried.

*boundary
values*

One other technique to increase your confidence in a program is to use a variety of different types of test data. For example, if the datum is an integer, try large positive numbers, small positive numbers, zero, a small negative number, a large negative number, and any other categories that you can think of. For loops, try data that will cause the loop to be executed zero, one and more than one time (or as many of those cases as are possible for the loop in question). Be sure to use a representative sample of the possible *boundary values* as test data. There is no precise definition of the notion of a boundary value but you should develop an intuitive feel for what it means. If a loop will be executed some number of times between 1 and 10, depending on the data, then be sure to have a test run that executes it 1 time and one that executes the loop 10 times. If a procedure does something to only one element of an array, always test the first and last elements of the array. Of course, you should also test a "typical" (nonboundary) value.

*fully
exercising
code*

Still another testing technique consists of *fully exercising* the procedure or program. This technique consists of using a collection of test cases that will cause each part of the procedure to be executed. That means executing each statement and substatement and also making each boolean expression that controls a loop assume the value **true** at least once and assume the value **false** at least once. For example, consider the following piece of code:

```
if X > 0 then Procedure1
else if Y <= 0 then Procedure2
else if Z >= 0 then Procedure3
else Procedure4
```

The call to **Procedure4** will never take place unless the test data cause **X** to be less than or equal to zero and at the same time cause **Y** to be greater than zero and at the same time cause **Z** to be less than zero. The call to **Procedure3** will never

if ⟨boolean exp⟩
    then ⟨statement 1⟩
    else ⟨statement 2⟩

To test both statements requires at least two test runs: one that makes ⟨boolean exp⟩ **true** and one that makes it **false**.

while ⟨boolean exp⟩ **do** ⟨statement⟩

**Figure 11.3
Fully exercising
code.**

There should be at least two test runs: one that makes ⟨boolean exp⟩ **false** and so skips the loop and one that makes it **true** and so executes at least one iteration of the loop.

take place unless the test data cause **X** to be less than or equal to zero and at the same time cause **Y** to be greater than zero but at the same time cause **Z** to be greater than or equal to zero. Fully exercising a program is difficult to do. However, if the program is divided into procedures and the procedures are small, then it is possible to fully exercise each procedure separately. Figure 11.3 illustrates some other examples of fully exercising code.

*testing
all paths*

An even better test of a program is something called *testing all paths*. When testing all paths, the tests not only cause each statement to be executed at least once but also cause each possible combination of branch and loop behaviors to take place. Some combinations may be impossible to achieve, but the test set should cause all other combinations to occur.

To see the difference between fully exercising a piece of code and testing all paths, consider the following code:

```
if X > 0
      then A := B
      else A := X;
if Y > 0
      then C := B
      else C := Y
```

This piece of code can be fully exercised with two inputs, one in which both **X** and **Y** are positive, and one in which they are both negative. To test all paths requires four tests as shown in Figure 11.4. Testing all paths is a good testing strategy. Unfortunately it is often difficult to find a set of test cases that will test all paths. Frequently you must settle for fully exercising the procedure and then testing as many paths as you reasonably can.

debugging

Testing can tell you that a program or procedure contains an error. Moreover, if it is done correctly, it will tell you which procedure contains the error, but it usually will not tell you what the error is. Once you know that a procedure

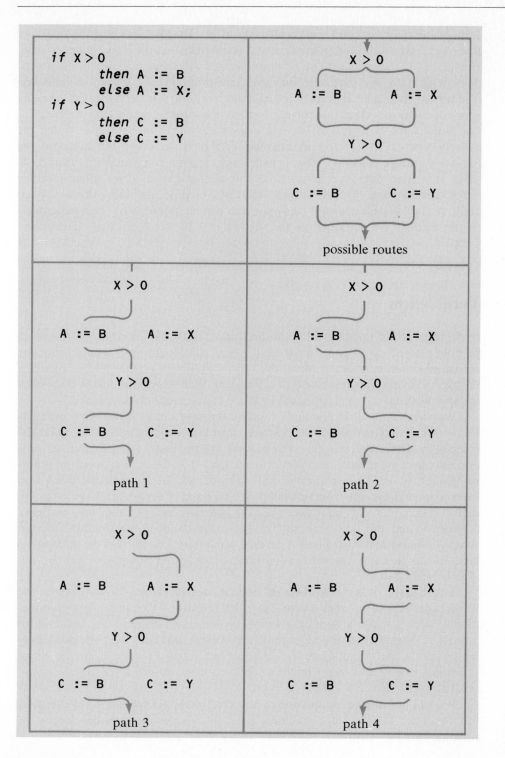

Figure 11.4
Testing all paths.

tracing

contains an error, you still must correct the error. That is the debugging stage. At that stage frustrated programmers are sometimes tempted to make random changes, in the hope that these random changes will magically correct the errors. They seldom do, and moreover, they make the program even less understandable. The way to correct an error is to test and analyze until you have located the exact cause of the error. Once the cause is located, the cure is usually easy to find.

Usually the best way to find the exact location of an error is to watch the procedure while it performs its calculation; that is, to watch the values of the various variables changing. This is called *tracing*. When a variable is traced, its value is written out either every time it is changed or at some other specified times. Some systems provide special debugging facilities for doing this automatically. If your system does not, then you can use temporary `writeln` statements in the manner we described in the section of Chapter 8 entitled "Debugging Loops."

Verification

In the ideal world there would be no need for testing and debugging, because all programs would be correct. In the ideal world, the programmer would prove the correctness of a program in much the same way that a mathematician proves a theorem. Proving the correctness of a program, that is, proving that it does what the specifications say it is supposed to do, is called program *verification*.

Whether or not it is practical to prove the correctness of large programs is still a hotly debated issue. In practice, testing and debugging will never be completely eliminated, but they may become less necessary and program verification may become a more common practice than it is today. For small programs verification is usually a realizable task. The debate arises when the discussion turns to large programs. There certainly is little hope of verifying a large program, such as a compiler, if you are given just the program code (without very extensive comments) and the specifications. On the other hand, if the top-down design strategy is used and each piece is verified separately, then it may be a tractable task. In this scenario, the verification takes place as the program is written, not after it is finished.

The debate over verification is one of degree. How formal should the verification be and to what extent can it be relied on? Certainly a programmer should always make a serious attempt to somehow demonstrate (at least to himself or herself) that the algorithms are correct and that the code accurately represents the algorithm. Code should never be designed by simply writing down something that "looks like it might work" and then running a few test cases "to see if it works."

We will not discuss verification in any great detail. If you would like to get a feel for what a proof of correctness looks like, read the optional section of Chapter 8 called "Invariant Assertions and Variant Expressions."

Portability

A *portable* program is one that can be moved from one computer system to another with little or no change. Since programs represent a large investment in programmer time, it pays to make them portable.

One way to make a program portable is to adhere closely to a *standard version* of the programming language. There are national and international organizations that set standards for the syntax and other details of programming languages. All the standard Pascal programs in this book conform to the ANSI/IEEE standard and to the ISO standard. (The initials have the following meanings: ANSI, American National Standards Institute; IEEE, Institute of Electrical and Electronic Engineers; ISO, International Standards Organization.)

*standard
language*

As impressive as all those initials may look, it is still not true that all the standard Pascal programs in this text will run on any standard Pascal system. There are two reasons for this: the standards do leave some details unspecified, such as exactly how many characters the system will have and the value of `maxint`; also, real systems usually differ at least slightly from the prescribed standard. UCSD Pascal is becoming a de facto standard for personal computers, but there is no standards committee to oversee its development. Despite these shortcomings, standards do serve a purpose. If you adhere to the versions of Pascal described by them, or in this book, then your program will be more portable. For example, if your system initializes all `integer` variables to zero, then do not use this feature. Instead, always explicitly initialize all variables. That way your programs will also work on systems that do not initialize variables. (None of the standards require that variables be initialized and, in fact, most Pascal systems do not do so.)

In this book we have presented both standard Pascal and UCSD Pascal. If portability is very important, then it would pay to write your programs in standard Pascal. The reason is that UCSD Pascal differs from standard Pascal mostly (but not entirely) in that it has more features than standard Pascal has. Hence it is easier to translate a program from standard to UCSD Pascal than to make the translation in the other direction. The two versions are very similar, though, and UCSD Pascal is very widely used. So when a UCSD Pascal feature (such as a predefined string-manipulating function) is available and natural to a program, it usually makes sense to use it. The final decision on whether or not to use features that are available only in UCSD Pascal depends on whether the program is likely to later be moved to a standard Pascal system.

Sometimes implementation-dependent details are unavoidable. For example, there is no command in Pascal that will clear the screen. If you want to clear the screen, you must use some implementation-dependent feature. In order to keep your program more portable, isolate all such implementation-dependent details into clearly labeled procedures. Then, when the program is moved, the things that need to change are easy to find and easy to modify. Input and output tend to be very implementation-dependent. Hence, input and output should always be isolated into procedures.

304

**Program Design
Methodology**

*time
and
storage*

Efficiency

The *efficiency* of a program is a measure of the amount of resources consumed by the program. Traditionally, the only resources considered have been time and/or storage. The less time it uses, the more time efficient a program is. The less storage it uses, the more storage efficient it is.

When running small programs of the type you encounter when first learning to program, efficiency is not usually an issue. If the user waits a few extra seconds for an answer, that is insignificant. A small program is also unlikely to use more than a very small fraction of the available storage. Moreover, if the program is run just a few times, then the savings are likely to be minimal at best. However, when running large programs repeatedly over a long period of time, the amount of time and storage saved can be significant. Computer time and storage cost money. Hence, if a program can be changed so that it runs faster or uses less storage, then, *all other things being equal*, the change should be made.

In some specialized settings efficiency is critically important. If the computer is controlling a hospital patient monitoring system, a fraction of a second delay may mean the patient's life. A very sophisticated storm-predicting program is useless if it takes 2 hours to predict that a tornado will arrive in 1 hour. A program to work in a small wrist calculator or a small satellite may have to make do with very little storage.

*example:
searching
an array*

To illustrate the notion of efficiency, consider the task of searching an array of integers to see whether or not a particular integer is in the array. If the array is called **A** and the integer being searched for is called **Key**, then the following loop will accomplish the task (**First..Last** is the array index type):

```
I := First;
while (Key <> A[I]) and (I < Last) do
  I := I + 1;
if Key = A[I] then writeln(Key, ' is in the array.')
              else writeln(Key, ' is not in the array.')
```

The loop checks each element of the array until it either finds the value **Key** or gets to the end of the array without finding **Key**.

Now let us suppose that we know the array elements are ordered so that:

```
A[First] < A[First + 1] < A[First + 2] < ... < A[Last]
```

In this case we can make the loop run more efficiently, in the sense of taking less time. If we know the list is ordered, then we can stop looking for the value **Key** as soon as the following holds:

```
Key <= A[I]
```

This is because if **Key** equals **A[I]**, we have found the value of **Key**, and if **Key** is less than **A[I]**, then we know that **Key** is smaller than all the array elements that follow and so cannot possibly equal any of them. Hence assuming that the list is ordered, we can replace the boolean expression in the *while* loop with the following:

```
(Key > A[I]) and (I < Last)
```

With this second boolean expression the loop will frequently perform fewer iterations. If the value of **Key** is in the array, then the two loops perform exactly the same number of iterations, but if **Key** is not in the array, then, "on the average," the second loop will perform a little more than half the number of iterations that the first one does. A precise definition of what we mean by "on the average" is beyond the scope of this book. However, the important thing to observe is that the second version does save a large fraction of time on a large number of inputs. The program in Figure 11.5 illustrates the savings for one particular set of values.

Program

```
program Compare(input, output);

const First = 1;
      Last = 10;
type Index = First..Last;
     List = array[Index] of integer;
var A: List;
    I: Index;
    Key: integer;

procedure Search1(A: List; Key: integer);
{Outputs a message saying whether or not Key is
the value of an array indexed variable A[I], for some I.}
    var I: Index;
begin{Search1}
    I := First;
    while (Key <> A[I]) and (I < Last) do
      I := I + 1;
    if Key = A[I]  then writeln(Key, ' is in the array.')
                   else writeln(Key, ' is not in the array.');
    writeln('Search 1 executed ', I - 1, ' loop iterations')
end; {Search1}

procedure Search2(A: List; Key: integer);
{Outputs a message saying whether or not Key is
the value of an array indexed variable A[I], for some I.
Precondition: A[First]  <  A[First + 1] <  ... <  A[Last]}
    var I: Index;
```

Figure 11.5

Comparing two algorithms

(continues on p. 306)

```
begin{Search2}
   I := First;
   while (Key > A[I]) and (I < Last) do
     I := I + 1;
   if Key = A[I]  then writeln(Key, ' is in the array.')
                     else writeln(Key, ' is not in the array.');
   writeln('Search 2 executed ', I - 1, ' loop iterations')
end; {Search2}

begin{Program}
   writeln('Enter 10 integers in ascending order:');
   for I := First to Last do
      read(A[I]);
   readln;
   writeln('Enter a Key to search for:');
   readln(Key);
   Search1(A, Key);
   Search2(A, Key)
end. {Program}
```

Sample Dialogue

Enter 10 integers in ascending order:
2 4 6 8 10 12 14 16 18 2001
Enter a Key to search for:
11
        11 is not in the array.
Search 1 executed   9 loop iterations.
        11 is not in the array.
Search 2 executed   5 loop iterations.

Figure 11.5 (cont'd)

Occasionally, a simple change like the one we just described can improve efficiency significantly. More often, however, the savings due to a minor change is a correspondingly minor savings. In order to make substantial savings, a completely new and more complicated algorithm is usually required. In the next section we discuss the advisability of using a complicated, efficient algorithm as opposed to a simple, less efficient one.

Efficiency versus Clarity

The current trend is to pay less attention to time and storage efficiency. The reasons for this switch are that computer time and storage have become cheaper and other expenses, such as programmer time, have become more costly. It simply does not make sense to pay out thousands of dollars (or even much less) in programmer salary in order to realize a few dollars savings in computer usage.

Frequently there are also other hidden costs in making a program very "efficient." A typical way to arrive at an "efficient" program is to start with a simple, easy-to-understand, correctly running program and to then make changes to the program so that it runs faster or uses less storage. In the process of doing so a number of unfortunate things can happen. The changes may introduce an error. That produces the ultimately inefficient program. Getting the wrong answer quickly is never a bargain. Changing a program to make it run faster may make the program harder to understand. At some later time when the program needs to be changed, this will increase the time needed to change it and will make errors more likely. Large programs typically have a life span in which they are modified numerous times by a series of different programmers. In that situation, clarity is the critically important consideration. When the choice is between clarity and efficiency, it usually pays to choose clarity.

A good rule to follow is the following. First make sure the program is clear and correct. Within those constraints and the constraints of available programmer time, it pays to make the program more time and storage efficient.

Batch Processing

This book is written assuming an interactive computing environment consisting of a video screen and keyboard. In that mode the program is run, and as it is running, the program requests data from time to time and produces output from time to time, typically intermixing input and output. Sometimes computing is done in what is called *batch mode*. In batch mode the program and all the data are fed into the computer at one time, and the output is not available until after the program has run to completion. A typical scenario is to have the program and data on punched cards and to receive the output from a printer.

Until recently, batch processing was the most common method of running a program. Today most programs are designed in an interactive environment. Some problems and some installations do, however, still require batch processing. For example, programs that process large amounts of data normally work in batch mode or something similar to batch mode. If you write a program to do a statistical profile on 5000 families, you do not want the program to prompt the user for data 5000 times. It makes more sense to enter all the data at one time, possibly from the keyboard but more likely on punched cards made up as the data is collected in the field or from data stored on some electronic medium, such as magnetic tape.

As you might guess, a program written to work in batch mode differs from the kinds of interactive programs we have seen, primarily in how it handles input and output. It need not prompt the user to enter data; the data is always there waiting to be read. A second difference is that a batch program can count on the data always being in a fixed format. It need not write out detailed input instructions or echo input or have elaborate routines to recover from errors in entering the input. On the negative side, batch programs are not as "friendly." The user must have at least some technical knowledge about formatting and entering the data. The term *friendly* is used to refer to a program that is easy to interact with, usually because it handles input and output in a natural way, such as being flexible about the exact format of the input.

The modern trend is toward interactive use. Even for those tasks that naturally demand batch processing the tendency is to use a combination of batch and interactive techniques. The bulk of the data is entered into the computer before the program is run, rather like the data for a batch processing job. The program then interacts with the user via a keyboard and screen to let the user know what is happening and to receive directions on how to process the data. If there are large amounts of output, the program directs it to some output device other than the screen, again much like batch processing. That way the output can be studied at leisure. Chapters 13 and 16 deal with programs of this mixed variety. In those programs the bulk of the input is read from secondary storage and large amounts of output may be written to secondary storage, but the programs still carry on a dialogue with the user.

Coping with Large Programming Tasks

*what is
"large"?*

The programs presented in an introductory programming book are extremely small compared to the programs typically worked on by professional programmers. One widely used Pascal compiler consists of almost 7400 lines of high-level-language code. If written as small as the text of this book, that program would occupy over 150 pages! Programs that large are qualitatively as well as quantitatively different from the sorts of small programs we have seen. Like the servant in the Dickens story (quoted at the end of this section), the typical reader of this book has only had a "sip" of programming. It is a larger sip than the servant had, and the reader who completes this book will have tasted programming. However, large programs really do have a different flavor from small programs. All the design principles we have discussed, such as modularity and top-down design, are even more important when designing large programs. But there are some additional considerations that only come into play when programs are very large.

*group
effort*

A program as large as a compiler or a complete operating system is not written by a single person. The effort is too large for any single individual. To take an extreme case, F. P. Brooks reports that the design of the IBM OS/360 operating systems consumed 5000 "man-years." That figure includes support staff and possibly would be lower today. However, it is clear that the job is too large for any single programmer. The production of a piece of software of that size requires a major organizational effort. It is a management feat as well as a design feat. The book by Brooks, cited at the end of this chapter, gives a good description of the management problems involved in designing large programs.

Most of the book is understandable to anyone who has read the first few chapters of this book.

Another feature of large programs is that they represent a large investment of both time and money. Hence, if they are written clearly enough to be easily modified and adapted, rather than discarded in favor of a completely new program, then significant time and money can be saved. In fact, most large programs, like compilers and operating systems, are continually being changed. Bugs are discovered and must be fixed. New features are added. However, even large programs eventually become out of date or deteriorate in quality. Unless a large program is well written and suitable for the task at hand, then just as in the case of a small program, it is more efficient to write a new program than it is to fix the old one.

◇

"Did you ever taste beer?"

"I had a sip of it once," said the small servant.

"Here's a state of things!" cried Mr. Swiveller.... "She *never* tasted it—it can't be tasted in a sip!"

Charles Dickens, The Old Curiosity Shop

◇

Summary of Terms

batch processing   As used in this book, running a program in batch mode means entering the program and all its data at one time and waiting until the program finishes before receiving the output.

efficiency   The efficiency of a program is measured by the amount of resources that the program consumes. The less resources it consumes, the more efficient it is. Time and storage are the resources that are usually considered.

fully exercise   A technique for testing a piece of code (like a program or procedure). It consists of finding a set of test inputs such that running the program on the test inputs will cause each statement and substatement to be executed on at least one of the test runs and will cause each boolean expression that controls a loop to assume the value `true` on at least one run and `false` on at least one run.

logical error   A program error that is due to an error in the algorithm or an error in translating the algorithm into the programming language. Normally logical errors produce no error messages.

portability   A program is portable if it can be moved from one system to another with little or no changes.

run-time error A program error that is discovered by the computer system at the time that the program is run. See **syntax error**.

standard version of a programming language A version of a programming language that is defined by some official standards organization.

syntax error An error consisting of a violation of the syntax rules of a language. Syntax errors are discovered and reported by the compiler. See **run-time error**.

testing all paths A technique for testing a piece of code (like a program or procedure). It consists of finding a set of test inputs such that running the program on the test inputs will cause each possible combination of branch and loop behaviors to occur on at least one of the runs.

tracing Inserting **write** statements into a program so that the values of the variables will be written out as the program performs its calculations. Some systems have debugging facilities that do this automatically.

verification Verifying a program means proving that it meets the specifications for the task it is supposed to perform.

Exercises

Self-Test and Interactive Exercises

1. The following piece of code is supposed to set **Sum** equal to the sum of the first 100 positive numbers. It contains a bug. What is it?

```
Sum := 0;
I := 1;
repeat
  Sum := Sum + I;
  I := I + 1
until I >= 100
```

If you cannot find the bug, then replace **100** by **3** and trace the computation, either with pencil and paper or by embedding the code and a **writeln** statement in a program.

2. Choose some input values to fully exercise the following piece of code (all the variables are of type **integer**):

```
readln(X, B, C)
if X >= 5
    then A := B
    else A := C;
Sum := 0;
while X > 0 do
  begin
    Sum := Sum + X;
    X := X - 1
  end;
```

3. Choose some input values to test all paths in the code of the previous exercise.

4. Redesign the algorithm for computing average terminal session times that was given in the pseudocode in the section entitled "Testing and Debugging." As noted in the text, the pseudocode contains a logical error.

5. What is wrong with the following program? (It correctly computes the average of 100 integers.)

```
program Exercise(input, output);
  type Index = 1..100;
       List = array[Index] of integer;
  var A: List; I: Index; Sum: integer; Average: real;
begin{Program}
  writeln('Enter 100 integers:');
  for I := 1 to 100 do
     read(A[I]);
  Sum := 0;
  for I := 1 to 100 do
     Sum := Sum + A[I];
  Average := Sum / 100;
  writeln('The average is:', Average)
end. {Program}
```

6. If you have access to more than one computer with Pascal available, run some of your programs from previous exercises on two or more machines. Is it necessary to change the programs in any way?

Regular Exercises

7. Write a program to read in a list of 100 or fewer integers and then do any of the following, as the user requests: display the list in sorted order largest to smallest; display the list in sorted order smallest to largest; compute the average; compute the mean; compute percentiles (e.g., the tenth percentile is the 10% of the scores that are highest in value); list the scores in the order largest to smallest or smallest to largest showing how much each differs from the average and/or median. Do this jointly with two or three other people. Each person should do separate subtasks and the code should be integrated into a single program.

8. (To do this one you and another group must have done the previous exercise.) The two groups exchange programs and then each modifies the other's program as follows: The option of computing the standard deviation is added to the program (see Exercise 11 in Chapter 4 for definitions). The user is also given the option of listing the scores in order, either lowest to highest or highest to lowest, with an annotation indicating whether or not the score is within one standard deviation of the average.

9. Exercises 19 and 20 in Chapter 10 are appropriate for this chapter as well.

10. A polynomial

$$a_n x^n + a_{n-1} x^{n-1} + \cdots + a_0$$

can be evaluated in a straightforward way by performing the indicated operations and using the procedure **Power** given in Figure 9.3. An alternative method is to factor the polynomial according to the following formula, known as *Horner's rule*:

$$(\ldots((a_n x + a_{n-1})x + a_{n-2})x + \cdots + a_1) + a_0$$

Write two procedures to evaluate polynomials by these two different methods. The procedures will read n as well as the coefficients a_n, a_{n-1} and so forth from the keyboard. After completely debugging the procedures, insert extra code to count the number of additions and multiplications performed. (Do not forget to count multiplications and divisions performed by all the procedures such as **Power**.)

References for Further Reading

American National Standard Pascal Computer Programming Language, 1983, Institute of Electrical and Electronic Engineers, Inc., New York. A very technical document that is not easy to read, but you may find it interesting to look through.

J. L. Bently, *Writing Efficient Programs*, 1982, Prentice-Hall, Englewood Cliffs, N.J. A good source for more information on writing efficient programs.

F. P. Brooks, *The Mythical Man-Month*, 1975, Addison-Wesley, Reading, Mass. A good collection of essays to give you a feel for the problems involved in writing very large programs.

E. W. Dijkstra, *A Discipline of Programming*, 1976, Prentice-Hall, Englewood Cliffs, N.J. A good series of essays on programming techniques and programming style.

E. W. Dijkstra, "Notes on Structured Programming," in O.-J. Dahl, E. W. Dijkstra and C. A. R. Hoare, *Structured Programming*, 1972, Academic Press, New York. A good essay on programming techniques and programming style.

D. Gries, *The Science of Programming*, 1981, Springer-Verlag, New York. A good source for more information on program verification.

Gerald M. Weinberg, *The Psychology of Computer Programming*, 1971, Van Nostrand Reinhold, New York. A collection of essays on what the title says it is on.

12

Using Recursion

After a lecture on cosmology and the structure of the solar system, William James was accosted by a little old lady.

"Your theory that the sun is the center of the solar system, and the earth is a ball which rotates around it, has a very convincing ring to it, Mr. James, but it's wrong. I've got a better theory," said the little old lady.

"And what is that, madam?" inquired James politely.

"That we live on a crust of earth which is on the back of a giant turtle."

Not wishing to demolish this absurd little theory by bringing to bear the masses of scientific evidence he had at his command, James decided to gently dissuade his opponent by making her see some of the inadequacies of her position.

"If your theory is correct, madam," he asked, "what does this turtle stand on?"

"You're a very clever man, Mr. James, and that's a very good question," replied the little old lady, "but I have an answer to it. And it is this: the first turtle stands on the back of a second, far larger, turtle, who stands directly under him."

"But what does this second turtle stand on?" persisted James patiently.

To this the little old lady crowed triumphantly. "It's no use, Mr. James— it's turtles all the way down."

J. R. Ross, Constraints on Variables in Syntax

Chapter Contents

*recursive
procedures
and
functions*

We have encountered a few cases of circular definitions that worked out satisfactorily. The most prominent examples are the definitions of certain Pascal statements. For example, the definition of a **while** statement says that it must contain another (smaller) statement. Since one possibility for this smaller statement is another **while** statement, there is a kind of circularity in that definition. The definition of the **while** statement, if written out in complete detail, will contain a reference to "**while** statements." In mathematics these kinds of circular definitions are called "recursive definitions." In Pascal a procedure or function may be defined in terms of itself in the same way. To put it more precisely, a procedure or function declaration may contain a call to itself. In such cases the procedure or function is said to be *recursive*. In this chapter we will discuss recursion in Pascal, and more generally we will discuss recursion as a programming and problem solving technique. We start with an example.

Example of a Recursive Function

In Chapter 9 we defined a function called **Power** which computed integer powers of the form:

$$x^n$$

That function was not recursive, but it will set the stage for a recursive version of that function. The function declaration is reproduced in Figure 12.1.

Notice that the version of **Power** given in Figure 12.1 only works for nonnegative values of **N**. Suppose now that we wish to extend the declaration so that the function also works for negative values of **N**. To get a feel for what is needed, let us consider a concrete case. Let us say that **X** is **3.0** and **N** is **−2**. We want

```
Power(3.0, -2)
```

to return the value $(3.0)^{-2}$. But that is equal to:

$$1/(3.0)^2$$

Negative powers are the same as positive powers in the denominator. Hence, if we know that the function **Power** returns the correct answer when **N** is positive, then we can calculate the correct value for **Power(3, -2)** by the expression:

```
1 / Power(3, 2)
```

Now let us replace **−2** by **N**. That will produce the clause needed to extend the function declaration to accommodate negative values of **N**. The correct extra clause for the extended function declaration will be something equivalent to:

```
if N < 0 then Power := 1 / Power(X, -N)
```

```
function Power(X: real; N: integer): real;
{Returns X to the power N. Returns 1 when N equals 0.
    Precondition: N > = 0.}
    var I: integer;
        Product: real;
begin{Power}
    Product := 1;
    for I := 1 to N do
      begin
        Product := Product*X
        {Product is X to the Power I.}
      end;
    Power := Product
end; {Power}
```

Figure 12.1

A nonrecursive function.

Figure 12.2
A recursive function
declaration.

```
function Power(X: real; N: integer): real;
{Returns X to the power N. Returns 1 when N equals 0.
Precondition: If N is negative, then X is not zero.}
    var Product: real;
        I: integer;
begin{Power}
    if N >= 0 then
      begin {then}
        Product := 1;
        for I := 1 to N do
            Product := X*Product;
        Power := Product
      end {then}
    else {if N < 0 then} Power := 1/Power(X, -N)
end;{Power}
```

Remember, **N** is to take on negative values such as **-2**. So **-N** will take on positive values like **2**. (Minus a negative number is a positive number.)

recursive call

We can now put this all together to get a recursive declaration of **Power** that works for negative as well as nonnegative exponents. The declaration is shown in Figure 12.2. The function call

Power := 1 / Power(X, -N)

is called a *recursive call* because it occurs inside the declaration for **Power**.

Let us see what happens when this function is called with some sample values. First let us consider the simple expression:

Power(3.0, 2)

When the function is called, the value of **X** is set equal to **3.0**, the value of **N** is set equal to **2** and the code is executed. Since **2** is greater than zero, the *else* part is ignored. So in this case it is easy to see that the value returned is **9.0**.

example of a recursive call

Next let us try a set of parameters that exercise the recursive part of the declaration. Let us determine the value of:

Power(3.0, -2)

We proceed just as before. When the function is called, the value of **X** is set equal to **3.0**, the value of **N** is set equal to **-2** and the code is executed. Since **-2** is less than zero, the *else* part is executed. So the value returned is the following (remember that since the value of **N** is **-2**, the value of **-N** is **2**):

1 / Power(3.0, 2)

But we already decided that the value of **Power(3.0, 2)** is **9.0**. Hence the value of **Power(3.0, -2)** is **1 / 9.0**, which is approximately **0.11111111**.

A Closer Look at Recursion

Notice that in evaluating the recursive function call **Power(3.0, -2)**, we did not do anything new or different. We treated it just like any of the nonrecursive function calls we saw in previous chapters. We simply plugged in the actual parameters for the formal parameters and then executed the code. When we reached the recursive call **Power(3.0, 2)**, we just repeated this process one more time.

how recursion works

The computer keeps track of recursive calls in the following way. When a function is called, the computer plugs in the actual parameters for the formal parameters and begins to execute the code. If it should encounter a recursive call, then it temporarily stops its computation. This is because it must know the result of the recursive call before it can proceed. It saves all the information it needs to continue the computation later on, and proceeds to evaluate the recursive call. When the recursive call is completed, the computer returns to the outer computation and completes that outer computation. Figure 12.3 illustrates this for the example of the previous section. Notice that when a recursive call is encountered, the current computation is temporarily suspended, and a complete second copy of the function declaration is used to evaluate the recursive call. When that is completed, the value returned by the recursive call is used to complete the suspended computation. In the example, there are two levels of function calls. There may be several levels of recursive calls. The principle is the same no matter how many levels of recursive calls there are.

a highly recursive example

As a further example, let us rewrite the function **Power** one more time. Observe that for any number x and any positive integer n, the following relation holds:

$$x^n = x\left(x^{n-1}\right)$$

That means that an alternative way to define x^n is as follows:

The value is 1 when $n = 0$;

The value is x times x^{n-1} when $n > 0$;

The value is $1/x^{-n}$ when $n < 0$.

The Pascal version of a recursive function that computes in this way is given in Figure 12.4. To avoid confusion, we have used a slightly different name for this version of the function.

Evaluation of a recursive function such as **POW** can get fairly involved. Consider what happens when the following statement is executed:

```
Z := POW(2.0, 3)
```

recursion within recursion

The computer starts to evaluate **POW(2.0, 3)**, but must stop to compute **POW(2.0, 2)**. While computing **POW(2.0, 2)**, it must stop to compute **POW(2.0, 1)**. While computing **POW(2.0, 1)**, it must stop to compute **POW(2.0, 0)**. It can easily compute **POW(2.0, 0)** to be **1**. It then returns and completes the computation of **POW(2.0, 1)** and determines that it is **2**. It then uses this value to finish the computation of **POW(2.0, 2)**, which it calculates to

Evaluating `Power(3.0, -2)` requires evaluating code equivalent to:

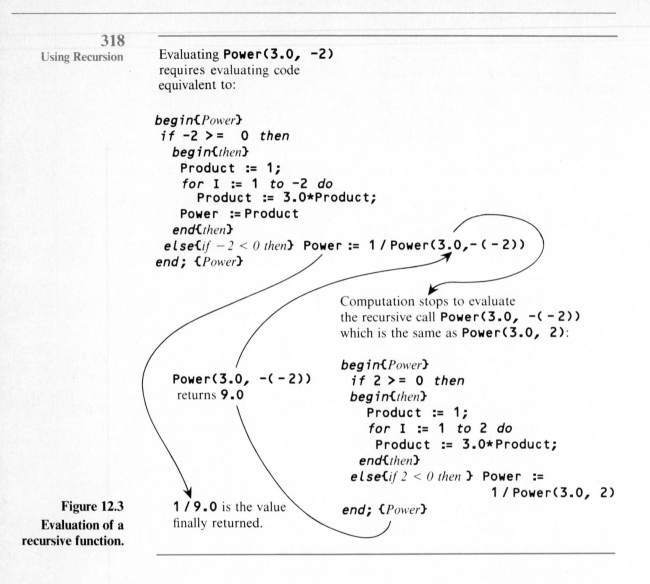

```
begin{Power}
 if -2 >= 0 then
   begin{then}
    Product := 1;
    for I := 1 to -2 do
      Product := 3.0*Product;
    Power := Product
   end{then}
  else{if −2 < 0 then} Power := 1 / Power(3.0,−(−2))
end; {Power}
```

Computation stops to evaluate the recursive call `Power(3.0, -(-2))` which is the same as `Power(3.0, 2)`:

```
begin{Power}
 if 2 >= 0 then
  begin{then}
    Product := 1;
    for I := 1 to 2 do
     Product := 3.0*Product;
   end{then}
  else{if 2 < 0 then } Power :=
                        1 / Power(3.0, 2)
end; {Power}
```

`Power(3.0, -(-2))` returns **9.0**

1 / 9.0 is the value finally returned.

**Figure 12.3
Evaluation of a
recursive function.**

```
function POW(X: real; N: integer): real;
{Returns X to the power N. Returns 1 when N equals 0.
Precondition: If N is negative, then X is not zero.}

begin{POW}
   if N = 0 then POW := 1
   else if N > 0 then POW := X*POW(X, N-1)
   else {if N < 0 then} POW := 1/POW(X, -N)
end; {POW}
```

**Figure 12.4
A "highly"
recursive function.**

Sequence of recursive calls:

```
POW(2.0, 3) := 2.0*POW(2.0, 2)
   POW(2.0, 2) := 2.0*POW(2.0, 1)
      POW(2.0, 1) := 2.0*POW(2.0, 0)
         POW(2.0, 0) := 1.0
```

How the final value returned is computed:

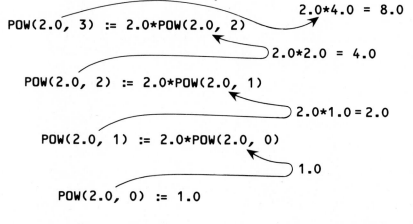

Figure 12.5
Evaluating the recursive function call POW(2.0, 3).

be **4**. It then uses that value to complete the computation of **POW(2.0, 3)**. The entire process is diagrammed in Figure 12.5. (To keep the figure uncluttered, we have simplified the code so that it uses the values of the actual parameters. Technically speaking, we should use the formal value parameters **X** and **N** as local variables and initialize them to these values. However, the idea is expressed more clearly by showing the values.)

Infinite Recursion

Pascal places no restrictions on how recursive calls are used in function and procedure declarations. However, in order for a recursive function declaration to be useful, it must be designed so that any call of the function will ultimately terminate with some piece of code that does not depend on recursion. The function may call itself, and that recursive call may call the function again. The process may be repeated any number of times. However, the process will not

how
recursion
terminates

terminate unless eventually one of the recursive calls does not depend on recursion in order to return a value.

Look back at Figure 12.5. To compute **POW(2.0, 3)**, the function makes the following sequence of recursive calls: **POW(2.0, 2)**, **POW(2.0, 1)** and **POW(2.0, 0)**. The call to **POW(2.0, 0)** returns a value by executing the code:

```
if N = 0 then POW := 1
```

That piece of code includes no recursive call. Hence, the code does eventually terminate; a value is returned for **POW(2.0, 0)** and the process works its way back to the original call, which terminates and returns a value for **POW(2.0, 3)**.

In the previous example, the series of recursive calls eventually reached a call of the function that did not involve recursion. If, on the other hand, every recursive call produces another recursive call, then a call to the function will, in theory, run forever. In practice, such a function will run until the computer runs out of resources and terminates the program abnormally. Phrased another way, a recursive declaration should not be "recursive all the way down." Otherwise, like the lady's explanation of the universe, a call of the function will never end, except perhaps in frustration.

example of infinite recursion

Examples of such infinite recursion are not hard to come by. The following is a syntactically correct Pascal function declaration, which might result from an attempt to declare an alternative version of the function **Power**:

```
function RecPower(X: real; N: integer): real;
  begin{RecPower}
    RecPower := 1 / RecPower(X, -N)
  end; {RecPower}
```

If embedded in a program that calls this function, the compiler will translate it to machine code and the machine code can be executed. Moreover, it even has a certain reasonableness to it. The relation

$$x^n = 1/x^{-n}$$

is true provided x is not zero. However, when called, this function will produce an infinite loop. An attempt to evaluate **RecPower(2.0, 3)** will stop to evaluate **RecPower(2.0, -3)**. That evaluation will in turn stop to evaluate an expression equivalent to **RecPower(2.0, 3)**. That in turn will attempt to compute **RecPower(2.0, -3)**. The process will proceed in a circle ad infinitum.

Stacks

In order to keep track of recursion, and a number of other things, most computer systems make use of a structure called a *stack*. A stack is a very specialized kind of memory structure which is analogous to a stack of paper sheets. In this analogy there is an inexhaustible supply of extra blank sheets. In order to place some information in the stack, it is written on one of these sheets of paper and placed on top of the stack of papers. To place more information in the stack, a clean sheet of paper is taken, the information is written on it and this new sheet of paper is placed on the stack. In this straightforward way more and more information may be placed on the stack. (This is a very common memory structure; a large number of office desks are organized in this fashion.)

Getting information out of the stack is also accomplished by a very simple procedure. The top sheet of paper can be read, and when it is no longer needed, it can be thrown away. There is one complication: only the top sheet of paper is accessible. In order to read, say, the third sheet from the top, the top two sheets must be thrown away. For this reason a stack is sometimes called a *last-in / first-out* memory structure.

Let us be a bit more precise about which pieces of paper are available to read and/or write on. In this analogy only the top sheet of paper on the stack is accessible. We will also allow one other sheet that is available to work on. That extra sheet is not part of the stack but it is still available. All sheets of paper in the stack other than the top one are not available. In order to access those sheets, some other sheets must be thrown away.

*stacks
and
recursion*

Using a stack, the computer can easily keep track of recursion. Whenever a function is called, a new sheet of paper is taken. The function declaration is copied onto the sheet of paper, and the actual parameters are plugged in for the formal parameters. Then the computer starts to execute the body of the function declaration. When it encounters a recursive call, it stops the computation it is doing on that sheet in order to compute the value returned by the recursive call. But before computing the recursive call, it saves enough information so that, when it does finally determine the value returned by the recursive call, it can complete the stopped computation. This saved information is written on the sheet of paper and placed on the stack. A new sheet of paper is used for the recursive call. It writes a second copy of the function declaration on this new sheet of paper, plugs in the actual parameters and starts to execute the recursive call. When it gets to a recursive call within the recursively called copy, it repeats the process of saving information on the stack and using a new sheet of paper for the new recursive call.

This process continues until some recursive call is completed and returns a value. When that happens, it takes the top sheet of paper off the stack. This sheet contains the partially completed computation, which needs the value just returned. So it is possible to proceed with that computation. The process continues until the computation on the bottom sheet is completed. The value returned by that bottom computation is the value returned by the function call. Depending on how many recursive calls are made and how the function declaration is written, the stack may grow and shrink in any fashion.

In Figure 12.6, we have redrawn the computation in Figure 12.5 showing how the stack behaves for this particular function call. Notice that the sheets in the stack can only be accessed in a last-in/first-out fashion, but that is exactly what is needed to keep track of recursive calls. The version currently being worked on is the one that was called by the version on top of the stack, and that is the one waiting for it to return a value.

Needless to say, computers do not have stacks of paper of this kind. This is just an analogy. The computer uses portions of memory rather than pieces of

*activation
record*

Evaluating POW(2.0, 3)

Figure 12.6
Stack contents
while evaluating
a recursive function.

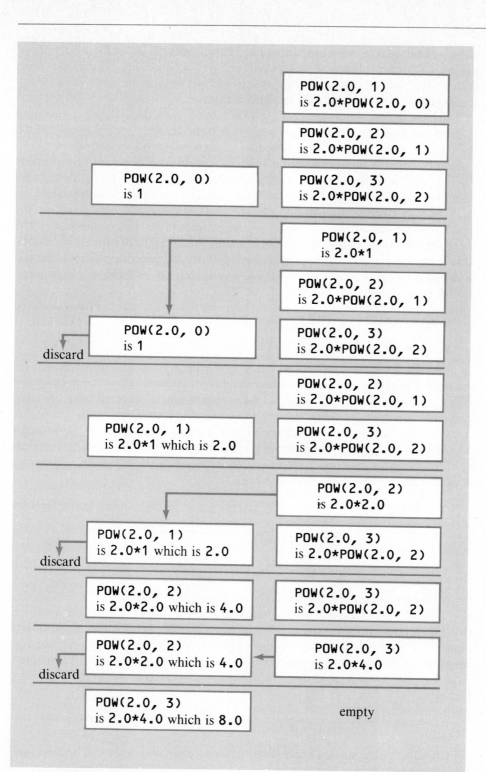

Figure 12.6 (cont'd)

paper. The analogy is very exact, though. The contents of one of these portions of memory ("sheets of paper") is called an *activation record*. These activation records are handled in this last-in/first-out manner and the memory dedicated to holding these activation records is called a *stack*.

Stacks are used for a number of things besides recursion. They are also used to keep track of local variables. Whenever a procedure calls another procedure, the computation of the calling procedure is suspended and an activation record ("sheet of paper") showing where it is in its computation is placed on the stack. Then a new activation record is started for the procedure just called. If an identifier, say **X**, is local to the just called procedure, then there may be values for **X** in both activation records. These are two different **X**'s: one local to the procedure just called and one local to the procedure on top of the stack. The computer knows they are different because they are in different activation records. This is the same process that we described for recursive functions. In fact, there is only one stack. Both things are aspects of one unified way of handling procedures.

Many systems limit the size of the stack for various reasons. Suppose the stack is limited to 20 activation records, suppose that the function **POW** is declared as shown in Figure 12.4 and suppose that the following statement is executed:

X := POW(2.0, 30)

In that case the system will try to place approximately 30 activation records on the stack. However, the stack is limited to 20 records. The system can not proceed within the constraints imposed. So the computation is aborted and an error statement is output. On many systems the error message will say *stack overflow*. A stack overflow simply means that the system tried to make the stack grow larger than what is permitted. One common cause of stack overflow is infinite recursion. If a procedure or function is recursing infinitely, then it will eventually try to make the stack exceed any stack size limit.

Since a recursive function has the potential to go on without stopping, it is similar to a loop. As with a loop, the programmer has a responsibility to make certain that a function with a recursive call will terminate whenever the precondition is satisfied. Fortunately, this can be done by the same technique that we used to demonstrate that loops terminate. To prove that a recursive function terminates, it is enough to find a *variant expression* and *threshold* with the following properties:

(0) Whenever the function is called, it will either terminate or make a recursive call.

(1) The value of the variant expression must decrease by at least one between one call of the function and any succeeding recursive call of that function.

(2) If the function is called and the value of the variant expression is less than or equal to the threshold, then the function will terminate without making any recursive calls.

Condition (0) is included to take account of factors other than recursion. For example, if the function declaration consists of a loop followed by a recursive call of the function, then the loop must be shown to terminate by means of the techniques discussed in Chapter 8. That has nothing to do with recursion, but it can affect termination.

Conditions (1) and (2) have to do with recursion. To see that they, together with (0), guarantee termination, reason as follows. Suppose the three conditions hold. Since (0) is true, every call of the function will either terminate or produce a recursive call. Since (1) is true, every recursive call will decrease the variant expression. This means that either the function will terminate, which is fine, or else the variant expression will decrease until it reaches the threshold. But if condition (2) holds, then once the variant expression reaches the threshold, the function will terminate. That covers all the cases.

Interestingly enough, the preceding conditions are themselves recursive. Conditions (0) and (2) include a test for termination and it is termination which we are testing for. However, this is not a problem, since the conditions only discuss termination when there are no recursive calls of the function, and that kind of termination can be checked by the techniques we discussed in Chapter 8. A complete list of our conditions would also summarize those tests for termination.

As an example, consider the recursive function **POW** declared in Figure 12.4. The variant expression can be taken to be:

> **abs(N) + 1**, *for negative values of* **N** *and*
> **N**, *for nonnegative values of* **N**.

With a threshold of zero, the conditions (0) through (2) hold and so we know that any call of the function will eventually terminate and return a value.

In addition to checking that a recursive function terminates, you should also check that it always returns the correct value. The usual technique for that is called *induction*. (If you have heard of mathematical induction, it may help to note that this is the same thing.) To show that a recursive function returns the correct value, all you need show is the following:

induction

(3) If the function returns without making any recursive calls, then it returns the correct value. (This is sometimes called the *base case*.)

(4) If the function is called and if all subsequent recursive calls return the correct value, then the original call will also return the correct value. (This is sometimes called the *inductive step*.)

By the *correct value* we mean whatever it is you want the function to return. That is part of the specification of the task of the function.

The conditions are numbers (3) and (4) to emphasize that they only ensure correctness if you know that the function calls always terminate. You must also insure that conditions (0) through (2) hold in order to guarantee that a recursive function declaration performs its task as desired.

To complete our example, let us return to the function **POW** defined in Figure 12.4. To complete our demonstration that it performs as desired, we must show that (3) and (4) hold.

It is easy to see that (3) holds. The only way that the function can terminate without a recursive call is if the value of **N** is zero. In that case it returns **1**, which is the answer we said we wanted. Any number to the power **0** is **1** by definition. (There is a reason for that definition, but that is a topic in algebra not program verification.)

To see that (4) holds we need only recall the algebraic identities:

$$x^n = x(x^{n-1})$$

and

$$x^n = 1/x^{-n}$$

Recursive Procedures—A Simple Example

All our remarks about recursive functions apply equally well to recursive procedures. As a first example, consider the task of writing an integer to the screen with its decimal digits reversed. For example, the number **1234** should be output as:

4321

A simple solution is the following:

> *if* the number is one digit long
>   *then* write that digit
>   *else begin*
>   write the last digit;
>   remove the last digit;
>   write the rest to the screen backwards
>   *end*

In the example, **4** is the last digit and **123** is the rest. This algorithm is recursive because the last step is an instance of the same task of writing a number backwards. It is routine to implement it as a recursive procedure. The implementation is shown in Figure 12.7. The arithmetic is straightforward. The last digit is always the remainder on division by **10**; that is,

> (the number) *mod* **10**.

For example, **(1234 *mod* 10)** is **4**. "The rest" is just the quotient when the number is divided by **10**; that is,

> (the number) *div* **10**.

For example, **(1234 *div* 10)** is **123**.

Program

```
program ReverseTheDigits(input, output);

var Number: integer;

procedure WriteBackwards(Number: integer);
{Writes the decimal digits of Number to the screen
in reverse order. Precondition: Number > = 0.}
    var LastDigit, TheRest: integer;
begin{WriteBackwards}
    if Number < 10 then write(Number:1)
    else
      begin{else}
        LastDigit := Number mod 10;
        TheRest := Number div 10;
        write(LastDigit:1);
        WriteBackwards(TheRest)
      end {else}
end; {WriteBackwards}

begin{Program}
    writeln('Enter a nonnegative whole number');
    readln(Number);
    writeln(Number,' written backwards is:');
    WriteBackwards(Number);
    writeln
end. {Program}
```

Sample Dialogue

Enter a nonnegative whole number
1066
1066 written backwards is:
6601

Figure 12.7
Program with a
recursive procedure.

Binary Search— A More Complicated Example of Recursion

In this section we will develop a recursive procedure that searches an array to find out if a given value is in the array. For example, the array may contain a list of serial numbers of stolen automobiles and we may wish to search it to see if a suspicious automobile is stolen. Let us call the array **A**. The indexes of the array **A** are the integers **First** through **Last**. **First** and **Last** are some specified integers, but their values are not relevant to the discussion. To simplify the problem, we will assume that the array is sorted. So if the array is **A**, then

$$A[First] \leq A[First + 1] \leq ... \leq A[Last]$$

When searching an array, we are likely to want to know both whether the value is in the list and (if it is) where it is in the list. For example, if we are searching for a serial number on a list of stolen automobiles, then the array index may serve as a record number. Another array indexed by these same indexes may hold the list of legal owners of the automobiles.

problem
definition

We will design the procedure to use two variable parameters to return the outcome of the search. One parameter, called **Found**, will be of type **boolean** and will be set to **true** if the value is found. If it is found, then another parameter, called **Location**, will be set to the index of the value found. If we use **Key** to denote the value being searched for, the task to be accomplished can be formulated precisely as follows:

Precondition: **First** ≤ **Last**; **A[Low]** *through* **A[High]**
   are sorted into increasing order.
Postcondition: if **Key** *is not one of the values*
          A[First] *through* **A[Last]**,
   then **Found** *is* **false**
   else **First** ≤ **Location** ≤ **Last**
      and **A[Location]** = **Key** *and* **Found** = **true**.

Now let us proceed to produce an algorithm to solve this task. In at least one special case the solution is easy:

if **First** = **Last** *then* test (**Key** = **A[First]**?) and set
Found and **Location** accordingly.

divide
and
conquer

However, it is more likely that the array contains a number of elements. In that case we will use a variation of the "divide and conquer" strategy. We will divide the big task into two smaller tasks of the same general type but with shorter lists to search. In order to determine if the **Key** is anywhere in the list, we will divide the list in half, determine which half it lies in and then search that half. In doing this we will make use of the fact that the list is sorted.

A variable **Mid** can be set to an approximate midpoint by the assignment:

Mid := (Last + First) *div* **2**

Now it is easy to tell which half of the array that **Key** can possibly be in. If **Key** ≤ **A[Mid]**, then **Key** might be one of the values **A[First]** through **A[Mid]**, but it can not be any of the values **A[Mid + 1]** through **A[Last]**. Otherwise, the situation is reversed and **Key** might possibly be in the second half of the array but cannot be in the first half. The following pseudocode gives an algorithm for the case of an array with two or more elements.

Mid := (Last + First) *div* **2;**
if **Key <= A[Mid]** *then* search **A[First]** through **A[Mid]**
                    else search **A[Mid + 1]** through **A[Last]**

We have just designed a recursive algorithm. The subtasks of searching half the array are the same as the big task of searching the array, and so we can can solve them by a recursive call. To summarize, we now put together the various pieces of pseudocode to get a complete, though still rather informal, version of the recursive algorithm:

algorithm

```
if First = Last
then test (Key = A[First]?) and set Found and Location accordingly
else
  begin{outer else}
    Mid := (Last + First) div 2;
    if Key <= A[Mid] then search A[First] through A[Mid]
                     else search A[Mid + 1] through A[Last]
  end {outer else}
```

This pseudocode is a bit too imprecise to be easily translated into Pascal. The problem has to do with the recursive calls. There are two recursive calls shown:

search **A[First]** through **A[Mid]**
search **A[Mid + 1]** through **A[Last]**

In order to implement that recursive call we need two more parameters. The recursive call specifies that a subrange of the array is to be searched. In one case it is the elements indexed by **First** through **Mid**. In the other case it is the elements **Mid + 1** through **Last**. The two extra parameters will specify the lower and upper bounds of the search. Let us call these two parameters **Low** and **High**. Using these parameters instead of **First** and **Last**, we can express the pseudocode more precisely as follows:

pseudocode

```
if Low = High
then test (Key = A[Low]?) and set Found and Location accordingly
else
    begin {outer else}
      Mid := (High + Low) div 2;
      if Key <= A[Mid] then search A[Low] through A[Mid]
                       else search A[Mid + 1] through A[High]
    end {outer else}
```

To search the entire array, the algorithm would be executed with **Low** set equal to **First** and **High** set equal to **Last**. The recursive calls will use other values for **Low** and **High**. Now we can routinely translate the pseudocode into Pascal. The result is shown in Figure 12.8. The procedure **Search** is an implementation of the above recursive algorithm.

Notice that the procedure **Search** solves a more general problem than the original task. Our goal was to design a procedure to search an entire array of type **List**. Yet the procedure will let us search any interval of the array by specifying the index bounds **Low** and **High**. This is a common phenomenon when designing recursive procedures. Frequently, it is necessary to solve a more general problem in order to be able to express the recursive algorithm. In this case, we only wanted

*solve a
more general
problem*

```
program BinarySearch(input, output);

const First = 1; Last = 100;
type Index = First..Last;
     List = array[Index] of integer;
var A: List;
    Key: integer;
    Found: boolean;
    Location: Index;

procedure Search(A: List; Low, High: Index; Key: integer;
                 var Found: boolean; var Location: Index);
```

{ *Precondition: First < = Low < = High < = Last;*
A[Low] through A[High] are sorted into increasing order.
Postcondition: A and Key are unchanged; if Key does not equal
one of A[Low] through A[High], then Found is false
else Found = true and A[Location] = Key.}

```
    var Mid: integer;
begin{Search}
    if High = Low
    then
      if A[Low] = Key
        then
          begin{inner then}
            Found := true;
            Location := Low
          end {inner then}
        else Found := false
    else
      begin{outer else}
        Mid := (High + Low) div 2;
        if Key <= A[Mid]
            then Search(A, Low, Mid, Key, Found, Location)
            else Search(A, Mid+1, High, Key, Found, Location)
      end {outer else}
end; {Search}

begin{Program}
```

· · ·

Figure 12.8

Program with a recursive procedure for binary search.

This portion of the program contains some code to fill the array **A**. The exact details are irrelevant to the example.

```
   . . .
   writeln('Enter number to be located');
   readln(Key);
   Search(A, First, Last, Key, Found, Location);
   if Found
      then writeln(Key, ' is in location ', Location)
      else writeln(Key, ' is not in the array')
end. {Program}
```

Figure 12.8 (cont'd)

the answer in the case where **Low** and **High** are set equal to **First** and **Last**. However, the recursive calls will set them to values other than **First** and **Last**.

Towers of Hanoi— An Example of Recursive Thinking

Recursion can be a very powerful programming tool. Sometimes a problem that appears to be difficult when tackled with any other programming techniques can turn out to be very simple when thought of in terms of recursion. One dramatic example of this is provided by a children's game called Towers of Hanoi. As with any programming task, the first step is to understand the problem.

The game consists of three pegs and a collection of rings that fit over the pegs, rather like phonograph records on a spindle. The rings are of different sizes. The initial configuration for a six-ring game is shown in Figure 12.9. Notice that the rings are stacked in decreasing order of their size. A move consists of transferring a single ring from the top of one peg to that of another. The object of the game is to move all the rings from the first peg to the second peg. The difficulty is that you are never allowed to place a ring on top of one with a smaller radius. You do have the one extra peg to temporarily hold rings, but the prohibition against placing a larger ring on a smaller ring applies to it as well as the other two pegs. A solution for the case of three rings is given in Figure 12.9.

This game apparently has an impressive and long history. Legend has it that it was invented by God at the dawn of time and was given to man as one of the major tasks of humanity. The task of solving it eventually fell to the monks of a certain monastery in what was then an obscure eastern village called Hanoi. The legend goes on to say that when the game is completed, the last task assigned to humanity will have been accomplished and that will mark the end of the world. The version God presented to mankind had 64 rings. So do not worry about trying it with three or four rings. (Besides, the game can not end the world unless the rings and pegs are made of stone and it is played in Hanoi.)

The game sounds simple enough but a solution has not been easy to derive, at least until very recently. It is easy to solve it for the case of three rings, but even four can take some thought. Ten rings boggle the mind. Sixty-four are almost

Initial configuration for a six-ring game

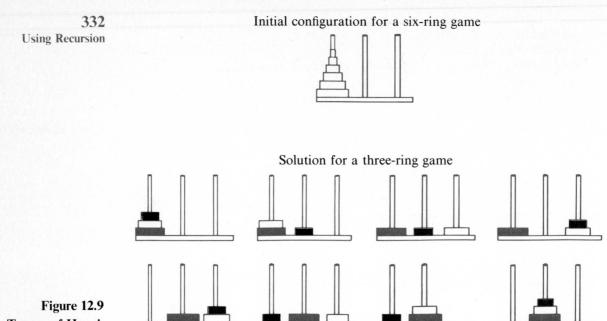

Solution for a three-ring game

**Figure 12.9
Towers of Hanoi.**

unimaginable. To get the feel of it, try to solve it for the case of four rings. If you succeed, then try the six-ring case.

thinking recursively

Although it is very difficult to solve by other means, the solution is almost trivial if you think recursively. The trick is to reduce the problem to a smaller one of the same type. The trick is illustrated in Figure 12.10. First we move all but one ring onto the spare peg. We do that by a recursive call. Then we move the last ring to where it belongs. After that we move the rings from the spare peg to the

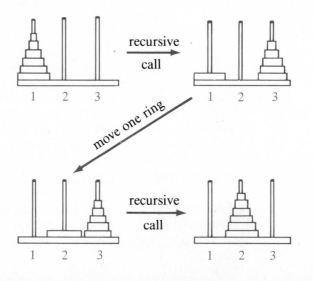

**Figure 12.10
Idea of a recursive
solution.**

Program

```
program Hanoi(input, output);

type PegNumber = 1..3;
var N: integer;

procedure WriteMoves(N: integer; Peg1, Peg2, Peg3: PegNumber);
{Outputs the moves needed to move N rings
from Peg1 to Peg2, using Peg3 as the extra peg.}
begin{Moves}
   if N = 1
     then writeln('Move a ring from ', Peg1:1, ' to ', Peg2:1)
     else
     begin{else}
       WriteMoves(N - 1, Peg1, Peg3, Peg2);
       writeln('Move a ring from ', Peg1:1, ' to ', Peg2:1);
       WriteMoves(N - 1, Peg3, Peg2, Peg1)
     end {else}
end; {Moves}

begin{Program}
   writeln('Enter the number of rings and');
   writeln('I''ll explain how to play Towers of Hanoi.');
   readln(N);
   writeln('To move ', N,' rings');
   writeln('from peg 1 to peg 2 proceed as follows:');
   WriteMoves(N, 1, 2, 3);
   writeln('That does it.')
end. {Program}
```

Sample Dialogue

Enter the number of rings and
I'll explain how to play Towers of Hanoi.
2
To move 2 rings
from peg 1 to peg 2 proceed as follows:
Move a ring from 1 to 3.
Move a ring from 1 to 2.
Move a ring from 3 to 2.
That does it.

Figure 12.11
Program to play
Towers of Hanoi.

goal peg by another recursive call. All the pegs are identical. So we can mix up their roles like this. Moving all the rings from the first peg to the second using the third as a spare is exactly the same problem as moving them from, say, the first to the third using the second as a spare. A program with a recursive procedure to write out the moves is given in Figure 12.11.

Recursive versus Iterative Procedures and Functions

iterative version

Recursion is not absolutely necessary. In fact, many programming languages do not allow it. Any task that can be accomplished using recursion can also be done in some other way without using recursion. For example, Figure 12.4 contains a recursive function declaration. A nonrecursive version of that function is given in Figure 12.12. In such cases the nonrecursive version typically uses a loop of some sort in place of recursion. For that reason, the nonrecursive version is usually referred to as an *iterative* version.

inefficiency of recursion

On many computer systems, the recursive version of **POW** given in Figure 12.4 will run much slower and use much more storage than the iterative version given in Figure 12.12. The reason is that the recursive version uses a large amount of time and a large amount of storage to keep track of the recursive calls. Recall our discussion of how recursion is implemented using a stack. Suppose the recursive version is called to evaluate:

POW(3.0, 10)

The computer will make about 10 extra copies of the procedure and place them on the stack. This consumes a large amount of time and memory. On the other

```
function POW(X: real; N: integer): real;
{Returns the value of X to the N. Returns 1 whenever N is 0.
Precondition: If N is negative, then X is not zero.}
    var I: integer;
        Product, Factor: real;
begin{POW}
    Product := 1.0;
    if N >= 0 then Factor := X
             else Factor := 1/X;
    for I := 1 to abs(N) do
        Product := Factor*Product;
    POW := Product
end; {POW}
```

**Figure 12.12
Iterative version
of the function in
Figure 12.4.**

hand, the iterative version does not do all this extra manipulating of the stack. It just performs ten simple multiplications and returns the answer.

The **POW** example is typical. A recursively written function will usually run slower and use more storage than an equivalent iterative version. The difference in efficiency depends on how large the stack grows when the recursive version is used; that is, on how long the string of recursive calls is. For example, the version of the function **Power** given in Figure 12.2 returns the same value as **POW**, is recursive and yet is not much less efficient than the iterative version of **POW**. That is because no call of **Power** ever produces a long string of recursive calls.

If efficiency is an important issue, then it may make sense to avoid recursion. However, the efficiency issue is a subtle one. First of all, not all recursive declarations are equally inefficient. As discussed in the previous paragraph, the inefficiency introduced by the recursive call in the function **Power** of Figure 12.2 is negligible. Moreover, the recursion makes the code easier to read, since it reflects our normal manner of thinking about this computation. Also, recursion can sometimes make a procedure or function so much easier to understand that it would be foolish to avoid it. Consider the Towers of Hanoi procedure. If we did not think recursively, we might not have produced a solution at all. If we convert that procedure to an iterative procedure it will be much more complicated and, as a result, will most likely contain bugs. No procedure can be considered efficient unless it gives the correct answers.

Finally, we should note that this discussion about efficiency assumes that recursive procedures are implemented with a stack using a method like the one we described. They need not be implemented in exactly that way. Some compilers will try to convert a recursive function declaration to an iterative one before they translate the declaration into machine code. On one of these compilers, recursive and iterative versions of a function will probably be equally efficient.

Forward Declarations
(Optional)

Normally you declare a procedure or function before the place where it is first used. However, there is a way around this rule. If you wish to declare a procedure after the declaration of some other procedure that uses it, you can provided you warn the compiler by including a *forward declaration* before the first location where the procedure is called. A forward declaration consists of the procedure heading followed by the identifier **forward** and terminated by a semicolon. For example:

```
procedure Reject(var Ans: char); forward;
```

The procedure declaration can then be placed anywhere after the forward declaration. Since the formal parameter list is given in the forward declaration, it is not given again when the procedure is declared. (However, it is a good idea to

Using Recursion

Program

```
program Test(input, output);
{Tests the mutually recursive procedures GetAnswer and Reject.}

var Ans: char;

procedure Reject(var Ans: char); forward;
{Outputs a message saying Ans is not an acceptable
answer and then calls the procedure GetAnswer(Ans).}

procedure GetAnswer(var Ans: char);
{Sets the value of Ans to 'Y' or 'N' depending on what the user
types in. Repeats the process until the user types in one of these
two characters. Mutually recursive with the procedure Reject.}
begin{GetAnswer}
    writeln('Answer cap Y for Yes or cap N for No.');
    readln(Ans);
    if not (Ans in ['Y', 'N']) then Reject(Ans)
end; {GetAnswer}

procedure Reject;
{var Ans: char}
begin{Reject}
    writeln(Ans, ' is not an acceptable response.');
    GetAnswer(Ans)
end; {Reject}

begin{Program}
    writeln('This is a test.');
    GetAnswer(Ans);
    writeln('Value of Ans is ', Ans);
    writeln('That ends the test.')
end. {Program}
```

Sample Dialogue

This is a test.
Answer cap Y for Yes or cap N for No.
y
y is not an acceptable response.
Answer cap Y for Yes or cap N for No.
OK
O is not an acceptable response.
Answer cap Y for Yes or cap N for No.
Y
The value of Ans is Y
That ends the test.

Figure 12.13
Example of a
forward declaration.

include the parameter list in a comment.) Functions as well as procedures may be given forward declarations in this way.

The program in Figure 12.13 requires a forward declaration. In that program the procedures **GetAnswer** and **Reject** each include a call to the other. Such a phenomenon is called *mutual recursion* and the two procedures are called *coroutines*. Forward declarations can also be used for less essential reasons, such as for putting all the most important procedures together in one place.

Summary of Problem Solving and Programming Techniques

A problem that does not easily yield to other methods of reasoning can sometimes be very simple when thought of in terms of recursion. If the problem can be reduced to smaller instances of the same problem, then a recursive solution is usually easy to find. Examples of this were the binary search technique and the Towers of Hanoi game discussed in this chapter.

When writing recursive procedures or functions, always check to see that the procedure will not produce infinite recursion.

If a procedure or function produces a long series of recursive calls (i.e., the procedure calls itself, that called copy calls itself, and so forth for very many calls) and if efficiency is an issue, then consider the possibility of translating your recursive procedure into an iterative procedure. Even when efficiency dictates that an iterative procedure should be used, it sometimes still makes sense to first find a recursive solution. Sometimes the recursive solution will be the only obvious way to solve the problem. In that case, think recursively until you solve the problem and, if need be, you can later translate your recursive algorithm into an iterative algorithm.

◇

"I remembered too that night which is at the middle of the Thousand and One Nights when Scheherazade (through a magical oversight of the copyist) begins to relate word for word the story of the Thousand and One Nights, establishing the risk of coming once again to the night when she must repeat it, and thus to infinity."

Jorge Luis Borges, The Garden of Forking Paths

◇

Exercises

Self-Test and Interactive Exercises

1. What is the output of the following program?

```
program Test(input, output);
function Rose(N: integer): integer;
  begin{Rose}
    if N = 1 then Rose := 0
             else Rose := Rose(N div 2) + 1
  end; {Rose}
begin{Program}
  writeln(Rose(8))
end. {Program}
```

2. What is the output of the following program?

```
program Test2(input, output);
procedure Cheers(N: integer);
  begin{Cheers}
    if N = 1 then writeln('Hurray')
             else begin{else}
               write('Hip ');
               Cheers(N - 1)
             end {else}
  end; {Cheers}
begin{Program}
  Cheers(3)
end. {Program}
```

3. Embed the following function in a program and run it. The program should take an integer **N** as input and then output the value of **RecSum(N)**. Run the program four times using the input values 3, 10, 100 and −10. Predict the output before you run it.

```
function RecSum(N: integer): integer;
  begin
    writeln('RecSum called with argument ', N);
    if N = 1 then RecSum := 1
             else RecSum := N + RecSum(N - 1)
  end;
```

4. Write an iterative version of the function in the previous exercise.

5. Write a recursive procedure that has one parameter which is a positive integer and that writes out that number of asterisks '*' to the screen.

6. Take a pad of paper to use as the inexhaustible supply of paper for a stack. Simulate the following procedure call using a stack of real paper. First, use the one word sentence *Hi*. Next, use a sentence of your own choice, which is about ten characters long. After that, type up the program and run it.

```
program ReverseInput(input, output);
procedure RecReadWrite;
    const Period = '.';
    var Letter: char;
begin{RecReadWrite}
  read(Letter);
  if Letter <> Period then RecReadWrite;
  write(Letter)
end; {RecReadWrite}
begin{Program}
  writeln('Type in a sentence ending with a period.');
  RecReadWrite;
  writeln
end. {Program}
```

7. Get hold of a real Towers of Hanoi game. Run the program in Figure 12.11 and follow its instructions for playing the game. Also, simulate the program using a stack of paper as in the previous exercise. The stack simulation is worth doing even if you do not have the game available.

Regular Exercises

8. The factorial function is often written as $n!$. Its value is the product of the integers 1 through n. By definition 0! is 1. So $0! = 1$, $1! = 1$, $2! = 2$, $3! = 1*2*3 = 6$ and so forth. Write an iterative function declaration for the factorial function. Embed it in a program and test it. Then write a recursive version and test it. Use local variables of type **real** and have it return a value of type **real**; otherwise, you might encounter integer overflow even for relatively small arguments.

9. Write a recursive function with one argument **N** of type **integer** that returns the **N**th Fibonacci number. See Exercise 14 in Chapter 8 for the definition of Fibonacci numbers.

10. Write a recursive procedure that has as arguments an array of characters and two bounds on array indexes. The procedure should reverse the order of those entries in the array whose indexes are between the two bounds. For example, if the array is:

  A[1] = 'A' A[2] = 'B' A[3] = 'C' A[4] = 'D' A[5] = 'E'

and the bounds are **2** and **5**, then after the procedure is run the array elements should be:

  A[1] = 'A' A[2] = 'E' A[3] = 'D' A[4] = 'C' A[5] = 'B'

Embed the procedure in a program and test it.

11. Write an iterative version of the procedure in the previous exercise. Embed it in a program and test it.

12. Write a recursive procedure to sort an array of integers into ascending order using the following idea: First place the smallest element in the first position, then sort the rest of the array by a recursive call.

13. Write a procedure that takes two parameters which are arrays of integers of the same size and one array parameter which is an array of integers of twice that size. The procedure assumes that the two smaller arrays are sorted and copies their contents into the larger array. It does so in such a way that the integers in the larger array are also sorted. Embed the procedure in a program in order to test it.

14. Use the ideas of the previous exercise to design a recursive sorting procedure that works along the following general lines. The array is divided in half. Each half is sorted by a recursive call and then the two halves are merged into a single sorted array. Embed the procedure in a program and test it.

15. Write an iterative version of the procedure **Search** from Figure 12.8.

16. Write an iterative version of the procedure **WriteMoves** (Figure 12.11) from the Towers of Hanoi program.

17. Write a set of procedures for using an array of characters as a stack. There should be one procedure to add a character to the stack, one to remove one and one to read the "top" character on the stack.

18. Write a recursive procedure that takes an array of characters as a parameter and outputs a random permutation of the characters in the array. The array can hold a maximum of five characters, but need not be full. One other parameter tells how many array elements are being used.

19. Find a formula for the number of times a disk is transferred from one peg to another in the Towers of Hanoi game with *n* rings. Compute the value for *n* equal to 5, 10 and 20.

20. Rewrite the Towers of Hanoi procedure so that it draws a stylized picture of the game being played. The output should be a series of pictures showing the game configuration after each ring is moved.

21. Redo Exercise 19 in Chapter 10, but this time use a recursive procedure.

References for Further Reading

N. Wirth, *Algorithms + Data Structures = Programs*, 1976, Prentice-Hall, Englewood Cliffs, N. J., Chapter 3.

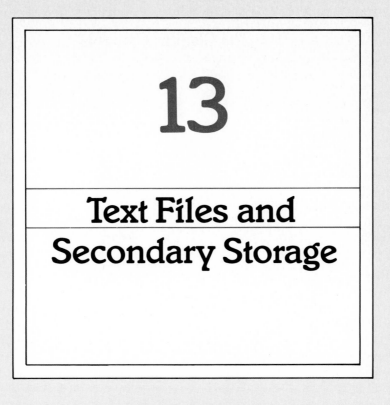

13

Text Files and Secondary Storage

Polonius: What do you read, my lord?
Hamlet: Words, words, words.
                William Shakespeare, Hamlet

Chapter Contents

PART I

Chapter 1 presented a description of the main components of a computer. That description emphasized what is called *main memory*. Virtually all computers have an additional form of memory called *secondary storage* or *external storage*. On a personal computer this secondary storage is likely to be a device called a *floppy disk drive*. On a large system it is likely to be a device called a *hard disk drive*. These storage mediums are called disks because they are disk shaped. They have some similarity to phonograph records in that they store information on tracks of a disk and read the information via an arm that rests over the disk. However, their physical properties are closer to those of the magnetic tape commonly used to record music than they are to those of a phonograph record. In any event, it is their characteristics as viewed by the programmer that are important to us. We will not need to know about the physics of how they work.

Main memory is of the type called *volatile*, which means that when you shut off the computer, the data stored in memory goes away. In fact, for all practical purposes, the data goes away as soon as the program is finished running. Secondary storage is nonvolatile. It can be used to store data for as long as is needed. In this chapter we will describe a method whereby a Pascal program can store text data in secondary storage. We will also describe how another program can access that data.

UCSD Pascal and standard Pascal handle secondary storage slightly differently. Some Pascal systems even combine some features from standard and some features from UCSD Pascal. So you may need to do a bit of experimenting and questioning in order to completely figure out your system. We will first discuss some features common to all Pascal systems and then give separate sections for standard and UCSD Pascal. After that, we will return to a unified discussion that applies to both versions of Pascal, but we will still need to present different sample programs for the two systems and occasionally even separate sections.

Text Files

In Pascal, a *file* is a named collection of data in secondary storage. The important properties of a file are that a program can write data to it, that it can remain in storage after the program has finished running, that it has a name and that later on other programs can access it by asking to read the file with that name. In a later chapter we will describe all the types of files which are available in Pascal. For now we will only discuss one special kind of file called a "text file."

A *text file* is a file that contains the same sort of data as the output screen. More precisely, a text file contains a long stream of characters divided into units called *lines*. One way to think of a text file is as a very long sheet of paper that a program can write on and that the same or a different program can later read. These conceptual sheets of paper are divided into lines in the same way that output to the screen is divided into lines. This is of course all done electronically and there are no real sheets of paper.

the type
text

Inside a Pascal program, a text file is named by a Pascal identifier chosen by the programmer. The exact way that this identifier is associated with the file is different for UCSD and standard Pascal, but in both systems the name is declared as a variable. The Pascal type name for text files is **text**. So to declare **Stuff** to be the name of a text file, include the following in the variable declaration section of your program:

var **Stuff: text;**

file
variables

The file name, such as **Stuff**, is called a *file variable* and it is declared just like a variable. Although a file variable is a kind of variable, it is a very atypical kind of variable. It can not appear in an assignment statement, nor can it be used in many of the other ways that the usual kinds of variables are used. It has special standard procedures and special syntax rules of its own. It is probably better to just think of it as a file name and not think of it as a variable at all.

Writing and Reading of Text Files

write
and
writeln

Data is outputted to text files in the same way that it is outputted to the screen, that is, by **write** and **writeln** statements. In order to output to a text file, the **write** statement must contain the name of the file; otherwise, the output will go to the screen. For example, to write the string `'Hello'` to the file **Stuff**, the following statement will suffice:

writeln(Stuff, 'Hello')

Unfortunately, this syntax is confusing. The identifier **Stuff** looks like a variable whose value is to be written out. It is not. It is the name of the file that the output is being sent to. There is no way to figure this out by looking only at the **writeln** statement. The only way that you, or the compiler, can figure this out is to look at the variable declaration section. If **Stuff** is declared to be a file variable, then this first argument is the name of the file that is to receive the output. If, on the other hand, we had declared **Stuff** to be a variable of some type such as **char** or **integer**, then this statement would instead write the value of **Stuff**, as well as the word `'Hello'`, to the screen.

When reading or writing to text files, numbers are handled just as they are handled when reading from the keyboard or writing to the screen. The system automatically converts numbers to characters when outputting numbers and automatically converts characters to numbers when filing variables of type **integer** or **real**. A text file can contain nothing but characters divided into lines. It can not contain numbers, but because of automatic type conversion, the following statement will cause no problems:

write(Stuff, 5)

Just as with output to the screen, numbers are handled as you would hope. The system changes the number **5** to the character `'5'` and it is the character `'5'` that is written into the text file.

Text files can be read by means of **read** and **readln** statements. There are problems associated with mixing **read** and **write** statements to the same text file. So for now, we will assume that different programs are doing the reading and the writing. Suppose some other program contains the following declarations:

```
var Stuff: text;
    FirstLetter, SecondLetter: char;
```

The program can then associate the same file with the name **Stuff**. (We will explain how later on.) After that, the program can read from the file by a **read** statement such as:

```
read(Stuff, FirstLetter, SecondLetter)
```

This will set the value of **FirstLetter** to ´H´ and set the value of **SecondLetter** to ´e´. Reading starts with the first character of the first line of the file and proceeds through the file. The first **read** statement reads the first so many characters, the next **read** executed reads the next so many characters and so forth. There is no backspace command.

The statements **read** and **readln** behave the same for text files as they do for the sort of keyboard reading we have used so far. The only difference is that if the name of a text file is given as the first argument, then the data is read from the text file rather than from the keyboard. Just as with a **write** statement, this is confusing syntax. The only way to tell that the first argument of a **read** or **readln** statement is the name of a text file is to look at the declarations section to see if it is declared to be of type **text**.

Since standard and UCSD Pascal differ on how they associate a file with a file variable name, we will have to treat them separately.

345
Text Files and
Secondary Storage

*read
and
readln*

Standard Pascal

In standard Pascal the names of the files accessed or created by a program are listed in the program heading. We have already been doing that for the files called **input** and **output**. The keyboard and the screen are considered to be special kinds of files called **input** and **output**. A program that reads from a text file called **ReadStuff** and writes to a text file called **WriteStuff** would start as follows:

```
program Sample(input, output, ReadStuff, WriteStuff);
```

The order of the file names is unimportant.

Even though the files are named in the program heading, they must be declared in the variable declaration heading. Hence the following declaration must appear in the program:

```
var ReadStuff, WriteStuff: text;
```

Some standard Pascal systems have provisions to allow the user to specify the name of a file when the program is run. Those user specified files are not listed in

*opening
files*

rewrite

the program heading. The other syntax details for these user specified files vary from system to system, but tend to be similar to that of UCSD Pascal.

All files must be *opened* before a program can read from a file or write to a file. Opening a file instructs the system to prepare the file for reading or writing. In standard Pascal a file may be opened for reading or for writing but not for both.

A file is opened for writing with the standard procedure **rewrite**. The procedure has one parameter, which is the name of the file to be opened. For example, the following opens the file called **TestFile** for writing:

```
rewrite(TestFile)
```

After this statement is executed, the program may use **write** or **writeln** statements with the file named **TestFile**. The **rewrite** procedure always gives a blank file, a "clean sheet of paper" so to speak. If there already is a file named **TestFile**, it is erased. If there is no file called **TestFile**, the **rewrite** procedure will create one.

A complete example is given in Figure 13.1. This program writes the numbers **3** and **4** to a text file called **TestFile**. The numbers will be on two lines. If **TestFile** did not exist before the program was run, the program will create it. If

---

Program

```
program Writer(input, output, TestFile);
{Writes the numbers 3 and 4 into the text file TestFile.}
    var TestFile: text;
        N: integer;
begin{Program}
    writeln('Start program');
    rewrite(TestFile);
    writeln(TestFile, 3);
    N := 4;
    writeln(TestFile, N);
    writeln('End of program')
end. {Program}
```

Output to Screen

Start program
End program

Output to TestFile

**Figure 13.1
Standard Pascal
program that writes
to a text file.**

3
4

there was a file called **TestFile**, the previous contents of that file will be lost. After the program is run, the file will only contain the two numbers **3** and **4**. The first and last **writeln**'s do not contain the identifier **TestFile** and so their output goes to the screen. If those two **writeln** statements are omitted, the program will output nothing at all to the screen.

Reading from a text file is similar. The file name must be given in the program heading in the same way as in Figure 13.1. The file name must be declared as a file variable in the same way. The file must be opened, but the standard procedure that opens a file for reading is called **reset**. For example, suppose the program in Figure 13.1 has been run and so has created the file **TestFile**. Another program can open that same text file for reading with the following statement:

```
reset(TestFile)
```

After this statement is executed, the program may use **read** or **readln** statements with the file named **TestFile**. A complete example of reading from a text file is given in Figure 13.2. That program will read from the text file created by the program in Figure 13.1.

Program

```
program Reader(input, output, TestFile);
{Reads two numbers from the text file TestFile, places them in variables N1
and N2 and then outputs the contents of N1 and N2 to the screen.}
    var TestFile: text;
        N1, N2: integer;
begin{Program}
    reset(TestFile);
    readln(TestFile, N1);
    readln(TestFile, N2);

    writeln(N1);
    writeln(N2);
    writeln('End of program')
end. {Program}
```

Output
(Assuming that the program in Figure 13.1 was run first.)

3
4
End of program

Figure 13.2
Standard Pascal program to read from a text file.

UCSD Pascal

All files must be *opened* before a program can read from the file or write to a file. Opening a file instructs the system to prepare the file for reading or writing. In UCSD Pascal a text file is normally opened for reading or for writing but not for both.

In UCSD Pascal a file has two names, a permanent name which all programs that refer to it use to open it and a temporary name that an individual program uses to refer to the file once that file has been opened. The permanent name of a text file is a string called its *directory name*. On most systems it must be of the form:

    `´⟨identifier⟩.TEXT´`

That is, some identifier followed by `´.TEXT´`. This is the name that the system programs, such as the filer and the editor, use to refer to the file. In order to read a text file or to write to a text file, a UCSD Pascal program must rename the file with a file variable. This is done as part of the process of opening the file. After it is opened, the file is always referred to by its file variable name and never by its directory name. This point will become clearer after we do an example.

A text file is opened for writing with the standard procedure **rewrite**. In UCSD Pascal, the procedure **rewrite** has two arguments. The first is a file variable name that has been declared to be of type **text**. The second is a string that is the directory name of the file being opened. For example, the following opens the file `´DATA.TEXT´` for writing and renames it with the file variable **TestFile**:

    rewrite(TestFile, ´DATA.TEXT´)

After executing this statement, the program may use **write** or **writeln** statements with the file. When doing so, the file is always referred to by the name **TestFile**. The **rewrite** procedure always gives a blank file, a "clean sheet of paper" so to speak. If there already is a file named `´DATA.TEXT´`, that file is erased. If there is no file called `´DATA.TEXT´`, the **rewrite** procedure will create one.

A complete example is given in Figure 13.3. That program will write the numbers **3** and **4** to a text file called `´DATA.TEXT´`. The numbers will be on two lines. If `´DATA.TEXT´` does not exist before the program is run, the program will create it. If there is a file called `´DATA.TEXT´`, the previous contents of that file will be lost; after the program is run the file will only contain the two numbers.

In UCSD Pascal, all files should be *closed* after the program has finished writing to, or reading from, the file. Closing a file tells the system that the program is through reading from or writing to the file. This is done with the predefined UCSD procedure **close**. **close** takes two arguments. The first argument is the file variable name of the file. The second argument is an optional instruction specifying the manner in which the file is to be closed.

Program

```
program Writer;
{Writes the numbers 3 and 4 into text file 'DATA.TEXT'}
   var TestFile: text;
       N: integer;
begin{Program}
   writeln('Start program');
   rewrite(TestFile, 'DATA.TEXT');
   writeln(TestFile, 3);
   N := 4;
   writeln(TestFile, N);
   close(TestFile, lock);
   writeln('End of program')
end. {Program}
```

Output to Screen

Start program
End program

Output to 'DATA.TEXT'

3
4

Figure 13.3
UCSD Pascal
program that writes
to a text file.

The most common option for closing a file is **lock**. With this option the program actions are "locked in place" in the file. This is the option shown in Figure 13.3. Another option is the **purge** option. If the word **purge** is used instead of **lock**, then the file will be removed from the directory and lost forever. These are the only options you are likely to want. All the various options are summarized in Appendix 6.

Most UCSD Pascal systems will automatically close any file that is left opened when the program terminates. However, it is best to explicitly close all files with a call to **close**.

There are a number of items to note in the program of Figure 13.3. The directory name for the file is only used when the file is opened. Thereafter the file is always referred to by the file variable **TestFile**. Also note that the directory name **'DATA.TEXT'** is in quotes. That is because it is a constant of type **string**. It is also possible to use a variable of type **string** here, but whatever expression is used, it must evaluate to something of type **string**. Finally, notice that the first and last **writeln** statements do not contain the file variable **TestFile** and so their output goes to the screen. If those two **writeln** statements are omitted, the program will output nothing at all to the screen.

Program

```
program Reader;
{Reads two numbers from the text file 'DATA.TEXT', places them in variables
N1 and N2 and then outputs the contents of N1 and N2 to the screen.}
    var TestFile: text;
        N1, N2: integer;
begin{Program}
    reset(TestFile, 'DATA.TEXT');
    readln(TestFile, N1);
    readln(TestFile, N2);

    writeln(N1);
    writeln(N2);

    close(TestFile, lock);
    writeln('End of program')
end. {Program}
```

Output

(Assuming that the program in Figure 13.3 was run first.)

3
4
End of program

Figure 13.4
UCSD Pascal
program to read
from a text file.

reset

A file is opened for reading with the standard procedure **reset**. **reset** takes two arguments of the same type as **rewrite**. For example, the following opens the file with the directory name `'DATA.TEXT'` for reading and renames it with the file variable **TestFile**:

`reset(TestFile, 'DATA.TEXT')`

The second argument, in this example `'DATA.TEXT'`, should be the directory name of a file that already exists. For example, the preceding **reset** might be used in another program that is to be run after the one in Figure 13.3 is run. After executing this statement, the program may use **read** or **readln** statements with the file. When doing so, the file is always referred to by the file variable name, **TestFile**. A complete example is given in Figure 13.4. As shown in that example, a file that is opened for reading should be closed when the program is through reading.

Avoid the Silent Program

It is quite common to write a program so that all the data that is output is directed to a text file. If you do this, then the program will produce no output to the screen. This can be bewildering. If you write programs that way, the user may not even be able to tell when the program has finished. To let the user know what is going on, there should always be some output to the screen, even if it just says when the program starts and when it ends.

Self-Test and Interactive Exercises

1. Suppose the text file named by the file variable **Arthur** contains the following:

5 63 75
5 63 75

Suppose variables are declared as follows:

```
var Arthur: text;
    Number: integer;
    Letter1, Letter2: char;
```

What will be the output produced by the following, provided it is embedded in a complete program that opens **Arthur** with **reset** and that declares variables as shown above?

```
read(Arthur, Number); write(Number);
read(Arthur, Number); write(Number);
readln(Arthur); writeln;
read(Arthur, Letter1); write(Letter1);
read(Arthur, Letter1, Letter2);
write(Letter1, Letter2)
```

2. Write a program that will write your name to a text file. Look at the text file after the program is run. On most systems, programs are kept in text files and can be written and read using an editor program. Hence if your system is typical, you already know how to look at a text file.

3. Create a text file using the editor (like you do when you write a program) and write three numbers in the text file. Write a program to read the three numbers and write them to the screen. After running the program once, go back and change the numbers. Then rerun the program.

4. Using the editor, change the text file from the previous example so that the three numbers are two digits long, with one space between them, and so that there are no spaces at the front of the line. For example, the text file might contain:

25 36 47

Rerun the program from the previous exercise. Next write a slightly different program that will read three characters from the same text file into three variables of type **char** and will then output them to the screen. Run this new program on the same text file.

PART II

◇

The Moving Finger writes; and, having writ,
Moves on: nor all your Piety nor Wit
Shall lure it back to cancel half a line,
Nor all your Tears wash out a Word of it.
Omar Khaẏyam, The Ruba'iyat
(*Fitzgerald translation*)

◇

readln and writeln Reexamined

It will help to have a more precise notion of how the statements **read**, **readln**, **write** and **writeln** work.

arrow   When a text file is opened, a location marker is placed somewhere in the file. For purposes of explanation, let us call this location marker an *arrow* and think of it as pointing to a file location that contains, or could contain, one character. This arrow tells where the next character to be read is or where the next character to be written will go.

writing   When a file is opened with the **rewrite** statement, the file is erased and the arrow is placed at the first location in the file. Every time the program writes a character, the character is written at the location of the arrow and then the arrow is advanced to the next location. Some sample code and its effect on the text file **TestFile** are shown in Figure 13.5. Notice that a second line is started when the

---

The file is called **TestFile**.

Program action:	File after the action
rewrite the file	↑
write(TestFile, 'a')	a ↑
write(TestFile, 'b')	ab ↑
write(TestFile, 'c')	abc ↑
writeln(TestFile)	abc ↑
write(TestFile, 'd')	abc d ↑

Figure 13.5
Writing to a text file, intuitive picture.

writeln statement is executed. This is the only way that a new line is initiated. There is no limit to the length of a line in a text file.

Also notice that in the example the output is written from the beginning of the file and continues on through the file. The arrow did not "back up." When using a text file, it is not possible to backspace and change a character. With text files, the moving arrow "writes and having writ moves on," much like the finger of fate described by Omar Khayyam. The only way to get the arrow back to another position is to use a **reset** or **rewrite** statement, and these do not allow the program to change a portion of the file. The **rewrite** statement will erase the entire contents of the file. The **reset** will move the arrow all the way back to the first character in the file and will only allow the program to read from the file. It will not allow it to write to the file.

lines

In order to fully understand text files, we need to examine the notion of a *line* more carefully. Figure 13.5 is the way we normally think of lines, and text files are implemented so as to reflect this intuition. However, there are no physical lines in a text file. Instead, a text file is just one continuous stream of characters. The "end of a line" is indicated by inserting a special marker. This marker is a character of sorts, but it is not possible to see it on the screen. The computer can recognize it, though, and it is this character which indicates the intuitive end of a line. In Figure 13.6 we have redone Figure 13.5, but this time we have indicated the end of a line by this marker. In the diagram the marker is denoted ⟨eoln⟩. The way to insert an ⟨eoln⟩ marker in a text file is with a **writeln**.

end-of-line marker

An existing file is opened for reading with the **reset** statement. When a file is opened in this way, the arrow is placed at the first character of the first line of the file. Every time a character is read, the arrow is advanced to the next character. The situation is diagramed in Figure 13.7. Notice that the **readln**

reading

The file is called TestFile.

Program action	File after the action
rewrite the file	↑
write(TestFile, 'a')	a ↑
write(TestFile, 'b')	ab ↑
write(TestFile, 'c')	abc ↑
writeln(TestFile)	abc⟨eoln⟩ ↑
write(TestFile, 'd')	abc⟨eoln⟩d ↑

Figure 13.6
Writing to a text file, the "real" picture.

The file is called `TestFile`.

Program action	File after the action		Value of X after action
	Intuitive picture	Real picture	
reset the file	abcd (↑ under a) / ef	abcd⟨eoln⟩ef (↑ under a)	?
read(TestFile, X)	abcd (↑ under b) / ef	abcd⟨eoln⟩ef (↑ under b)	'a'
read(TestFile, X)	abcd (↑ under c) / ef	abcd⟨eoln⟩ef (↑ under c)	'b'
readln(TestFile)	abcd / ef (↑ under e)	abcd⟨eoln⟩ef (↑ under e)	'b'
read(TestFile, X)	abcd / ef (↑ under f)	abcd⟨eoln⟩ef (↑ after f)	'e'

Figure 13.7
Reading from a text file.

statement moves the arrow to the beginning of the next line and all the characters on the old line are thus ignored. If the program runs out of characters on one line, its behavior can be unpredictable. Usually, the programmer must ensure that the arrow is explicitly moved to the next line by means of a **readln**. An exception is made for numbers. If the program is reading into a variable of type **integer** or **real** and there is no more data on the current line, it will automatically go to the next line.

The ⟨eoln⟩ symbol is a symbol in the file and hence can be read into a variable of type **char**. It can then be written to another text file. Although this is theoretically possible, in practice it seldom works. Due to implementation-dependent details, it is likely to be written as some character other than ⟨eoln⟩. In practice, the only safe way to insert the ⟨eoln⟩ symbol into a text file is with a call to **writeln**.

eof and eoln

eof

When a program is reading from a text file, it is often helpful if the program can detect the end of the file. Pascal provides a special boolean valued function which does just that. The function **eof** is officially called the *end-of-file function*, but is usually pronounced by reading the letters "e-o-f." It takes one argument, a file variable, and it returns **true** if the program is at the end of that file. More specifically,

eof(⟨file variable⟩ **)**

evaluates to **true** if the arrow in the file named by ⟨file variable⟩ is past the last line in the file; otherwise, it evaluates to **false**.

```
program Standard(input, output, OldFile, NewFile);
    var Buffer: integer;
        OldFile, NewFile: text;
begin{Program}
    writeln('Copying program started');
    reset(OldFile);
    rewrite(NewFile);
    while not eof(OldFile) do
      begin{while}
        readln(OldFile, Buffer);
        Buffer := 2 * Buffer;
        writeln(NewFile, Buffer)
      end; {while}
    writeln('Numbers in OldFile doubled');
    writeln('and result copied to NewFile')
end. {Program}
```

Figure 13.8(s)
Standard Pascal
program using
eof.

As an example, the programs in Figures 13.8(s) and 13.8(u) each read a list of numbers from a file named by the file variable **OldFile**, multiply each number by two and copy the result into a second (new) file called **NewFile**. The version in Figure 13.8(s) gives the program in standard Pascal and Figure 13.8(u) gives the UCSD Pascal version of the program. The function **eof** is used to detect when all the numbers in the file have been read. Suppose the file **OldFile** contains the following when the program is run:

1
2
3

The body of the **while** loop in the program will then be executed three times. Each time one of the following three lines will be written to the file **NewFile**:

2
4
6

At this point the arrow in the file **OldFile** has moved beyond the third and last line. So **eof(OldFile)** evaluates to **true** and the following boolean expression evaluates to **false**:

not eof(OldFile)

Since the controlling boolean expression now evaluates to **false**, the **while** loop is terminated.

The function **eoln** is similar to **eof** except that it tests for the end of a line rather than the end of the entire file. In terms of the arrow discussed above, **eoln**

eoln

```
program UCSD;
    var Buffer: integer;
        OldFile, NewFile: text;
begin{Program}
    writeln('Copying program started');
    reset(OldFile, 'Old.TEXT');
    rewrite(NewFile, 'New.TEXT');
    while not eof(OldFile) do
      begin{while}
        readln(OldFile, Buffer);
        Buffer := 2 * Buffer;
        writeln(NewFile, Buffer)
      end; {while}
    close(OldFile, lock);
    close(NewFile, lock);
    writeln('Numbers in Old.TEXT doubled');
    writeln('and result copied to New.TEXT')
end. {Program}
```

**Figure 13.8(u)
UCSD Pascal
program using
eof.**

can be explained as follows. When the arrow in the file named by ⟨file variable⟩ is pointing to the end-of-line marker (what we have been denoting by ⟨eoln⟩ in the diagrams), then

eoln(⟨file variable⟩**)**

returns **true**; otherwise it returns **false**. (Do not confuse **eoln** and ⟨eoln⟩. ⟨eoln⟩ is a symbol in the text file. **eoln** is a function that tests to see if the arrow in a text file is pointing to ⟨eoln⟩.)

In order to construct an example using **eoln**, suppose that a program contains the following declarations:

```
var OldFile, NewFile: text;
    Buffer: char;
```

If both files are opened properly and the arrow is at the start of a line, then the following loop will copy one line of text from **OldFile** into **NewFile**:

```
while not eoln(OldFile) do
  begin
    read(OldFile, Buffer);
    write(NewFile, Buffer)
  end
```

The effect of this loop on some sample file contents is shown in Figure 13.9. After the two characters on the line have been read, the arrow in **OldFile** is at the end-of-line marker, and so **eoln(OldFile)** becomes **true**. That causes the boolean expression for the **while** loop to become **false**, and so the loop

OldFile	NewFile	Buffer	eoln(Oldfile)
ab⟨eoln⟩*cd*⟨eoln⟩ ↑	 ↑		false
then program executes	`read(OldFile, Buffer)`		
ab⟨eoln⟩*cd*⟨eoln⟩ ↑	 ↑	´a´	false
then program executes	`write(NewFile, Buffer)`		
ab⟨eoln⟩*cd*⟨eoln⟩ ↑	*a* ↑	´a´	false
then program executes	`read(OldFile, Buffer)`		
ab⟨eoln⟩*cd*⟨eoln⟩ ↑	*a* ↑	´b´	true
then program executes	`write(NewFile,Buffer)`		
ab⟨eoln⟩*cd*⟨eoln⟩ ↑	*ab* ↑	´b´	true
then program executes	`readln(OldFile)`		
ab⟨eoln⟩*cd*⟨eoln⟩ ↑	*ab* ↑	´b´	false
then program executes	`writeln(NewFile)`		
ab⟨eoln⟩*cd*⟨eoln⟩ ↑	*ab*⟨eoln⟩ ↑	´b´	false

Figure 13.9
Copying a line from one text file to another.

terminates after one more **write** statement. Typically, this loop would be followed by:

```
readln(OldFile);
writeln(NewFile)
```

This moves the arrow in each file to the beginning of the next line.

The standard functions **eof** and **eoln** may be applied to the file **input**. In fact if no argument is given, then the file is assumed to be **input**; that is, **eof** by itself is equivalent to **eof(input)** and **eoln** by itself is equivalent to **eoln(input)**. The end-of-line marker at the keyboard is usually the return key. The end-of-file marker at the keyboard varies from system to system. Since the exact details vary from system to system, using **eof** with the file **input** is usually more trouble than it is worth.

Using a Buffer

In Chapter 10 we briefly introduced the term "buffer." The word is frequently used in discussions about files and has a semitechnical meaning. A *buffer* is a location where some data is held on its way from one place to another. That is why we chose `Buffer` as the name of the character variable in the previous loop example. The program reads a character from one file into `Buffer` and then writes it from `Buffer` into the other file. The variable serves as a temporary location for one character. (The phrase "buffer variable" also has a technical meaning in Pascal, which is really a special case of this general notion of a buffer, but that topic comes later.)

Pragmatics of eoln and eof

Text files are designed for holding characters. When reading or writing numbers, a type conversion is performed. The exact details of how a system handles numbers in text files will vary from one installation to another. When dealing with numeric data, these details can cause the behavior of `eoln` and `eof` to vary in an unpredictable way from one system to another. The easiest way to avoid any problems when using `eof` with numeric data is to always use `readln` and `writeln` rather than `read` and `write`. The function `eoln` is best avoided completely when processing numeric data. When processing data of type `char`, there are no such problems. However, there are still some other problems in how `eof` and `eoln` interact.

When `eof(TextFile)` is `true`, the value of `eoln(TextFile)` is undefined. Hence it is not possible to mix these two functions in a single boolean expression. For example, the value, if any, of the following is unpredictable:

> `eof(TextFile)` *or* `eoln(TextFile)`
> {*This should not be used.*}

When `eof(TextFile)` is `true`, you might expect this expression to evaluate to `true`. However, the normal way to evaluate a boolean expression using *or* is to first evaluate both arguments and then apply the *or*. In this case `eof(Text-File)` evaluates to `true`, but the attempt to evaluate `eoln(TextFile)` produces an error condition, since that function has no value. On most systems this will produce an error message.

Text Files as Parameters to Procedures

In standard Pascal and most versions of UCSD Pascal, a text file may be a parameter to a procedure just like things of other data types. There is, however, one qualification. Text file parameters must be variable parameters; they can never be value parameters.

example:
copying
a file

As an example, we will design a procedure that has two text file parameters called `OldFile` and `NewFile`. The procedure will copy the contents of the file `OldFile` into the file `NewFile`. A precise definition of the task to be accom-

```
while not eof(OldFile) do
  begin{a line}
```

  {*The arrows in OldFile and NewFile are
  both at the start of a line*}

  Copy a line from `OldFile` to `NewFile`;

  {*The arrows in OldFile and NewFile are
  both at the end of a line*}

```
    readln(OldFile); {Moves the arrow to the next line}
    writeln(NewFile) {Inserts an end-of-line marker}
  end; {a line}
```

Figure 13.10

**The basic outline
of the procedure
in Figure 13.11.**

plished is:

> *Precondition:* `OldFile` *has been opened with* **reset***;*
> `NewFile` *has been opened with* **rewrite***;*
> *but no reading or writing has taken place yet.*
> *Postcondition:* `OldFile` *is unchanged; the contents of*
> `NewFile` *is made the same as that of* `OldFile`.

The basic outline of the procedure is given in Figure 13.10.

In order to convert that piece of pseudocode into Pascal, all we need to do is to design some Pascal code for the informal instruction:

> Copy a line from `OldFile` to `NewFile`

That is exactly what we did in the section on **eoln**. The Pascal code we developed there is:

```
while not eoln(OldFile) do
  begin
    read(OldFile, Buffer);
    write(NewFile, Buffer)
  end
```

If we now put together all the details, we obtain the procedure **Copy** shown in Figure 13.11.

Portability

The handling of files is different for UCSD and standard Pascal. Moreover, even implementations that claim to be UCSD or standard will frequently treat files in a slightly different way from what we have described. Thus, a program that deals

```
procedure Copy(var OldFile, NewFile: text);
```
{*Precondition: OldFile has been opened with reset; NewFile has been opened with rewrite; but no reading or writing has taken place yet. Postcondition: OldFile is unchanged; the contents of NewFile is made the same as that of OldFile.*}
```
    var Buffer: char;
begin{Copy}
    while not eof(OldFile) do
    begin{a line and outer while}

        while not eoln(OldFile) do
          begin{inner while}
            read(OldFile, Buffer);
            write(NewFile, Buffer)
```
            {*The current lines of NewFile and OldFile contain exactly the same thing up to (but not including) the positions of their arrows.*}
```
          end; {inner while}
```
        {*The arrow in OldFile is at the end of a line*}
```
        readln(OldFile);
        writeln(NewFile)
```
        {*The arrows in both files are at the beginning of the next line.*}
```
    end {a line and end outer while}
end; {Copy}
```

Figure 13.11
Procedure with text
file parameters.

---

with files cannot be completely portable. Moving it from one implementation to another will require rewriting part of the program. In order to make this rewriting task as easy as possible, all file handling should be isolated into self-contained procedures or at least easy to find isolated code. Then if the program is moved to a new system, only these isolated sections need to be rewritten.

Basic Technique for Editing Text Files

As we have already noted, there is no way to change part of a text file. The only way to write to a text file is to create a new file or to completely erase an old file. However, there is a way to get the effect of changing a file. In order to change part of a text file, a Pascal program must do something like the following: copy the entire contents from the given file into some temporary file, making changes as the copying is done; then copy the entire contents of the temporary file back to the original file.

Standard Pascal—Internal Files

What we have been describing are called *external* text files. They exist before and/or after the program is run. In standard Pascal there are also files that only exist for the duration of the program. These are called *internal* text files. The name of an internal file is local to a program. Thus it is wise to make any temporary file an internal file. In particular, if a program edits a text file in the manner outlined in the previous section, then it will need an extra temporary file. That extra file should be an internal file.

*external
versus
internal
files*

It is very easy to make a file internal to a program. Simply omit it from the program heading. An internal file is manipulated in exactly the same way as an external file, but when the program ends, the file disappears. For example, suppose you wish to write a program to edit a file called `DataFile` and your program uses a file called `TempFile` to temporarily hold some text. The program heading should be:

```
program Edit(input, output, DataFile);
```

If there coincidently happens to be a file called `TempFile` in the system, it will not be affected by the program because `TempFile` is an internal file.

An internal file is like a local variable. It is perfectly correct to think of an internal file variable as one that is local to the program. However, the way to make it internal is to omit it from the program heading. Simply making it a local variable in some procedure will not make it an internal file.

Example—Editing Out Excess Blanks

Suppose you wish to write a program to edit excess blanks from a text file containing some ordinary English text. To be more precise, let us say that the program is to delete all initial blanks on a line and is to compress every other string of two or more blanks down to a single blank. So, for example, consider the lines below:

*problem
definition*

```
    The    Answer to the    question of  Life,
    the    Universe   and Everything is:
```

They should be edited to look like:

```
The Answer to the question of Life,
the Universe and Everything is:
```

We will use the basic technique outlined above for editing files. Let us use `DataFile` as the name of the file to be edited. We will need one temporary file. We will call the temporary file `TempFile`. The basic outline of the program is:

subtasks

1. Open `DataFile` using `reset`; open `TempFile` using `rewrite`.
2. (`CleanBlanks`:) Copy `DataFile` into `TempFile` but delete excess blanks as this is done. (That is, copy all characters except the unwanted blanks from `DataFile` to `TempFile`.)

3. Reopen `TempFile` using `reset`; reopen `DataFile` using `rewrite`.
4. (**Copy**:) Copy the contents of `TempFile` into `DataFile`.

We will implement subtasks 2 and 4 as procedures named `CleanBlanks`
and `Copy`. The Pascal program, with some details still missing, is shown in Figure
13.12(s) for standard Pascal and in Figure 13.12(u) for UCSD Pascal. The
procedure `Copy` is the one in Figure 13.11. So all that remains is to design an
algorithm for subtask 2 and to translate that algorithm into some Pascal code.
That code will complete the procedure declaration for `CleanBlanks`.

mixing
reading
and
writing

Before designing the code for the procedure `CleanBlanks`, let us observe a
few things about the program outline. Notice that the programs in Figures
13.12(s) and 13.12(u) both read from and write to the same file. This is permitted
as long as the reading and writing are not mixed. The program must first read
from the file and then reopen it for the purpose of writing. (In UCSD Pascal the

```
program Edit(input, output, DataFile);
{Edits out excess blanks from the text file DataFile.}

var DataFile, TempFile: text;

procedure CleanBlanks(var DirtyFile, CleanFile: text);
{Precondition: DirtyFile has been opened with reset; CleanFile has
been opened with rewrite; but no reading or writing has taken place yet.
Postcondition: DirtyFile is unchanged; the contents of CleanFile is made
the same as that of OldFile except that superfluous blanks are deleted.}
            .   .   .
            .   .   .
procedure Copy(var OldFile, NewFile: text);
{Precondition: OldFile has been opened with reset; NewFile has been
opened with rewrite; but no reading or writing has taken place yet.
Postcondition: OldFile is unchanged; the contents of NewFile is
made the same as that of OldFile.}
            .   .   .
            .   .   .
begin{Program}
   writeln('Program is running');

   reset(DataFile); rewrite(TempFile);
   CleanBlanks(DataFile, TempFile);

   reset(TempFile); rewrite(DataFile);
   Copy(TempFile, DataFile);

   writeln('End of program')
end. {Program}
```

**Figure 13.12(s)
Standard Pascal
program that edits
a text file.**

```
program Edit;
{Edits excess blanks from a file specified by the user.}

var DataFile, TempFile: text;
    DataName, SpareName: string;

procedure CleanBlanks(var DirtyFile, CleanFile: text);
```
{Precondition: DirtyFile has been opened with reset; CleanFile has
been opened with rewrite; but no reading or writing has taken place yet.
Postcondition: DirtyFile is unchanged; the contents of CleanFile is made
the same as that of OldFile except that superfluous blanks are deleted.}

      • • •

      • • •

```
procedure Copy(var OldFile, NewFile: text);
```
{Precondition: OldFile has been opened with reset; NewFile has been
opened with rewrite; but no reading or writing has taken place yet.
Postcondition: OldFile is unchanged; the contents of NewFile is
made the same as that of OldFile.}

      • • •

      • • •

```
begin{Program}
    writeln('Enter the directory name of');
    writeln('the file to be cleaned of blanks:');
    readln(DataName);

    writeln('I need a temporary file name.');
    writeln('Enter a directory name which');
    writeln('is NOT the name of any file.');
    readln(SpareName);

    reset(DataFile, DataName); rewrite(TempFile, SpareName);
    CleanBlanks(DataFile, TempFile);
    close(DataFile, lock); close(TempFile, lock);

    reset(TempFile, SpareName); rewrite(DataFile, DataName);
    Copy(TempFile, DataFile);
    close(TempFile, purge); close(DataFile, lock);

    writeln('End of program')
end. {Program}
```

**Figure 13.12(u)
UCSD Pascal
program that edits
a text file.**

algorithm

file must be closed before it is reopened.) It is also possible to write first and then read, but every change from reading to writing and every change from writing to reading requires that the file be reopened. This is a nontrivial restriction, since opening the file for writing completely erases the file.

We now turn to the task of designing the procedure **CleanBlanks**. It can be very much like the procedure **Copy**. In fact, the only difference between **CleanBlanks** and **Copy** is that **CleanBlanks** will sometimes read a character and decide not to copy it to the second file. Hence we need to design a test to

```
procedure CleanBlanks(var DirtyFile, CleanFile: text);
{Precondition: DirtyFile has been opened with reset; CleanFile has
been opened with rewrite; but no reading or writing has taken place yet.
Postcondition: DirtyFile is unchanged; the contents of CleanFile is made
the same as that of OldFile except that superfluous blanks are deleted.}
    const Blank = ' ';
    var Current, Last: char;
begin{CleanBlanks}
    while not eof(DirtyFile) do
      begin{a line and outer while}
        Last := Blank; {This ensures that a blank at the
        start of a line will be deleted}

        while not eoln(DirtyFile) do
          begin{inner while}
            read(DirtyFile, Current);
            if not( (Last = Blank) and (Current = Blank) )
              then write(CleanFile, Current);
            Last := Current
            {The current lines of NewFile and OldFile
            contain the same thing up to (but not including)
            the positions of their arrows, except that any
            excess blanks do not appear in NewFile. Last
            contains the last character considered and possibly
            copied to CleanFile.}
          end; {inner while}
        {The arrow in DirtyFile is at the end of a line}

        readln(DirtyFile);
        writeln(CleanFile)
        {The arrows in both files are at
        the beginning of the next line.}
      end {a line and end outer while}
end; {CleanBlanks}
```

**Figure 13.13
Procedure to copy
with excess blanks
omitted.**

determine if a character should or should not be copied. For the moment let us ignore the problem of initial blanks and concentrate only on strings of blanks within a line. We want to compress every string of two or more blanks to a single blank. One solution is to copy only the first blank out of any string of blanks and not to copy the rest of the string of blanks. To express this condition, it is easier to think in terms of those characters that are not copied. The procedure should copy a character provided the following does **not** hold:

1. The character is a blank and
2. The character that precedes it on the same line is also a blank.

This test requires that the program remember two characters instead of just one. Hence we will use two variables of type **char** as buffer variables. One, called **Current**, will contain the current symbol, which either does or does not get copied to the second file. One, called **Last**, will contain the previous character in the file being copied from. Our test now can be expressed as follows:

Copy the symbol **Current** provided:
not((Last = Blank) *and* (Current = Blank))

This is not yet a complete solution. It does not make sense for the first symbol of a line. To make it work for the first symbol of a line, recall that we want to copy the first symbol as long as it is not a blank. Hence if we set **Last** equal to the blank symbol before we start each line, then this test works for the first symbol of a line as well. The complete details are shown in Figure 13.13.

Text Editing as a Programming Aid

A Pascal program is a piece of text and is stored in a text file. Hence it can be edited by another program in the ways we have been describing. This can sometimes be a helpful programming aid. As an example, consider the task of tracing a program, which we discussed in Chapter 8. Tracing is a technique to aid in debugging programs. Specifically, it consists of inserting temporary **write** statements that output intermediate results. Once the program is debugged, we want to remove these extra **write** statements used for tracing. To aid us in finding and removing trace statements or for that matter any other sort of temporary lines, we suggested marking them by a comment like the following sample of a temporary **writeln**

    {TEMP} ; writeln(SUM);

The extra semicolon is there for reasons explained in Chapter 8, but its inclusion or omission is irrelevant to what we are discussing here.

Suppose all our temporary statements are marked in the way we described. Then to remove the temporary statements, all we need to do is locate those lines that begin with {TEMP} and delete them. This sort of tedious and uninteresting task is best left to the computer. In Exercise 17 you are asked to write a program for the computer to do this editing. After writing the program, it would be a good idea to actually use the program as a programming tool from then on. It is not just a "toy problem."

Summary of Problem Solving and Programming Techniques

Text files are used for storing data that is to remain in secondary storage after a program terminates. The data is stored as strings of symbols like the data displayed on the output screen. The text file can later be read by other Pascal programs. The exact details of file handling will vary from one installation to another. Hence file handling should be isolated into procedures in order to make any needed changes easy to carry out.

A text file may not be opened for reading and writing at the same time. Hence when editing a text file, the usual technique is to use an additional temporary file. The contents of the text file are copied into the temporary file and the editing changes are made in the process of copying. After that, the edited version of the text is recopied back into the original file. One application of text editing is to edit the temporary trace statements out of a debugged Pascal program.

◇

In *theory*,
there is no difference between *theory* and *practice*;
but in *practice*,
there is.
Remark overheard at a computer science conference.

◇

Summary of Pascal Constructs

Constructs Common to All Versions of Pascal

the type for text files
Syntax:

```
text
```

The Pascal type name for text files.

text variables
Syntax:

```
var ⟨file variable⟩: text;
```

Example:

var `DataFile: text;`

Declaration of a file variable of type **text**. Except possibly in statements that open a file, a text file is always referred to by such a file variable name.

write statement

Syntax:

`write(`⟨file variable⟩`,` ⟨argument list⟩ `)`

Example:

`write(DataFile, 'Hello', X, Y)`

Just like using **write** to write to the screen, but when done this way, the things in ⟨argument list⟩ are written to the text file named by ⟨file variable⟩. ⟨file variable⟩ is a variable of type **text**. The file named by ⟨file variable⟩ must have been opened with a call to **rewrite**. ⟨argument list⟩ is a list of variables and quoted strings separated by commas.

writeln statement

Syntax:

`writeln(`⟨file variable⟩`,` ⟨argument list⟩`)`

Example:

`writeln(DataFile, 'Hello', X, Y)`

Same as the previous definition with the addition that it inserts an end-of-line marker \ in the text file. In other words, it causes any subsequent output to ⟨file variable⟩ to be written on the next line.

read statement

Syntax:

`read(`⟨file variable⟩`,` ⟨variable list⟩`)`

Example:

`read(DataFile, X, Y, Z)`

Just like using **read** to read from the keyboard, but done this way, the values are read from the text file named by ⟨file variable⟩. ⟨file variable⟩ is a variable of type **text**. The file named by ⟨file variable⟩ must have been opened with a call to **reset**. The ⟨variable list⟩ is a list of variables separated by commas.

readln statement

Syntax:

`readln(`⟨file variable⟩`,` ⟨variable list⟩`)`

Example:

`readln(DataFile, X, Y, Z)`

Same as the previous definition with the addition that it causes any subsequent read from the file named ⟨file variable⟩ to start at the beginning of the next line.

end-of-file function
Syntax:

> **eof(**⟨file variable⟩**)**

Example:

> **eof(DataFile)**

⟨file variable⟩ is a variable of type **text**. This is a boolean valued function that returns **true** if all of the text file named by ⟨file variable⟩ has been read. More precisely, it evaluates to **true** if the arrow (described in the chapter) has moved past the last line in the file.

end-of-line function
Syntax:

> **eoln(**⟨file variable⟩**)**

Example:

> **eoln(OldFile)**

⟨file variable⟩ is a variable of type **text**. This is a boolean valued function that returns **true** if all of the data on the current line of the file named by ⟨file variable⟩ have been read. More precisely, it evaluates to **true** if the arrow (described in the chapter) is pointing to the end-of-line marker.

Standard but Not UCSD Pascal

program heading
Syntax:

> **program** ⟨program name⟩**(** ⟨file list⟩**);**

Example:

> **program Standard(input, output, File1, File2);**

⟨file list⟩ is a list of (external) files which are used in the program. The file name **input** may be omitted if the program does not read from the keyboard. On most systems the file **output** must be listed because any error messages are written to the file **output**. All text files, except **input** and **output**, must also be declared to be variables of type **text**.

reset
Syntax:

> **reset(**⟨file variable⟩**)**

Example:

> **reset(File1)**

Opens the text file named by ⟨file variable⟩ for reading. ⟨file variable⟩ is a variable of type **text**. Reading starts at the first character of the first line of the text file and proceeds through the file.

Syntax:

rewrite(⟨file variable⟩**)**

Example:

rewrite(File2)

Opens the text file named by ⟨file variable⟩ for writing. ⟨file variable⟩ is a variable of type **text**. This always produces a blank file. If no file named ⟨file variable⟩ exists, a blank one is created. If there already is a file named ⟨file variable⟩, the file is erased.

UCSD but Not Standard Pascal

reset

Syntax:

reset(⟨file variable⟩**,** ⟨directory name⟩**)**

Example:

reset(DataFile, ´DATA.TEXT´)

Opens a text file for reading. ⟨file variable⟩ is a variable of type **text**. ⟨directory name⟩ is an expression of type **string** that evaluates to the directory name of the text file being opened. In the rest of the program the file is always referred to by the name ⟨file variable⟩. Reading starts at the first character of the first line of the text file and proceeds through the file. It is not possible to reread a character of the text file unless it is **reset** again.

rewrite

Syntax:

rewrite(⟨file variable⟩**,** ⟨directory name⟩**)**

Example:

rewrite(SecondDataFile, ´DATA2.TEXT´)

Opens a text file for writing. ⟨file variable⟩ is a variable of type **text**. ⟨directory name⟩ is an expression of type **string** that evaluates to the directory name of the text file being opened. In the rest of the program the file is always referred to by the name ⟨file variable⟩. This always produces a blank file. If no file named ⟨directory name⟩ exists, then a blank file is created. If there already is a file named ⟨directory name⟩, then it is erased.

close

Syntax:

close(⟨file variable⟩**,** ⟨option⟩**)**

Example:

close(DataFile, lock)

The procedure for closing the file named by the ⟨file variable⟩. The ⟨option⟩ specifies how the file is to be closed. If 〈option〉 is **lock**, the program actions are preserved and the file is stored as the program actions left it. If 〈option〉 is **purge**, the file is removed from the directory.

Exercises

Self-Test and Interactive Exercises

5. Suppose the text file named by the file variable **Sally** contains the following:

abcdef〈eoln〉*ghijk*〈eoln〉*lmnop*〈eoln〉

Suppose variables are declared as follows:

```
var Sally: text;
    L1, L2, Buffer: char;
```

What will be the output produced by the following, provided it is embedded in a complete program that opens **Sally** with **reset** and that declares variables as shown above?

```
readln(Sally, L1, L2); writeln(L1, L2);
while not eoln(Sally) do
  begin
    read(Sally, Buffer);
    write(Buffer)
  end;
writeln('Hi')
```

6. (This is only for readers using standard Pascal.) Standard Pascal has no provisions whereby a program may read a file name from the keyboard. However, many standard Pascal systems have been extended to allow this. Find out if your system allows programs to read in a file name, and if it does, find out how this is done.

7. Write a program to write the numbers **1** through **10** to a text file, one per line. Run the program and then look at the text file.

8. Write a program that reads the list of numbers from the text file of the previous exercise, computes their sum and outputs the sum to the screen. The program should use **eof** to detect the end of the file.

9. Write a program to read a line of text from a text file and display it on the screen. Use **eoln**. Use the editor or another program to create the text file.

Regular Exercises

10. Write a program that computes the average number of characters per word and the average number of words per sentence for the text in some text file.

11. Write a procedure that will append the contents of one text file to the end of another text file. The contents of the first file should be unchanged after the procedure is called.

12. Write a program that will create a table telling how to give change using quarters, dimes and pennies. It should show the coins for all amounts from 1 to 99 cents. There should be a heading for the table. The program should output the table to a text file.

13. Write a program that will output a table for converting from Celsius (centigrade) temperatures to Fahrenheit temperatures. Show all temperatures from -10 Celsius to 100 Celsius. A Celsius (centigrade) temperature C can be converted to an equivalent Fahrenheit temperature F according to the following formula:

$$F = (9/5)C + 32$$

The program should output the table to a text file.

14. Write a procedure that will fill one variable parameter of type **integer** with a value read from the keyboard. The procedure will read the input as a string of characters and will check and recover from input typing mistakes as follows: It will skip over all characters other than the 10 digits. So, it will interpret the input: *$12**%5* as the number **125**. It will then echo the integer value and allow the user to try again if it is not correct.

15. Write a program that gives and takes advice on program writing. The program should open by writing a piece of advice to the screen. It should then ask the user to type in a different piece of advice. The next user of the program receives the advice typed in the last time the program was run. Be sure that the first person to run the program gets some advice.

16. Write a program that merges two lists of alphabetically sorted words into a single list of alphabetically sorted words. The words are to be read from two text files and written to a third text file. The words should appear one per line with no blanks in the line.

17. Write a program to delete all temporary lines from a text file containing a Pascal program. See the section on "Text Editing as a Programming Aid" for a discussion of this problem.

18. (This is an exploratory exercise for those who did the previous exercise.) In writing the program for Exercise 17, you may have added some temporary **write** or **writeln** statements. If you did not, then go back and add some. Now you have a copy of the program with lines that need to be deleted. Run this program on the text file containing the program; that is, "run the program on itself." The program will clean itself, so to speak. (Some systems may require that you have two copies of the program to do this, but most systems will let you do it with just one copy. In any event, you should have an extra copy of the program just in case some mistake causes the program to damage itself.)

19. The organization Professional Programmers for Purity in Pascal Programs has declared ´**P**´ to be a dirty letter and has hired you to write a program to eliminate this letter from text files. Write a program that will replace all occurrences of the letter ´**P**´ in a text file with the letter ´**X**´.

20. Write a program to generate personalized junk mail. The program will work with a text file that contains a letter in which the location of the name of the recipient is indicated by some special string of characters, such as ´#**name**#´. The program will ask for the name from the keyboard, read it in and then make a copy of the letter with the name inserted where indicated. The letter with the name inserted should be written to another text file.

21. Pascal allows either the pair ´**{}**´ or the pair ´**(**)**´ to enclose a comment. The reason for including the pair ´**(**)**´ is that some systems do not have the symbols ´**{**´ and ´**}**´ available. In order to run a Pascal program written using ´**{}**´ on a system that does not have these symbols, all occurrences of ´**{**´ need to be replaced by ´**(***´ and all occurrences of ´**}**´ need to be replaced by ´***)**´. Write a program that will change the text file containing a Pascal program so that this substitution of comment delimiters is made.

22. Write a program that will produce a list of all the words used in a text file as well as the number of times each word is used. The list should be output to the screen as well as to another text file. The list should be in alphabetical order. Do not forget to consider punctuation marks, such as periods and commas, when determining the ends of words. The program should treat upper- and lower-case letters as being the same. For example, `'Word'` and `'word'` should be treated as the same word.

23. Write a program to generate pseudorandom test data for other programs. The data is written to a text file which contains `NumLINES` lines of `NumPerL integer` values per line. The values of `NumLINES` and `NumPerL` as well as a range of possible integer values are to be read from the keyboard. If your system has a predefined pseudorandom number generator, then you may use it; otherwise, use the function `Random` described in Chapter 9.

24. Books and newspapers contain text that is right-justified; that is, all lines are the same length. This is accomplished by copying as many words as possible onto one line and then adding extra blanks between the words so that the line is filled out to the prescribed line length. The line breaks in the original unjustified text are ignored in determining line lengths in the justified text. Write a program that produces right-justified text. The program will read from one file and write the right-justified text to another file. Use 80 characters, or whatever is convenient, as the line length.

25. Write a program to generate random English sentences. The program will use two text files, one containing a list of nouns and one containing a list of verbs, and will use a random number generator to choose words from these files.

26. Enhance the program of the previous exercise so that it outputs a series of sentences that seem to be related. Do this by repeating the nouns and verbs used. Specifically, once a noun or verb is used, the program remembers it and uses it more often than the other words on the lists. To make the output seem even more reasonable, you might try grouping related words and have the program choose words related to those already chosen. Use your imagination in forming word groupings and the other details of the algorithm.

27. Since the rules of grammar are not as rigid for poetry as they are for prose, it is usually easier to write a poetry-writing program that produces human-like output than it is to produce a reasonable prose-writing program. Use the techniques discussed in the previous two exercises to write a program that outputs free verse poetry.

28. Design a version of Pascal in a foreign language of your choice. To do this choose a fixed translation for each reserved word and standard identifier. Write a program that will take a text file containing a Pascal program and translate it into the foreign language version by replacing each reserved word and standard identifier with its translation. Then enhance your program so that it can also translate the foreign language version into English Pascal; the user specifies which language to translate the program into.

29. A *pretty print* program takes a program, which may not be indented in any particular way, and produces a copy with the same program indented so that *begin/end* pairs line up with inner pairs indented more than outer pairs and so that *if - then - else* statements are indented with the *if*, *then* and *else* lined up and with comments lined up and so forth. Write a program that reads a Pascal program from one text file and produces a pretty print version of the program in a second text file. To make it easier, simply do this for the body of the program, ignoring the declarations, and assume that all substatements of complex statements (other than compound statements themselves) are compound statements enclosed in *begin/end* pairs. To make it harder add any or all of the features omitted from the easy version.

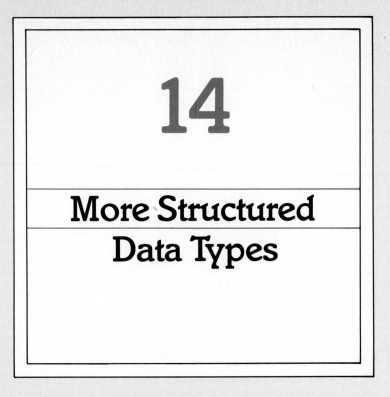

14

More Structured Data Types

The time has come the walrus said
to talk of many things;
of shoes and ships and sealing wax
of cabbages and kings.
Lewis Carroll,
Through the Looking-Glass

Chapter Contents

In Chapter 10 we discussed the notion of a structured data type and introduced arrays as a first example of a structured type. In this chapter we will extend the notion of an array. The arrays we discussed previously are called one-dimensional arrays. In the next section we introduce multidimensional arrays. After that we go on to discuss another class of structured types called "records." We complete the discussion of Pascal sets that we began in Chapter 7. We discuss techniques for using each of these data types as well as techniques for deciding which data type to use.

Multidimensional Arrays

In Chapter 10 we discussed simple arrays, such as the array **L** in the declaration:

>*var* L: *array*[1..80] *of* char;

Using the array **L**, we can associate a value of type **char** with each index in the range **1..80**. Frequently, we desire a more complicated structure. For example, suppose we wish to hold a page of text in an array. We could number the characters of the text consecutively and use a larger array index range. If there are 100 characters per line and 30 lines per page, we could make it an array of characters indexed by the type **1..3000**. However, it would be much more convenient to use two different indexes, one for the line and one for the character on that line. In Pascal and most other high level programming languages this is possible. It is possible to have an array, for example, called **P**, that has two indexes, one for the line and one for the character in that line. Although Pascal does not insist on it, it is traditional to make the first index count the lines and the second index count the position in the line. The array declaration in this case would be written:

>*var* P: *array*[1..30, 1..100] *of* char;

With **P** declared this way, the first character of the first line can be stored as the value of **P[1,1]**, that of the second character on the first line as the value of **P[1,2]** and so forth. As another sample, the value of

>**P[5, 38]**

is the thirty-eighth character on the fifth line. To write out the entire fifth line to the screen, the following will do:

>*for* I := 1 *to* 100 *do*
>   write(P[5, I]);
>writeln

*two-dimensional
example*

   An array with more than one index is called a *multidimensional* array. The diagram in Figure 14.1 may help to explain this choice of terminology. The array **A** diagramed there contains a list of average grades for a small class with four students numbered **1** through **4**. The array can be thought of as a simple list. Such lists are one-dimensional objects. The array **G** shows more details of the class grading. It gives three quiz scores for each of the four students. This can be visualized as a two-dimensional arrangement, with one row for each student and one column for each quiz.

*sample
declarations*

   Multidimensional arrays are declared in the same way as one-dimensional arrays. The syntax for a multidimensional type definition is described in Figure 14.2. Just as in the one-dimensional case, the index types must be subrange types. The various index types need not be subranges of the same type. The index types are separated by commas. There may be any number of them, so long as there is at least one. (If there is just one, then we have the one-dimensional case.) The component type may be any type we have seen except that it may not be a file

```
var A: array[1..4] of real;
```

Layout   Sample values

	Average			Average
Student 1	A[1]		Student 1	10.0
Student 2	A[2]		Student 2	8.3
Student 3	A[3]		Student 3	0.3
Student 4	A[4]		Student 4	6.7

```
var G: array[1..4, 1..3] of 0..10;
```

Layout   Sample values

	Quiz 1	Quiz 2	Quiz 3		Quiz 1	Quiz 2	Quiz 3
Student 1	G[1,1]	G[1.2]	G[1,3]	Student 1	10	10	10
Student 2	G[2,1]	G[2,2]	G[2,3]	Student 2	9	7	9
Student 3	G[3,1]	G[3,2]	G[3,3]	Student 3	1	0	0
Student 4	G[4,1]	G[4,2]	G[4,3]	Student 4	7	8	5

**Figure 14.1
One- and
two-dimensional
arrays.**

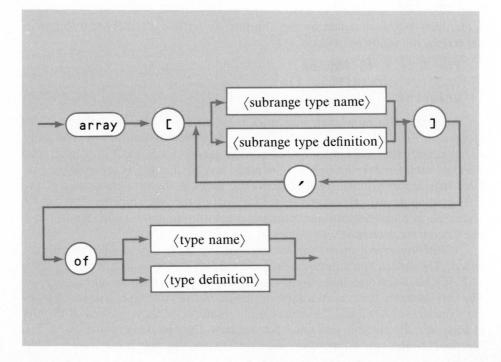

**Figure 14.2
Syntax of array
definitions.**

type, such as the type **text**. Some sample multidimensional array type declarations are:

```
type Matrix = array[1..10, 1..5] of real;
     Count = array[1..100, 'A'..'B'] of integer;
     Picture = array[0..4, 0..9] of char;
     WOW =
       array[-89..7, 'M'..'R', boolean] of boolean;
```

The last type is not likely to arise in practice but it does illustrate some of the possibilities for index types. Recall that the type **boolean** is the same as the type **false..true**. All the other type declarations are quite plausible. Arrays of the first type might hold real numbers for some scientific or engineering calculation. The type **Count** can be used in text processing. Suppose **C** is declared as:

*sample
applications*

```
var C: Count;
```

The array **C** might be used to count occurrences of each letter in a 100 line text. With the two-dimensional array, the program can easily keep a separate count for each line. The number of occurrences of, say, **'M'** on, say, line 20 would be the value of **C[20, 'M']**. Arrays of type **Picture** might be used to hold patterns consisting of five lines of 10 characters each, which when displayed on the screen form a geometric pattern.

Aside from the fact that multidimensional arrays may have more than one index, their usage is the same as that of the simple one-dimensional arrays we introduced in Chapter 10.

Grading—An Example Using a Two-Dimensional Array

To illustrate the use of multidimensional arrays, we will solve a simple class grading problem. The program we design will be a program to compute grade averages and to display the grades and the averages. It could be used by an instructor to obtain an overview of class grades.

The definition of the task is as follows. The quiz scores are to be read into the computer. A screen display is then written out consisting of each student's number followed by the student's average grade and a list of all the quiz scores for that student.

We need to devise some method for keeping track of each student's score. A natural way to do this is with a two-dimensional array, such as the array **G** illustrated in Figure 14.1. One index can be the student number; the other index can be the quiz number. If the array is called **G**, then **G[SNum, QNum]** will contain the grade that student number **SNum** received on quiz number **QNum**. If **NumStudents** and **NumQuizzes** are constants equal to the number of students and the number of quizzes, and if each quiz is scored on a zero to 10 points, then the declaration for the two-dimensional array **G** can be:

```
type Score = 0..10;
     StudentIndex = 1..NumStudents;
     QuizIndex = 1..NumQuizzes;
     GradeArray =
        array[StudentIndex, QuizIndex] of Score;
var G: GradeArray;
```

Figure 14.1 illustrates one possible set of values for **G**. There, and in our program, **NumStudents** is set to **4** and **NumQuizzes** is set to **3**.

*parallel
arrays*

We will use a second array **A** to hold the averages. The array **A** will be a one-dimensional array indexed by student numbers in the range **1..NumStudents**. The array **A** is not absolutely necessary for this simple problem, but it would be needed if we expanded the program to do more complicated tasks such as displaying the averages in sorted order. Two related arrays with the same index type(s), such as **G** and **A**, are frequently called *parallel arrays*.

The task to be solved by this program can be decomposed into three subtasks:

1. Read in the quiz grades.

2. Compute the averages.

3. Display the grades and the averages.

Each task is accomplished by a separate procedure. The complete program is shown in Figure 14.3.

Program

```
program QuizAve(input, output);
{Reads quiz scores for each student into a two-dimensional
array G; computes each student's average and stores it in an
array A; displays each student number followed by the student
average followed by a list of quiz scores.}

const NumStudents = 4;
      NumQuizzes = 3;
type Score = 0..10;
     StudentIndex = 1..NumStudents;
     QuizIndex = 1..NumQuizzes;
     GradeArray =
        array[StudentIndex, QuizIndex] of Score;
     AveArray = array[StudentIndex] of real;
var G: GradeArray;
    A: AveArray;
```

```
procedure ReadQuizzes(var G: GradeArray);
{Postcondition: For each student number SNum, G contains the quiz
scores for student SNum in indexed variables G[SNum, 1], G[SNum, 2],...}
    var SNum: StudentIndex;
        QNum: QuizIndex;
begin{ReadQuizzes}
    for SNum := 1 to NumStudents do
      begin{Student number SNum}
        writeln('Enter the ', NumQuizzes:3, ' quiz scores');
        writeln('for student number ', SNum:3);
        for QNum := 1 to NumQuizzes do
            read(G[SNum, QNum]);
        readln
      end {Student number SNum}
end; {ReadQuizzes}

procedure CompAverage(G: GradeArray; var A: AveArray);
{Precondition: G contains the quiz scores for student SNum in
indexed variables G[SNum, 1], G[SNum, 2],... Postcondition: A contains
the average quiz score for student SNum in the indexed variable A[SNum].}
    var SNum: StudentIndex;
        QNum: QuizIndex;
        Sum: integer;
begin{CompAverage}
    for SNum := 1 to NumStudents do
      begin{Student number SNum}
        Sum := 0;
        for QNum := 1 to NumQuizzes do
            Sum := Sum+G[SNum, QNum];
        {Sum contains the sum of the quiz scores for student SNum.}
        A[SNum] := Sum/NumQuizzes
      end {Student number SNum}
end; {CompAverage}

procedure Display(G: GradeArray; A: AveArray);
{Precondition: Scores for student SNum are in G[SNum, 1],
G[SNum,2], etc. and the student's average score is in A[SNum].
Postcondition: The scores and average are displayed on the screen.}
    const Space = ' ';
    var SNum: StudentIndex;
        QNum: QuizIndex;
begin{Display}
    writeln( 'Student':8, 'Ave':5, Space:4,'Quizzes');
    for SNum := 1 to NumStudents do
```

Figure 14.3
continues on p. 380

```
begin{outer for loop}
   write(SNum:8, A[SNum]:5:1, Space:4);
   for QNum := 1 to NumQuizzes do
      write(G[SNum, QNum]:3);
   writeln
end {outer for loop}
end; {Display}

begin{Program}
   ReadQuizzes(G);
   CompAverage(G, A);
   Display(G, A);
   writeln('Now you know the scores!')
end. {Program}
```

Sample Dialogue

Enter the 3 quiz scores for student number 1
10 10 10
Enter the 3 quiz scores for student number 2
9 7 9
Enter the 3 quiz scores for student number 3
1 0 0
Enter the 3 quiz scores for student number 4
7 8 5

Student	Ave	Quizzes
1	*10.0*	*10 10 10*
2	*8.3*	*9 7 9*
3	*0.3*	*1 0 0*
4	*6.7*	*7 8 5*

Now you know the scores!

Figure 14.3 (cont'd)

As illustrated in the procedure **Display**, the usual and natural way to step through all the elements of a multidimensional array is to use *for* loops nested inside of one another. Each *for* loop steps through one of the array indexes.

Storage Efficiency

It is very easy to use unreasonably large amounts of storage when programming with multidimensional arrays. Even a modest looking multidimensional array declaration can sometimes cause the computer to use a huge amount of storage.

For example, consider the following reasonable looking array declaration:

> *var* A: *array*[0..50, 0..50, 0..50] *of* integer;

The compiler must allocate storage for $51 \times 51 \times 51 = 132,651$ integers. Many computer installations simply will not have enough storage available to accommodate such a program.

In Chapter 10 we made a number of remarks about storage efficiency and one-dimensional arrays. These remarks apply to multidimensional arrays as well. In particular, multidimensional arrays may be declared to be of a **packed** type in the same way that one-dimensional arrays are.

Another way to economize on storage is to use variable parameters rather than value parameters for arrays, even if their value is not changed. Chapter 10 contains an explanation of why this saves storage. In this chapter we have ignored the question of storage. If storage is an issue, then our procedures and type declarations should be modified to use packed arrays and variable parameters.

Introduction to Records

Sometimes it is useful to have a unified name for a collection of values of different types. For example, an inventory for a mail-order house might contain the following entry:

> atomic can opener
> item #2001
> price $1,999.99

In this example each inventory record consists of a name, a stock number and a price. Although the record is conceptually a unit, the components are items of different data types. In Pascal it is possible to define a structured data type consisting of a number of components, each of a possibly different type. These kinds of structured types are called *records*.

The individual components of a record are commonly referred to as *fields* or *components* or *component fields*. Each field has a name called a *field identifier*, which is some identifier chosen by the programmer when the record type is declared. Each field also has a type, which is specified when the record type is declared. A possible record declaration for the inventory record mentioned in the last paragraph is:

*component
field*

```
type StockItem =
        record
          Name: array[1..20] of char;
          Number: integer;
          Price: real
        end;
```

Name, **Number** and **Price** are the field identifiers. **StockItem** is the name of the type. To declare **Item1** and **Item2** to be variables of this type, the

component
values

component
variable

declaration is:

```
var Item1, Item2: StockItem;
```

The values of a record type are lists of values. There is one value on the list for each field and the type of each value on the list is the type specified for that field in the record type declaration. For example, a value of type **StockItem** is a list of three values: one is an array of characters, one is of type **integer** and one is of type **real**. The individual values on the list are called the *component values* of the record.

The field identifiers of a record are similar to the indexes of an array. They provide a way to name each individual value on the list of values that make up the record. By adding the field name to a record variable, we can specialize the variable to one of its components. A component of a record variable is, as you might expect, called a *component variable*. To specify a component variable, a period and the field identifier are appended to the record variable. For example, the component variable of **Item1** named by the field identifier **Price** is written as follows:

```
Item1.Price
```

It is a variable of type **real** and can be used just like any other variable of type **real**. For example, the following will write the **real** value **9.95** on the screen:

```
Item1.Price := 9.95;
writeln(Item1.Price);
```

Similarly, the component variable **Item1.Number** is a variable of type **integer**, and the component variable **Item1.Name** is an array of characters.

When reading expressions involving records and arrays, always proceed from left to right. Consider the expression:

```
Item1.Name[2]
```

The identifier **Item1** names a record variable of type **StockItem**. By adding the field identifier we specify a particular component variable. So **Item1.Name** denotes the component variable called **Name**. As specified in the type declaration, that is an array and so we can add an array index to it. The complete expression thus refers to the second indexed variable of this array. To be very concrete it refers to the second letter in the name of the item stored in record **Item1**. Figure 14.4 fills a record variable of type **StockItem** and illustrates this notation.

The values of a record type are lists of values of the component types specified in the declaration of that record type. This list can sometimes be treated as a single (structured) value. For example, a procedure parameter of a record type is written without any field identifiers. The situation is similar to that of arrays. Also, the value of an entire record variable can be set by a single assignment statement. The following two statements consist of a procedure call, followed by an assignment:

```
ReadRecord(Item1);
Item2 := Item1
```

```
type StockItem =
        record
          Name: array[1..20] of char;
          Number: integer;
          Price: real
        end;

procedure ReadRecord(var Item: StockItem);
{Sets the value of each component variable of Item
to a value read from the keyboard.}
    var I: integer;
begin{ReadRecord}
    writeln('Enter name of item. Add blanks');
    writeln('to make it 20 characters long.');
    writeln('Extra blanks are OK.');
    for I := 1 to 20 do
        read(Item.Name[I]);
    readln;

    writeln('Enter stock number.');
    readln(Item.Number);

    writeln('Enter price.');
    writeln('Do not include a dollar sign.');
    readln(Item.Price)
end; {ReadRecord}
```

**Figure 14.4
Procedure to fill
a record variable.**

If the declarations are as we gave them, then the first statement is a procedure call that sets the value of the record variable **Item1** by setting the value of each component variable. The second statement sets the value of each component variable of **Item2** equal to the value of the corresponding component of **Item1**.

Records and arrays are similar in many ways. They both provide a way to give a single name to a list of values. They both refer to elements of the list by means of some sort of name. In the case of an array, the name is an index. In the case of a record, the name is a field identifier. A variable of either type can be thought of as a list of variables of the component types.

comparison of arrays and records

On the other hand, arrays and records do have some important differences. The elements in an array list must all be of the same type. The component values of a record may be of different types. The index of an array may be computed by the program. If the index type is **1..50**, then a variable of this type may be used as the index. So the name of an array index variable (such as **A[I]**) may be computed by the program (by computing the value of **I**). The name of a component variable of a record (such as **Item.Price**) must include a field identifier (such as **Price**) and there is no way for the program to compute a field identifier. The programmer must write it into the program.

The Syntax of Simple Records

Type definitions of records follow the pattern of the inventory record in the previous section. The list of field identifiers is enclosed within the two identifiers **record** and **end**. Each field identifier is followed by a colon and the type of that field. A component type may be a structured type such as an array or even another record type. The only thing it cannot be is a file type, such as **text**. The various field identifier parts are separated with semicolons. If two successive field identifiers are of the same type, their declaration may be combined by separating them with commas and only listing the component type once. For example, the following two type declarations are equivalent:

```
type Employee =
      record
        Number: integer;
        BaseRate: real;
        OvertimeRate: real
      end;

type Employee =
      record
        Number: integer;
        BaseRate, OvertimeRate: real
      end;
```

The syntax for type definitions is summarized in Figure 14.5.

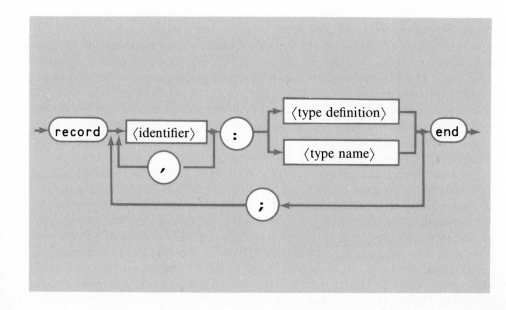

**Figure 14.5
Syntax for simple
record type
definitions.**

Hierarchies of Structured Types

Simple record types are seldom used by themselves. They are more often combined into other more complex structured types. One very common example of this is an array of records. For example, if **StockItem** is the record type defined in our introduction to records, then we are likely to use the records in an array of records. If there are 100 items in the inventory, a likely additional declaration would be the following:

arrays of records

```
type List = array[1..100] of StockItem;
var Inventory: List;
```

The complete list of the inventory could be read into the array by the code:

```
for I := 1 to 100 do
    begin
      writeln('Next item:');
      ReadRecord(Inventory[I])
    end;
```

The procedure **ReadRecord** is described in Figure 14.4.

When programming with these nested structures, expressions can sometimes get quite complicated. To interpret them correctly, you must patiently work your way through them from left to right. As a sample, review the declaration of the type **StockItem** and then try to figure out the following expression, before reading on:

syntax for nested structures

```
Inventory[2].Name[3]
```

The expression is interpreted as follows. **Inventory** is an array of records of type **StockItem**. Hence each indexed variable of that array is a record of that type. **Inventory[2]** is the second indexed variable of this array and hence is a record variable of type **StockItem**. Since it is of this record type, it makes sense to refer to the component called **Name**. The way to specify a component variable of any record variable is to append a period followed by the field name. In this case the following is the component variable of the record variable **Inventory[2]** that has the field name **Name**:

```
Inventory[2].Name
```

The component named **Name** is an array of type:

```
array[1..20] of char
```

Hence the third index variable of the array **Inventory[2].Name** is:

```
Inventory[2].Name[3]
```

This expression is an indexed variable of type **char**. Its value is the third letter in the name of the second item on the inventory list.

Sometimes it makes sense to structure a record in a hierarchical way by making some component or components themselves records. For example, an

records within records

alternative type for the inventory records we have been discussing is the following:

```
type Specs = record
                Number: integer;
                Price: real
             end;
     StockItem =
       record
         Name: array[1..20] of char;
         Info: Specs
       end;
```

A record variable might then be declared as follows:

```
var SaleItem: StockItem;
```

If this record variable **SaleItem** has its value set to an inventory record, then the price of the item in that record is:

```
SaleItem.Info.Price
```

As always, the way to read these expressions is very carefully and from left to right. **SaleItem** is a record. The component with field name **Info** is:

```
SaleItem.Info
```

This component variable is itself a record of type **Specs**. Hence it has two components, one of which is called **Price**.

It is important to be able to understand these complicated expressions. Until you do, you will not completely understand Pascal records. Unfortunately, such complicated expressions are confusing. Fortunately they can frequently be avoided by using the construction described in the next section.

The With Statement

Look back at the procedure **ReadRecord** given in Figure 14.4. The entire procedure deals with a single record called **Item**. Every field identifier refers to **Item**. It would be convenient to have a way to say that all references to a record of type **StockItem** are references to the record **Item**. Then we could simply write the field identifiers and not have to write **Item** each time. The *with* statement lets us do just that.

As an even simpler example, consider the following declarations:

```
type Sample = record
                F1: integer;
                F2: char
              end;
var X: Sample;
```

The following code uses a *with* statement:

```
with X do
    begin
        F1 := 5; F2 := 'A'
    end;
writeln(X.F1, X.F2)
```

In the statement following *with* **X** *do*, all references to component field names **F1** and **F2** refer to **X.F1** and **X.F2**, respectively. Hence if the preceding code is embedded in a complete program, then it will produce the following output:

```
5 A
```

Using a *with* statement we can rewrite the procedure **ReadRecord** so that the record name **Item** need be written only once. The procedure in Figure 14.6 does this and is equivalent to the one in Figure 14.4.

The syntax for a *with* statement is summarized in Figure 14.7. As indicated there, it is possible to have more than one record variable on the record variable

```
type StockItem =
        record
            Name: array[1..20] of char;
            Number: integer;
            Price: real
        end;

procedure ReadRecord(var Item: StockItem);
{Sets the value of each component variable of Item to
a value read from the keyboard.}
    var I: integer;
begin{ReadRecord}
    with Item do
    begin{with}
      writeln('Enter the name of the item.');
      writeln('Add blanks to make it 20 characters long.');
      writeln('Extra blanks are OK.');
      for I := 1 to 20 do
          read(Name[I]);
      readln;

      writeln('Enter stock number.');
      readln(Number);

      writeln('Enter price. Do not include a dollar sign.');
      readln(Price)
    end {with}
end; {ReadRecord}
```

Figure 14.6

Figure 14.4 redone using a **with** statement.

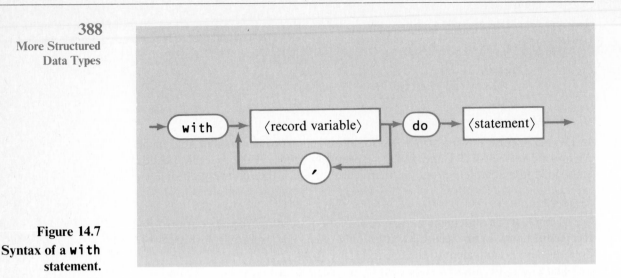

Figure 14.7
Syntax of a **with**
statement.

list of a *with* statement. However, you must be careful to avoid any ambiguities when doing so. In particular, you cannot have two record variables of the same record type on the record variable list. This is because there would be no way to tell which record variable a field identifier refers to.

Parimutuel Betting Odds— An Example Using Records

problem definition

In this section we use an array of records data structure in designing a program to compute horse-race payoffs. The task of the program is to read in a list of horses, assign a number to each, record all bets and then announce the amount of payoff on the horses that finish first, second and third. As is traditional, first place is called *win*, second is called *place* and third is called *show*. A bet is a wager that the horse will do at least that well. So, for example, if you bet a horse to show and it wins, then your bet succeeds and you receive a payoff, although usually not as large as that received by those who bet that it would win.

computing payoffs

The payoffs are to be computed according to a *parimutuel* formula, which means that a certain percent of all the money wagered is taken by the race track and the rest is divided among those with successful bets. Win, place and show payoffs are calculated completely separately.

We will simplify the problem by treating all place payoffs as equal. Everybody whose horse placed will get paid the same. Similarly, we will treat all show bets as equal. For example, suppose $10,000 was bet on the race and that $2,000 of that was in *place* bets on one horse or another. The track gets 10% of everything, that is, $1,000. Of the $2,000 wagered on *place* bets, the track gets $200 (which is included in the track's $1,000), leaving $1,800 to divide among all bets that the first and second place horses would *place*. The payoff to those who bet that the first place horse would win are calculated separately and do not affect the amount paid off to those who bet that it would *place*. You can bet any dollar amount you want and the payoff (if any) is proportionate to the amount you bet. By tradition, the results are announced in terms of a $2 bet.

Once we understand the problem, the next step is to choose a data structure. In this case we need to keep track of a horse's name, number, the total amount bet on that horse to win, the total amount bet on that horse to place and the total amount bet on that horse to show. If we use an array, then we can use the array index as the horse's number. If we make it an array of records, then a single array will suffice. The following hierarchical data structures are well suited to the problem:

choosing a data structure

```
type NameString = array[1..MaxNameLength] of char;
     FirstToThird = 1..3;
     Horse =
       record
         Name: NameString;
         Bets: array[FirstToThird] of integer
         {1 for Win, 2 for Place, 3 for Show.}
       end;
     Numbers = 1..MaxNumHorses;
     Field = array[Numbers] of Horse;
var A: Field;
```

For example, the amount bet on horse number five to show will be the value of:

```
A[5].Bets[3]
```

Now that we have a data structure, we proceed to design the algorithm. The problem subdivides as follows:

subtasks

1. Step through the horse numbers and read the name of horse number `HorseNumber` into the array `A[HorseNumber].Name`.
2. Record the bets.
3. Find out which horses came in first, second and third.
4. Calculate the payoffs.
5. Display the payoffs.

Each of these subtasks is accomplished by a procedure or function. The complete program is shown in Figure 14.8.

Program

```pascal
program Parimutuel(input, output);
{Records horse race bets and computes race payoffs
according to a simplified parimutuel formula.}
const MaxNameLength = 20;
      MaxNumHorses = 12;
      ProfitRatio = 0.1; {Fraction of each pot kept by track.}
type NameString = array[1..MaxNameLength] of char;
     FirstToThird = 1..3;
     Horse =
       record
         Name: NameString;
         Bets: array[FirstToThird] of integer
         {1 for Win, 2 for Place, 3 for Show.}
       end;
     Numbers = 1..MaxNumHorses;
     Field = array[Numbers] of Horse;
var A: Field;
    NumHorses, WinNum, PlaceNum, ShowNum: integer;

procedure ReadName(var Name: NameString);
{Reads a name into array Name; fills extra places with blanks.}
   const Blank = ' ';
   var Count, I: integer;
       Character: char;
begin{ReadName}
   writeln('Enter name, terminate it with a ! :');

   read(Character);
   Count := 1;
   repeat
     Name[Count] := Character;
     Count := Count + 1;
     read(Character)
   until (Character = '!') or (Count > MaxNameLength);

   for I := Count to MaxNameLength do
     Name[I] := Blank;
   readln
end; {ReadName}
```

Figure 14.8
Program using
records.

```
procedure EnterHorses(var A: Field;
                      var NumHorses: integer);
{Postcondition:NumHorses contains the number of horses in the race;
A[1].Name through A[NumHorses].Name set to the horses' names.}
    var HorseNumber: integer;
begin{EnterHorses}
    writeln('How many horses are running?');
    readln(NumHorses);
    if NumHorses > MaxNumHorses
      then writeln('Too many horses for this program')
      else for HorseNumber := 1 to NumHorses do
        begin{for in else}
          writeln('Horse number ', HorseNumber:2);
          ReadName(A[HorseNumber].Name)
        end {for in else}
end; {EnterHorses}

procedure PlaceBets(var A: Field; NumHorses: integer);
{Records bets until user signals end of betting.
Postcondition: A[N].Bets[P] contains the total amount of all
bets that horse N will finish in position P or better.}
    var Amount: integer;
        Horse: Numbers;
        WPS: FirstToThird;
begin{PlaceBets}
    for Horse := 1 to NumHorses do
      for WPS := 1 to 3 do
        A[Horse].Bets[WPS] := 0;
    {Amount bet on each horse is zero so far.}
    writeln(NumHorses:2, ' horses are in the next race.');
    writeln('Enter a bet of zero to end betting.');

    writeln('Enter bet:');
    writeln('(Amount<sp>Horse number<sp>1, 2 or 3)');
    readln(Amount, Horse, WPS);
    while Amount > 0 do
      with A[Horse] do
      begin{with in while loop}
        Bets[WPS] := Bets[WPS] + Amount;
        {A[Horse].Bets[1], A[Horse].Bets[2], A[Horse].Bets[3] contains
          the amounts bet so far on Horse to win, place and show, respectively.}
        writeln('Enter bet:');
        writeln('(Amount<sp>Horse number<sp>1, 2 or 3)');
        readln(Amount, Horse, WPS)
      end; {with in while loop}

    writeln('They''re off!!')
end; {PlaceBets}
```

Figure 14.8
continues on p. 392

```
procedure RunRace(var WinNum, PlaceNum, ShowNum: integer);
   begin{RunRace}
     writeln('Enter horse numbers for');
     writeln('win, place and show:');
     readln(WinNum, PlaceNum, ShowNum)
   end; {RunRace}

function Payoff(A: Field; Position: FirstToThird;
                         NumHorses, WinNum, PlaceNum,
                              ShowNum: integer): real;
```

{*Returns the payoff on a $2 bet. Computes either win, place
or show return depending on whether Position is 1, 2 or 3, respectively.
Precondition: Horse number WinNum finished the race in first position,
PlaceNum in second position and ShowNum in third position.*}

```
   var Horse: Numbers;
       Total: integer;
       TrackCut, Pot, DollarPayoff: real;
       BetsToPayoff: integer;
begin{Payoff}
   Total := 0;
   for Horse := 1 to NumHorses do
     Total := Total + A[Horse].Bets[Position];
```
   {*Total contains the total amount of all money bet on
   any horse to finish in position Position.*}
```
   TrackCut := ProfitRatio * Total;
   Pot := Total - TrackCut;
```
   {*Pot contains the amount to be divided among all successful
    bets that some horse would finish in position Position or better.*}

```
   if Position = 1
   then BetsToPayoff := A[WinNum].Bets[1]
   else if Position = 2
```
       {*Pay off place bets on the first and second place horses.*}
```
       then BetsToPayoff := A[WinNum].Bets[2]
                               + A[PlaceNum].Bets[2]
   else {If Position = 3 then pay off show bets placed on
```
       the first, second and third place horses.}
```
       BetsToPayoff := A[WinNum].Bets[3]
                           + A[PlaceNum].Bets[3]
                           + A[ShowNum].Bets[3];
   if BetsToPayoff > 0
       then DollarPayoff := Pot / BetsToPayoff
       else DollarPayoff := 10.0; {When nobody wins,
```
           the amount of the payoff does not matter.}

Figure 14.8 (cont'd)

```
    {DollarPayoff contains the payoff on $1.}
    Payoff := 2 * DollarPayoff
end; {Payoff}

procedure DisplayResults(A: Field;
    NumHorses, WinNum, PlaceNum, ShowNum: integer);
    const PayLength = 6; {Total field width for payoff amounts}
    var WinAmount, PlaceAmount, ShowAmount: real;
        I: integer;
begin{DisplayResults}
    WinAmount :=
      Payoff(A, 1, NumHorses, WinNum, PlaceNum, ShowNum);
    PlaceAmount :=
      Payoff(A, 2, NumHorses, WinNum, PlaceNum, ShowNum);
    ShowAmount :=
      Payoff(A, 3, NumHorses, WinNum, PlaceNum, ShowNum);

    for I := 1 to MaxNameLength do
      write(A[WinNum].Name[I]);
    writeln(' Number ', WinNum:2);
    writeln('paid $', WinAmount:PayLength:2,' to win.');
    writeln('paid $', PlaceAmount:PayLength:2,' to place.');
    writeln('paid $', ShowAmount:PayLength:2,' to show.');

    for I := 1 to MaxNameLength do
      write(A[PlaceNum].Name[I]);
    writeln(' Number ', PlaceNum:2);
    writeln('paid $', PlaceAmount:PayLength:2,' to place.');
    writeln('paid $', ShowAmount:PayLength:2,' to show.');

    for I := 1 to MaxNameLength do
      write(A[ShowNum].Name[I]);
    writeln(' Number ', ShowNum:2);
    writeln('paid $', ShowAmount:PayLength:2,' to show.')
end; {DisplayResults}

begin{Program}
    EnterHorses(A, NumHorses);
    PlaceBets(A, NumHorses);
    RunRace(WinNum, PlaceNum, ShowNum);
    DisplayResults(A, NumHorses, WinNum, PlaceNum, ShowNum)
end. {Program}
```

Figure 14.8
continues on p. 394

How many horses are running?
4
Horse number 1
Enter name, terminate it with a ! :
Fancy Dancer!
Horse number 2
Enter name, terminate it with a ! :
Pascal's Pleasure!
Horse number 3
Enter name, terminate it with a ! :
Montezuma's Revenge!
Horse number 4
Enter name, terminate it with a ! :
Person Of War!
  4 horses are in the next race.
Enter a bet of zero to end betting.
Enter bet:
(Amount⟨sp⟩Horse number⟨sp⟩1, 2 or 3)
10 3 1
Enter bet:
(Amount⟨sp⟩Horse number⟨sp⟩1, 2 or 3)
5 2 1
Enter bet:
(Amount⟨sp⟩Horse number⟨sp⟩1, 2 or 3)
2 4 3
Enter bet:
(Amount⟨sp⟩Horse number⟨sp⟩1, 2 or 3)
10 4 2
Enter bet:
(Amount⟨sp⟩Horse number⟨sp⟩1, 2 or 3)
5 3 2
Enter bet:
(Amount⟨sp⟩Horse number⟨sp⟩1, 2 or 3)
0 1 1
They're off!!
Enter horse numbers for
win, place and show:
2 4 1
Pascal's Pleasure   Number 2
paid $ 5.40 to win.
paid $ 2.70 to place.
paid $ 1.80 to show.

Figure 14.8 (cont'd)

Person Of War   Number 4
paid $ 2.70 to place.
paid $ 1.80 to show.
Fancy Dancer   Number 1
paid $ 1.80 to show.

Standard Pascal—Use of
Packed Arrays of Characters
(Optional)

Records frequently include a field that is a string. In all our examples, we have used an ordinary array of characters to hold strings. It sometimes makes more sense to declare these strings to be **packed** arrays of characters. That would save memory space, and since a packed array of characters can be an argument to **write**, it would make it easier to output the string to the screen. An alternative type declaration for the inventory records of the type we discussed earlier would be:

```
type StockItem =
        record
          Name: packed array[1..20] of char;
          Number: integer;
          Price: real
        end;
```

UCSD Pascal—
Use of Strings in Records

Records frequently include a field that is a string. In all our examples, we have used an array of characters to represent strings. In UCSD Pascal it would make more sense to declare these fields to be of type **string**.

One disadvantage of using the type **string** is that it can consume a large amount of storage; if there are many records, this storage consumption can get quite large. A component variable of type **string**, or any other variable of type **string**, is allocated enough storage for 80 characters. It can be declared to reserve less room by specifying a smaller maximum number of characters. (This technique can also be used to obtain string variables that can hold strings of length more than 80 characters.) The syntax for these different size string types is:

string[⟨max characters⟩**]**

⟨max characters⟩ must be a positive integer which is at most **256**.

A preferable UCSD Pascal type declaration for inventory records of the type we discussed earlier would be:

```
type StockItem =
        record
          Name: string[20];
          Number: integer;
          Price: real
        end;
```

Variant Records
(Optional)

It is frequently convenient and natural to have records in which the field identifiers and component types vary from record to record. For example, a list of publications might naturally be thought of as an array of records. Normally the records would contain slightly different entries for articles and for books. Both articles and books would have author, title and date. Books normally also have a publisher and city listed, while articles normally have a journal name, volume number and pages listed. Pascal allows records which have some fields that vary from record to record. These sorts of records are called *variant records*. They are most often used in conjunction with enumerated types. (If you have not read the section on enumerated types, you should go back and read it before reading the rest of this section. Enumerated types are covered in Chapter 10.)

fixed part   The syntax of a variant record type declaration uses something analogous to a *case* statement in order to specify the fields that vary from record to record. For example, Figure 14.9 defines two types. The type **Form** is an enumerated type. The type **Publication** is a variant record type for records each of which is an entry for either a book or an article. The part before the identifier *case* is

```
type Form = (Book, Article);
     Publication =
     record
       Author, Title: array[1..30] of char;
       Date: 1600..2000;
       case Kind: Form of
       Book:
          (Pub, City: array[1..20] of char);
       Article:
          (Journal: array[1..20] of char;
          Vol, FirstP, LastP: integer)
     end;
```

Figure 14.9
A variant record type.

called the *fixed part*. It is just like the record types we have seen. Suppose we have the following variable declaration:

> *var* `PubRec: Publication;`

Then the following component variables are exactly like the ones we have seen for the ordinary records discussed in previous sections:

> `PubRec.Author, PubRec.Title, PubRec.Date`

The part of the type declaration that starts with the identifier ***case*** is called the *variant part*. The identifier **Kind** is called the *tag field* identifier. It is a component of type **Form**. Every record has this component. Hence **PubRec.Kind** can be used as an ordinary component variable. However, this component has an additional property. The value of the component **Kind** determines the form of the rest of the record. If the value of **Kind** is **Book**, then the record will have the following additional two components:

*variant
part*

*tag
field*

> `PubRec.Pub`
> `PubRec.City`

If the value of **Kind** is **Article**, then these two fields will not exist; instead, the following four fields will be present:

> `PubRec.Journal`
> `PubRec.Vol`
> `PubRec.FirstP`
> `PubRec.LastP`

In all cases the types of the components are the ones specified in the declaration.

A complete syntax diagram for record type definitions that can include a variant part is given in Figure 14.10. Notice that there is only one ***case*** type structure and it always comes last. (There can be a ***case*** within the ***case***, but such nesting is rare.) All the various field identifiers must be distinct. The ⟨tag field id⟩ is a normal field identifier. The ⟨type name⟩ may name any subrange or other ordinal type. It must be a type name; it can not be a type definition, such as **1..4**.

It is possible to omit the tag field identifier. In the example, that would be done by replacing:

*omitting
tag field
identifier*

> *case* `Kind: Form of`

with

> *case* `Form of`

If this is done, there will be no component called **Kind**. The programmer must somehow ensure that the various cases are used consistently. If a record has its value set using **Pub**, it cannot later try to read the component **FirstP**. If it does, the result is unpredictable. Notice that the tag type must be included even if there is no tag field. The syntax diagram in Figure 14.10 describes all the possible variations.

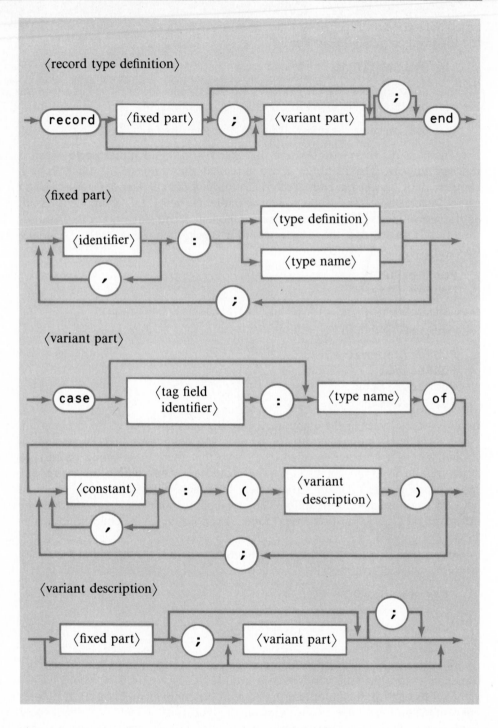

**Figure 14.10
Complete syntax
diagram for record
type definitions.**

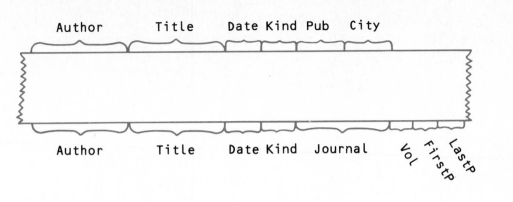

**Figure 14.11
Memory allocation
for a variant record.**

Variant records are not absolutely necessary. For example, we could have defined the type **Publication** to have all 10 possible fields and could then write the program so that it uses whatever fields are needed. However, on most systems the variant record form will use less storage, because the same storage is used for the **Book** fields as is used for the **Article** fields. Hence the storage needed is the maximum of the two cases rather than the sum of the two. This kind of storage allocation is illustrated in Figure 14.11.

*storage
efficiency*

More about Sets
(Optional)

In Chapter 7 we had a brief introduction to *sets*. The context of that discussion was certain boolean expressions such as:

X *in* **[1, 3, 5]**

The subexpression **[1, 3, 5]** is a set.

A *set* is almost identical to what most people call a "list." However, there are some differences. The elements of a list have an order and that order is part of the identity of the list. So the following two lists are different:

*sets
versus
lists*

1, 3, 5

and

1, 5, 3

A set is like a list except that the order in which the elements are named is unimportant. For example, the following two Pascal sets are equal:

[1, 3, 5]
[1, 5, 3]

One other difference between sets and lists is that, unlike a list, a set cannot have any repetitions.

elements

The values in a set are called *elements* of the set. In Pascal the elements of a set must all be of the same type and that type must be an ordinal type. Thus a set may contain integers only or characters only, but not a combination of integers and characters. There are different sorts of set types depending on the type of the individual elements. A set type definition is of the form

> *set of* ⟨base type⟩

where the ⟨base type⟩ is an ordinal type. A program can declare variables to be of a set type in the usual ways. For example:

> *var* Scores, CheckOn: *set of* 0..10;
> Symbols: *set of* char;

Once a variable is declared, it can have its value changed by an assignment statement, such as:

> Scores := [1, 3, 5]

set constants

Expressions such as [1, 3, 5] are constants of a set type. A *set constant* is written by giving a list of elements of the base type separated by commas and enclosed in square brackets. If some of the elements of a set constant form a subrange, then it is possible to abbreviate the list of elements by listing a subrange type, for example:

> CheckOn := [0..5, 10]

This statement sets the value of **CheckOn** equal to:

> [0, 1, 2, 3, 4, 5, 10]

set operators

Sets may be manipulated with the operators given in Figure 14.12 and may be compared using the relational operators given in Figure 14.13. For example, the following boolean expressions all evaluate to **true**:

> ['A', 'B', 'C'] = ['B', 'C', 'A']
> ['A', 'B'] <> ['A', 'B', 'C']
> [1, 2] <> [5, 7, 22]
> [1, 2] <= [1, 2, 3]
> [1, 2] <= [1, 2]
> [1, 2, 3] >= [1, 2]
> [1, 3] + [3, 5, 7] = [1, 3, 5, 7]
> [1, 3] * [3, 5, 7] = [3]
> [1, 2, 3, 4] - [4, 2] = [1, 3]

The operator *in* as well as the operators in Figures 14.12 and 14.13 can be applied to set variables as well as to set constants.

empty set

Figure 14.14 contains a sample program using set variables. Notice that [] is used to denote the set with no elements in it. As you might easily guess, that set is called the *empty set*. Also notice that a variable of the base type can be used within a set expression, such as in the following line, which appears in the

Pascal Form	Definition of Value Returned
⟨set 1⟩ **+** ⟨set 2⟩	Union: the set containing all the elements that are in ⟨set 1⟩ or ⟨set 2⟩ or both
⟨set 1⟩ ***** ⟨set 2⟩	Intersection: the set containing those elements that are in both ⟨set 1⟩ and ⟨set 2⟩
⟨set 1⟩ **−** ⟨set 2⟩	Set Difference: the set containing those elements that are in ⟨set 1⟩ but not in ⟨set 2⟩

procedure **ReadSentence**:

```
ChSet := ChSet + [Character];
```

Finally notice that defined set constants are not allowed in Pascal. It would be nice to define **Terminators** to be a constant rather than a variable. Unfortunately, that is not allowed in Pascal.

There are some shortcomings in the way Pascal handles sets. First of all, the size of the base type of a set type is limited. The exact limit varies from system to system, but you can expect the limit to be relatively small. In virtually any implementation, the type **set of integer** is not allowed because the number of integers exceeds this limit. Most, but not all, implementations make this limit large enough to allow the type **set of char**. However, the only way to be sure that your programs will run on almost all systems is to use small subrange types as the base type. Also, in most versions of Pascal, there is no efficient way to step through all the elements in a set. For example, in the procedure **WriteLetters** (Figure 14.14) we had to test every letter to see if it was in the set **ChSet**. This is inefficient, but we have no other alternative in Pascal.

*limitations
of sets*

Pascal Form	Definition of Value Returned
⟨set 1⟩ **=** ⟨set 2⟩	Equality: evaluates to **true** if ⟨set 1⟩ and ⟨set 2⟩ contain exactly the same elements; otherwise, it evaluates to **false**
⟨set 1⟩ **<>** ⟨set 2⟩	Inequality: evaluates to **true** if ⟨set 1⟩ and ⟨set 2⟩ are not equal; otherwise, it evaluates to **false**
⟨set 1⟩ **< =** ⟨set 2⟩	Subset: evaluates to **true** if every element of ⟨set 1⟩ is also an element of ⟨set 2⟩; otherwise, it evaluates to **false**
⟨set 1⟩ **> =** ⟨set 2⟩	Superset: evaluates to ⟨set 2⟩ **< =** ⟨set 1⟩

**Figure 14.13
Set relational
operators.**

Program

```
program Letters(input, output);
```
*{Requests a sentence from the keyboard, forms a set consisting of all symbols
in the sentence, writes out a list of those letters used in the sentence.}*

```
const FirstLetter = 'A';
```
*{The first letter in the ordered set of
values for the type char; May vary from system to system.
On most systems it is either 'a' or 'A'.}*

```
      LastLetter = 'z';
```
*{The last letter in the ordered set of
values for the type char; May vary from system to system.
On most systems it is either 'z' or 'Z'.}*

```
type SetOfChar = set of char;
```
*{Procedure declarations
require named types. Hence, this silly looking type definition.}*

```
var ChSet: SetOfChar;

procedure ReadSentence(var ChSet: SetOfChar);
```
*{Requests a sentence from the keyboard, then reads the sentence
and sets the value of ChSet equal to the set of all characters in the
sentence. Sentence must terminate with a period, question mark
or exclamation mark. The terminator is not put in the set ChSet.}*

```
    var Character: char;
        Terminators: SetOfChar;
begin{ReadSentence}
   writeln('Enter a sentence. End it with');
   writeln('a ''?'', ''!'' or a period.');

   Terminators := [ '.', '?', '!'];

   ChSet := [];
   read(Character);
   repeat
     ChSet := ChSet + [Character];
```
{ChSet contains the characters read so far.}
```
     read(Character)
   until Character in Terminators
end; {ReadSentence}

procedure WriteLetters(ChSet: SetOfChar);
```
*{Writes out the letters in the set ChSet to the screen.
Each letter is written once.}*
```
    const Blank = ' ';
    var Character: char;
```

Figure 14.14
Program using set
variables.

```
begin{WriteLetters}
    for Character := FirstLetter to LastLetter do
        if Character in ChSet
            then write(Character, Blank);
    writeln
end; {WriteLetters}

begin{Program}
    ReadSentence(ChSet);
    writeln('Your sentence contains');
    writeln('the following letters:');
    WriteLetters(ChSet)
end. {Program}
```

Sample Dialogue

Enter a sentence. End it with
a '?', '!' or a period.
May the hair on your toes grow long and curly!
Your sentence contains
the following letters:
M a c d e g h i l n o r s t u w y

Figure 14.14
(cont'd)

Choosing a Data Structure

A *data structure* is a way of organizing data values. The various structured types that we have seen, such as arrays and records, are all data structures. Even simple variables of types such as **integer** or **char** are data structures, although of a particularly simple kind. We now have a number of data structures available. We will eventually learn how to create other data structures within a Pascal program. Not infrequently we have a choice of structures. For example, our grade-averaging program used two arrays. Alternatively, we could have used an array of records of the following type:

data
structures

```
type GradRec =
    record
        Quizzes: array[1..NumQuizzes] of Score;
        Average: real
    end;
    GradeBook =
    array [1..NumStudents] of GradRec;
```

The array of records data structure is closer to our intuition of how grade information is naturally kept and organized and so is often preferable to the two parallel arrays we used in Figure 14.3.

On the other hand, suppose we expand our grading program so that it does many things that do not depend on the average of the quizzes such as displaying the highest and lowest score for each student. It would then be somewhat inefficient to always include the average in parameters passed to procedures. Perhaps more importantly, it would clutter our reasoning and make the program less clear if we were to always include but seldom use the averages. Hence, in such cases, we should choose the two parallel arrays as the data structure.

When designing a program, the choice of a data structure can be just as important as the designing of an algorithm for the program. The efficiency and clarity of a program can depend heavily on what data structures are used. Unfortunately, there is no algorithm for choosing a data structure. There are, however, a few useful guidelines.

Always consider the possibility of alternative data structures. Just because you find one that works does not mean that you have found the best one. All other things being equal, choose the one that is easiest to understand and manipulate.

Just as hierarchical control structures make a program easier to understand, so do hierarchical data structures. It pays to combine the basic data-structuring techniques to obtain hierarchical structures such as arrays of records, records of arrays, arrays of records of records and so forth.

There are some rules that apply to choosing between the various options for array types and/or record types. If all the items to be stored are of the same simple type, then a single array with that simple type as its component type can be used. If the items are of different types, then an array of records type can be used. An alternative to the array of records data structure is to use parallel arrays; that is, a collection of arrays with the same indexes. The grading example in Figure 14.3 uses two parallel arrays, one for holding the averages and one for holding the quiz scores. Some other programming languages do not have *record* types. When programming in these languages, parallel arrays are an even more important data structure.

Summary of Problem Solving and Programming Techniques

In this chapter we discussed two data structures, arrays and records. These two basic structures can be combined to obtain complex hierarchical data structures, such as arrays of records and records with array and record components. Arrays, records, and other data structures still to be introduced are ways of organizing data so that it is easier to design algorithms to manipulate the data. Often a well-chosen data structure will be the key to finding a clear and efficient algorithm.

◇

Algorithms + Data Structures = Programs
Niklaus Wirth

◇

Summary of Pascal Constructs

array type declaration
   Syntax:

> **type** ⟨name⟩ **=**
> **array[**⟨type 1⟩**,** ⟨type 2⟩**,** ... **,**⟨type *n*⟩**] of** ⟨component type⟩**;**

Example:

> **type ArrayName =**
>   **array[0..5, 'A'..'F'] of real;**

The *n* index types must be subrange types. There may be any number of index types as long as there is at least one. The component type may be any type that does not involve a file.

simple record type declaration
   Syntax:

> **type** ⟨type name⟩ **=**
>   **record**
>   ⟨field ident 1⟩**:** ⟨component type 1⟩**;**
>   ⟨field ident 2⟩**:** ⟨component type 2⟩**;**
>   .
>   .
>   .
>   ⟨field ident *n*⟩**:** ⟨component type *n*⟩
>   **end;**

Examples:

> **type Person =**
>   **record**
>   **Name: array[1..20] of char;**
>   **Age: 1..100;**
>   **Height: real;**
>   **Weight: real**
>   **end;**
>   **Sample =**
>   **record**
>   **A: integer;**
>   **B: char**
>   **end;**

The ⟨type name⟩ is an identifier that will name the record type. The field identifiers ⟨field ident 1⟩, ⟨field ident 2⟩,...,⟨field ident *n*⟩ may be any nonreserved word identifiers. All these identifiers must be different. The component types may be any types that do not involve files. The component types may be different from one another. If two successive field identifiers are of the same type, then their declaration may be combined by separating them with commas and only listing the component type once, like so:

```
type Person =
      record
         Name: array[1..20] of char;
         Age: 1..100;
         Height, Weight: real
      end;
```

The above type declaration is equivalent to the first type of the sample declarations given at the start of this entry.

record variable declaration

Syntax:

> **var** ⟨variable name⟩**:** ⟨type name⟩**;**

Example:

```
var MsX, MrY: Person;
    Sam: Sample;
```

This is the same form as any other variable declaration. Note that no field identifiers are used.

component variable of a record variable

Syntax:

> ⟨record variable⟩**.**⟨field identifier⟩

Example:

```
MsX.Height
```

This is a variable of the type given after ⟨field identifier⟩ in the type definition for the type of the ⟨record variable⟩.

with statement

Syntax:

> **with** ⟨record variable list⟩ **do** ⟨statement⟩

Example:

```
with MsX, Sam do
     begin
        Height := 5.5;
        A := 8
     end
```

The ⟨record variable list⟩ is a list of record variables with no field names in common.

Within the ⟨statement⟩ the component variables of the record variables on the list may be referred to by using only the field identifier. For example, given the declarations in the above entries, the preceding **with** statement is equivalent to the following compound statement:

```
begin
    MsX.Height := 5.5;
    Sam.A := 8
end
```

Exercises

Self-Test and Interactive Exercises

1. Write a program to fill a two-dimensional array **A** of the type shown below, display it to the screen in the natural way and then allow the user to type in any pair of indexes **I, J** and have the program write out the value of **A[I,J]**.

```
array[1..3, 1..2] of integer
```

Include a loop to let the user enter different values of **I** and **J** for as long as the user wishes. The procedures **ReadQuizzes** and **Display** from Figure 14.3 can be used as models for the general method of reading in the array and displaying the array. They will not work without changes, but they do give the general outline of what is to be done.

2. Consider the following type declarations:

```
type Sample = record
                  F1: integer;
                  F2: char
              end;
var X1, X2: Sample;
```

What will the output of the following piece of code be (provided that it is embedded in a correct Pascal program with the preceding type declarations)?

```
X1.F1 := 5; X1.F2 := 'A';
writeln(X1.F1, X1.F2);
X2 := X1;
X2.F1 := 6;
writeln(X2.F1, X2.F2);
```

3. Write a type declaration for a record type called **Sue** with one field of type **integer**, one of type **real** and one of type **char**.

4. Write a program to fill (with data read from the keyboard) one record of the type described in the previous exercise and then display the record to the screen.

5. Write a type declaration for a student record that contains one field for the name, room for 10 quiz scores between zero and 10, a midterm, a final exam score and a final numeric grade, each in the range zero to 100, and a final letter grade.

6. Write a program to fill (with data read from the keyboard) one record of the type described in the previous exercise and then display the record to the screen. Use a *with* statement.

7. The inventory of a shoe store lists shoes by a stock number. With each stock number there is associated a style number in the range 0 to 50, the number of pairs in each size between 3 and 10 and a price. A program is to be written to keep track of the inventory. Give type declarations for two different ways to structure the inventory data: as parallel arrays and as an array of records.

8. (This is for the optional section on sets.) Determine the value returned by each of the following expressions:

```
[7, 8, 9] + [8, 1, 3]
[7, 8, 9] + []
[7, 8, 9] * [8, 1, 3]
[7, 8, 9] * [31, 19]
[7, 8, 9] - [8, 9]
[7, 8, 9] = [8, 9, 7]
[7, 8, 9] = [1, 2, 3]
[7, 8, 9] <> [1, 2, 3]
[9, 8, -5] >= [8, 9]
['A', 'C', 'D'] <= ['A', 'C']
['A', 'B', 'C'] >= ['B', 'A']
```

Regular Exercises

9. Write a program that does the following: Asks the user to type in nine numbers in three rows of three numbers each, reads the numbers into a two-dimensional array, computes the sum of each row and each column, then outputs the array as well as the row and column sums in the following format:

ARRAY:	*ROW SUMS:*
1 2 3	*6*
3 3 3	*9*
3 2 1	*6*

COLUMN SUMS:
      7 7 7

10. Write a program to assign passenger seats in an airplane. Assume a small airplane with seat numberings as follows:

A	1	2	3	4
B	1	2	3	4
C	1	2	3	4
D	1	2	3	4
E	1	2	3	4
F	1	2	3	4
G	1	2	3	4

The program should display the seat pattern, with an **X** marking the seats already assigned.

For example, after seats A1, B2 and D3 are taken, the display should look like:

A	X	2	3	4
B	1	X	3	4
C	1	2	3	4
D	1	2	X	4
E	1	2	3	4
F	1	2	3	4
G	1	2	3	4

After displaying the seats available, the program prompts for the seat desired, the user types in a seat and then the display of available seats is updated. This continues until all seats are filled or until the user signals that the program should end. If the user types in a seat that is already assigned, then the program should say that seat is occupied and ask for another choice.

11. Write a program that takes as input the name and the annual sales of four companies and then displays a bar graph of this data. That is, three bars (formed by writing the character '**\$**' some number of times) are displayed and the ratios of the lengths of the bars are equal to the ratios of the sales. Each bar is labeled by the company name. The bars should be vertical, not horizontal.

12. A graph with **NumVert** vertices can be represented by an array of the type:

```
var G: array[1..NumVer, 1..NumVert] of boolean;
```

If **G[I, J]** has value **true**, that means that there is an arc from node **I** to node **J**. Write a program that takes as input the array representation of a graph and two nodes in the graph and that outputs a path from the first node to the second or else announces that no path exists. Assume that the arcs are "one-way" arrows, so that if there is an arc from **I** to **J**, then the path can go from **I** to **J** but not necessarily in the other direction. (It may help to think recursively.)

13. The game of *Life*, invented by J. H. Conway, is played by choosing an arrangement of marks on a rectangular grid and watching them change according to the following rule: if two or three of the four immediately neighboring positions are marked, then the mark is left; otherwise, it disappears; an unmarked cell becomes marked if exactly three of its immediately neighboring positions are marked. Write a program that accepts a pattern and then shows the series of patterns it produces. Have the program stop after the pattern stabilizes or after 10 changes if it does not stabilize by then. Use a grid size of at least 10 by 10. All changes occur simultaneously, so the program will need two copies of the configuration, one for the old pattern and one for the new one.

14. Write a program that will do the following: read in a screen display consisting of 20 lines of 20 characters each, write the display out rotated onto its side, then rotated more until it is upside down, then rotated to three quarters of a complete rotation and finally rotated back to its original orientation.

15. An *n* by *m* matrix is a rectangular array of numbers. For example, the following is a 4 by 3 matrix:

$$\begin{pmatrix} 1 & 2 & 3 \\ 0 & 5 & 9 \\ 1 & 3 & 9 \\ 6 & -3 & 5 \end{pmatrix}$$

The entries of a matrix are normally numbered by two subscripts, one for the row and one for the column. The following illustrates the numbering of a 4 by 3 and a 3 by 2 matrix:

$$\begin{pmatrix} a_{11} & a_{12} & a_{13} \\ a_{21} & a_{22} & a_{23} \\ a_{31} & a_{32} & a_{33} \\ a_{41} & a_{42} & a_{43} \end{pmatrix} \qquad \begin{pmatrix} a_{11} & a_{12} \\ a_{21} & a_{22} \\ a_{31} & a_{32} \end{pmatrix}$$

The product of an m by n matrix with entries a_{ij} and an n by p matrix with entries b_{ij} is an m by p matrix whose entries c_{ij} are defined as follows:

$$c_{ij} = a_{i1}b_{1j} + a_{i2}b_{2j} + \cdots + a_{in}b_{nj}$$

Write a program that will read in an m by n matrix row by row, then read in an n by p matrix row by row, then compute the product matrix and display the two matrices as well as their product matrix on the screen. Use integer values for the matrix entries. Use 3, 4 and 5 for the values of m, n and p, but declare constant names for them so that they can easily be changed.

16. Write a program that will read an n by n matrix into a two-dimensional array **A** and then determine which, if any, of the following special classes the matrix falls into:

Symmetric: **A[I,J] = A[J,I]** for all indexes **I** and **J**.

Diagonal: **A[I,J] = 0** whenever **I** and **J** are different.

Upper triangular: **A[I,J] = 0** whenever **I < J**.

Lower triangular: **A[I,J] = 0** whenever **I > J**.

Use 6 as the value of n.

17. Write a program that will allow two users to play tic-tac-toe. The program should ask for moves alternately from player X and player O. The program displays the game positions as follows:

```
1 2 3
4 5 6
7 8 9
```

The players enter their moves by entering the position number. After each move, the program displays the changed board. A sample board configuration is:

```
X   X   O
4   5   6
O   8   9
```

18. Redo the previous exercise, but this time have the computer be one of the two players.

19. Enhance the program in Figure 14.3 so that student names are stored in a parallel array, so that the student records are displayed in sorted order from the lowest to the highest average score and so that the student name is displayed as well.

20. Write a program that will allow the user to make a pattern on the screen using the keyboard and will then store the pattern in a two-dimensional array and echo it back to the user. It continues to do this until the user indicates that the program should end. Use any array dimensions that are convenient, but allow at least a four by four pattern of characters.

21. Change the program of the previous exercise so that it reads in a large version of each letter of the alphabet and stores the 26 patterns in an array of type:

array['A'..'Z'] of Picture

(If your implementation is one in which there are symbols between the capital letters, then use some other indexing scheme such as **1..26**.) After that, this entire array should be stored in a text file according to some convenient format. For example, the pictures can be stored in order from ´**A**´ to ´**Z**´.

22. Write another program that will read the text file produced by the previous exercise and fill an array of type

    array[´**A**´..´**Z**´] *of* **Picture**

with the 26 patterns. So, now you are in some sense back where you started from after filling the array of the previous program. The program should then output the alphabet in the large letter format.

23. Modify the program from the previous exercise so that it does not simply output the alphabet, but instead asks for the user's name and then outputs the name in large letters using the patterns in the array.

24. Redo the grading program in Figure 14.3, but this time use an array of records of the type discussed in the section on "Choosing a Data Structure."

25. Enhance the parimutuel betting program in Figure 14.8 in the following ways: When entering a horse's name, the name is terminated with a carriage return rather than an exclamation mark. The name is stored in a **packed** array of characters. (UCSD Pascal users use the type **string** rather than a **packed** array.) After each bet is placed, the program displays the current odds for each horse. The current odds for a horse are the ratio of the amount it would pay a $1 win bet if the betting stopped and that horse won the race. For example, if it would pay $4 on a $2 ticket, then the odds are 2 to 1. (Extra touch: enhance the odds computation so that it outputs odds such as 5 to 3.) The first three horses are chosen using a random number generator; use some calculated quantity for the seed such as the amount bet on horse number one multiplied by the number of letters in the horse's name. Calculate the place and show payoffs differently for the different horses; specifically, payoff in reverse ratio to that of the amount bet. For example, if there is twice as much bet on horse one to place than on horse two to place and they both do place, then the payoff on horse two is double that of horse one. Also, write the program so that it repeats the entire cycle until the user tells it to stop.

26. Further enhance the program from the previous exercise so that the program generates the names of the horses in the race. The program should use a random number generator to choose names from a text file filled with names.

27. Write a program that will keep the inventory for a shoe store in an array of records. Use the type declaration from Exercise 7. The program should be designed to run indefinitely, keeping track of changes in stock. The user should be allowed to report when an item has arrived and when it is sold. The user should also be able to enter a price change. The program will answer queries about how many of a particular item are in stock, or its price, or sizes in stock. The array index can be used as a stock number. The user is allowed to query using either the style number or the stock number.

28. Write a procedure declaration for a procedure called **Deal** that sets the values of two variable parameters to values which represent a card chosen at random from a standard 52 card deck. The function should also keep track of the cards already dealt out, so that it does not deal a card twice. A card will be represented as two values, one for the "value" ace, two etc. and one for the suit, diamonds, clubs etc. Use an array of records parameter to keep track of the cards already dealt out.

29. Write a program to play "clock patience," displaying the game configurations on the screen. *Clock patience* is a solitaire card game played as follows. The cards in a 52 card

deck are dealt into 12 piles of four each in a "clock" circle with the remaining four cards in the middle. A move consists of taking a card from a pile and placing it under the pile where it belongs, and this pile provides the card for the next move. (Cards are ordered clockwise: ace for one, then two, three, and so forth to queen.) The center pile is for the kings. The game terminates when the four kings have been placed on the center pile. The game is considered successful if all the other cards are correctly placed.

29. Write a program to score five-card poker hands into one of the following categories: nothing, one pair, two pairs, three of a kind, straight (in order), flush (all the same suit), full house (one pair and three of a kind), four of a kind, straight-flush (both straight and flush). Use an array of records to store the hand. The array index type is **1..5**, the records have one field for the value and one for the suit of a card.

30. Write a program to play five-card draw poker with the user. The user and the program each get five cards. They may discard and receive replacements for up to three cards. The hands are then scored according to the order given in the previous exercise. Do not forget to keep track of the cards already dealt so that no card is dealt twice. In the easy version only the above ordering is used, so any two hands with three of a kind, for example, are equal. In the harder version, the hands are compared further; for example, three aces beat three jacks.

References for Further Reading

N. Wirth, *Algorithms + Data Structures = Programs*, 1976, Prentice-Hall, Englewood Cliffs, N. J., Chapter 1.

C. A. R. Hoare, "Notes on Data Structuring," in O.-J. Dahl, E. W. Dijkstra and C. A. R. Hoare, *Structured Programming*, 1972, Academic Press, New York.

A. M. Tenenbaum and M. J. Augenstein, *Data Structures Using Pascal*, 1981, Prentice-Hall, Englewood Cliffs, N. J.

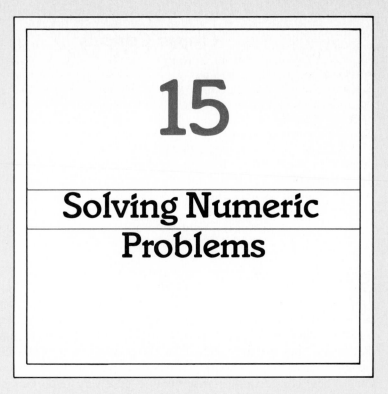

15

Solving Numeric Problems

"I confess that I can not recall any case within my experience which looked at first glance so simple, and yet which presented such difficulties."
Arthur Conan Doyle (*Sherlock Holmes*),
The Man with the Twisted Lip

Chapter Contents

Most of the computing done by scientists
and engineers involves computing with numbers, and more often than not with
fractional numbers rather than with integers. The general program design rules
that we have presented throughout this book apply to numeric calculations. There
are also some additional considerations that apply specifically to numeric calculations. These considerations arise because of a very important but perhaps not
obvious principle. To illustrate the principle, consider the following very simple
piece of code, and predict its output:

```
X := 1/3 + 1/3 + 1/3;
writeln(X)
```

The calculation hardly needs a computer. The expected output is one. Yet many
computers will give an output such as:

```
0.9999
```

One need not be Sherlock Holmes to observe that the computer's performance is
either incorrect or more subtle than our simple mental model of arithmetic. As it
turns out, the second alternative is the better explanation. The numbers inside a
computer are not like the numbers you have learned about in mathematics classes
from grade school through calculus. Hence you must learn to think quite
differently when performing involved numeric calculations on a computer. A
detailed treatment of numeric programming techniques is beyond the scope of
this book, but in this chapter we will describe some of the basic principles
involved.

A Hypothetical Decimal Computer

Most computers work in binary notation and some of the problems that arise when doing numeric calculations are due to the differences between binary and decimal notation. However, the difference between binary and decimal notation is small and the problems caused by this difference are typically small. We will discuss numeric calculations in terms of a fictitious computer that works in base ten rather than in binary notation. Since we normally think in base ten, this will make the entire process easier to understand. Aside from the fact that it works in base ten, our hypothetical computer handles numbers in a typical way.

In Chapter 1 we observed that most computers have their main memory divided into a series of locations called *words*. Numeric values are usually stored one value per word. The size of a word will vary from machine to machine, but usually all words are of the same size. One word of our hypothetical computer has room for eight symbols, each either a sign or a decimal digit. So a word may be diagramed as follows:

word size

Each of the small boxes within a word can hold any one of the twelve symbols: 0, 1, 2, 3, 4, 5, 6, 7, 8, 9, +, − .

In our hypothetical computer, values of type **integer** are stored as their usual base ten numeral preceded by a sign. For example, the number 2957 would be stored as:

storing integers

+	0	0	0	2	9	5	7

The number −67543 would be stored as:

−	0	0	6	7	5	4	3

The largest integer that can be stored in our computer is thus

+	9	9	9	9	9	9	9

which is one less than ten million. With Pascal implemented on our computer we would expect **maxint** to be **9999999**. Similarly, we would expect the smallest possible negative integer value to be minus this amount.

maxint

On our computer, values of type **real** are stored in what is called *floating point* notation. This is a variation on the **E** notation used to write **real** constants in Pascal. The computer word is divided into two parts. On our hypothetical computer one part consists of five boxes and the other part consists of three boxes. The value of each real is first converted to a form consisting of a decimal fraction multiplied by a power of ten. For example, the value **123.4** would be converted to the equivalent form:

floating point (real) numbers

$$+ 0.1234 \times 10^{+3}$$

*fraction
part*

*exponent
part*

*significant
digits*

The number with the decimal point in it is called the *fraction part*. The fraction part (including the sign) is stored in the first five boxes, and the exponent of ten (including its sign) is stored in the last three boxes. So **123.4** is stored as:

+	1	2	3	4	+	0	3

The position of the decimal point is assumed to be before the first digit. It is not marked in any way in the computer word. The division between the exponent part and the fraction part is also fixed and understood by the computer. It is not marked in any way. (In our hypothetical computer the boundary can be inferred by the presence of a plus or minus sign. However, in a typical computer, plus and minus would be represented by two digits such as 0 and 1.)

Other examples of storing values of type **real** are given in Figure 15.1. Notice that all numbers are normalized so that the fractional part has the decimal point immediately in front of the first nonzero digit. This is an attempt to preserve the maximum number of significant digits. Consider the number **0.01234**. If the computer merely stores the first four digits after the decimal point, then the final digit **4** would be lost. However, because the computer normalizes the position of the decimal point, this number is stored as follows:

$$+ 0.1234 \times 10^{-1}$$

The normalization has saved that last digit. This moving of the decimal point is the origin of the term *floating point*.

There is only room for four decimal digits in our computer. For this reason, the value stored is sometimes only an approximation of the value we might expect

−0.1234E + 03

−	1	2	3	4	+	0	3

0.01234

+	1	2	3	4	−	0	1

−0.001234

−	1	2	3	4	−	0	2

0.1234123

+	1	2	3	4	+	0	0

Figure 15.1
Storing real (floating point) values.

a Pascal expression to represent. For example, **0.1234123** and **0.12340** have the same representation in our computer. Hence on our hypothetical computer, the following boolean expression evaluates to **true**:

0.1234123 = 0.12340

As this example indicates, testing for equality between two values of type **real** is pointless and even dangerous.

Our computer rounds numbers when they have too many digits to fit in a word. So **765.46** is rounded to **765.5**. Some systems truncate (i.e., discard the extra digits) instead. If our computer were to truncate instead of round, then the number **765.46** would be stored as **765.4** instead of **765.5**.

On our computer the largest positive value of type **real** that we can store would look as follows in memory:

*largest
real
number*

+	9	9	9	9	+	9	9

Expressed more conventionally, this is the value:

0.9999×10^{99}

Hence, the largest possible value of type **real** is about 10^{99}. By contrast, the largest possible value of type **integer** is only **9999999** or about 10^{7}.

If a program attempts to compute a value of type **real** whose absolute value is too large to fit into a memory location, we get what is called *real overflow* or *floating point overflow*. Similarly, if a program attempts to compute a value of type *integer* which is larger than **maxint** or smaller than the smallest integer that can be held in one word, that is called *integer overflow*. Whenever any sort of overflow occurs, an error message should be produced. However, many systems, including most UCSD Pascal systems, do not give any such error message. They simply produce some meaningless value and keep on computing. At that point, the entire computation becomes meaningless.

overflow

In addition to a largest magnitude that can be stored as a value of type **real**, there is also a smallest possible magnitude. The smallest positive number of type **real** that can be stored in our machine will be produced by the following word configuration:

*smallest
fraction*

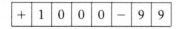

+	1	0	0	0	−	9	9

That is, the number

0.1000×10^{-99}

which is a decimal point followed by ninety-nine zeros and then a one. Certainly a very small number. However, calculations involving such small quantities do occur. When the computer attempts to produce a nonzero number whose absolute value is smaller than this quantity, we have what is called *underflow*. On many systems any such small quantity is simply replaced by zero, which usually is a satisfactory approximation. Some systems give an error message in the case of underflow. Unfortunately, a few other systems produce a meaningless result and

underflow

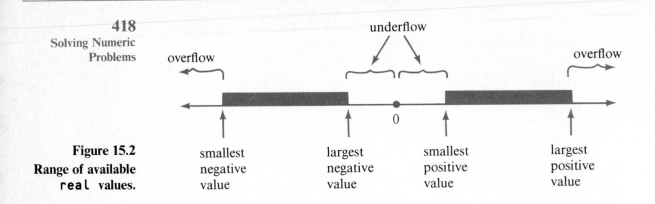

Figure 15.2
Range of available
real values.

continue the computation. The situation is similar to that of overflow but generally produces fewer problems. The situation with respect to overflow and underflow is diagramed in Figure 15.2.

As you can see from the preceding discussion, the types **integer** and **real** are implemented in different ways. As an illustration, consider the difference between the constants **123412** and **123412.0**. The first is of type **integer** and is stored exactly as:

+	0	1	2	3	4	1	2

The second is of type **real** and so is stored only as the approximate value:

+	1	2	3	4	+	0	6

Most problems peculiar to numeric calculations arise because of the approximate nature of **real** values. When studying mathematics, we frequently think in terms of an ideal world where quantities are represented as exact values called "real numbers." These exact numbers are not available on a computer. If the quantity we need has more than four nonzero decimal digits after the decimal point, then it will not be represented exactly in our computer. If it consists of a decimal point followed by five or six nonzero digits, then we could use a computer with a larger word size. However, some quantities, such as the number pi used in geometry, cannot be represented exactly by any finite string of digits. For these "real numbers" even a computer with a word size of one million digits could only store an approximation to the quantities they represent. Many of the "real numbers" of classical mathematics are simply not available on computers. Moreover, the missing numbers are not always very exotic ones. Recall the example which opened this chapter. It performs the calculation:

X := 1 / 3 + 1 / 3 + 1 / 3

The number one-third has no representation as a finite string of decimal digits. Our computer will represent **1 / 3** as:

$$0.3333 \times 10^0 = 0.33330$$

When three of these are added together the result is **0.99990**, rather than the value **1.0** that is predicted by the usual idealized model of arithmetic.

419
Solving Numeric
Problems

Binary Numerals
(Optional)

Most computers represent numbers in *binary notation* rather than in the more familiar base ten notation. On occasion, this can have a significant effect on the outcome of a numeric calculation. The basic idea of binary notation is quite simple. It is just like the base ten notation we normally use, except that the role of ten is replaced by the number two. Base ten notation uses the ten digits, 0 through 9. Base two notation uses only two digits, 0 and 1. In base ten each change in position, from the rightmost to the leftmost digit, represents multiplying by ten. In base two each change in position, from the rightmost to the leftmost digit, represents multiplying by two.

For example, consider the ordinary base 10 numeral 3019. It satisfies the following equality:

$$3019 = 3 \times 10^3 + 0 \times 10^2 + 1 \times 10^1 + 9 \times 10^0$$
$$= 3 \times 1000 + 0 \times 100 + 1 \times 10 + 9 \times 1 = 3000 + 0 + 10 + 9$$

The meaning of any base ten numeral is decomposed in a similar way.

Next consider an example of a binary numeral, such as 100101. The situation is the same except that now each digit position represents some power of two. For example,

example

(*the base two numeral*) $100101 =$
(*the base ten expression*) $1 \times 2^5 + 0 \times 2^4 + 0 \times 2^3 + 1 \times 2^2 + 0 \times 2^1 + 1 \times 2^0$
$$= 1 \times 32 + 0 \times 16 + 0 \times 8 + 1 \times 4 + 0 \times 2 + 1 \times 1$$
$$= 32 + 4 + 1 = 37 \ (base \ ten)$$

In binary notation the rightmost digit represents that digit multiplied by $2^0 = 1$, the next digit to the left represents that digit multiplied by $2^1 = 2$, the next multiplied by $2^2 = 4$, the next multiplied by $2^3 = 8$ and so forth. Any integer can be represented in this binary notation.

whole numbers

The treatment of fractions in binary notation is similar to that of decimal fractions. In decimal fractions, the digit positions after the decimal point represent smaller and smaller fractions. Each shift to the right represents dividing by ten. For example, in base ten:

fractions

$$0.103 = 1/10 + 0/10^2 + 3/10^3$$
$$= 1/10 + 0/100 + 3/1000$$

Fractions in binary notation follow the same principle, but with 10 replaced by 2.

For example:

> (*the base two numeral*) 0.1101
> = (*the base ten expression*)$1/2 + 1/2^2 + 0/2^3 + 1/2^4$
> = $1/2 + 1/4 + 0/8 + 1/16 = 0.8125$ (*base ten*)

In binary notation the "point" is called a *binary point*, rather than a decimal point. The first digit after the binary point represents that number divided by $2^1 = 2$, the next digit after the binary point represents that digit divided by $2^2 = 4$, the next digit represents the digit divided by $2^3 = 8$ and so forth.

In both decimal and binary notation any quantity between zero and one can be represented by a point followed by a string of digits. In both binary and decimal notation, this may require an infinite string of digits. For example, in base ten:

> $1/3 = 0.3333333333333333...$

As we add more 3s we get a better approximation to $1/3$, but no finite number of digits after the decimal point will yield a number exactly equal to $1/3$.

A similar phenomenon occurs in binary notation. In binary notation, the fraction $1/4$, for example, can be expressed as the finite string 0.01, but the exact representation of $1/5$ requires an infinite string of binary digits after the binary point.

> $1/5 = $ (*in binary*) $0.00110011001100110011...$

Any finite string of binary digits can only approximate the value $1/5$. In decimal notation $1/5$ can be represented exactly as 0.2. As this example indicates, some quantities that we express exactly in decimal notation can become approximate quantities when stored in a binary computer.

In both binary and decimal notation you can combine the notation for whole numbers and that for fractions. In base ten, 12.34 means 12 plus 0.34. In base two, 10.101 means 10 (base two) plus 0.101 (base two).

binary arithmetic

Arithmetic on binary numerals is very similar to arithmetic on base ten numerals. In particular, shifting the binary point is similar to shifting the decimal point in base ten. In base ten shifting the point to the right one position is the same as multiplying by ten. In base two it is the same as multiplying by two. For example, in base two, 1.011 multiplied by two is 10.11 and 1.011 multiplied by four is 101.1.

Machine Representation of Numbers in Binary
(Optional)

bits

Like our hypothetical decimal computer, most real computers have a memory that is divided into locations called *words*. However, these words usually store strings of zeros and ones rather than strings of decimal digits. Recall that a digit that must always be either zero or one is called a *bit*. Computer word sizes are usually described as being some number of bits. Some typical word sizes are sixteen, thirty-two and sixty-four bits. When people refer to a "sixteen bit machine," they mean that each word of the machine holds sixteen binary digits. (They do not mean that the computer costs $2.)

Since computer words usually hold bits, most computers store numbers in binary notation. Aside from the fact that the numbers are expressed in binary notation, the method of representing numbers is the same as we described for our hypothetical decimal machine.

integers

Numbers of type **integer** are stored as binary numerals either in the exact form we described in the previous section or in some variant of that notation. Each value of type **integer** is stored in one word. For example, the number five has the binary representation 101 and, in a sixteen bit word, it might be stored as:

+	0	0	0	0	0	0	0	0	0	0	0	0	1	0	1

A word holds only zeros and ones. What we have written as the sign + must be represented as a zero or one. If we take 0 to stand for plus and 1 to stand for minus, then in this eight-bit computer, the preceding word contents is an abbreviation for:

0	0	0	0	0	0	0	0	0	0	0	0	0	1	0	1

We will always use the plus and minus sign rather than 0 and 1 to denote the sign of a number in storage. It helps avoid confusion.

largest integer

Since one bit is occupied by the sign, the largest integer that can be stored in a sixteen-bit computer is the number with binary representation consisting of fifteen 1's. In base ten that number is written 32767. You can compute this base ten numeral by evaluating the sum:

$$1 \times 2^{14} + 1 \times 2^{13} + 1 \times 2^{12} + 1 \times 2^{11} + 1 \times 2^{10} + 1 \times 2^9 + 1 \times 2^8 +$$
$$1 \times 2^7 + 1 \times 2^6 + 1 \times 2^5 + 1 \times 2^4 + 1 \times 2^3 + 1 \times 2^2 + 1 \times 2^1 + 1 \times 2^0$$

(If you understand a bit of binary arithmetic, you can calculate it more quickly as follows:

111111111111111 (*base two*) = 1000000000000000 − 1 (*base two*)
= (*in base ten*) $2^{15} - 1 = 32768 - 1 = 32767$

However, if you are uncomfortable with binary arithmetic, simply do it the long way.)

So if you are working on a sixteen-bit machine you can expect the value of **maxint** to be about 32767. The smallest negative number your sixteen-bit machine can hold will probably be about −32767. This is not part of the definition of the Pascal language. The exact way that numbers are represented is left up to the implementors. So the value of **maxint** and the value of the smallest negative integer in your machine might vary somewhat from these figures. However, these values will be approximately correct for most sixteen-bit machines.

*real
numbers*

Aside from the fact that binary notation is used, numbers of type **real** are stored in the same way as we described for our decimal computer. For example, a sixteen-bit word might be divided to allow four digits to express the exponent and twelve digits to express the fraction part. On a binary machine, the exponent represents a power of two rather than a power of ten. For example, consider the following word configuration for such a machine:

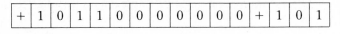

It represents the number:

$$(in\ binary)\ 0.1011 \times 2^{101} = (in\ decimal)(1/2 + 0/4 + 1/8 + 1/16) \times (2^5)$$

We have taken the liberty of using the digit 2 in our binary expression. This mixed notation is sometimes easier to understand than absolutely pure binary notation.

Although numbers are invariably stored in binary notation, that notation normally has little, if any, effect on the outcome of a numeric computation. So we will end our discussion of binary arithmetic here and return to using our hypothetical decimal computer.

Extra Precision
(Optional)

Some computer installations have facilities to store numbers in more than one word and so obtain a more accurate representation for values of type **real**. It is not part of the definition of Pascal and not available on most Pascal systems. However, it is a common feature of other programming languages and does occur in some Pascal implementations.

*double
precision*

One common method for obtaining extra accuracy when storing **real** values is called *double precision*. In double precision, each **real** number is stored in two words. This yields more than double the number of meaningful digits because all the extra digits of the second word normally go into the fractional part. Our hypothetical decimal computer had an eight-decimal-digit word size. On that computer, a typical double precision implementation would store one **real** value in two words as illustrated by the example in Figure 15.3. In our hypothetical

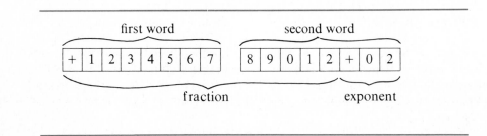

**Figure 15.3
Example of a
double precision
number.**

decimal computer, this accurately represents the decimal number:

12.3456789012

With this sort of double precision, the largest possible **real** value that can be stored is about the same as it is for the normal one-word representation. However, a full twelve decimal digits of accuracy can be represented. The ordinary one-word representation only allowed for four decimal digits of accuracy.

The disadvantages of double precision are that it uses more storage and that it usually causes programs to run more slowly.

There is no standard Pascal syntax for double precision numbers. You will have to consult the documentation for your particular system in order to see if it is available and, if available, to see how to use it in a Pascal program.

UCSD Pascal—Long Integers
(Optional)

In some versions of UCSD Pascal it is possible to have "integers" that are larger than **maxint**. These other "integers" are of a type referred to as *long integers*. The type definition is illustrated by the following:

type Digits20 = integer[20];

A variable of type **Digits20** is then declared in the usual way and may contain any whole number with up to twenty decimal digits. The number twenty was just an example. Any number of digits up to thirty-six may be specified.

For purposes of type compatibility, the type **integer** is considered a subrange type of all long integer types. Hence, if **X** is of type **Digits20** (declared above) and **Y** is of type **integer**, then the following assignment is legitimate:

X := Y

Most of the usual arithmetic operations may be applied to long integers and will return values of a long integer type. An exception is the operation *mod*, which is not defined for long integers.

Sources of Error in Real Arithmetic

When computing with values of type **real**, errors arise because numbers are stored as approximate values. These approximations are sometimes accurate enough and other times very inaccurate. In this and the next section we will discuss some common sources of inaccuracy in programs that compute values of type **real**.

overflow

As you will recall, overflow results when the computer tries to compute a number larger than it can hold in memory. The problem of integer overflow can sometimes be avoided by using variables of type **real** to do calculations involving large numbers, even if the quantities involved are whole numbers. The computer can store much larger values of type **real** than it can values of type **integer**. There is a certain loss of accuracy in doing this, but often this loss of accuracy is tolerable.

underflow

Recall that underflow results when the computer attempts to produce a nonzero value of type **real** that is too small in absolute value. These values are too close to zero and so cannot be represented in memory. Most computers, including our hypothetical decimal computer, simply estimate such values by zero and store a zero as the result of the calculation. This is called *rounding to zero*. If your computer rounds to zero on underflow, then underflow is unlikely to be a problem. If your computer does anything else, then you must be careful to avoid underflow.

*multiplication
and
division*

When a multiplication or division is performed, the answer usually has more digits than either of the two numbers being combined. Frequently, these extra digits cannot be represented in memory and so are lost, along with a little bit of accuracy. For example, consider the following code. (Here and in the examples which follow, we will set the value of variables by means of assignment statements. This is to keep the examples small. In practice, those values would be read from the keyboard or would be the results of other calculations.)

```
X := 912.0;
Y := 0.11;
Z := X * Y
```

The value that should be stored in **Z** is:

$$912.0 \times 0.11 = 100.32$$

However, our hypothetical decimal computer only stores four digits in the fraction part of a **real** value. Hence, it will store the value of **Z** as

+	1	0	0	3	+	0	3

which represents the value:

$$0.1003 \times 10^3$$

That means that the last digit is lost, and the value of **Z** becomes **100.30**. Even if the values of **X** and **Y** were completely accurate, the value of **Z** has lost one digit of accuracy as the result of a simple multiplication.

In all the examples of this section and the next section, we will use our hypothetical decimal computer. So we are only allowed four digits after the decimal point.

*simple
addition*

Even a very simple addition or subtraction can produce a slightly inaccurate result. If the computer adds the number **9.222** to itself, the result should be:

$$9.222 + 9.222 = 18.444$$

However, our computer only retains four digits and so will store the answer as:

$$0.1844 \times 10^2$$

This means that **18.444** was rounded to **18.440** and one digit of the answer was lost.

Under some circumstances, the loss of accuracy in addition can be dramatic. Consider the following piece of code:

```
X := 2000.0;
Y := 0.5;
X := X + Y
```

The values of **X** and **Y** are stored as:

0.2000×10^4
0.5000×10^0

Like most computers, our hypothetical decimal machine can not add two numbers unless they have the same exponent part. Hence it must change one of the two numbers. On our machine the second number is changed to:

0.00005×10^4

Then the following addition is performed:

$$\begin{array}{r} 0.2000 \ \ \times 10^4 \\ +0.00005 \times 10^4 \\ \hline 0.20005 \times 10^4 \end{array}$$

This answer is what we might expect as the value of **X**, but unfortunately that is not the value stored. Since our computer only stores four digits after the decimal point, the computer stores the following as the value of **X**:

0.2000×10^4

The adding in of **Y** had absolutely no effect on the value of **X**.

Situations like the preceding example are common. To avoid this sort of problem, you must somehow avoid adding or subtracting two values of very different size. Sometimes this can be done by rearranging the order in which numbers are combined. As an example, consider the following code:

adding large and small numbers

```
X := 2000.0;
Y := 0.5;
Z := 0.6;
X := X + Y;
X := X + Z
```

As we have just seen, adding **Y** has no effect on the value of **X**. Similarly, adding **Z** has no effect. This calculation leaves the value of **X** unchanged at:

0.2000×10^4

However, if we first combine **Y** and **Z**, then we will get **X** set to something close to the value we expect.

Consider the following slightly different code for the same computation:

```
X := 2000.0;
Y := 0.5;
Z := 0.6;
W := Y + Z;
X := X + W
```

The values added to obtain the value of **W** are:

$$\frac{\begin{array}{r} 0.5000 \times 10^0 \\ +0.6000 \times 10^0 \end{array}}{1.1000 \times 10^0} = 0.1100 \times 10^1$$

This value is then added to the value of **X** as follows:

$$\frac{\begin{array}{r} 0.2000\ \ \times 10^4 \\ +0.00011 \times 10^4 \end{array}}{0.20011 \times 10^4}$$

The final value of **X** is stored as:

$$0.2001 \times 10^4$$

By rearranging the order of the additions, we have added one digit of accuracy to the answer. This is a standard trick. If the small numbers are first added together, then that will produce a somewhat larger value. This larger value can then be combined with other large values. In this way the numbers being combined are more nearly equal and so the results of their addition will be more accurate.

Error Propagation

Each individual operation on a value of type **real** is likely to introduce only a very small error. However, after a number of operations, these small errors may be compounded to produce a very large inaccuracy. Once again we illustrate the pitfall with a piece of code:

```
    . . .
B := 0.1232;
C := A - B;
D := 10000.0;
X := C * D
```

The three dots represent some computation that sets the value of **A**. Let us say that **A** gets set to **0.1234**, a value very close to that of **B**. The value of **C** gets set by the calculation:

$$\frac{\begin{array}{r} 0.1234 \times 10^0 \\ -0.1232 \times 10^0 \end{array}}{0.0002 \times 10^0} = 0.2000 \times 10^{-3}$$

The value of **X** is then computed by multiplying that value by 10,000 to obtain the following value of **X**:

$$0.2000 \times 10^1$$

So far things look fine. The answer appears to be **2**. However, as we have already seen, it is easy for a program to calculate a value that is slightly in error. Suppose that the value of **A** was slightly in error. Specifically, suppose the correct value of **A** is **0.1233**. Then the correct answer is:

$$(0.1234 - 0.1233) \times 10,000 = 1$$

The correct answer is **1**, but our code computed it as **2**. A slight mistake has been compounded, and our answer is now wrong by a factor of two.

The problem is that when subtraction is performed on two nearly equal numbers, the answer is the difference between the end digits of the two numbers. After the subtraction, only the last digits of the two almost equal numbers have any effect on the rest of the computation. But these are exactly the digits that are likely to be incorrect. Hence a program should somehow avoid subtracting two almost equal numbers of type **real**.

subtracting almost equal numbers

All the examples in this and the previous section are unrealistic in the sense that most computers represent **real** values with an accuracy equivalent to more than four decimal digits. In all other respects they are real pitfalls. Realistic examples can be manufactured by simply adding a few more digits to the initial values and leaving the rest of the code unchanged.

Example—Series Evaluation

One common numeric task is to sum a series. For example, consider the following series:

$$\frac{1}{2} + \frac{2}{2^2} + \frac{3}{2^3} + \cdots + \frac{N}{2^N}$$

Suppose that we have already declared a function called **Power** such that the value of **Power(**x, y**)** is:

$$x^y$$

The most obvious way to calculate the sum is as follows:

```
Sum := 0;
for I := 1 to 100 do
    Sum := Sum + (I / Power(2,I))
```

If the calculation is carried out with complete accuracy, this will set the value of **Sum** to the desired value. However, the operations are not carried out with complete accuracy. Moreover, the values of the successive terms rapidly become very small, while in comparison, the value of **Sum** remains moderately large.

*order of
summation*

Hence, after the first few iterations, the loop is adding two numbers of very different size. As we have seen, this can lead to inaccuracies in the answer.

We can avoid adding numbers of such greatly differing size by summing the series in the other direction, like so:

```
Sum := 0;
for I := 100 downto 1 do
    Sum := Sum + (I/Power(2,I))
```

The numbers being combined will then be more nearly equal, and hence the results of the additions are likely to be more accurate.

Example—Finding a Root of a Function

A common numeric programming task is to solve an equation. For example, consider the equation:

$$x^3 + 2x = 33$$

One solution is 3, since:

$$3^3 + 2 \times 3 = 33$$

By rearranging the equation, we can always get it into the form:

$$F(x) = 0$$

where $F(x)$ is some expression that can be made into a Pascal function having one argument of type **real** and returning a value of type **real**. For example, the equation

$$x^3 + 2x = 33$$

can be rearranged to the following equivalent equation:

$$x^3 + 2x - 33 = 0$$

The expression on the left-hand side is computed by the Pascal function declared as:

```
function F(X: real): real;
  begin
    F := X*X*X + 2*X - 33
  end;
```

roots

Viewed this way, solving equations of this form is equivalent to finding a value x such that the expression $F(x)$ on the left side of the rearranged equation is made equal to zero. Such a value x is called a *root* of the function $F(x)$. We will design a program that finds the approximate value of a root of the Pascal function **F**. The method works for a wide range of different functions **F**.

To make the task definition precise, we first list all the assumptions (preconditions) that we assume to be true. We assume that we are given two values x_1

and x_2 such that there is exactly one root between them. We also assume that the graph of the function can be drawn on paper as a smooth line. (The technically precise condition is that the function must be *continuous*. However, we will not stop to define that term. The informal notion of "easy to draw as a smooth line will do here.")

The method we will use is called the *bisection method* and is diagramed in Figure 15.4. The graph represents the function **F**. Two values, **Low** and **High**, are chosen so that exactly one root lies between these two values. We therefore know that the following relation holds:

> **Low** < *root* < **High**

The midpoint between these two values **Low** and **High** is then computed. In Figure 15.4 this midpoint is denoted **M**. The root is either between **Low** and **M** or else it is between **M** and **High**. In the figure the root is between **M** and **High**. All

bisection method

pseudocode

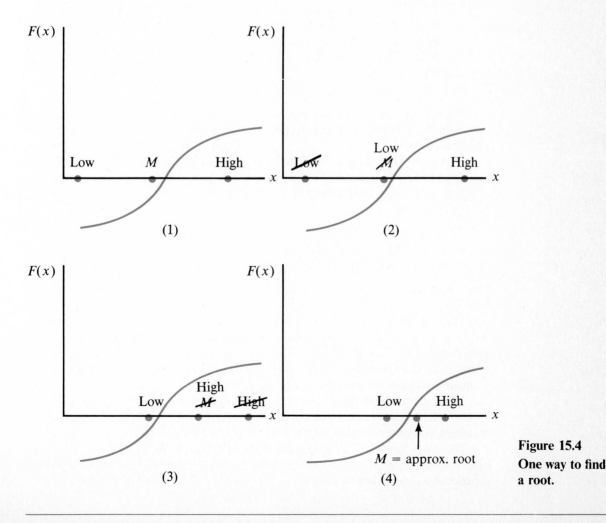

Figure 15.4 One way to find a root.

this has managed to narrow down the location of the root. Originally we knew it was between **Low** and **High**. Now we know that it is in the smaller interval between **M** and **High** (or, in other cases, between **Low** and **M**). Next, we change the values **Low** and **High** to these new end point values; in the figure example, **M** becomes the new value of **Low** and the value of **High** is unchanged. If we keep repeating this process, we eventually get a very small interval that contains the root. This gives us an approximation to the value of the root. The method is outlined in the following pseudocode:

request values x_1 and x_2 such that:
 $x_1 < root < x_2$;
Low := x_1; **High** := x_2;
M := **(Low + High)/2**;
RootFound := **false**;
while not(**RootFound**) *do*
 begin
  if (**F(M)** approx. equals **0.0**) *then* **RootFound** := **true**
  else if the root is between **Low** and **M** *then* **High** := **M**
  else if the root is between **M** and **High** *then* **Low** := **M**;
  M := **(Low + High)/2**
 end;
output: "The root is approximately **M**."

We still must design a subalgorithm to decide whether the root is between **Low** and **M** or between **M** and **High**. The interval containing the root can be determined from the signs of the values: **F(Low)**, **F(M)** and **F(High)**. One of the two values **F(Low)** and **F(High)** will be positive and one will be negative. If the sign of **F(M)** matches **F(High)**, then **High** gets its value changed to **M**. If the match is with **Low**, then **Low** gets changed. So the pseudocode for the guarded command can be refined to

if (**F(M)** approximately equals **0.0**) *then* **RootFound** := **true**
else if **SameSign(F(High), F(M))** *then* **High** := **M**
else if **SameSign(F(Low), F(M))** *then* **Low** := **M**

where **SameSign** is a boolean-valued function that tests two values to see if they have the same sign.

The test for approximate zero will depend on a constant called **Threshold**. As long as a number is less than **Threshold** in absolute value, it will be considered close enough to zero. The value of **Threshold** will depend on the accuracy of the computer and the accuracy needed for the particular application. Hence we will ask the user to supply the value.

If incorrect initial values are used, the program can go into an infinite loop. Hence, a limit is set on the number of loop iterations allowed. When that limit is exceeded, the program halts and reports that something is likely to be amiss.

The final program is in Figure 15.5. The function declaration for **F** is indicated by three dots. It can be filled in with any function definition that satisfies the assumptions we made.

```pascal
program FindRoot(input, output);
{Finds a root of the function F by the bisection method.}
const MaxIterations = 1000;
var Low, High, M: real;
    Threshold: real;
    RootFound: boolean;
    Count: 0..MaxIterations;

function F(X: real): real;
{The function whose root is being sought}
    . . .

function SameSign(V1, V2: real): boolean;
{Returns true if V1 and V2 have the same sign; otherwise returns false.}
    begin{SameSign}
      if (V1 >= 0.0) and (V2 >= 0.0)
              then SameSign := true
      else if (V1 <= 0.0) and (V2 <= 0.0)
              then SameSign := true
      else SameSign := false
    end; {SameSign}

procedure ReadInterval(var Low, High: real);
{Reads in two values which are supposed to have exactly one root
between them. Makes a test to see if they are plausible values.}
begin{ReadInterval}
    repeat
      writeln('Enter two values.');
      writeln('The first less than the root');
      writeln('The second greater than the root.');
      writeln('Be sure there is');
      writeln('exactly one root between them.');
      readln(Low, High);
      if SameSign(F(Low), F(High))
        then
          begin
            writeln('Those cannot be right');
            writeln('Try again')
          end
    until not (SameSign(F(Low), F(High)))
end; {ReadInterval}

begin{Program}
    writeln('Enter accuracy desired');
    readln(Threshold);
    RootFound := false;
    ReadInterval(Low, High);
```

Figure 15.5
**Program to find
a root of a function.**

```
M := (Low + High)/2;
Count := 0;

while not(RootFound) and (Count < MaxIterations) do
  begin {while}
    {Low  <  (the root) <  High and M = (Low + High) / 2}
    if abs(F(M)) <= Threshold
        then RootFound := true
    else if SameSign(F(High), F(M))
        then High := M
    else if SameSign(F(Low), F(M))
        then Low := M
    else writeln('Something is wrong!');

    M := (Low + High)/2;
    Count := Count + 1
  end; {while}

if Count = MaxIterations
  then writeln('Exceeded iteration limit')
  else writeln('The root is approximately ', M)
end.{Program}
```

Figure 15.5
(cont'd)

Summary of Problem Solving and Programming Techniques

Values of type **real** are stored as approximate quantities. Hence computations involving these numbers yield only approximations of the desired results. Unless particular care is taken to minimize errors, these approximations can often be very inaccurate. Some common sources of error are round-off error in any arithmetic operation such as addition or multiplication, but most especially in certain combinations such as adding two numbers of very different sizes or subtracting two numbers of almost equal size.

◇

> As a wise programmer once said, "Floating point numbers are like sandpiles: every time you move one, you lose a little sand and you pick up a little dirt." And after a few computations, things can get pretty dirty.
>
> *B. W. Kernighan and P. J. Plauger,*
> *The Elements of Programming Style*

◇

floating point numbers In Pascal, numbers of type **real**.

overflow The condition that results when a program attempts to compute a numeric value that is larger than the largest value of that type which the computer can represent in memory or is smaller than the smallest value of that type which the computer can represent in memory.

underflow The condition that results when a program attempts to compute a value of type **real** such that the value is smaller in absolute value than the smallest positive **real** value that the system can represent in memory. In other words, the condition that results when a program attempts to compute a nonzero value that is too close to zero to be represented in memory (except possibly by the approximately equal value of zero).

Exercises

Self-Test and Interactive Exercises

1. Describe how each of the following **integer** and **real** constants is represented in our hypothetical decimal computer:

```
123456          -123456
123.456         -123.456
0.00123456       -0.00123456
3.14159265358979323846
```

2. Find (approximately) the largest value for the constant **Epsilon** that will cause the following **writeln** to be executed on your system.

```
X := 1.0 + Epsilon;
if X = 1.0
  then writeln('It''s really nothing')
```

3. Our hypothetical decimal computer had a word size of eight. To store values of type **real**, it used five digit positions for the fraction part and three digit positions for the exponent part. Suppose that we instead used other combinations. At what value would **real** overflow occur if we instead used the following combinations?

Fraction part uses four digit positions and exponent part uses four.

Fraction part uses three digit positions and exponent part uses five.

Fraction part uses six digit positions and exponent part uses two.

4. (Applies to the optional section "Binary Numerals.") Convert the following binary numerals into equivalent decimal numerals: 111, 101, 100, 11011, 010110, 0.1, 0.01, 0.001, 0.101, 1.001, 101.101.

5. (Applies to the optional section "Machine Representation of Numbers in Binary.") What would you expect as the value of **maxint** in a thirty-two-bit machine? Assume that numbers are stored as described in this chapter. What about a sixty-four-bit machine?

Regular Exercises

6. Write a function declaration for a function called **Digit** that returns the value of the nth digit from the right of an **integer** argument. The value of n should be a second argument. For example, **Digit(9635,1)** returns **5** and **Digit(9635,3)** returns **6**.

7. If e denotes the base of the natural logarithm then the value e^x can be calculated by the series:

$$e^x = 1 + x + \frac{x^2}{2!} + \frac{x^3}{3!} + \frac{x^4}{4!} + \frac{x^5}{5!} + \cdots$$

Write a program that computes an approximate value of e by summing that series for **N** terms. Have the program compute the series from left to right and from right to left and output both results. The value e^x can also be computed by the standard function **exp(** x **)**. Have the program also output the value of e calculated by **exp(1.0)**. Compare the three results. Embed these three calculations in a loop that repeats the calculation for values of **N** from **1** to **100**. To avoid integer overflow, store the factorials as values of type **real**.

8. Write a program to sum the following series from left to right until a term of absolute value less than **0.00001** is encountered and to then output the answer:

$$4 - \frac{4}{3} + \frac{4}{5} - \frac{4}{7} + \frac{4}{9} - \cdots$$

(The denominators are the positive odd numbers 1, 3, 5, 7, 9, 11, ...) Have the program then recalculate the sum from right to left using the same number of terms and output that value as well. Compare the two results.

9. (Applies to the optional section "Binary Numerals.") Write a program that takes base two numerals (for whole numbers) as input and outputs the equivalent base ten numeral.

10. (Applies to the optional section "Binary Numerals.") Write a program that takes base ten numerals (for whole numbers) as input and outputs the equivalent base two numeral.

11. (Applies to the optional section "Binary Numerals.") A *hexadecimal numeral* is a numeral written in base 16. Write a program that takes a hexadecimal numeral (for a whole number) as input and outputs the equivalent base ten numeral. Use the first six letters of the alphabet for the digits "ten" through "fifteen."

12. (Applies to the optional section "Binary Numerals.") Write a program that takes base 10 numerals (for whole numbers) as input and outputs the equivalent hexadecimal numerals. (See Exercise 11.)

13. One way to obtain extra digits is to store numbers as arrays of digits. Write a program that will read in two whole numbers with up to 20 digits each and store their digits in arrays of type:

array[0..20] *of* **integer**

The program then computes the sum of the two numbers, stores the result in an array of the same type and then outputs the result to the screen. Use the ordinary addition algorithm that you learned in grade school. Be sure to issue an "overflow" message if the result is more than twenty digits long.

14. It is wasteful to store just one digit in an array location that can hold about the number of digits in **maxint**. Redo the previous exercise, but this time store **L** digits in

each array variable, where **L** is two less than the length of **maxint** written in base ten. You will need to modify the addition algorithm slightly, but the idea is still the same. Use **0..4** as the array index type.

15. Do the previous exercise for multiplication instead of addition.

16. Use the ideas in the previous exercise to design a program that can do multiplication of "real" numbers that yields at least twice as many significant digits as your system's ordinary Pascal **real** multiplication does.

17. (This exercise assumes that you know what a derivative is.) If x is a maximum or minimum of a function f and f has a derivative at x, then the derivative of f is zero at x. Use this idea to design a program to find local minima and maxima of polynomials of degree two. Use any input format that is convenient.

18. Redo the previous exercise, but allow polynomials of arbitrary degree and use the bisection method to find the roots of the derivatives.

References for Further Reading

B. W. Kernighan and P. J. Plauger, *The Elements of Programming Style*, 1978, McGraw-Hill, New York. Includes material on pitfalls in both numeric and nonnumeric programming. The examples are in Fortran and PL/I, not in Pascal.

D. E. Knuth, *The Art of Computer Programming, Volume 2, Seminumerical Algorithms*, 2nd ed., 1981, Addison-Wesley, Reading, Mass. Also does not use Pascal, but the text can be read without reading the programs.

J. Stoer and R. Bulirsch, *Introduction to Numerical Analysis*, 1980, Springer-Verlag, New York. Uses Algol, a language similar to Pascal.

16

More File Types

A little more than kin, and less than kind.

William Shakespeare, Hamlet

Chapter Contents

T ext files, which we have already used, are a special case of the more general construct known as "files." In this chapter we discuss Pascal files in complete generality and also discuss techniques for using files of types other than **text**.

The General Notion of a File

In Pascal, a *file* type is a structured data type. Associated with each file type is a simpler type called its *component type*. A file consists of sequences of items called *components*, all of which are values of the component type. The component type of a general file can be any data type other than another file type. It may be a simple type such as **integer** or **char**. It might be an array type. It very frequently is a record type.

component type

This description makes a file sound very much like an array, and indeed a file is conceptually very much like a one-dimensional array. There are, however, three important conceptual differences between a file and an array. First, the size of an array must be declared and so is bounded by some fixed number. On the other hand, there is no limit to the size of a file. The number of components that are placed in a file is not declared anywhere in the program, and there is no limit to the number of such components. Any particular implementation will impose an upper bound on the size of a file, but this is typically so large that, for most purposes, it can be considered unbounded. Second, files can be kept in secondary storage. Finally, files are normally accessed sequentially. For example, to get to the tenth component of a file, a program normally steps through the first nine components before it reaches the tenth component. In standard Pascal, this is the only way that a file component can be accessed. With an array, a program can go directly to any element of the array.

comparison to arrays

A type definition for a file type consists of the two words **file of** followed by the component type. The component type may be given either as a type name or a type definition. For example, if you want **FileInt** to be the name of a type consisting of a file of integers, then the type declaration is as follows:

syntax for type definitions

```
type FileInt = file of integer;
```

Some other sample file types are:

```
file of real
file of array[0..10] of integer
file of
    record
      Name: array[1..20] of char;
      Number: integer;
      Price: real
    end
```

A text file is almost the same thing as a **file of char**. The only difference is that a text file is divided into lines and a **file of char** is not. Despite their similarities, text files and other types of files are usually thought of as two different categories of files. Moreover, on many systems, text files and other files are treated slightly differently by the standard procedures for manipulating files. Because of these small differences, it is best to treat text files as a special category of files; when compared to other types of files, text files are "more than kin and less than kind." To avoid problems, use the descriptions presented in this chapter

text files

for files other than text files and use the descriptions presented in Chapter 13 for text files.

File Variables

Like other types, programs can have variables of the various file types. The declaration for a variable **Y** of the type that is to be a file of integers is:

var Y: *file of* integer;

An alternative, and usually preferable, way to declare **Y** would be to declare the type **FileInt** as in the previous section and to declare **Y** by:

var Y: FileInt;

file
names

On some systems the file variable name is the only name a file has. On other systems a file may have a directory name in addition to its file variable name. As with text files, once any file is opened it is always referred to by its file variable name. All types of files must be opened before a program can access the file.

Standard Pascal—Opening Files

external
files

In standard Pascal a file is opened for writing with the standard procedure **rewrite** and is opened for reading with the standard procedure **reset**. The syntax is identical to that of text files. Any type of file may be either external or internal. If the file is external, then it must be listed in the program heading. For example, if the file **IntData** is a file of **integer** values which is in secondary storage, then a program that accesses this file would open as follows:

program Sample(input, output, IntData);

internal
files

Internal files only exist for the duration of the program and are not listed in the program heading. The details are identical to those of text files.

rewrite
reset

A **write** statement may be used with any file that has been opened with the standard procedure **rewrite**. A **read** statement may be used with any file that has been opened with the standard procedure **reset**. In addition, files opened with **rewrite** may have data added to them by means of the standard procedure **put** described later in this chapter. Files opened with **reset** may have data "read" from them by means of the standard procedure **get**, also described later in this chapter. **writeln** and **readln** can only be used with text files, since this is the only type of file that is divided into lines.

UCSD Pascal—Opening Files

reset
rewrite

In UCSD Pascal any file that already exists in secondary storage is opened with the standard procedure **reset**. A new file is created by means of the standard procedure **rewrite**. All files have both a directory name of type **string** and a file variable name. Once a file has been opened, the file is always referred to by its file variable name and never by its directory name. The syntax of **rewrite** and **reset** for general files is identical to what it is for text files.

In many versions of UCSD Pascal it is difficult to have two files open for writing at the same time. Two **rewrite** statements in a row usually do not work. At first it is best to simply avoid this possibility. If you need to have two files open for writing, consult the documentation on your local system or consult a local expert.

On all systems, "writing" and "reading" can be done by means of the standard procedures **put** and **get**, respectively. (They are described below.) On most systems, the standard procedures **write** and **read** can also be used. **writeln** and **readln** can only be used with text files, since this is the only type of file that is divided into lines. In UCSD Pascal it is possible to mix "reading" and "writing" to a file of any type except the type **text**. However, doing so can be a little tricky. It may be safer and easier at first to only "read" from files opened with **reset** and only "write" to files opened with **rewrite**.

All files must be closed when a program is through "reading" from and/or "writing" to the file. The syntax and effect of the various options for **close** are identical to what we described for text files.

close

Windows and Buffer Variables

Before we go on to discuss syntax and give examples, there is one other concept connected with files that we must explicate, namely, the notion of a *window*. As we already said, a file is a sequence of components all of the same type. Every file has a window that is positioned at exactly one of these components. If these components are records, then the window is positioned at one record. If the file is a file of integers, then the window is positioned at one integer. As the term "window" indicates, the program has access to (can "see") only one component in the list, namely, the component at which the window is positioned. To "read" things in a file, the program must somehow move the window to the position of the component to be read. Similarly when "writing" to a file, the program can only "write" at the current position of the window. That means that files can only be accessed one component (record or integer or whatever) at a time. This window has no name in a Pascal program. However, a very closely related object called a "buffer variable" does have a Pascal name and can appear in Pascal programs.

Whenever any type of file variable is declared, a variable called the *buffer variable* for the file is automatically declared. In Pascal programs, this file variable is always written as the identifier for the file variable followed by the "up arrow" symbol ↑. (The up arrow symbol may look a bit different on some screens. Some systems even use the totally different symbol @ in place of ↑.) The type of the buffer variable is the same as the component type of the file variable. The value, if

window

buffer variable

any, of the buffer variable is some item of the component type that typically either is in the window or can easily be placed in the window.

To illustrate the notion of a buffer variable, suppose that a program contains the declarations:

```
type FileInt = file of integer;
var File1: FileInt;
```

As a side effect of this file variable declaration, a buffer variable spelled as follows is automatically declared:

```
File1↑
```

This buffer variable is of type **integer**. It need not be explicitly declared. In fact, it is an error to do so. Including the following line in the program will cause a syntax error message:

```
var File1↑: integer;
{THIS LINE IS NOT ALLOWED IN ANY PROGRAM.}
```

Still, **File1↑** is a variable of type **integer** and may be manipulated in many of the same ways that any other **integer** variable is manipulated. So under some but not necessarily all conditions, the following are valid Pascal statements:

```
File1↑ := 5;
X := File1↑;
readln(File1↑); {This reads from the keyboard.}
writeln(File1↑); {This writes to the screen.}
Proc4(File1↑) {Proc4 is a procedure name.}
```

The buffer variable is designed to be used with the standard procedures **put** and **get**.

put—"Writing" to Files

Entering data into a file is called *writing* even if the procedure **write** is not used. The standard procedure **put** can be used to write one component to a file. For example, suppose **File1** is the file variable name for a file of integers and that the file has been opened appropriately. A call to **put** is of the form:

```
put(File1)
```

This command "puts," or "writes," the value of the buffer variable **File1↑** into the window of **File1** and then moves the window to the next position. For example, writing the number **5** to **File1** can be accomplished by the two statements:

```
File1↑ := 5;
put(File1)
```

Writing the number **6** into the next position in the file can be accomplished by next executing the two statements:

```
File1↑ := 6;
put(File1)
```

After execution of the procedure **put**, the value of the buffer variable is undefined. Hence, the buffer variable must be given a value before an additional call to **put**.

In standard Pascal, a file must be opened with **rewrite** in order to use **put**, and the new components are always appended to the end of the file. In standard Pascal the window always moves in one direction.

When a file is created using **rewrite**, the window is at the location to receive the first component, but since the file is empty, there is no value in the window. The value of the buffer variable is also undefined at this point and must be given a value before a **put** is executed. The process is diagramed in Figure 16.1.

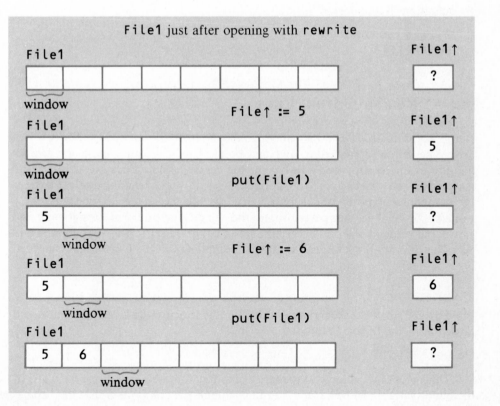

Figure 16.1
Use of **put**.

The Procedure write

In standard Pascal and some versions of UCSD Pascal the standard procedure **write** may be used with files of any type, not just with files of type **text**. Suppose that **File1** is the file variable name for a file of integers, as in the previous section, and suppose that the file **File1** has been opened appropriately. Now suppose that we wish to write some new components to the file. Specifically, suppose we wish to write the three values **5**, **4** and the value of the **integer** variable **N**. The following statement will accomplish the writing:

```
write(File1, 5, 4, N)
```

As with text files, the first argument is the file variable name of the file. The rest of the arguments must be expressions that evaluate to values of the component type. If the component type is **integer**, then the values written must all be of type **integer**. If the component type is a record type, then the values written must all be of that record type.

write defined

The precise effect of **write** is defined in terms of **put**. To illustrate, consider the statement:

```
write(File1, X)
```

By definition that statement is equivalent to:

```
File1↑ := X;
put(File1)
```

get—"Reading" from Files

Retrieving data from a file is called *reading* even if the procedure **read** is not used. The standard procedure **get** can be used to read one component from a file. For example, suppose **File1** is the file variable name for a file of some type (say, *file of* **integer** to be specific, but the same remarks apply whatever the component type is) and suppose that the file has just been opened with a **reset**. The call to **reset** positions the window at the first component and causes the value of the buffer variable **File1↑** to be set to this first component. So to set the variable **X1** equal to the first component in the file, all that is needed is an assignment statement, like so:

```
X1 := File1↑
```

To "get" the next component in the file, the function **get** can be used. A call to **get** is of the form:

```
get(File1)
```

eof

This moves the window to the next component in the file and sets the value of the buffer variable **File1↑** equal to the value of the component that then comes into the window. If there is a next component so that all this can be carried out, then the call to **get** also sets the value of **eof(File1)** to **false**. If there is no next component, then the location of the window and the value of **File1↑** are undefined and the value of **eof(File1)** is set to **true**.

As an example, the following piece of code sets the values of **X1** and **X2** equal to the first and second components (in that order) of the file **File1**:

{*The file File1 has been opened with* **reset** *and*
has not been manipulated since being opened.}
```
X1 := File1↑;
get(File1);
X2 := File1↑
```

The process is illustrated in Figure 16.2.

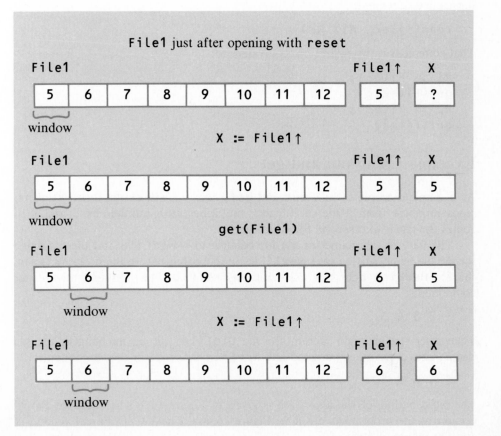

Figure 16.2
Use of get.

The Procedure read

In standard Pascal and some versions of UCSD Pascal the standard procedure **read** can be used with files of any type. The first argument is the file variable name, and the remaining arguments are variables of the component type. The call will set the values of the variables equal to as many of the components of the file as there are variables. The use is essentially the same as for text files except that all variables must be of the component type.

read defined

The precise effect of **read** is defined in terms of **get**. For example, suppose a program contains the following declarations:

```
type Item = record
              First: real;
              Second: array[1..10] of integer
            end;
var File2: file of Item;
    R1, R2: Item;
```

Assume that **File2** has been opened appropriately and consider the following illustrative statement:

```
read(File2, R1, R2)
```

That statement is, by definition, equivalent to:

```
R1 := File2↑;
get(File2);
R2 := File2↑;
get(File2)
```

Example Using put and get

As a simple example of how **put** and **get** work, we will design a program that reads numbers from a file of integers, multiplies each number by **2** and then copies the result to a second file of integers.

The file variable name for the file being read is **OldFile** and the file name for the file being written to is **NewFile**. Suppose that before the program is run, the file **NewFile** does not exist and the file **OldFile** contains the integer components:

```
1 2 3 4 5
```

Then after the program is run, the file **OldFile** will be unchanged, the file **NewFile** will have been created and **NewFile** will contain the components:

```
2 4 6 8 10
```

The basic outline of the algorithm is given in Figure 16.3. The standard Pascal version of the program is given in Figure 16.4(s). The UCSD Pascal version is given in Figure 16.4(u).

```
open OldFile with reset;
create NewFile with rewrite;
{The window is at the first component of OldFile;
NewFile is blank.}
while not eof(OldFile) do
    begin
        NewFile↑ := 2 * OldFile↑;
        put(NewFile);
        get(OldFile)
        {Up to but not including the position of the windows, the
        components of NewFile are those of OldFile multiplied by 2.}
    end
```

Figure 16.3
**How to copy
modified
components from
one file to another.**

```
program StandardFiles(input, output, OldFile, NewFile);
{Reads integers from the file called OldFile, multiplies each by 2
and writes the result to the file called NewFile. If NewFile does
not exist, it is created; if it already exists, the old contents are
lost. OldFile is not changed.}

type FileInt = file of integer;
var OldFile, NewFile: FileInt;

begin{Program}
    writeln('Manipulating files.');

    reset(OldFile);
    rewrite(NewFile);
    {The window is at the first component of OldFile;
    NewFile is blank.}

    while not eof(OldFile) do
      begin{while}
        NewFile↑ := 2 * OldFile↑;
        put(NewFile);
        get(OldFile)
        {Up to but not including the position of the windows, the
        components of NewFile are those of OldFile multiplied by 2.}
      end; {while}

    writeln('End of program')
end. {Program}
```

**Figure 16.4(s)
Standard Pascal
program using put
and get.**

```
program UCSDFiles;
```
{Reads integers from the file called 'Data1' in the directory, multiplies each by 2 and writes the result to the file called 'Data2' in the directory. If 'Data2' does not exist, it is created; if it already exists, the old contents are lost. 'Data1' is not changed.}

```
type FileInt = file of integer;
var OldFile, NewFile: FileInt;

begin{Program}
    writeln('Manipulating files.');

    reset(OldFile, 'Data1');
    rewrite(NewFile, 'Data2');
```
{The window is at the first component of OldFile; NewFile is blank.}

```
    while not eof(OldFile) do
      begin{while}
        NewFile↑ := 2 * OldFile↑;
        put(NewFile);
        get(OldFile)
```
{Up to but not including the position of the windows, the components of NewFile are those of OldFile multiplied by 2.}
```
      end; {while}

    close(OldFile, lock);
    close(NewFile, lock);

    writeln('End of program')
end. {Program}
```

Figure 16.4(u)
UCSD Pascal
program using put
and get.

In standard Pascal the programs can be made clearer by using the standard procedures **read** and **write**. To get an equivalent program that uses **read** and **write**, replace the *while* loop by the one below. (The same replacement works on some, but not all, UCSD Pascal systems.)

```
while not eof(OldFile) do
  begin{while}
    read(OldFile, Buffer);
    Buffer := 2 * Buffer;
    write(NewFile, Buffer)
```
{Up to but not including the position of the windows, the components of NewFile are those of OldFile multiplied by 2.}
```
  end; {while}
```

The variable **Buffer** must be declared to be of type **integer**. It serves a role similar to that of the buffer variable **OldFile↑**, but is a different variable.

Files as Parameters to Procedures

Procedures may have parameters of any file type, but they must be variable parameters; they cannot be value parameters. The situation for other types of files is the same as it is for text files.

Deciding What Type of File to Use

Since **integer** and **real** values can be stored in text files, there may seem to be no need for the file types *file of* **integer** and *file of* **real**. This is not quite true. When storing numbers in a file of type **text**, a type conversion is performed whenever a number is read from or written to the file. With the other file types, no type conversion is needed. Hence, if all the data in a file is of type **integer**, then a program will run more efficiently if the type of the files used is *file of* **integer** rather than **text**. In the case of the type **real**, accuracy is also an issue. When using a text file, each reading or writing of a value of type **real** can introduce inaccuracies in the values stored. This loss of accuracy is a result of the type conversion calculation.

When choosing a file type, remember that the components of a file can be of a structured type. If your program needs to place an array of **real** values in secondary storage, then a *file of* **real** will work acceptably. However, a much simpler program can be written using a file with an array component type. For example, consider the following:

```
type ArrayType = array[1..100] of real;
var A: ArrayType;
    DiskFile: file of ArrayType;
```

Once the file has been opened, the array can be placed in secondary storage with two simple statements:

```
DiskFile↑ := A;
put(DiskFile)
```

or the equivalent statement:

```
write(DiskFile, A)
```

This technique does have one disadvantage. You must know the number (or a good upper bound on the number) of values that will be stored. This is because the array dimensions must be specified in the type definition.

Standard Pascal— A File of Records Example

As an illustration of the use of files, Figure 16.5 contains a simple program for changing a file of records. The file **PayFile** holds the rate of pay for each employee in a company. The file components consist of records with two fields, one for an employee name and one for an hourly pay rate. The program changes each component in the file, so that the field containing the pay rate is increased by 10%. The records are copied from the file **PayFile** to the internal file **Temp**, changing each pay rate in the process. After that, the changed file contents are copied back to **PayFile**.

```
program Standard(input, output, PayFile);
{The external file PayFile is changed so that each component
record has the PayRate increased by (UpFactor*100) percent.
Precondition: The file PayFile exists in secondary storage
and the PayRate record fields of each component have a value.}

const UpFactor = 0.1; {For a pay raise of 10 percent}
type Spell = array[1..30] of char;
     Employee = record
                     Name: Spell;
                     PayRate: real
                 end;
        PayRecords = file of Employee;
var PayFile, Temp: PayRecords;
      {PayFile is an external file name;
       Temp is an internal file name.}
      OneRecord: Employee;

procedure Copy(var Source, Dest: PayRecords);
{Copies the contents of the file Source into the file Dest.
Previous contents of Dest are lost.}
    var OneRecord: Employee;
begin{Copy}
    reset(Source);
    rewrite(Dest);
    {The window is at the first component of Source.  Dest is blank.}
    while not eof(Source) do
      begin{while}
        read(Source, OneRecord);
        write(Dest, OneRecord)
        {Up to but not including the position of the windows,
         the components of Dest are the same as those of Source.}
      end; {while}
end; {Copy}
```

Figure 16.5
Standard Pascal program using a file of records.

```
begin{Program}
  writeln('I''m going to give everyone a raise.');
  {First copy each record to Temp adjusting
  the value of PayRate in each record.}
  reset(PayFile);
  rewrite(Temp);
  while not eof(PayFile) do
    begin{while}
      read(PayFile, OneRecord);
      with OneRecord do
        PayRate := PayRate + UpFactor*PayRate;
        write(Temp, OneRecord)
    end; {while}

  Copy(Temp, PayFile);

  writeln('Everybody is now richer.')
end. {Program}
```

UCSD Pascal—seek
(Optional)

In UCSD Pascal, programs can both read and write to the same file. The **reset** statement opens an existing file. The **rewrite** statement creates a new file. In either case the file can be both read from and written to. Hence a UCSD Pascal program can mix **read** and **write** statements to the same file. (That is, provided these procedures work at all. On some systems, the procedures **read** and **write** are not defined for files of the types under discussion.) Similarly, **put** and **get** statements to the same file can also be mixed. Unfortunately, it is usually difficult to mix **read** and **write** to the same file or **put** and **get** to the same file in an effective way. UCSD Pascal allows them to be mixed, but because of the way they move the window, it is hard, though not impossible, to get much use out of this feature. In order to use them together, it is usually necessary to position the window with the **seek** command described in the next paragraph.

UCSD Pascal allows random access to files. In other words, the window can move backward as well as forward and can jump directly to any desired location. This is done with the predefined procedure **seek**. For example, the following will move the window in the file named by the file variable **PayFile** to component number **7** in the file:

seek

```
seek(PayFile, 7)
```

```
program UCSD;
{The file called 'PayData' in the directory is changed so that each
component record has the PayRate increased by (UpFactor*100) percent.
Precondition: The file 'PayData' exists in secondary storage
and the PayRate record fields of each component have a value.}

const UpFactor = 0.1; {For a pay raise of 10 percent}
type Employee = record
                    Name: string;
                    PayRate: real
                end;
     PayRecords = file of Employee;
var PayFile: PayRecords;
    ComponentNum: integer;

begin{Program}
   writeln('I''m going to give everyone a raise.');

   reset(PayFile, 'PayData');
   ComponentNum := 0;
   seek(PayFile, ComponentNum);
   get(PayFile);
   {The value of the buffer variable PayFile↑ is equal to the value of
   component number ComponentNum, i.e., component number 0.}

   while not eof(PayFile) do
    begin{while}
      with PayFile↑ do
        PayRate := PayRate + UpFactor*PayRate;
      seek(PayFile, ComponentNum);
      put(PayFile);
      {Components zero through ComponentNum
      have had the value of PayRate adjusted.}
      ComponentNum := ComponentNum + 1;
      seek(PayFile, ComponentNum);
      get(PayFile)
    end; {while}

   close(PayFile, lock);

   writeln('Everybody is now richer.')
end. {Program}
```

Figure 16.6
UCSD Pascal
program using a
file of records.

The procedure **seek** takes two arguments: the first is a file variable name and the second is an expression that evaluates to a nonnegative **integer** value. The call to **seek**, more or less, moves the file window to the component whose number is specified by the **integer** expression. The precise effect of this command is that the next **put** or **get** executed applies to that component. The components are numbered starting with **0** rather than **1**. So the first component is component number **0**, the next component is numbered **1** and so forth. The **seek** statement does not work for text files.

For example, suppose **X** is a variable of some type called **Employee** and **PayFile** is a file variable name for a file of component type **Employee**. In order to set the value of **X** equal to component number **7** in the file **PayFile** you can use the following code (declarations as in Figure 16.6):

```
seek(PayFile, 7);
get(PayFile);
X := PayFile↑
```

To change component **9** to the value of **X**, the following code will suffice:

```
seek(PayFile, 9);
PayFile↑ := X;
put(PayFile)
```

Because of the way **seek** is implemented, there must always be a **put** or **get** executed between every two executions of a **seek**. Otherwise, unpredictable things can happen to the window position. Also, the only safe way to mix **put** and **get** to the same file is to precede each call to either **put** or **get** with a call to **seek**. That is what is done in the sample program in Figure 16.6.

Summary of Problem Solving and Programming Techniques

Data of almost any type, including record types, may be kept in secondary storage by using a file with that particular component type. This provides a way to make a permanent file with data of types other than the simple types that can be written to text files. Although numeric data can be stored in a text file, it is usually more efficient and clearer to store it in a file whose component type matches the type of the data. Text files are best used for text and numbers are best stored in files of one of the two types *file of* **integer** or *file of* **real**.

Summary of Pascal Constructs

Constructs Common to All Versions of Pascal

file types
Syntax:

> *file of* ⟨component type⟩

Example:

> *file of record*
>   Field1: integer;
>   Field2: *array*[1..10] *of* real
> *end*

Type of a file to hold components of type ⟨component type⟩. The ⟨component type⟩ may be any type other than a file type.

file variable declarations
Syntax:

> *var* ⟨file var⟩: *file of* ⟨component type⟩;

Example:

> *var* File1: *file of* integer;

Declaration of a file variable of type ⟨component type⟩. (A type name that has been declared to name the file type can be used instead of the type definition.)

buffer variable
Syntax:

> ⟨file var⟩↑

Example:

> File1↑

Buffer variable for the file named by the file variable ⟨file var⟩. A variable whose type is the component type of the file variable ⟨file var⟩. The buffer variable is meant to be used in conjunction with the standard procedures **put** and **get**.

put
Syntax:

> **put(** ⟨file var⟩ **)**

Example:

> **put(File1)**

Writes the value of the buffer variable ⟨file var⟩↑ into the window in the file ⟨file var⟩

and moves the window to the next position. After execution, the value of the buffer variable ⟨file var⟩↑ is undefined.

get

Syntax:

> **get(** ⟨file var⟩ **)**

Example:

> **get(File1)**

If the window is at some component other than the last component, then this moves the window in ⟨file var⟩ to the next component, sets the value of the buffer variable ⟨file var⟩↑ equal to this next component and sets the value of **eof(** ⟨file var⟩ **)** to **false**. If the window is at the last component, this sets **eof(** ⟨file var⟩ **)** to **true** and leaves both the window position and the value of ⟨file var⟩↑ undefined.

read

Syntax:

> **read(** ⟨file var⟩ **,** ⟨component type variable⟩ **)**

Example:

> **read(File1, X)**

The standard function **read** used with a file of type other than **text**. ⟨file var⟩ is the file variable name of the file and ⟨component type var⟩ is a variable of the component type of the file. There may be any number of variables. Equivalent to:

> ⟨component type variable⟩ **:=** ⟨file var⟩↑ **;**
> **get(** ⟨file variable⟩ **)**

Not implemented in some versions of UCSD Pascal.

write

Syntax:

> **write(** ⟨file var⟩ **,** ⟨expression⟩ **)**

Example:

> **write(File1, X+9)**

The standard function **write** used with a file of type other than **text**. ⟨file var⟩ is the file variable name of the file and ⟨expression⟩ is an expression that evaluates to a value of the component type of the file. There may be any number of expressions. Equivalent to:

> ⟨file var⟩↑ **:=** ⟨expression⟩ **;**
> **put(** ⟨file var⟩ **)**

Not implemented in some versions of UCSD Pascal.

eof

Syntax:

> **eof(** ⟨file var⟩ **)**

Example:

```
eof(File1)
```

Boolean function that returns **true** if the window in the file named by the file variable ⟨file var⟩ is beyond the last component and **false** when a file component is in the window. Also see **get** and **put**.

Standard Pascal but Not UCSD Pascal

reset

Syntax:

```
reset(⟨file var⟩)
```

Example:

```
reset(File1)
```

Opens the file named by the file variable ⟨file var⟩ for reading, positions the window at the first component in the file and sets the value of the buffer variable ⟨file var⟩↑ equal to the first component. If the file is empty, the position of the window and the value of the buffer variable ⟨file var⟩↑ are undefined.

rewrite

Syntax:

```
rewrite(⟨file var⟩)
```

Example:

```
rewrite(File1)
```

Creates a new file named by the file variable ⟨file var⟩, opens the file for writing and positions the window to receive the first component. If there already is a file called ⟨file var⟩ and ⟨file var⟩ is an external file name (i.e., appears in the program heading), then the contents of the old file are lost.

UCSD Pascal but Not Standard Pascal

reset

Syntax:

```
reset(⟨file var⟩, ⟨string⟩)
```

Examples:

```
reset(File1, 'Data10')
reset(File1)
```

Used to open existing files. Associates the file called ⟨string⟩ in the directory with the file variable ⟨file var⟩, positions the window at the first component in that file and sets the value of the buffer variable ⟨file var⟩↑ equal to the first component in the file. (The first component in the file is numbered zero.) ⟨string⟩ may be any expression that evaluates to a string which is an allowable file name. If the file named by ⟨file var⟩ is already open, then the argument ⟨string⟩ may be omitted; in that case, the file associated with ⟨file var⟩ will be the same as it was before the call to **reset**.

rewrite

Syntax:

rewrite(⟨file var⟩**,** ⟨string⟩**)**

Example:

rewrite(File1, 'Data10')

Creates a new file called ⟨string⟩ in the directory and ⟨file var⟩ in the program and positions the window to receive the first component. ⟨string⟩ may be any expression that evaluates to a string that is an allowable file name. The first argument ⟨file var⟩ is a file variable of the desired component type. If there already is a file named ⟨string⟩ in the directory, that file is lost. It is difficult to have two or more files, which were opened with **rewrite**, open at the same time. See your system manuals for details about opening two files for writing.

close

Syntax:

close(⟨file var⟩**,** ⟨option⟩**)**

Example:

close(File1, lock)

Closes the file named by the file variable ⟨file var⟩ in the manner indicated by the option ⟨option⟩. In most situations the option **lock** is appropriate. The option **purge** will remove the file from the directory. See Appendix 6 for a complete list of options.

seek

Syntax:

seek(⟨file var⟩**,** ⟨index⟩**)**

Example:

seek(File1, 89)

Causes the next **put** or **get** to the file named by the file variable ⟨file var⟩ to apply to component number ⟨index⟩. The argument ⟨index⟩ can be any expression that evaluates to a nonnegative integer. The components are numbered 0, 1, 2, 3,.... The **seek** statement cannot be used with files of type **text**.

Exercises

Self-Test and Interactive Exercises

1. Give a suitable type declaration for a file that is to hold student records consisting of a name, final exam score in the range 0 to 100 and a letter grade.

2. Suppose **Stuff** is a file variable of some type other than **text**. What does the following mean? (Answer in terms of **put** and/or **get**.)

```
read(Stuff, X)
```

3. Write a program to create a file of type *file of* **integer** and to write the numbers 1 through 10 to the file.

4. Write a program that will display to the screen the contents of the file created by the program of the previous exercise.

5. Write a program to search an existing file of integers to see if it contains a particular integer. The particular integer should be read in from the keyboard.

6. Write a program to create a file of records and fill the file with data read from the keyboard. The record should have two fields, one of type **integer** and one of type **char**.

7. Write a program to display on the screen the contents of the file created by the program of the previous exercise.

8. Write a program that will fill an array with ten integers read from the keyboard and then store the array value in a file of the type defined as follows:

```
type List = array[1..10] of integer;
     AFile = file of List;
```

9. Write a program that will fill an array from the file created by the program of the previous exercise and will then display the array values to the screen.

Regular Exercises

10. Write a program to search an existing file of integers and find the largest integer in the file.

11. Write a program that will read 10 **integer** values from a *file of* **integer** into an array, sort the array and then write the sorted list to another file of the same type.

12. Write a program that sorts a file of type *file of* **integer** so that the numbers appear in numeric order from the smallest to the largest. The final sorted list should be in the same file as the one originally containing the integers.

13. A record for describing a person is to consist of the following items: last name, initial of first name, sex, age, height, weight and telephone number. The records are to be stored in an array indexed by integers in the range **1** to **Limit**. **Limit** is to be declared as a constant. Write a program that will read in up to **Limit** records from the keyboard, store them in an array, write them out to the screen and then write them to a file. The file should

be a file of records, not a text file or a file of arrays. Your program should allow the possibility of fewer than **Limit** records being read in.

14. Write a program which reads the file created in the previous exercise, places the components into an array, sorts the records in the array according to the alphabetic order of the last names, writes the sorted records to the screen and then copies the records back to the file in alphabetic order.

15. Modify your program from Exercise 13 so that the second and succeeding times that it is run the contents of the file are copied into an array, and then the user has the option of either clearing all records and starting over or adding more records to those already in the array. Modify your program further to allow the user to delete individual records by specifying the last name for the record to be deleted. The user should also have the option of clearing all records without having to specify every name. Modify your program further to allow the user to see all records of a given category (such as all records for individuals between two specified ages) on the screen. All manipulations should be done with the array. When the user is finished, the program should copy the modified collection of records back to the file so that the file then contains the same records as the array.

16. Redo the previous assignment, but this time have your program deal directly with the file and not use an array.

17. Write a program for a computerized dating service. The information on individuals should be kept in a file of records and should include all the information described in Exercise 13, plus other information such as a hobbies, favorite color, etc. A user should be able to request a list of all dates that satisfy the user's specifications. Include a "best match" option that finds the date that is best suited to the user based only on the user's own record. Use a file of records.

18. Write a program to sort a file of records of the type described in Exercise 13. The files are to be arranged into alphabetic order according to last names. (One simple way to do this is to use a second file; the alphabetically first record is copied to the file, then the alphabetically next and so forth. There are also more efficient ways to do the sorting.)

19. Write a procedure that takes two sorted files of the type described in the previous exercise and merges them to produce a single sorted file that contains all the records from the two files.

20. Write a program to keep track of airline flight reservations and seat reservations. Allow any number of flights. Display seating plans as described in Exercise 10 of Chapter 14. The program should be able to add or delete flights. It should keep track of who is in what seat, as well as which seats are reserved. Keep the information in a file so that the program can be rerun and the information will be as it was left the last time the program was run. Use some file type other than **text**.

21. Write a program that will fill a two-dimensional array of characters with a pattern typed in from the keyboard and will then echo back the pattern on the screen. Next write a program that uses a file whose component type is the type of the two-dimensional array. This program should store one array for each letter of the alphabet. When displayed, the array for each letter should display that letter as a large block letter. Finally, write a program that uses this file of arrays to read a word from the keyboard and to echo it back to the screen in block letters.

22. If you are enrolled in a programming (or other) course, write a program that will serve as a record keeper for grades in your course. The program should allow the entry, display

and changing of any particular grade, such as the grade for a particular quiz or exam. If there is a formula for the final numeric grade, the program should calculate it. The program should allow the user to ask the average of any particular grade, such as a quiz or exam grade. Use a file of records, one for each student.

References for Further Reading

The reference manuals for your particular system are likely to be your best source of detailed information. The reference by Tiberghen listed in Chapter 3 is also helpful. For UCSD Pascal see the UCSD Pascal books listed in Chapter 3.

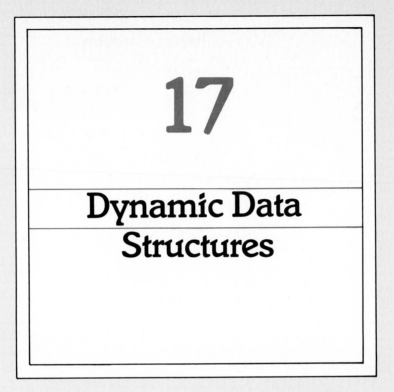

17

Dynamic Data Structures

"You are sad," the Knight said in anxious tone: "let me sing you a song to comfort you."

"Is it very long?" Alice asked, for she had heard a good deal of poetry that day.

"It's long," said the Knight, "but it's very, *very* beautiful. Everybody that hears me sing it —either it brings the *tears* into their eyes, or else—"

"Or else what?" said Alice, for the Knight had made a sudden pause.

"Or else it doesn't, you know. The name of the song is called '*Haddocks' Eyes*.'"

"Oh, that's the name of the song, is it?" Alice said, trying to feel interested.

"No, you don't understand," the Knight said, looking a little vexed. "That's what the name is *called*. The name really is '*The Aged Aged Man*.'"

"Then I ought to have said 'That's what the *song* is called'?" Alice corrected herself.

"No, you oughtn't: that's quite another thing! The *song* is called '*Ways and Means*': but that's only what it's *called*, you know!"

"Well, what *is* the song, then?" said Alice, who was by this time completely bewildered.

"I was coming to that," the Knight said. "The song really *is* '*A-sitting On A Gate*': and the tune's my own invention."

Lewis Carroll, Through the Looking-Glass

Chapter Contents

A *static* data structure is one whose structure is completely specified at the time the program is written and which cannot be changed by the program. Most of the data structures we have seen so far are static data structures. Arrays and simple records are examples of static data structures. The values of the various components in these structures may change, but the structures themselves do not change. A program cannot change the number of items in an array or the number of indexes for the array. The structure is fixed.

Dynamic data structures may have their structure changed by the program. (So far we have seen very few examples of dynamic data structures. A file is a dynamic data structure because the number of components can be changed by the program. The rest of the structure of a file is, however, fixed. So a file does not exhibit many dynamic features. Variant records, which were discussed in an optional section of Chapter 14, are dynamic data structures with more dynamic properties.) In this chapter we introduce a construct, called a *pointer,* that can be used to construct a wide variety of dynamic data structures.

The Notion of a Pointer

A *pointer* is, quite plain and simply, something that points. That definition is very abstract. To make it concrete, we will give it a geometric interpretation in terms of figures drawn on paper. These figures will always be configurations of boxes connected by arrows. In these figures a pointer is represented by an arrow drawn on paper. Each of these arrows, or pointers, usually points to an object called a *node*. In these drawings a node is represented by a box, of any shape, in which things may be written or, more abstractly, in which data may be stored. For example, a list of integers might be represented as nodes and pointers in the manner of Figure 17.1.

Before we present any more discussion of dynamic data structures, we will stop and discuss the Pascal syntax for pointers and nodes. That will allow us to express our algorithms as Pascal programs.

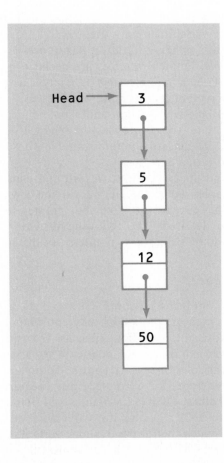

Figure 17.1

A data structure containing pointers.

Pascal Pointers and Dynamic Variables

In Pascal there is a special class of variables called *dynamic variables*. These dynamic variables are designed to be used as the nodes in dynamic data structures. In many ways dynamic variables are like the ordinary variables we have been using. Dynamic variables have a type that can be any of the types that ordinary variables can have. The only exception is that a dynamic variable cannot have a file type. Dynamic variables can be assigned a value by means of an assignment operator, or a **read** statement, or by any other means that the value of an ordinary variable can be set. Similarly, the value in a dynamic variable can be accessed in any of the ways that the value of an ordinary variable can be accessed: for example, by a **write** statement or by being an actual parameter to a procedure.

*dynamic
variables*

Dynamic variables differ from ordinary variables in only two ways. First, they may be created and destroyed by the program, and hence the number of such dynamic variables need not, indeed cannot, be determined at the time the program is written. Second, they have no names in Pascal; there is no identifier that names them in the way that ordinary variables are named by identifiers. For these reasons, dynamic variables are not declared.

*pointer
variables*

In order to refer to a dynamic variable, Pascal uses another type of variable called a *pointer variable*. Pointer variables are declared and do have identifiers associated with them. Pointer variables also have a type associated with them, and this type specifies the type of the dynamic variables they can be used with. The value of a pointer variable is a pointer, and a pointer may point to a dynamic variable of the appropriate type. In this way, a dynamic variable may be referred to indirectly by giving the name of a pointer variable whose value is a pointer that points to the dynamic variable.

To help understand the basic ideas, we will first consider some very simple types of dynamic variables. To be specific, we will first consider dynamic variables of type **integer**. They are not declared, but pointer variables that can hold pointers to them are declared. The following declares the variable **P** to be a pointer variable whose values are pointers to dynamic variables of type **integer**:

 var **P:** ↑**integer;**

The symbol ↑ is the "up arrow" symbol. (It may look a bit different on some screens. Some systems even use the totally different symbol @ in place of ↑.)

*domain
type*

The type of the dynamic variables, such as **integer** in this example, is sometimes called the *domain type* of the pointer. The variable **P** can only contain pointers to dynamic variables of type **integer**. To hold a pointer to a dynamic variable of some other type, for example, **char**, requires a different pointer variable of the type ↑**char**. Dynamic variables and pointer variables both have types and, in order to hold a pointer to a dynamic variable, the type of the pointer variable must match that of the dynamic variable.

new

Of course, a pointer variable is of no use unless there is something for it to point to. In order to create a dynamic variable, the standard procedure **new** is used. For example, suppose that **P** is as previously declared and consider the following statement:

```
new(P)
```

This will create a new dynamic variable of type **integer** and set the value of **P** equal to a pointer that points to this new dynamic variable. This dynamic variable can then be referred to as "the thing pointed to by **P**." In Pascal the phrase "the thing pointed to by **P**" is denoted **P↑**. (For those who have already read Chapter 16, we should note that this syntax is identical to that used for buffer variables. However, this has nothing to do with files or buffer variables. We are simply using the symbol ↑ in another and different context.) In order to set the value of this new dynamic variable equal to **5**, the following would suffice:

```
P↑ := 5
```

The value of the dynamic variable can be written to the screen in the usual way:

```
writeln(P↑)
```

Similarly, **P↑** can be used anyplace else that it is appropriate to use a variable of type **integer**.

Manipulating Pointers

Before going any further, we had best stop and clarify the common English syntax used by programmers when discussing pointers and pointer variables. In the preceding example, **P** was a pointer variable. Technically speaking, it does not point to anything. It has values that are pointers, and these pointers point to dynamic variables. It may help to think of the pointer as an arrow and the pointer variable as something or somebody that can hold one pointer arrow at a time. This distinction between a pointer and a pointer variable is sometimes important. However, we will follow common usage and will usually blur this distinction. We will usually write, for example, "**P** points to a dynamic variable" when we really mean "the value of **P** points to a dynamic variable."

Dynamic variables may have more than one pointer pointing to them. Also, pointers may be changed so that they point to different dynamic variables at different times. These changes are accomplished with the assignment operator **:=** . Technically speaking, there is nothing new here. The assignment operator works in exactly the same way with pointer variables as it does with the other types of variables we have seen. However, interpreting the result can be a bit subtle. A sample program will help to illustrate the concepts. The workings of the program in Figure 17.2 are illustrated in Figure 17.3.

:= and
pointers

In Figure 17.2 the statement

```
P1 := P2
```

changes the value of **P1** to that of **P2**. The value of **P1** is a pointer and the only property a pointer has is that it points to something. Hence, the effect of this

**Figure 17.2
Program that
illustrates pointers.**

Program

```
program Test(input, output);

type IntPointer = ↑integer;
var P1, P2: IntPointer;

begin{Program}
   new(P1);
   P1↑ := 1;
   writeln(P1↑);
   new(P2);
   P2↑ := 2;
   writeln(P2↑);
   P1 := P2;
   P2↑ := 3;
   writeln(P1↑, P2↑)
end. {Program}
```

Output

1
2
3 3

statement is to give **P1** a value that is a pointer which points to the same dynamic variable as the value of **P2** does. Stated this way, it makes it sound like the two pointers in Figure 17.3(e) are the same pointer, and in a sense they are, just as two values of the number **5** stored in two different **integer** variables are the same integer **5**. Those who find this too confusing, or too philosophical for their liking, can instead remember the more prosaic rule that if **X** and **Y** are pointer variables, then the statement

X := Y

changes **X** so that it points to the same thing that **Y** is currently pointing to.

When dealing with pointer variables, the distinction between a pointer variable, **P1**, for example, and the thing it points to, **P1↑**, is very important. When using the assignment operator always be sure to check that you are referring to objects of the appropriate type. The distinction is illustrated in Figure 17.4.

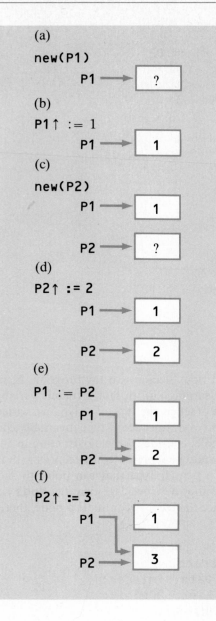

Figure 17.3
Explanation of
Figure 17.2.

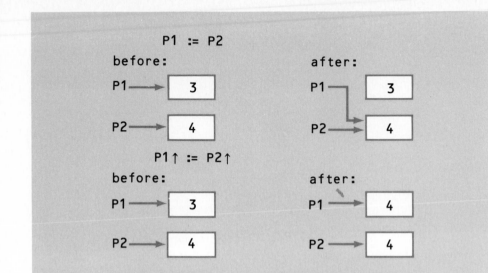

Figure 17.4
The distinction
between P1 and
P1↑.

Nodes

*type
declaration*

The program in the previous section is a toy program. Nobody would use it for anything other than a learning aid. In fact, dynamic variables of type **integer** have almost no uses. In practice, the type of a dynamic variable is inevitably some sort of record type. Moreover, this record type invariably contains a field that is a pointer type. For example, consider the data structure in Figure 17.1. The nodes in that data structure would be represented by records with two fields, one of type **integer** and one of a pointer type that can point to such nodes. The Pascal declaration would be as shown below. The identifier **Node** can be replaced by any other identifier, but since the record represents a node, there is a tendency to call the type **Node**.

```
type NPointer = ↑Node;
     Node = record
               Data: integer;
               Link: NPointer
            end;
var Head, Last: NPointer;
```

This declaration is blatantly circular. **NPointer** is defined in terms of **Node** and **Node** is defined in terms of **NPointer**. As it turns out, there is nothing wrong with this circularity and it is allowed in Pascal. One indication that this definition is not logically inconsistent is the fact that we can draw pictures representing such structures. Figure 17.1 is one such picture. This is very fortunate, since we must use some sort of circularity if we are to have data structures of this kind. After all, we want each node to contain a pointer to other nodes of the same type. If this is to be the situation, then the straightforward definition of the node type must refer to the pointers, and the straightforward definition of the pointer type must refer to the nodes. (In an attempt to avoid circularity, one clever programmer suggested defining a "pointer" as an arrow that points to "anything." But alas, the programmer's definition of "anything" referred to nodes, and the definition of "nodes" referred to pointers.) This is yet another example of how circular definitions can be not only meaningful but also extremely useful in writing computer programs.

Now we have pointers inside records and have these pointers pointing to records that contain pointers and so forth. In these situations the syntax can sometimes get involved, but in all cases the syntax follows those few rules we have described for pointers and records. As an illustration, suppose the declarations are as above, the situation is as diagramed in Figure 17.1 and we want to change the value of the **Data** field of the second node to **7**; in other words, we want to change the **5** to a **7**. One way to accomplish this is with the following statement:

```
Head↑.Link↑.Data := 7
```

To understand the expression on the left-hand side of the assignment operator, read it carefully from left to right. **Head** is a pointer; **Head↑** is the thing it points to, namely, the node (dynamic variable) containing **3**. (This node can be referred to as **Head↑**, "but that's only what it's called, you know!" What it really is is the first node.) This node, referred to by **Head↑**, is a record, and the field of this record, which contains a pointer, is called **Link**, and so **Head↑.Link** is the name of a pointer pointing to the node containing **5**. Since **Head↑.Link** is the name of a pointer pointing to the node containing **5**, **Head↑.Link↑** is a name for the node itself. Finally, **Head↑.Link↑.Data** is a name for the **Data** field of this node containing **5** and has its value changed to **7** by the assignment statement. One can usually avoid such long expressions involving pointers, but occasionally they are useful, and they are a good test of whether or not you understand the syntax and semantics of pointers.

The Pointer nil

There is one last Pascal construct that we need to describe before going on to discuss the applications of pointers. That is the constant *nil*. This constant *nil* is a predefined constant in the same sense that **maxint** is a predefined constant, although *nil* is of a different type than **maxint**. The constant *nil* is used to give a value to pointer variables which do not point to anything. As such it can be used as a kind of end marker. For example, in the data structure shown in Figure 17.1 it would be reasonable to set the pointer field of the last node equal to *nil*. Then the program can test for the end of the list by checking to see if the pointer field equals *nil*. The usage of *nil* as an end marker is illustrated in the next section.

To avoid syntax errors, remember that *nil* is a pointer and not the thing pointed to. For example, suppose the declarations are as in the previous section, and suppose the situation is as diagramed in Figure 17.5(a). In order to set the pointer field of the last node to *nil*, the Pascal statement would be:

    Last↑.Link := *nil*

The effect of this assignment is diagramed in Figure 17.5. Before this assignment, one pointer field had no value. Afterwards it has the value *nil*. Notice that the type of the expression on the left-hand side of the assignment operator is a pointer type, namely, the type **NPointer**.

*type
of nil*

The type of *nil* is a bit unorthodox since its type can be that of a pointer to a dynamic variable of any type. To make this seem less strange, it should be pointed out (after a while the pun is unavoidable or perhaps just irresistible) that *nil* does not point to anything and, since it is a constant, it cannot be changed so that it does point to something.

Linked Lists—An Example of Pointer Use

head

Structures like those in Figures 17.1, 17.5 and 17.6 are called *linked lists*. The pointer **Head** (in any of these figures) is not part of the linked list but is inevitably present when manipulating a linked list. A linked list consists of nodes each of

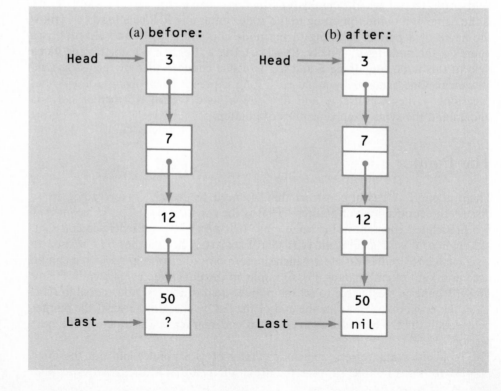

Figure 17.5
Last↑.Link
:= *nil*

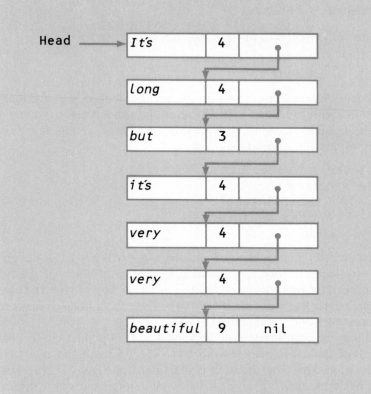

**Figure 17.6
A linked list.**

which has one pointer field. The pointers are set so that they order the nodes into a list. There is always one node called the *head* such that if you follow the arrows starting from that node, you will pass through each node exactly once. To put it less formally, the head is the first node in the list. The pointers called **Head** in these figures point to the heads of the linked lists given in the figures.

Linked lists are used for many of the same things that arrays are used for, namely, for storing lists of data. The linked list in Figure 17.1 holds a list of integers. The one in Figure 17.6 holds a sentence in the form of a list of words. As we will see, a program can change the size of a linked list. Also, it is relatively easy to efficiently insert or delete nodes in a linked list. For these reasons, linked lists are preferable to arrays for some applications.

As illustrated in Figure 17.6, the nodes may contain more than one kind of data. The nodes in that list contain a word, as an array of characters, and a count of the number of characters in the word. One possible type declaration for the nodes in that linked list is:

```
type WPointer = ↑WordNode;
     WordNode = record
                     Word: array[1..10] of char;
                     Count: 1..10;
                     Next: WPointer
                end;
```

The Pascal code designed in this section will apply to linked lists of integers, such as the ones in Figures 17.1 and 17.5. However, the same techniques apply no matter what sort of data is stored in the nodes. For reference, we repeat the type declarations we will use for a linked list of integers:

```
type NPointer = ↑Node;
     Node = record
                  Data: integer;
                  Link: NPointer
            end;
```

searching
a list

We will first consider the problem of locating a node. We want to design a procedure that will locate a node in a linked list made up of nodes of the type **Node**. More precisely, the procedure has a value parameter **Key** of type **integer** and a variable parameter **Here** of type **NPointer**. The procedure must make the pointer **Here** point to a node containing **Key**.

We assume that the head (first) node is pointed to by a pointer called **Head** and that the end of the list is marked with *nil*. The pointer **Head** is another parameter to the procedure. The situation is diagramed in Figure 17.8(a). Since empty lists present some minor problems that would clutter our discussion, we will assume that the linked list contains at least one node. Our assumptions can be summarized by the following precondition:

Precondition: **Head** *points to a linked list of integers containing at least one node; the end of the list is marked by* **nil**.

Our goal can be expressed precisely by the postcondition:

Postcondition: If there is a node that contains the integer **Key**, *then* **Here** *points to the first such node. If no node contains* **Key**, *then an error message is written to the screen.*

The only way to move around a linked list, or any other data structure made up of nodes and pointers, is to follow the arrows. So we will place the pointer **Here** at the first node and then move it from node to node, following the pointers until we find a node containing the integer **Key** or until we encounter the end of the linked list.

Since the pointer **Head** points to the first node, the following will leave **Here** pointing to the first node:

```
Here := Head
```

In order to move the pointer **Here** to the next node, we must think in terms of the named pointers we have available. The next node is the one pointed to by the pointer field of the current node. The node currently pointed to by **Here** is **Here**↑. The pointer field of that node is:

```
Here↑.Link
```

In order to move **Here** to the next node, we want to change **Here** so that it points to the node that is pointed to by the above-named pointer field. Hence, the following will move the pointer **Here** to the next node in the list:

```
Here := Here↑.Link
```

The complete procedure is given in Figure 17.7. The way the procedure works is illustrated in Figure 17.8.

In order to have a large linked list, a program must be able to add nodes to the linked list. A procedure to add nodes is given in Figure 17.9. In that procedure nodes are always added at the head of the list as indicated by the sample before and after diagrams. To help explain the procedure, a few extra comments have been added.

*adding
nodes*

```
type NPointer = ↑Node;
     Node = record
               Data: integer;
               Link: NPointer
            end;
procedure Find(Key: integer; Head: NPointer;
                       var Here: NPointer);
```

{*Precondition: Head points to a linked list of integers containing
at least one node; the end of the list is marked by nil.
Postcondition: If there is a node that contains the integer Key,
then Here points to the first such node. If no node contains Key,
then an error message is written to the screen.*}

```
begin{Find}
   Here := Head;
   while (Here↑.Data <> Key) and (Here↑.Link <> nil) do
      Here := Here↑.Link ;
   {Here is either pointing to a node containing Key or
   is pointing to the last node in the list (or both).}
   if Here↑.Data <> Key then
      writeln('ERROR ', Key,' is not in the list')
end; {Find}
```

**Figure 17.7
Procedure to locate
a node in a linked
list.**

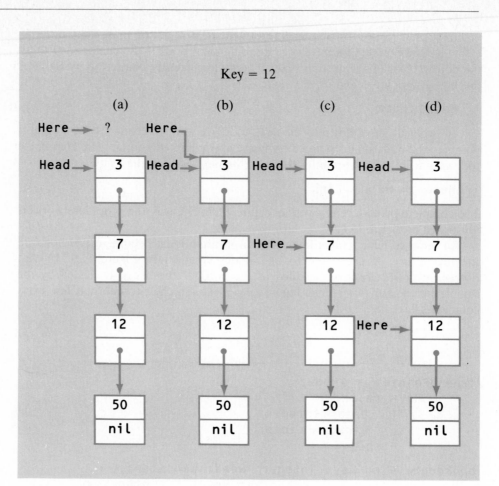

Figure 17.8
How the procedure
Find works.

The procedure **HeadInsert** in Figure 17.9 inserts nodes at the head of a list. With a linked list a node can be inserted anywhere in the list by a similar technique. Consider the linked list in Figure 17.10(a). The numbers in the nodes are in numeric order. Suppose we wish to add a node that contains the integer 8 to the linked list and to do this in such a way that the integers are still in ascending order. The resulting linked list should look like the one in Figure

Figure 17.9
Procedure to add
a node to a linked
list.

```
type NPointer = ↑Node;
     Node = record
               Data: integer;
               Link: NPointer
            end;
```

```
procedure HeadInsert(NewData: integer;
                    var Head: NPointer);
```
*{Inserts a node containing the number NewData at the head
of the linked list headed by Head ↑; assumes there already is
at least one node in the linked list.}*

```
    var PNew: NPointer;

begin{HeadInsert}
    new(PNew); {Creates a new node to hold NewData}
    PNew↑.Data := NewData;
    PNew↑.Link := Head;
        {Places the new node at the head of the list.}
    Head := PNew
        {Moves Head so it points to the new head of the list.}
end; {HeadInsert}
```

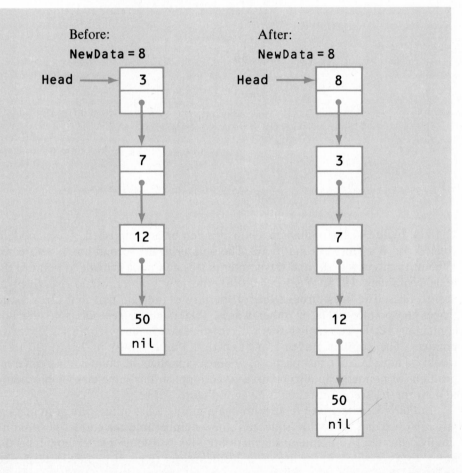

Figure 17.9 (cont'd)

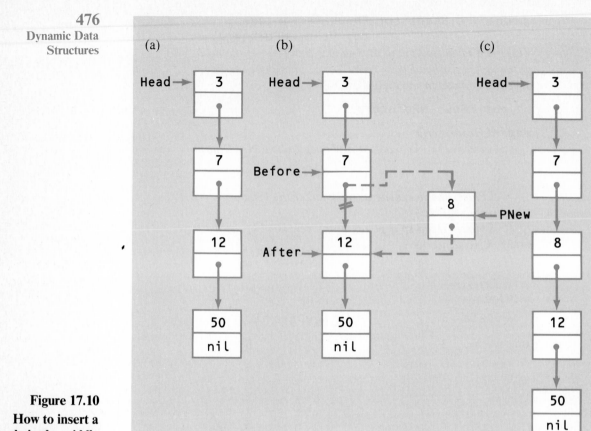

Figure 17.10
How to insert a node in the middle of a linked list.

17.10(c). Figure 17.10(b) illustrates how this can be accomplished. A new node is created and **8** is stored in that node. The pointer in the second box is redirected to point to this new node, and the pointer in this new node is made to point to the node containing **12**. In Figure 17.10(b), the new pointer values are given as dashed lines. The lines through one of the arrows indicate that that arrow is no longer the pointer value, in other words, that it no longer points to the box containing **12**. To accomplish this with reasonable efficiency requires a few extra pointers. The pointers **Before**, **After** and **PNew** shown in Figure 17.10(b) would be adequate for this purpose. Different numbers of pointers and different positions of pointers can also be used to accomplish this same task. A procedure to perform this sort of insertion is given in Figure 17.11.

In the preceding example we were maintaining a list of integers in numerical order. Notice that we could "squeeze" a new number into the correct position by simply adjusting two pointers. Furthermore, this is true no matter how long the linked list is or where in the list we want the integer to go. If we had instead used an array, then much, and in extreme cases all, of the array would have to be

```
type NPointer = ↑Node;
     Node = record
               Data: integer;
               Link: NPointer
             end;
procedure Insert(NewData: integer;
                 Before, After: NPointer);
{Inserts a node containing the number NewData
between the two nodes pointed to by Before and After.}

   var PNew: NPointer;

begin{Insert}
   new(PNew);
   PNew↑.Data := NewData;
   Before↑.Link := PNew;
   PNew↑.Link := After
end; {Insert}
```

Figure 17.11
Procedure to insert a node in a linked list.

copied over in order to make room for a new integer in the correct spot. In spite of the overhead involved in positioning the pointers, inserting into a linked list is frequently more efficient than inserting into an array.

deleting nodes

Deleting a node from a linked list is also quite easy. Figure 17.12 illustrates the method. Once the pointers **Before** and **Here** have been positioned, all that is required to delete the node is the following Pascal statement:

```
Before↑.Link := Here↑.Link
```

dispose
(Optional)

Look again at Figure 17.12(c). The node containing **12** is no longer on the linked list, but it has not been destroyed. Unless the program explicitly eliminates the node, it will remain in storage and will waste storage. The standard procedure **dispose** can be used to eliminate dynamic variables and so free some storage for other purposes. For example, the following will eliminate the node pointed to by **Here**:

```
dispose(Here)
```

The procedure **dispose** is not implemented in all versions of UCSD Pascal.

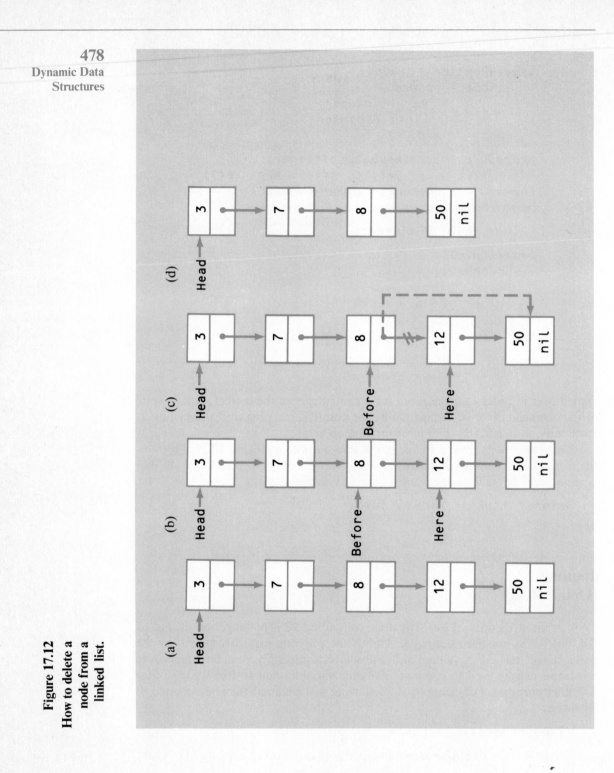

Figure 17.12
How to delete a node from a linked list.

Doubly Linked Lists—
A Variation on Simple Linked Lists

A variant of the linked list is the doubly linked list, such as the one shown in Figure 17.13. A doubly linked list is like a simple linked list, except that in a doubly linked list, there are pointers pointing backward as well as forward. Doubly linked lists illustrate the point that a node may contain more than one pointer. Doubly linked lists are handled very much like ordinary linked lists except that they allow the program to move along the list in both directions. This can sometimes be useful. Our handling of linked lists would have been easier if they were doubly linked. In that case we would usually not need trailer pointers such as the pointer **Before** in Figure 17.12. Doubly linked lists do, however, require more storage than ordinary linked list because of the extra pointer in each node.

A possible set of type declarations for a doubly linked list is:

```
type Link: ↑Node;
     Info = record
               Number: integer;
               Price: real;
               Style: 1..8
            end;
     Node = record
               Data: Info;
               Back: Link;
               Forward: Link
            end;
```

Notice that in the preceding type declarations nodes have three fields, one of which is itself a record. A node can be almost any sort of record and a hierarchical arrangement, such as that shown above, can sometimes be very useful.

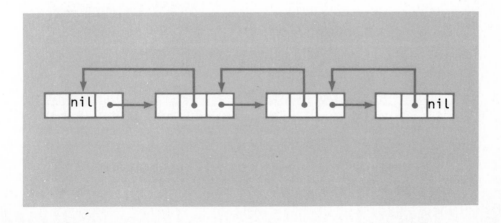

Figure 17.13
A doubly linked list.

Trees

*binary
trees*

An extremely useful type of data structure that is significantly different from the linked list structure is the *binary tree*. A sample binary tree is shown in Figure 17.14. A reasonable type declaration for the nodes of a binary tree is the following:

```
type Pointer = ↑TreeNode;
     TreeNode = record
                   Info: integer;
                   LeftLink: Pointer;
                   RightLink: Pointer
                end;
```

To understand why structures such as that shown in Figure 17.14 are called "trees," turn the page upside down. The resulting branching structure should, with a little bit of help from your imagination, look like the branching structure of a tree.

*root
node*

The pointer **Root** in Figure 17.14 points to a special node called the *root* node. The name comes from the fact that if you turn the picture upside down, then that node is located where the root of the tree would start. The root node is the only node from which every other node can be reached by following the pointers. It serves a function similar to that of the head node in a linked list.

*binary
search
trees*

There are numerous applications for trees. These include compiler programs as well as game-playing programs and other artificial intelligence programs. One of their most common applications is the storing of data for rapid retrieval. The numbers in the tree in Figure 17.14 have been stored in a way that makes it easy to find out if a specified number is in the tree. Such trees are called *binary search*

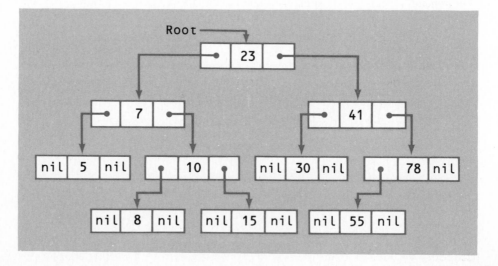

**Figure 17.14
A binary tree.**

trees. At each node of a binary search tree one number is stored. If we follow the `LeftLink` out of the root (to the left in the figure), it leads to a smaller tree that contains all the numbers smaller than the one in the root node. If we follow the `RightLink` out of the root (to the right in the figure), it leads to a smaller tree that contains all the numbers larger than the one in the root node. This same pattern is repeated at each node. Each node is the root node of a smaller tree. If we consider only the numbers stored in that smaller tree, the numbers are divided into two groups: the ones smaller than the number in the root node of the subtree can be reached via the pointer to the left, and the numbers greater than the number in the root node of the subtree can be reached via the right pointer.

For example, the root node contains **23**. The numbers **5**, **7**, **8**, **10** and **15** are less than **23** and are all in the smaller tree to the left. The numbers **30**, **41**, **55** and **78** are greater than **23** and are all in the smaller tree that hangs off the right pointer. Now consider the node containing **7**. The subtree below that node contains four numbers besides **7**, namely, **5**, **8**, **10** and **15**. The number **5** is less than **7** and so is to the left. The numbers **8**, **10** and **15** are greater than **7** and so are in the subtree that is suspended below the right pointer field.

searching a tree

To find a number stored in a binary tree like the one in Figure 17.14, a program need not look at every node. For example, to decide if the number **15** is in the tree, the program can first compare it to the number in the root node. The number **15** is less than the number in the root node. Hence, **15** is either not in the tree or else is in one of the nodes that can be reached by following pointers starting with the pointer `LeftLink` out of the root node. Following that pointer leads to the node containing **7**. Since **15** is greater than **7**, the search for **15** proceeds to follow the pointer field `RightLink`. That leads to the node containing **10**. The number **15** is greater than **10**, and so the search again follows the pointer `RightLink` and that leads to the node containing **15**.

As another example consider searching for the number **35**. Since **35** is greater than the number stored in the root node, **35** either is not in the tree or else is in one of the nodes that can be reached by following pointers starting with the pointer `RightLink` of the root node. Following that pointer leads to the node containing **41**. Since **35** is less than **41**, the search for **35** proceeds to follow the pointer field `LeftLink`. That leads to the node containing **30**. Since **35** is greater than **30**, **35** either is not in the tree or is in one of the nodes that can be reached by following the pointers starting with the pointer `RightLink` of the node containing **30**. But that pointer is *nil*, indicating that it leads to no nodes. Hence, **35** is not in the tree.

The function `TreeSearch` given in Figure 17.15 uses the above described method to determine whether or not a particular number is stored in a binary search tree.

building a search tree

Searching a binary search tree is easy. Building one for a given collection of data is slightly more complicated but is still not too difficult. Adding data nodes to an existing tree and deleting data nodes from such a tree are much more complicated techniques, and we will not discuss them here. They are discussed at length in the references at the end of this chapter. This chapter contains enough techniques to build a binary search tree for a fixed collection of data and to design programs to search such a tree and retrieve data. If the data will change over time, then the more sophisticated techniques given in the references will be needed.

Binary search trees can be used to store any sort of data that can be ordered. For example, they might hold employee records with several fields. One field might be the name of the employee. Using the alphabetic ordering in place of numeric ordering, these records can be stored in a binary search tree according to name, and the record containing a given name can be rapidly retrieved using the techniques described in this section.

Implementation
(Optional)

In order to program in a high level language, such as Pascal, you do not need to know how the language is implemented, any more than you need to understand the workings of the human larynx or of the human brain in order to use the English language. Pascal programs are implemented as the machine code that comes out of the Pascal compiler, and all you need to know is that the machine code makes the input and output behave as we have described for the language Pascal. Still, it is sometimes helpful, and invariably interesting, to know some details of the implementation. This is particularly true of pointers and dynamic variables. Since the description of their implementation is very much more concrete than the high level description of Pascal pointers, some people find it easier to understand pointers in terms of their implementation. Also, it gives you a pretty good idea of how the notion of pointers can be implemented in other programming languages, including many high level programming languages which do not have pointers as a basic predefined construction.

address

In order to describe a typical implementation for Pascal pointers and dynamic variables, we need to recall our discussion of the internal structure of computers. Recall that a computer's main memory consists of a very long sequence of numbered memory locations and that each memory location can hold one string of binary digits, which we can interpret as a number. The locations are frequently called *words* and the number of a location is frequently called its *address*. As this discussion indicates, a computer memory is structured much like a very large one-dimensional array.

To be concrete, let us say we want to implement a linked list of integers. One way to do this is to allocate two adjacent memory locations for each dynamic variable that is to serve as a node in the linked list. One of the two locations will hold the integer in the node, and the other location will hold some integer that can be interpreted as a pointer to a node.

What can be interpreted as a pointer to one of these dynamic variables? These dynamic variables are implemented as pairs of adjacent memory locations. Hence, one way to name one of these dynamic variables is to name the two addresses of these locations, specifically by giving the addresses of these two memory locations. That is exactly what we will do; however, we will use only the first address, since the other differs from it by exactly one. In our implementation a dynamic variable of the type under discussion is just two adjacent memory locations: the first holds the integer and the second holds the pointer. In this implementation the pointer is realized as the address of the first of the two memory locations that represent the dynamic variable that is pointed to.

By way of example, consider Figure 17.16. It shows a possible implementation of the linked list shown in Figure 17.10(a). The *nil* pointer is indicated by the number −1. Minus one is used for *nil* because we know there is no location with that address. Any other negative number would do as well. The right-hand figure is an abstraction that ignores the particular address numbers used. Since the particular address numbers used are not important to the realization, that right-hand figure is easier to deal with.

As a program proceeds to add nodes to and delete them from a linked list the picture of memory becomes a good deal more intricate. Suppose we wish to add a

adding nodes

```
type Pointer = ↑TreeNode;
     TreeNode = record
                    Info: integer;
                    LeftLink: Pointer;
                    RightLink: Pointer
                end;

function TreeSearch(Query: integer;
                    Root: Pointer): boolean;
```
{*Searches the binary tree whose root node is pointed to by Root. Returns true if the number Query is in some node of the tree. Returns false if Query is not in the tree.*}
```
begin{TreeSearch}
   if Root = nil then
          {empty tree}
          TreeSearch := false
   else if Query = Root↑.Info then
          {found Query}
          TreeSearch := true
   else if Query < Root↑.Info then
          {Search subtree to the left of the root.}
          TreeSearch := TreeSearch(Query, Root↑.LeftLink)
   else {if Query > Root↑.Info then}
          {Search subtree to the right of the root.}
          TreeSearch := TreeSearch(Query, Root↑.RightLink)
end; {TreeSearch}
```

**Figure 17.15
Function that
searches a binary
tree looking for
a node.**

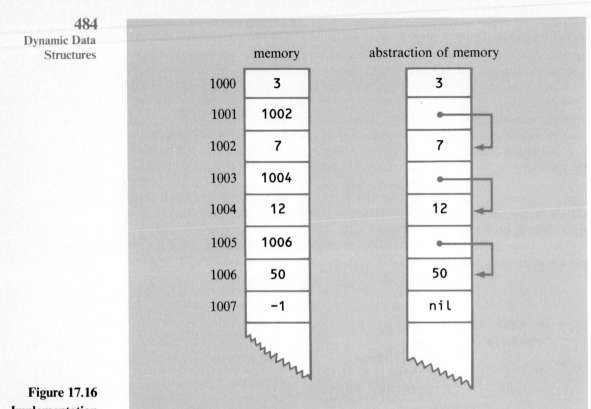

Figure 17.16
Implementation
of a linked list.

node containing **8** to our linked list and to keep the nodes in numeric order; the result should be as shown in Figure 17.10(c). Figure 17.17 shows the configuration of memory after a dynamic variable for a node containing the number **8** is added. Note that the dynamic variable for this node was implemented with the next two available memory locations. The way to think about a linked list is as if the new node is squeezed in. However, in this implementation all the old nodes stay where they are. Only the values of the pointer fields change.

deleting
nodes

Figure 17.18 shows the implementation of the same linked list after both adding the node containing **8** and then deleting the node containing the integer **12**.

garbage
collection

Notice that as we add nodes, the pattern of arrows gets to be rather messy, but that need not concern us. Ordinarily we need not be concerned with the actual memory addresses when we use pointers and dynamic variables. We need only think in terms of an abstraction of the pointer structure that ignores the actual location of the dynamic variables. If we have lots of memory, we can get away with thinking only on an abstract level, which ignores all the details of the particular memory addresses used. Unfortunately, there is some danger of wasting memory if we think exclusively on this abstract level. Look again at the memory

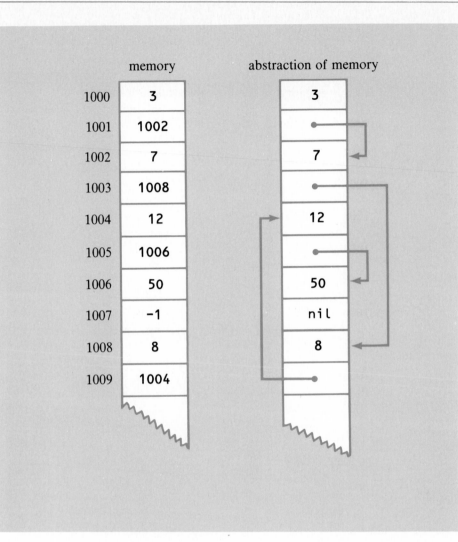

**Figure 17.17
Implementation
of a linked list with
added node.**

configuration shown in Figure 17.18. Notice that the dynamic variable in locations 1004 and 1005 still has an integer and a pointer in it. Yet the node
represented by that dynamic variable is no longer on the linked list. The program
will never be able to use the dynamic variable stored in locations 1004 and 1005,
and so those memory locations should be made available for other uses. Yet, if we
continue to add dynamic variables at the bottom of memory, then locations 1004
and 1005 will never be reused. Locations like 1004 and 1005 are frequently
referred to by the technical term *garbage*—not a very dignified word but a
descriptive one and the one that is generally used. A good implementation would
keep track of these garbage memory locations and reuse them. Locating such
garbage memory locations so that they can be reused is called, appropriately
enough, *garbage collection*.

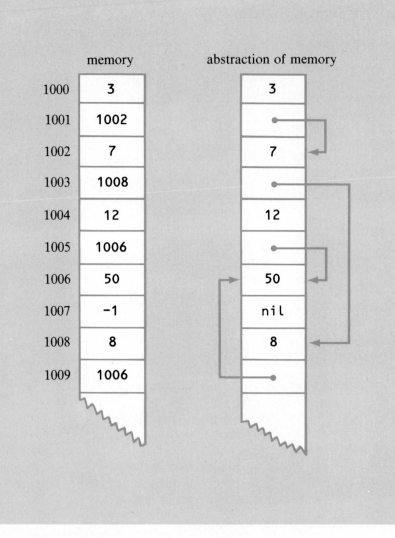

memory   abstraction of memory

1000	3		3
1001	1002		
1002	7		7
1003	1008		
1004	12		12
1005	1006		
1006	50		50
1007	−1		nil
1008	8		8
1009	1006		

**Figure 17.18
Implementation
of a linked list with
deleted node.**

Many implementations of Pascal do not have very good garbage collection and the system must be given some help in order to do the garbage collection. Specifically, the system must be told which dynamic variables are garbage. This is what the **dispose** command does. (In UCSD Pascal, the procedures **mark** and **release** are usually used instead of **dispose**.)

The idea of this implementation can be used in high level languages as well. If Pascal did not have pointers as a built-in feature, we could still implement something like pointers by using an array in the same way that we used the computer's main memory in the implementation just described.

UCSD Pascal—mark and release
(Optional)

In some versions of UCSD Pascal **dispose** is not implemented. However, in any UCSD Pascal system, the predefined procedures **mark** and **release** can be used to eliminate dynamic variables. These two procedures are not available in standard Pascal.

The procedures **mark** and **release** are best described in terms of the implementation of pointers and dynamic variables that was discussed in the previous section. Recall that the dynamic variables we were considering were records with two fields, one of type **integer** and one a pointer type. Such dynamic variables might be used as nodes in a linked list, but their specific use is not important. Each dynamic variable was implemented as two adjacent memory locations, one containing the **integer** and one containing a pointer. The pointer was implemented by storing the address of the dynamic variable it pointed to. A similar implementation is used for dynamic variables of other types. This particular type was just used to have a concrete example.

These implementations have no automatic garbage collection and so the amount of memory occupied by dynamic variables will grow larger and larger as more dynamic variables are created. The memory occupied by these dynamic variables increases in a very orderly way. When a new dynamic variable is added, it is placed in the next available memory location. That is, it is always added at the end of the list.

The memory allocated to dynamic variables is used as a list with new dynamic variables added to the end of the list. Another way to think of this memory is to consider it to be a stack with the end of the list serving as the top of the stack. The command **mark** can be used to mark a position in the stack. The command **release** can be used to release all the memory up to a marked location. The value of any pointer variable that points to a dynamic variable in the released memory space becomes undefined, and all the memory locations in the released memory space are made available for reuse.

marking the stack

mark and **release** are only approximately equivalent to **dispose**. They cannot be used to release one particular dynamic variable, unless it just happens to be the last one created. They always have to be used on a whole chunk of memory, a whole collection of dynamic variables. In this sense **mark** and **release** are not as versatile as **dispose**. However, **mark** and **release** are more powerful since they can be used to release dynamic variables that have no pointer pointing to them.

In order to use **mark** and **release**, the program uses a pointer variable of type ↑**integer**. The pointer is not used to point to dynamic variables but is instead dedicated to the marking process. For example, suppose **M1** is of type ↑**integer** and consider the following statement:

```
mark(M1)
```

The effect of this statement is to mark a position in memory by having **M1** "point to it." (We include the quotation marks because we are using the informal notion of "pointing," not the Pascal notion of pointing.) Later on, the program can release the memory occupied by all the dynamic variables that have been added in memory locations after the position marked by **M1**. To release that memory, the program executes:

release(M1)

This call to **release** releases all the memory between the position marked by **M1** and the next memory location available for dynamic variables. The value of a

---

```
procedure Reverse;
{UCSD Pascal procedure to read in a line of text
and write it out to the screen in reverse order.}

type ItemPointer = ↑Item;
     Item = record
                 Letter: char;
                 Link: ItemPointer
             end;
var Head, Next: ItemPointer;
    Spot: ↑integer;

begin{Reverse}
    mark(Spot);
    Head := nil;
    writeln('Enter a line of text:');
    while not eoln do
      begin{while}
        new(Next);
        read(Next↑.Letter);
        Next↑.Link := Head;
        Head := Next
      end; {while}
    readln;
    writeln('Spelled backwards it reads:');
    while Head <> nil do
      begin{Second while}
        write(Head↑.Letter);
        Head := Head↑.Link
      end; {Second while}
    writeln;
    release(Spot)
end; {Reverse}
```

Figure 17.19

UCSD
Pascal procedure
using **mark** and
release.

pointer variable used for marking memory, such as **M1**, must not be changed between the time it is used with **mark** and the time it is used with **release**.

By using several different pointer variables, in the same way as **M1**, you can mark several different positions in memory and later release all the memory up to any of these marked positions.

Figure 17.19 shows a sample procedure that uses **mark** and **release**. It reads a line of text into a linked list and then writes the line to the screen in reverse order. After that, all the memory used for the linked list is released. Because the procedure uses **mark** and **release** to manage garbage collection, it can be called many times and yet will only require enough storage to hold the longest line of text. Without such garbage collection, each successive call to the procedure would consume more and more memory in order to hold all the garbage nodes that are no longer needed.

Summary of Problem Solving and Programming Techniques

The choice of a data structure can make a profound difference in how clear and/or efficient a program is. Pointers provide a means for designing a wide variety of dynamic data structures. For example, a linked list has a number of advantages over an array as a data structure for certain tasks. In a linked list data items (nodes) can be "squeezed in" anyplace in the list. With a linked list the length of the list can be changed.

Another important dynamic data structure is the binary tree. Trees have numerous uses. They can be used to store data in a way that allows a program to retrieve individual data items very quickly. In this chapter we have only given a brief introduction to dynamic data structures. Research on trees in particular and dynamic data structures in general has produced a large number of nonobvious techniques for building and maintaining dynamic data structures. The references that follow include much more material on the subject.

◇

"Would you tell me, please, which way I ought to go from here?"

"That depends a good deal on where you want to get to," said the Cat.

Lewis Carroll, Alice in Wonderland

◇

Summary of Pascal Constructs

declaring pointer variables

Syntax:

> ***var*** ⟨identifier⟩**:** ↑⟨domain type⟩**;**

Example:

> ***var*** **P1:** ↑**Node;**

Declares ⟨identifier⟩ to be a pointer variable. The variable ⟨identifier⟩ can only take on values that are pointers to dynamic variables of the type ⟨domain type⟩.

naming the dynamic variable pointed to

Syntax:

> ⟨pointer variable⟩↑

Example:

> **P1**↑

One way to name the dynamic variable pointed to by ⟨pointer variable⟩.

new

Syntax:

> **new(**⟨pointer variable⟩**)**

Example:

> **new(P1)**

Creates a new dynamic variable of the domain type of the pointer variable ⟨pointer variable⟩ and leaves ⟨pointer variable⟩ pointing to this new dynamic variable.

pointer variables in assignment statements

Syntax:

> ⟨pointer variable1⟩ **:=** ⟨pointer variable2⟩

Example:

> **P1 := P2**

Makes the value of ⟨pointer variable1⟩ point to the same thing as the value of the pointer variable ⟨pointer variable2⟩.

nil

Syntax:

> ***nil***

Predefined constant of a type that is compatible with pointers to any type of dynamic variable. ***nil*** does not point to any dynamic variable but is used to give a value to pointer variables which do not point to any dynamic variable.

Self-Test and Interactive Exercises

1. What is the output produced by the following code? All the pointers are of type ↑`integer`.

```
new(P1); new(P2);
P1↑ := 10;
P2↑ := 20;
writeln(P1↑, P2↑);
P1 := P2;
writeln(P1↑, P2↑);
P1↑ := 30;
writeln(P1↑, P2↑);
P2↑ := 40;
writeln(P1↑, P2↑)
```

2. What is the output produced by the following code? All the pointers are of type ↑`integer`.

```
P1↑ := 10;
P2↑ := 20;
writeln(P1↑, P2↑);
P1↑ := P2↑;
writeln(P1↑, P2↑);
P1↑ := 30;
writeln(P1↑, P2↑);
P2↑ := 40;
writeln(P1↑, P2↑)
```

3. How would the output of the program in Figure 17.2 change if the line

```
P2↑ := 3;
```

were replaced by the following line?

```
P1↑ := 3;
```

4. Type up the program in Figure 17.2 and run it. Try running it a number of times with as many minor variations as you can think of.

5. Write a procedure to fill a linked list with the integers **1** through **N**. **N** should be a parameter.

6. Write a procedure to display to the screen all the integers in a linked list of integers.

7. What is the difference between the kind of node used in a binary tree and the kind used in a doubly linked list?

Regular Exercises

8. (This exercise assumes that you have read Chapter 16.) Write a procedure to copy the integers in a linked list of integers into a file of integers.

9. Write a procedure that takes as parameters a linked list of integers (literally the parameter will be a pointer to the head of the list) and two integers **L** and **U** such that **L** is less than **U**. The procedure should write to the screen all integers in the list which are between **L** and **U**. The list need not be sorted.

10. Redo Exercise 14 in Chapter 15, but this time use linked lists rather than arrays. With linked lists there is no limit to the number of digits in the two numbers being added.

11. Redo Exercise 15 in Chapter 15, but this time use linked lists rather than arrays. With linked lists there is no limit to the number of digits after the decimal point. Hence, this gives unlimited accuracy.

12. Write a program for a two-person maze game that is played as follows. The first player thinks of a maze consisting of five rooms numbered **1** through **5** and one-way corridors between the rooms. Each room must have exactly two corridors leading from it to two other rooms. The program asks the first player the numbers of the rooms at the end of the two corridors leading out of room **1**, then room **2** and so on up to room **5**. The program then uses pointers to build a graph of the maze. (You will probably want five extra named pointers to keep track of the rooms.) The second player then tries to guess a route from room number **1** to room number **5**. The route is input as a sequence of numbers. If the second player guesses correctly, he/she wins. If he/she guesses incorrectly, the program tells the first incorrectly guessed room connection. If the second player fails after three tries, then the first player must exhibit a route in order to win. A harder version allows the option of the program assuming the role of the first player and generating the maze using a random number generator.

13. Write a procedure that takes a linked list of integers and produces a linked list of the same integers sorted into ascending order.

14. Write a procedure that takes a (singly) linked list and reverses the order of the nodes in the linked list. For concreteness, make it a linked list of characters.

15. Modify the program from Exercises 14 and 15 in Chapter 16 so that they use a linked list instead of an array.

16. Write procedures to insert, find and delete nodes in a doubly linked list. For simplicity, suppose the nodes store integers.

17. A binary tree can be used to classify items according to a series of yes/no questions. Write a program that will build a tree to classify animals according to yes/no questions. The questions are stored in the nodes and the answer determines which pointer to follow. Each leaf (end) node of the tree contains the name of an animal for which the yes/no answers are correct. For example, *Is it very big? Is it hairy? Does it eat meat? Does it have big ears?* The answers *yes*, *no*, *no* and *yes*, respectively, might lead to the name *elephant*. The program asks the user to think of an animal and then asks the questions. When it gets to the end of the questions, it asks the animal name. In that way it can build the tree. After that the interaction changes. The program offers to guess the name of an animal. The user thinks of an animal and answers questions. The program works its way to an end node and then "guesses" the animal named in that node.

18. Write a recursive procedure which will write to the screen, in ascending order, all the integers stored in a binary search tree. The procedure should assume the integers are stored in order in the sense described in this chapter.

19. Redo the previous exercise, but this time do not make the procedure recursive.

20. Write a recursive procedure that takes a linked list of integers, already sorted into ascending order, and produces a binary search tree that contains the same integers, stored in order in the sense described in this chapter.

21. Write a procedure that takes a binary search tree with integers stored in order, in the sense discussed in this chapter, and copies them into a second tree. The second tree should

also have the integers sorted into order and should be as close to balanced as possible. A tree is balanced if for each node, the two subtrees led to by its two pointer fields contain the same number of nodes.

References for Further Reading

D. E. Knuth, *The Art of Computer Programming*, *Vol. 1/Fundamental Algorithms*, 1968 Addison-Wesley, Reading, Mass. You can skip Chapter 1 and go directly to Chapter 2. Refer back to Chapter 1 as needed.

N. Wirth, *Algorithms + Data Structures = Programs*, 1976 Prentice-Hall, Englewood Cliffs, N. J., Chapter 4. This one may be more immediately understandable to readers of this book than Knuth is, since Wirth uses a Pascal-like language to express algorithms.

Appendixes

Appendix 1
The goto Statement

The term *flow of control* refers to the order in which the statements and substatements of a program are executed. There is one Pascal mechanism for flow of control which we have not yet discussed. That mechanism is the *goto statement*. The method of using this statement; in fact the very question of whether or not it should be used at all, is very controversial. In this appendix we briefly explain the **goto** statement and the controversy surrounding it.

As an example, consider the following program fragment:

```
   writeln('First Statement');
42:writeln('Statement Labeled 42');
   writeln('Third Statement');
   goto 42;
```

The number **42** on the second line is called a *label*. It has no effect on the statement. It is just a way to give a name to the second **writeln** statement. The **goto** instructs the computer to next execute the statement labeled **42**. After executing the statement labeled **42**, the computer proceeds to the next statement after that; in other words, the computer forgets whether it arrived at a labeled statement via a **goto** or by some other means. Thus, the above example is an infinite loop with output:

```
First Statement
Statement Labeled 42
Third Statement
Statement Labeled 42
Third Statement
Statement Labeled 42
Third Statement
```

The last two lines are repeated indefinitely.

In Pascal all labels, such as **42**, must be integers in the range **0** to **9999**. However, they are used only as names of statements and not as numbers. In particular, a **goto** statement cannot contain an integer variable. All *labels* must be declared. The label declarations come before all other declarations in a block. The syntax consists of the reserved word **label** followed by a list of labels; the labels are separated by commas and terminated with a semicolon. For example, the following declares **100** and **42** to be labels:

label 100, 42;

Once a label is declared, it may be used to label a statement and then used in a **goto** statement. A **goto** statement consists of the identifier **goto** followed by a label. The identifier **goto** is a single word with no spaces. The execution of a **goto** statement is frequently called a *jump* because the execution "jumps" to the labeled statement specified after the **goto**.

There is one important restriction that applies to the use of **goto** statements. It is possible to use a **goto** statement to jump out of a structure such as a loop or procedure. However, a **goto** statement may not be used to jump into a structure. If a **goto** is used to jump into a structure, the effect is undefined and unpredictable.

The **goto** has a long history; at least, it is long when compared to other things in the young field of computer science. Although it was usually spelled differently, the **goto** was an important feature in virtually all early programming languages. Machine languages invariably have **goto** statements. In fact, most flow of control in machine language programs is typically by means of **goto** statements or similar constructs. Most high level languages include **goto** statements. Moreover, until very recently, most high level programming languages depended on the use of **goto** statements for much or even most flow of control.

Around 1960 a class of languages referred to as *structured programming languages* began to appear. A structured language is one that includes constructs for flow of control which allow for a systematic way to structure a program into meaningful subparts. Procedures and **while** statements are examples of such constructs. One of the earliest of these languages was ALGOL. Pascal is also a typical example of a structured language. These structuring constructs provided an alternative to the **goto** statement. Programs written with many **goto**'s have a structure that is usually not apparent to the reader. Programs written without the **goto** can more easily exhibit a clear structure for the flow of control.

Although there are varying views on the details of how and when **goto**'s should be used, some things about **goto** statements are clear. First of all, there is no absolute need for **goto**'s. Any program that is written with **goto**'s can be rewritten to do the same thing without any **goto** statements. The question is whether **goto** statements enhance or detract from good programming style. Even in the less exact domain of style some things are clear. A program which uses very many **goto**'s is harder to read than a well-written program which uses very few **goto**'s or no **goto** statements at all. A consensus is arising which says that **goto** statements should be avoided.

When first learning to program, it is best to avoid *goto*'s completely. Otherwise, it is difficult to learn that they are never needed and seldom even of any help. After you become proficient at programming, you may want to use an occasional *goto*, or you may agree with the school of thought that says they should never be used.

Situations in which *goto* statements may be reasonable are various sorts of exiting situations. When an error or other terminating condition is encountered, a *goto* can be used to jump directly to the end of a loop, a procedure or an entire program. For example, a program can be designed to terminate on detection of an error, by the following scheme:

```
program Sample(input, output);
label 100;
var . . .
    . . .
begin{Program}
    . . .
  if ⟨error condition⟩  then goto 100;
    . . .
100:end. {Program}
```

In this scheme the label **100** labels the empty statement. This trick produces the equivalent of labeling the *end*.

Additional material on *goto*'s can be found in the following references:

E. W. Dijkstra, "Go to statement considered harmful," *Communications of the ACM*, Vol. 11, No. 3, March 1968, 147–148, 538, 541.

D. E. Knuth, "Structured Programming with go to Statements," *Computing Surveys*, Vol. 6, No. 4, Dec. 1974, 261–298.

Appendix 2
Reserved Words

and	*end*	*nil*	*set*
array	*file*	*not*	*then*
begin	*for*	*of*	*to*
case	*function*	*or*	*type*
const	*goto*	*packed*	*until*
div	*if*	*procedure*	*var*
do	*in*	*program*	*while*
downto	*label*	*record*	*with*
else	*mod*	*repeat*	

Appendix 3
Precedence of Operators

Parentheses can be used to determine precedence; otherwise operators are evaluated as follows:

First: *not*

Second: ***** **/** *div* *mod* *and*

Third: **+** **−** *or*

Fourth: **< =** **=** **> =** **>** **<** **<>** *in*

Operators in the same group are evaluated left to right.

Appendix 4
Packed Structures

4A. The Procedures pack and unpack

To facilitate the transfer of elements between ordinary and packed arrays, the standard procedures **pack** and **unpack** are provided. Unfortunately, they are difficult to understand and confusing to use. Usually, it is clearer, easier and just as efficient to use a *for* loop. For completeness, they are described in the next paragraph. (The procedures are not available in most UCSD Pascal implementations.)

If **PA** is a packed array of any component type and **OA** is an ordinary array of the same component type, then the elements of **OA** can be copied to **PA** by the procedure call:

```
pack(OA, I, PA)
```

This will fill all of **PA** with elements of **OA** starting with element **OA[I]**. To copy in the other direction use:

```
unpack(PA, I, OA)
```

This will copy all of the elements of **PA** into **OA**, placing the first element in **OA[I]**. The arrays **PA** and **OA** do not have to have the same number of elements. The index **I** may be any expression; it need not be a variable.

4B. Other Packed Structures

Records, sets and files may be declared to be *packed*. The syntax and the effect on storage is essentially the same as that for packed arrays. When declaring a type to be packed, the identifier *packed* precedes the rest of the definition. For example:

```
type Sample = packed record
                    A: char;
                    B: integer
              end;
```

Appendix 5
Syntax Diagrams for
Standard Pascal

⟨program⟩

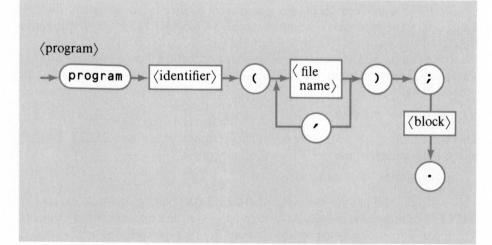

⟨block⟩

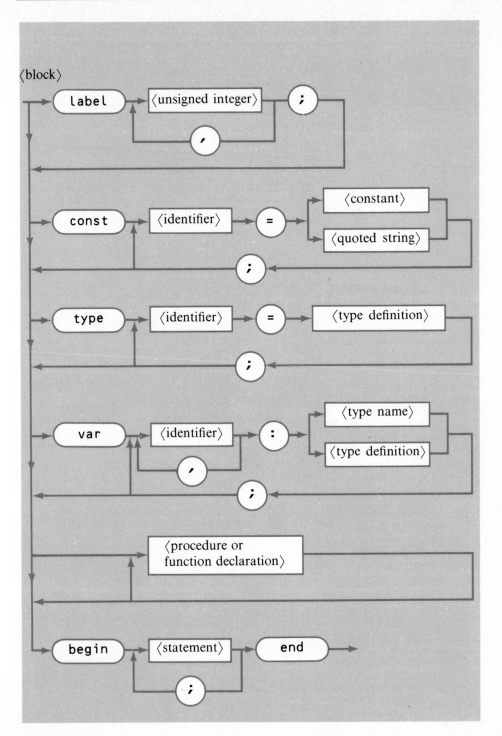

⟨quoted string⟩

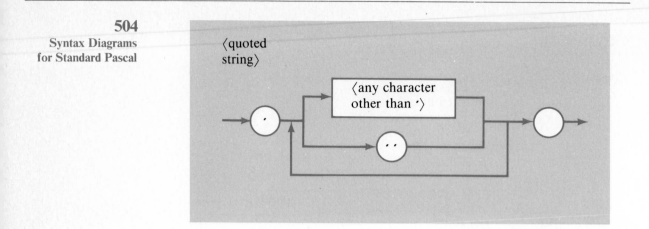

⟨type
definition⟩

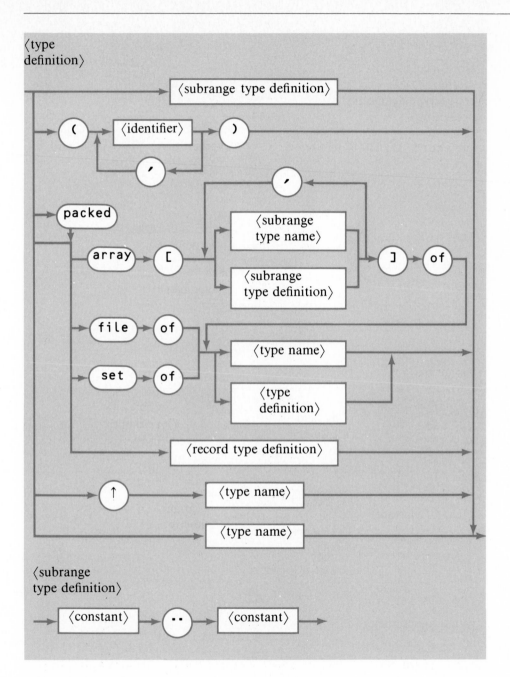

⟨subrange
type definition⟩

⟨record type definition⟩

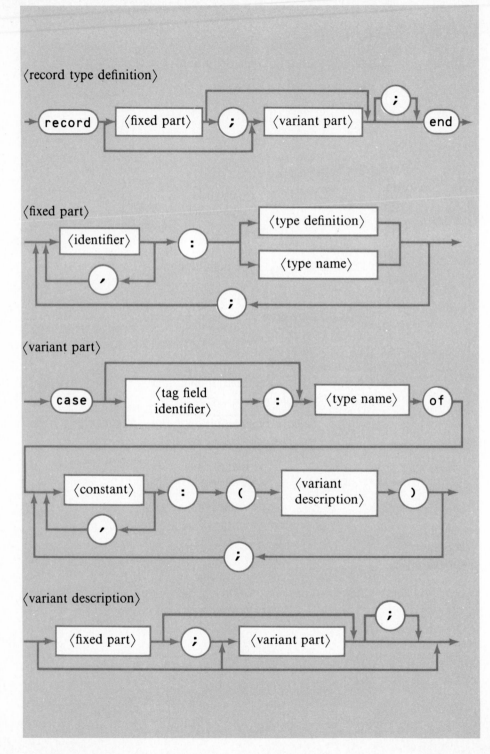

⟨fixed part⟩

⟨variant part⟩

⟨variant description⟩

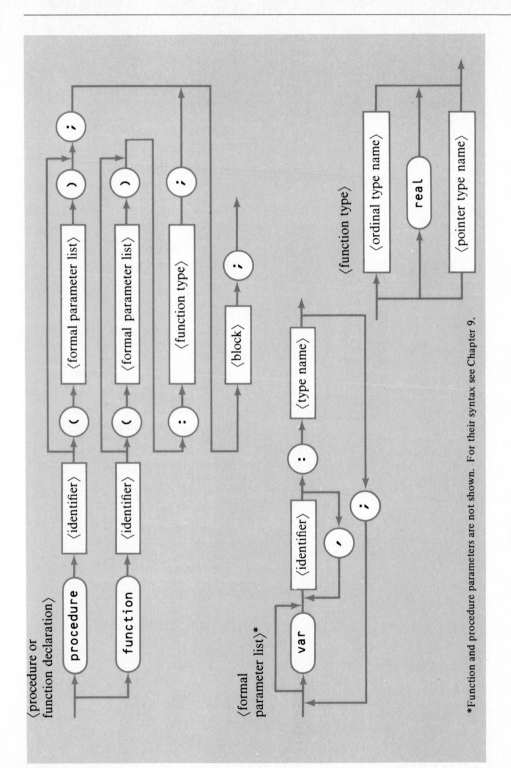

⟨procedure or
function declaration⟩

⟨formal
parameter list⟩*

⟨function type⟩

*Function and procedure parameters are not shown. For their syntax see Chapter 9.

⟨statement⟩

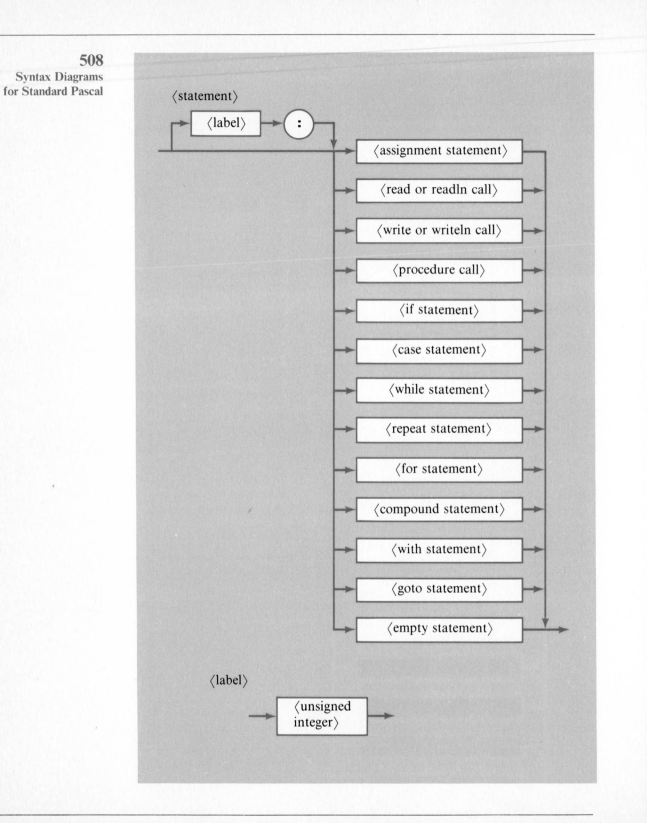

⟨assignment statement⟩

⟨read or readln call⟩

⟨write or writeln call⟩

⟨write parameter⟩

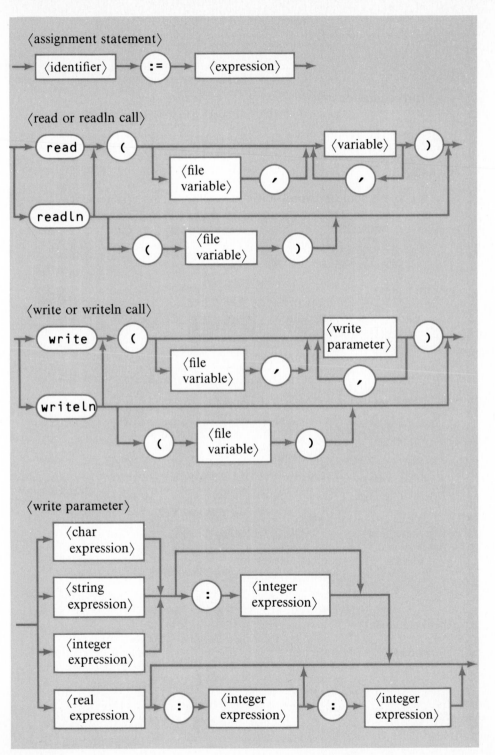

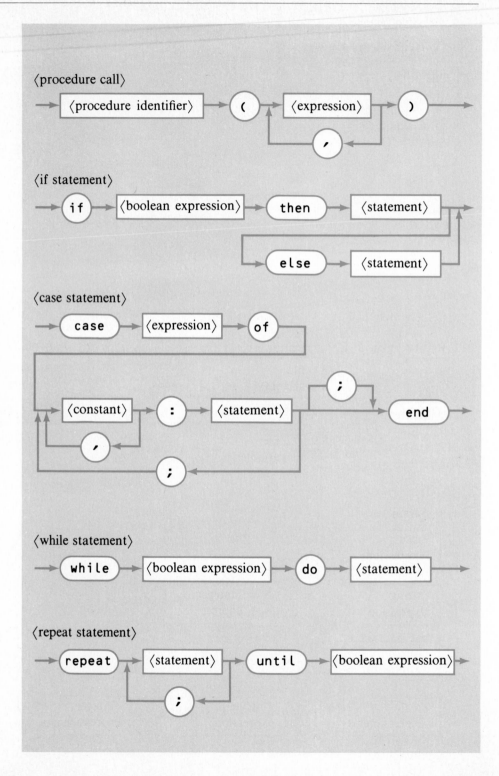

⟨for statement⟩

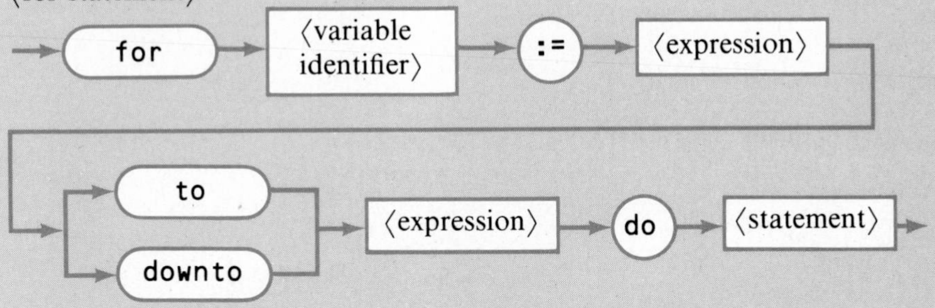

→──(for)──→[⟨variable identifier⟩]──→(:=)──→[⟨expression⟩]──┐

└──→┬──(to)────┬──→[⟨expression⟩]──(do)──→[⟨statement⟩]──→

   └──(downto)──┘

⟨compound statement⟩

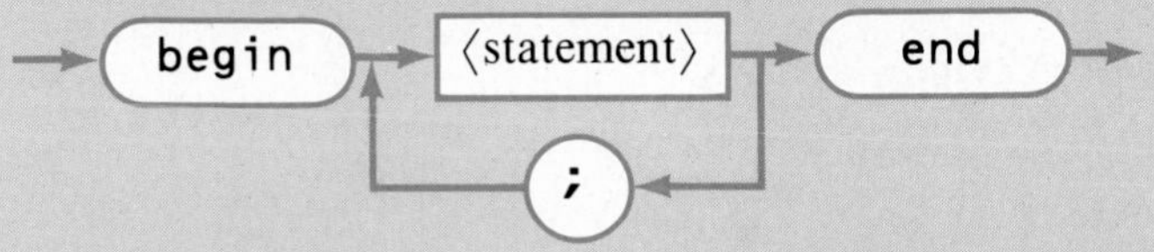

→──(begin)──→[⟨statement⟩]──→(end)──→

        ↑──(;)──┘

⟨with statement⟩

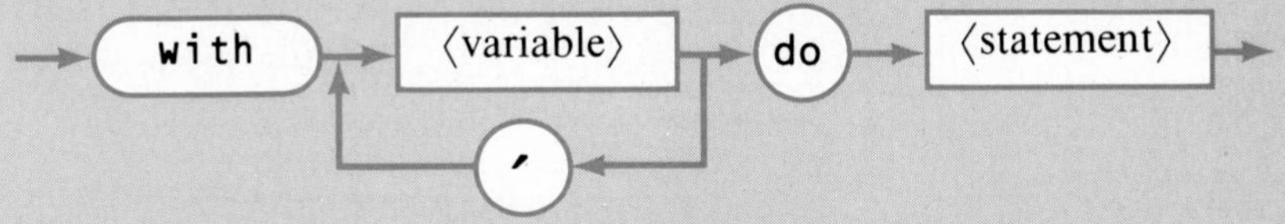

→──(with)──→[⟨variable⟩]──→(do)──→[⟨statement⟩]──→

        ↑──(,)──┘

⟨goto statement⟩

→──(goto)──→[⟨label⟩]──→

⟨empty statement⟩

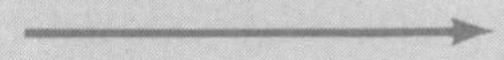

────────────────→

⟨boolean expression⟩

⟨test boolean expression⟩

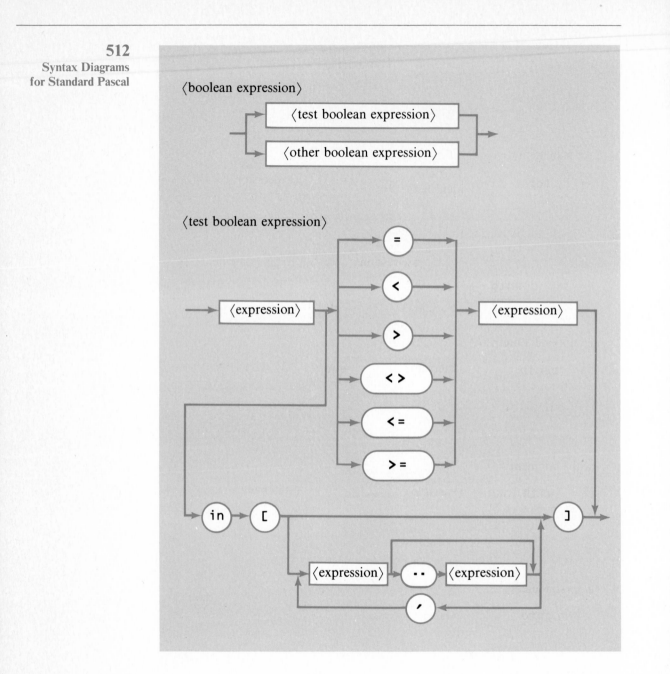

⟨other boolean expression⟩

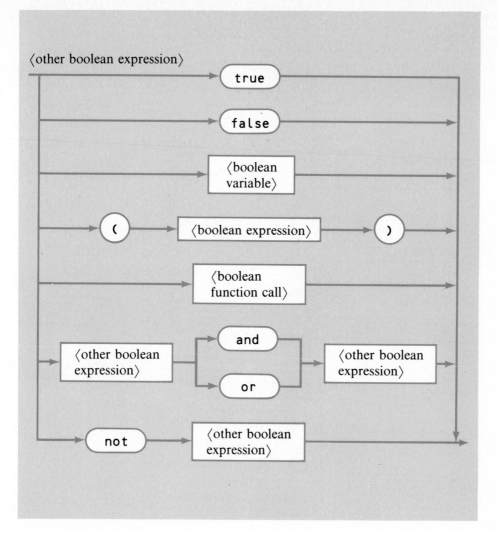

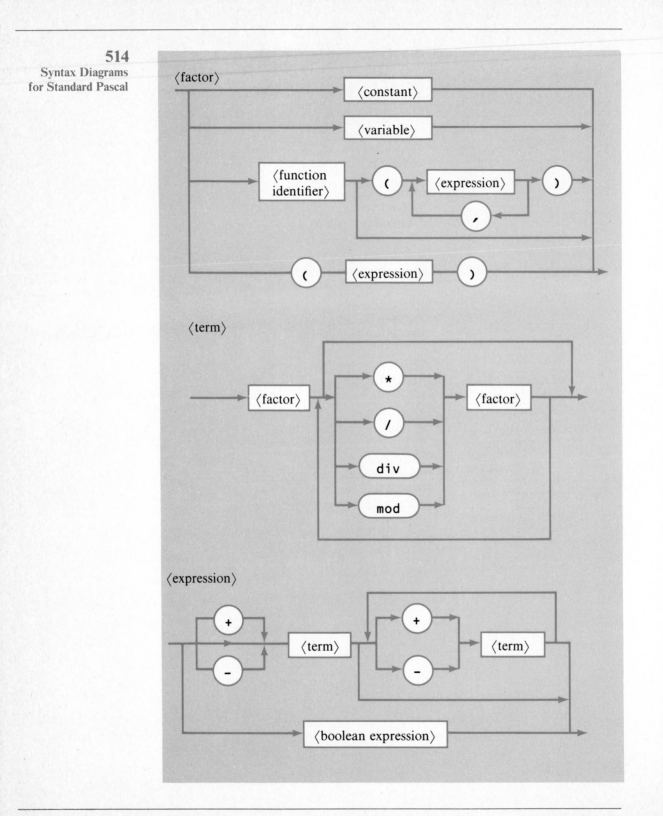

⟨variable⟩

⟨constant⟩

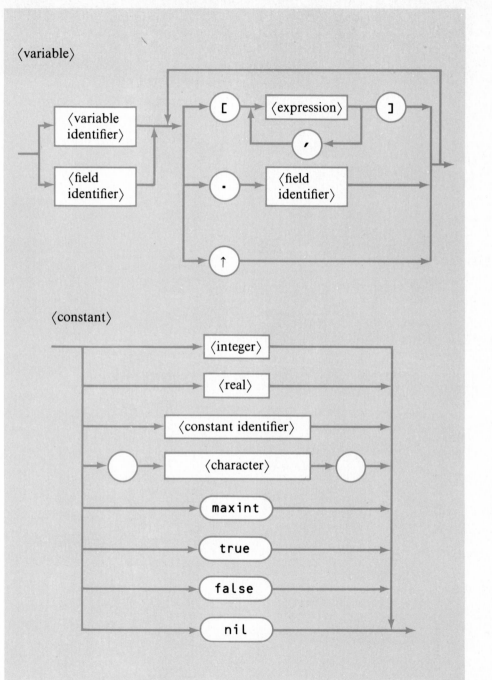

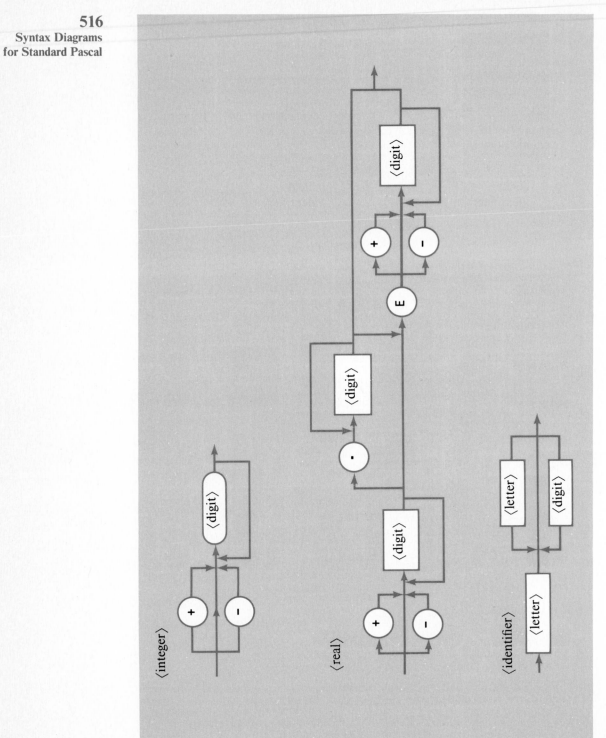

Appendix 6
UCSD Pascal Details

6A. The exit Statement

UCSD Pascal has a special statement that can be used to exit a procedure or an entire program. The statement is of the form:

exit(⟨procedure name⟩**)**

This statement is equivalent to a jump to the end of the procedure named by ⟨procedure name⟩. For example, the following scheme can be used to design a procedure that terminates immediately if a specified error is discovered:

procedure **Sample**...
.....
begin{*Sample*}
...
if ⟨error condition⟩ *then* exit(Sample);
...
end; {*Sample*}

6B. close Options

close(⟨file variable⟩**, normal)**
Leaves the file as it was before it was opened.

close(⟨file variable⟩**)**
Equivalent to **close(**⟨file variable⟩**, normal)**

close(⟨file variable⟩**, lock)**
Leaves the file as changed by the program.

`close(`⟨file variable⟩`, purge)`
    Removes the file from the directory.

`close(`⟨file variable⟩`, crunch)`
    Equivalent to **lock**, but all of the file after the last access (**get**, **put**, **read** or **write**) is removed. On some systems, this option is not available.

Note: On most systems, when a program is terminated normally (i.e., no run time errors), all files that have not yet been closed are automatically closed with the **normal** option.

6C. Turtle Graphics

Some UCSD Pascal systems include a *turtle graphics* package for generating line drawings. The commands consist of instructions to a "turtle" that "walks" on the screen drawing a line as it walks. The turtle is usually just the cursor. It only walks in straight lines, but by means of a series of short straight lines, the drawings can be made to look like they contain curved lines.

    Your system will probably require setting some sort of option in order to make the turtle graphics available to a Pascal program. One typical way of doing this is to insert the line:

    `uses turtlegraphics;`

or

    `uses turtle;`

immediately after the program heading. If this does not work, consult the documentation for your particular systems.

    The basic graphics commands are:

`initturtle`
    On some systems, a program can not mix writing text and doing graphics. On these systems, a program must always be in either *graphics mode* or *text mode*. The command **initturtle** (or something similar) puts the program in graphics mode. (This is in addition to the line **uses turtlegraphics**.) The command **textmode** (or something similar) puts it back into text mode.

`move(`⟨integer⟩`)`
    Instructs the turtle to move ⟨integer⟩ units in the direction it is facing. The size of a unit varies from system to system.

`moveto(`⟨integer⟩`, `⟨integer⟩`)`
    Moves the turtle to the coordinates specified by the two integers. The size of a unit and the location of the origin are implementation dependent.

`turn(`⟨integer⟩`)`
    Instructs the turtle to turn ⟨integer⟩ degrees.

turnto(⟨integer⟩**)**

Turns the turtle to face ⟨integer⟩ degrees from zero. Normally, **0** degrees is straight right; **90** degrees is straight up toward the top of the screen, and so forth. **turn** is for relative directions; **turnto** is for absolute directions.

pencolor(⟨color⟩**)**

Changes the color of the pen to ⟨color⟩. At least two colors are available, **white** and **black**. **white** is a line. **black** is like an eraser. Other colors may also be available. Use **none** to move the turtle without leaving a line.

clearscreen

Clears the screen. See next entry.

fillscreen(black)

Some systems use this instead of **clearscreen**. On these systems, **black** may be replaced by **white** to get a screen fully "marked."

Glossary

actual parameter A variable or expression that is substituted for a formal parameter when a procedure or function is called. See **value parameter** and **variable parameter** for an explanation of the two forms of substitution in Pascal.

address The address of a memory location is a number used as a way of naming that location. The memory locations are numbered 0, 1, 2, etc.

algorithm Detailed, unambiguous, step-by-step instructions for carrying out a task.

argument Another name for **parameter**, particularly an actual parameter to a function.

ASCII The American national Standard Code for Information Interchange. An arbitrary assignment of numbers to displayable characters and control signals.

assembly language Almost the same thing as machine language. The only difference is that assembly language instructions are expressed in a slightly more readable form, instead of being coded as strings of zeros and ones. See **machine language**.

assertion A comment which, if the program is correct, will be true when the program execution reaches the assertion.

auxiliary storage Another name for **secondary memory**.

batch processing As used in this book, running a program in batch mode means entering the program and all its data at one time and waiting until the program finishes before receiving the output.

binary search A search technique for finding the location of a value in an ordered list, or other structure for keeping ordered data values such as a binary tree. The list is divided in half and the search proceeds to search the half that is a candidate for the sought value, that half is divided in half to obtain one quarter of the list and so forth.

binary tree A tree in which each node has at most two descendants. See **tree**.

bit A binary digit; that is, a digit that may be either zero or one but can assume no other value.

block A set of statements enclosed with **begin** and **end** and separated by semicolons, together with the declarations that apply to them. Applied to programs and procedures.

bottom-up Applied to any method that goes from subparts to larger parts made up of the subparts. See **bottom-up testing** in the text for an example of usage.

buffer A location for holding data which is on its way from one place to another.

bug A mistake in a program.

byte 1. Eight bits. 2. A location, or part of a location, in memory that holds eight bits.

call The interruption of a program's execution in order to execute a procedure or function.

call-by-name parameter Approximately the same as **variable parameter**.

call-by-value parameter A synonym for **value parameter**.

central processing unit See **CPU**.

code Sometimes used to mean a program or part of a program.

compile 1. To translate a program using a compiler. 2. The action of a compiler.

compile-time error An error discovered by the compiler, typically a syntax error.

compiler A program that translates programs from a high level language to machine language.

component One unit of data stored in a file or other structured type value.

component variable 1. Of a record variable: the variable obtained by specializing the record variable to a single field; the syntax is to append a period followed by the field name. 2. Of an array: the same thing as an **indexed variable**.

constant In a Pascal program: the name of a value. It may be a number constant such as **5** or **3.5** or a quoted string or character. It also may be the name associated with one of these constants by a constant declaration.

control variable A variable of an ordinal type that is used to control a *for* loop.

CPU The *Central Processing Unit* of a computer. It performs the actual calculations and the manipulation of memory according to the instructions in a machine language program.

crash For a computer to suddenly stop working, often with disastrous results to the programs which are running at the time of the crash.

cursor A mark on a display screen which indicates where writing or other actions will take place; typically a rectangle or small line of light.

data 1. The input to an algorithm or program. 2. Any information that is available to an algorithm or to a computer.

data structure A structure for holding related data values in an organized way; examples are arrays, records, lists and trees.

disk A secondary memory device consisting of a disk that stores information in concentric tracks. There are two common types of disk: *hard* disks are semipermanently mounted and relatively large; *floppy* disks are smaller and are remounted at each session.

EBCDIC Extended Binary Coded Decimal Interchange Code. An arbitrary assignment of numbers to display characters and control signals.

echoing Displaying the data typed in at the keyboard on the display screen.

editor   A program that allows the computer to be used as a typewriter. An editor also has a number of commands that are more powerful than those of a typewriter, such as moving an entire piece of text from one place to another.

efficiency   The efficiency of a program is measured by the amount of resources that the program consumes. The fewer resources it consumes, the more efficient it is. Time and storage are the resources that are usually considered.

element   A single data item, typically of an array or set.

empty statement   In Pascal: a statement written by writing nothing and which does nothing when executed. Its main purpose is to allow the insertion of extra semicolons.

enumerated types   A user-defined type consisting of a list of identifiers.

execute   When an instruction is carried out by a computer, either directly or in some translated form, the computer is said to execute the instruction. When a computer follows the instructions in a complete program, it is said to execute the program.

expression   In Pascal: any representation of a value, such as a variable, constant, arithmetic expression or boolean expression.

field width   In Pascal: a specification that tells how many spaces to leave for an argument to **write** or **writeln**. It consists of a colon followed by an integer expression. For values of type **real** a second colon and integer expression may be used to specify the number of digits to output after the decimal point.

file   A named collection of data stored in secondary memory.

file manager   Also sometimes called a *filer* or *file system*. A program that allows the user to store and retrieve objects called *files*. Among other things, a file can contain a Pascal program. Hence, a file manager is the program used to store and retrieve Pascal programs.

flag   Any device that changes value to indicate that some event has taken place; boolean variables are often used as flags in Pascal programs.

floating point numbers   In Pascal: Numbers of type **real**, especially when written in the *E* notation.

formal parameter   An identifier in a procedure or function declaration heading that is changed when the procedure is called. See **value parameter** and **variable parameter**.

friendly   A program is said to be *friendly* if it is easy to interact with, usually because it is very free about the format for entering data.

fully exercise   A technique for testing a piece of code (like a program or procedure). It consists of finding a set of test inputs such that running the program on the test inputs will cause each statement and substatement to be executed on at least one of the test runs and will cause each boolean expression that controls a loop to assume the value **true** on at least one run and **false** on at least one run.

garbage collection Making no longer needed memory locations available for reuse. In standard Pascal this is done using **dispose**; in UCSD Pascal using **mark** and **release**.

global variable A variable declared in the main block of a program.

hard copy Output on paper, as opposed to output which goes to a file or other electronic means of storage.

hardware The actual physical parts of a computer or computer system.

heap The portion of memory allocated to dynamic variables.

hexidecimal numeral A base 16 numeral.

high level language A programming language which includes larger, more powerful instructions, and typically, a grammar that is somewhat like English. Programs in a high level language usually cannot be directly executed by computers. See **machine language**.

implementation-dependent A language detail that is different for different implementations; typically it is not fully specified in the definition of the language, but left up to the implementor to implement in any way that is convenient and reasonable.

index The value which specializes an array, such as **5** in **A[5]**.

initialize Giving the first value to a variable in a program.

intelligent Having properties similar to a computer. For example an *intelligent terminal* can do many computer functions without being connected to a computer.

interactive An interactive computer system is one that converses with the user via a terminal.

invalid index An error condition that occurs when a program attempts to either refer to an array location that is outside the declared range or to refer to a subrange type value that is outside the subrange declared for that type.

invoke a function or procedure To *call* a function or procedure.

iterate To repeat. Often used to mean an execution of the body of a loop.

K Abbreviation of *kilo*; stands for 1,000. For example, 64K bytes means 64,000 bytes.

kilo See **K**.

line printer A typewriter-like output device that writes an entire line of text at one time.

listing A copy of a program or the contents of a text file written on paper by some computer output device.

local identifier An identifier that is declared within a procedure or function, such as a local variable or local constant.

local variable A variable declared within a procedure or function.

logical error A program error that is due to an error in the algorithm or an error in translating the algorithm into the programming language. Normally logical errors produce no error messages.

machine language A language that can be directly executed by a computer. Programs in machine language consist of very simple instructions, such as "add two numbers." These simple instructions are coded as strings of zeros and ones. See **assembly language**.

main memory The memory that the computer uses as temporary "scratch paper" when actually carrying out a computation. See **secondary memory**.

matrix 1. A two-dimensional arrangement of numbers. 2. A two-dimensional array.

mega- A prefix meaning one million; for example, a *megabyte* is one million bytes.

micro-computer A small computer, usually for the use of a single person.

mini-computer A medium size computer, typically shared by a number of users simultaneously.

mnemonic A memory aid. It frequently refers to the spelling of identifiers so as to hint at their use.

modem A device for transmitting digital information (typically to a computer) over a line such as a telephone line.

modularity A *modular* program is one that is divided into units (such as procedures) in such a way that each unit has well-defined means of communicating with the rest of the program (such as via parameters).

monitor 1. A display screen. 2. A program to trace another program.

nesting Placing one unit inside another unit. For example, nesting a smaller statement inside an *if-then* statement.

object program The translated version of a program produced by a compiler is called the *object program*. See **source program**.

octal numeral A base 8 numeral.

operating system A program that is part of the system software of a computer. It is the program that controls and manages all other programs.

operator In Pascal: a symbol, such as **+** or *****, or certain identifiers, such as *div*, which are used to combine two values and produce a third value.

ordinal type A type that is considered to be an ordered list of values. In Pascal, the only ordinal types are: **integer**, **char**, **boolean**, enumerated types and subrange types.

overflow The condition that results when a program attempts to compute a numeric value that is larger than the largest value of that type which the computer can represent in memory, or is smaller than the smallest value of that type which the computer can represent in memory. See also **stack overflow**.

parameters   The mechanism for passing information to or accepting information from a procedure or function. See *formal parameter*.

pass a parameter   The value or name of an actual parameter is said to be *passed* when the procedure (or function) is called.

peripheral device   An input, output or secondary storage device of a computer.

pop   To remove an element from a stack.

portability   A program is *portable* if it can be moved from one system to another with little or no change.

precedence   If an expression contains several different operations, the precedence is the order in which the operations are performed.

program   An algorithm that a computer can either follow directly or translate and then follow the translated version.

prompt-line   A line of output telling the user to enter input.

pseudocode   A mixture of English and Pascal (or some other combination of a natural language and a programming language).

pseudorandom number   A number produced by a function or procedure designed to enumerate random-looking numbers.

push   To add an element to a stack.

radian   A unit for measuring angles. There are 2π radians in 360 degrees.

reference parameter   Another term for *variable parameter*.

reserved word   An identifier whose meaning is defined by the specification of the Pascal language and whose meaning cannot be changed by the programmer.

root   See **tree**.

running a program   When a program and some data are given to a computer in such a way that the computer is instructed to carry out the program using the data, that is called running the program (on the data).

run-time error   A program error that is discovered by the computer system at the time the program is run. See **syntax error**.

scalar type   Sometimes used as another term for ordinal type. Sometimes used to mean a type which is either an ordinal type or the type **real**.

secondary memory   The memory a computer uses to store information in a permanent or semipermanent state. (When the computer does not have sufficient main memory for a computation, then it is also used as an addition to main memory.) See **main memory**.

semantics The meaning of a program or program construct or part of a program.

side-effect Something done by a procedure or function other than changing an actual variable parameter or returning a function value and which has an effect beyond the procedure or function itself. Changing a global variable is an example of a side effect.

simple type A type which is either an ordinal type or the type **real**.

software Another term for programs.

source program The input program to be translated by a compiler is called the *source program*. See **object program**.

stack A particular data structure used, among other things, for keeping track of recursion. See the index for the location of the section which explains this.

stack overflow An error condition that results when a data structure called a *stack* is given more data than it can hold. It is a run-time error. One likely cause is infinite recursion.

standard version of a programming language A version of a programming language that is defined by some official standards organization.

statement The unit of action in a Pascal program. Statements are usually separated by semicolons. See the syntax diagrams in the appendix.

step-wise refinement A method of developing a program by dividing the entire task into subtasks.

structured programming A method of programming that includes step-wise refinement for designing programs and includes coding the program in a form consisting of well-defined modules in a hierarchical arrangement.

structured type A type whose values are made up of other simpler values, such as an array, file or record type.

subscript Of an array: the same thing as an index.

subscripted variable An indexed variable of an array.

syntax The grammar rules of a language. The syntax rules of Pascal tell which strings of symbols are allowed as programs, statements, etc.

syntax error An error consisting of a violation of the syntax rules of a language. Syntax errors are discovered and reported by the compiler. See **run-time error**.

system software Refers collectively to all the programs that handle user programs. Included under this heading are such programs as compilers and operating systems.

terminal A device for communication with a computer, typically consisting of a keyboard and a display screen.

testing all paths A technique for testing a piece of code (like a program or procedure). It consists of finding a set of test inputs such that running the program on the test inputs will cause each possible combination of branch and loop behaviors to occur on at least one of the runs.

top-down   Any method that goes from the entire task or program to subparts, then sub-subparts, etc. For example, *top-down design* means the same as *step-wise refinement*.

tracing   Inserting **write** statements into a program so that the values of the variables will be written out as the program performs its calculations. Some systems have debugging facilities that do this automatically.

tree   A data structure consisting of nodes connected by pointers and satisfying certain conditions. Informally, these conditions require that, when drawn on paper, the structure exhibit a branching structure similar to a tree or upside-down tree. The nodes pointed to by a given node are called its *descendant* or *children* nodes. There is one node called the *root* node which has the property that any other node can be reached from it by following pointers.

truth table   A table showing the value of a boolean expression for each possible set of argument values.

type clash   A mismatch of types in the assignment of expressions to variables or in actual parameters of a procedure call or anyplace else.

underflow   The condition that results when a program attempts to compute a value of type **real** such that the value is smaller in absolute value than the smallest positive **real** value that the system can represent in memory. In other words, the condition that results when a program attempts to compute a nonzero value that is too close to zero to be represented in memory (except possibly by the approximately equal value of zero).

value parameter   Formal and actual parameters come in pairs. The pair is either a pair of value parameters or a pair of variable parameters. If the formal parameter is not prefaced by *var* in the formal parameter list of the procedure heading, then the pair is a pair of value parameters. If the pair is a pair of value parameters, the actual parameter may be anything that evaluates to the type of the corresponding formal parameter. A formal value parameter is a local variable. When the procedure is called, the value of the formal value parameter is initialized to the value of the corresponding actual value parameter.

variable parameter   Formal and actual parameters come in pairs. The pair is either a pair of value parameters or a pair of variable parameters. If the pair is a pair of variable parameters, then a *var* is written in front of the formal parameter in the formal parameter list of the procedure heading. If the pair is a pair of variable parameters, the actual parameter must be a variable. A formal variable parameter is a labeled blank. When the procedure is called, the actual variable parameter is substituted for the corresponding formal variable parameter.

verification Verifying a program means proving that it meets the specifications for the task it is supposed to perform.

volatile memory Memory that loses its data contents when the power is shut off or when a program is finished running.

word 1. A location in main memory. 2. The contents of a location in main memory. 3. Any unit of storage or data.

Answers to Self-Test
Exercises

Chapter 1

2. The enhanced algorithm will compute the amount that is to be paid to the tax collector. If the amount is negative, then a refund is due. An outline of the algorithm is:

begin

1. Compute the amount of tax owed and call this amount **TAX**; (this subpart is accomplished by the algorithm developed in the chapter).
2. Determine the amount of income withheld and call this **Withheld**; (this amount will be part of the input data to the algorithm).
3. Subtract **Withheld** from **Tax** and call the result **AmountToPay**;
4. If **AmountToPay** is positive,
     then that is the amount due to the tax collector;
   if **AmountToPay** is negative,
     then the refund is equal to the absolute value of this amount;
   if **AmountToPay** is zero,
     then there is no payment or refund

end.

3. Algorithm to add two whole numbers:

begin

1. Write the two numbers down one above the other so that they line up digit by digit with the rightmost digits one above the other (if the two numbers are not of the same length, then add extra zeros to the front of the shorter number until they are of equal length);
2. Add the two rightmost digits, obtaining a one- or two-digit number;

3. Write the rightmost of these two digits down as the rightmost digit of the answer and remember the leftmost digit; Call the digit that needs to be remembered by the name **Carry**;

4. Do 4a, 4b and 4c again and again until you run out of digits (if the two numbers are each only one digit long, then you "run out" before you start and so do 4a, 4b and 4c zero times, i.e., not at all);

4a. Move to the next pair of digits to the left;

4b. Add these two digits and the **Carry**, obtaining a new one- or two-digit number;

4c. Write the rightmost digit of the number so obtained as the next (reading right to left.) digit of the answer and use the leftmost digit of this number as the new (possibly changed) value of **Carry** (if the number has only one digit, then the new value of **Carry** is zero);

5. If **Carry** is zero at this point (i.e., at the left end of the two numbers), then you are done;

6. If **Carry** is not zero, then write down the value of **Carry** as the leftmost digit of the answer

end.

5. As with virtually all problems, there is more than one algorithm for this problem. One algorithm is:

begin

1. Write the word down on one line;

2. Write it down on the line below, but this time write it backwards; (Align the letters on the two lines.)

3. For each letter in the word: compare the letter to the one written just below it;

4. If all letters match then the word is a palindrome; if at least one mismatch is found, then it is not a palindrome

end.

6. This algorithm assumes that the input word is written on a sheet of paper.

begin

1. Write the letters of the alphabet down on a sheet of paper, one per line;

2. Write zero after each letter;

3. Place your finger on the first letter of the word;

4. Repeat the following until you run out of letters (at the end of the word):

4a. Read the letter pointed to by your finger;

4b. Add one to the number written after that letter on the sheet of paper (the old number is erased or crossed out).

4c. Move your finger to the next letter in the word (provided there is one);

5. The number of occurrences of each letter is written on the sheet of paper

end.

Chapter 2

1. *2 2*

If your system outputs

22

(i.e., no blanks between the numbers), then on your system you need to explicitly insert a blank between any two consecutive numbers output. If you are on one of these systems, then modify the **writeln** statement as follows and run the program again.

```
writeln(X, ' ', Y)
```

(The second parameter is a blank in single quotes.)

2. The output is the single number:

   3

3. *BCB*

5. Type it up and compile it; the compiler will tell you the first mistake as well as a guess of the other mistakes. Correct the first mistake, and compile it again. Continue until you have corrected all the mistakes. (The first mistake is that the first line needs a semicolon. The second mistake is that the double quotes are used where single quotes should be used. The other mistakes are all missing punctuation marks: a closing single quote, a semicolon and the final period.)

8. They are all incorrect except for the constant **4** (with no decimal point).

9. The first two are correct; all the rest are incorrect. The last constant, **4**, is a correctly formed constant of type **integer** and so it can be used anyplace that a constant of type **real** can be used; that makes **4** pragmatically as good as correct.

10. *START* $-1234.567END$
    (There is one blank before the minus sign.)

12. (a) Correct as is. (Even though the spacing is less than elegant.)
    (b) The identifier *var* should only be used once.
    (c) The first semicolon should be a comma.
    (d) It needs a semicolon at the end.

Chapter 3

3. | | |
   |---|---|
   | 15 *div* 12 is 1 | 15 *mod* 12 is 3 |
   | 24 *div* 12 is 2 | 24 *mod* 12 is 0 |
   | 123 *div* 100 is 1 | 123 *mod* 100 is 23 |
   | 200 *div* 100 is 2 | 200 *mod* 100 is 0 |
   | 99 *div* 2 is 49 | 99 *mod* 2 is 1 |

6. `3X, 3*X + Y, (X + Y)/7, (3*X + Y)/(Z + 2)`

7. `4, 3, 6, -6, 7, -7, 6.8,`
   `6.8, 4, 4, 4`

8. `sqr(X + (Y/(X + Z)) + W)`
   `  or sqr(X + Y/(X + Z) + W)`
   `( (2*X*X*X)/(4*A) ) + B`
   `  or (2*X*X*X)/(4*A) + B`
   `sqrt(((X + 3*Z)/W) + Y)`
   `  or sqrt((X + 3*Z)/W + Y)`

11. The following are incorrect; the rest are correct.
    .99; 57; 57E3.7; 57.9E3.7
    The constant **57** is a correctly formed constant of type **integer** and so can be used anyplace that a constant of type **real** can be used.

1. Begin Conversation
    Goodbye
    Hello
    One more time:
    Hello
    Goodbye
    End conversation

2. One
    One Two
    One Two Three

3. *1 2*
    2 2
    2 1

5.  ```
    program Practice(input, output);
    var A, B: integer;
    procedure Exercise(var X, Y: integer);
    begin{Exercise}
     writeln(X, Y);
     X := Y;
     writeln(X, Y)
    end; {Exercise}

    begin{Program}
     writeln('Enter values for A and B:');
     readln(A, B);
     Exercise(A, B);
     writeln('After procedure A = ', A, ' B = ', B);
     writeln('End exercise')
    end. {Program}
    ```

Chapter 5

1. *4 5 6*
    4 5 3

2. *4 5 6*
    1 2 3

3. *4 5 6*
    5 4 3

4. *5 5 6*
    5 2 3

5. *4 5 6*
    4 2 5

6. *A B*
    X B
    ```

9.
```
program Mixed(input, output);

   var Area: real;

   procedure ComputeArea(Length, Width: real; var A: real);
   begin{ComputeArea}
    A := Length * Width
   end; {ComputeArea}

   begin{Program}
    ComputeArea(4, 3, Area);
    writeln('A rectangle of dimensions 4 by 3 inches');
    writeln('has area ', Area, ' square inches.')
   end. {Program}
```

Chapter 6

1.
```
program ShowCase(input, output);

   var MonthNum: integer;

   begin{Program}
    writeln('Enter a month as a number between 1 and 12.');
    writeln('I''ll tell you how many days it has in it.');
    readln(MonthNum);
    case MonthNum of
       4, 6, 9, 11: writeln('30 days');
       1, 3, 5, 7, 8, 10, 12: writeln('31 days');
       2: writeln('28 days (29 if leap year)')
    end; {case}
    writeln('That''s it !')
   end. {Program}
```

3.
```
program Exercise3(input, output);
   var N1, N2: integer;
   begin{Program}
    writeln('Enter two integers:');
    readln(N1, N2);
    if N1 < N2
      then writeln('In order: ', N1, N2)
      else writeln('In order: ', N2, N1);
    writeln('End program')
   end. {Program}
```

5. The two on the first line evaluate to **false**; the other two evaluate to **true**.

6.
```
sqrt(X) <= (Y + 1)
Z > 0
W <> 0
X mod 12 = 0
```

7. *Start*
First writeln
Next
Enough

Chapter 7

1. `false true`
   incorrectly formed, incorrectly formed
   `false`
   `false`
   `false`

2. `2 + 2 = 4`
   `X + 7 > 100`
   `('Z' <> 'A') and ('Z' <> 'B') and ('Z' <> 'C')`
   `(X <= Y + 2) and (Y + 2 <= Z)`

3. `if X < 0 then writeln(X, ' is Negative.')`
   `else if (0 <= X) and (X <= 100)`
   `        then writeln(X, ' is between 0 and 100.')`
   `else {if X > 100} writeln(X, ' is greater than 100.')`

5. `not(FootLoose) and not(FancyFree)`
   is equivalent to (always evaluates to the same value) as:
   `not(FootLoose or FancyFree)`
   The other two expressions are equivalent to each other, but not equivalent to the above two.

7. `(A or B) and not(A and B)`
   There are other equivalent expressions that would be correct here.

Chapter 8

2. -2

3. A `repeat` is always executed at least once; a `while` may be executed zero times.

5. *1 3*
   2 2
   3 2

7. `    while ⟨boolean⟩ do ⟨statement⟩`
   is equivalent to:
   `    if ⟨boolean⟩`
   `        then`
   `        repeat`
   `            ⟨statement⟩`
   `        until not(⟨boolean⟩)`

   `    repeat ⟨body⟩ until ⟨boolean⟩`
   is equivalent to:
   `    begin`
   `      ⟨body⟩`
   `    end;`
   `    while not(⟨boolean⟩) do`
   `      begin`
   `        ⟨body⟩`
   `      end`

1. `function Half(A: integer): real;`
   {*Returns A divided by 2.*}
   `begin`{*Half*}
     `Half := A / 2`
   `end;` {*Half*}

2. All the following are allowed: `integer`, `real`, `char` and `boolean`. The type `string` is not allowed. (That is almost a complete list, but later on we will introduce a few other types that may be returned.)

3. `function Area(Length, Width: real): real;`
   {*Returns the area of a rectangle of the given dimensions.*}
   `begin`{*Area*}
     `Area := Length*Width`
   `end;` {*Area*}

4. The function name, `TwoPower`, is not a variable but is being used as a variable. The following is not allowed:
       `TwoPower := TwoPower*2`

5. `function Divides(A, B: integer): boolean;`
   {*Returns true if A evenly divides B; otherwise, returns false.*}
   `begin`{*Divides*}
     `Divides := (B mod A = 0)`
   `end;` {*Divides*}

   The following also works, but is poor style:

   `function Divides(A, B: integer): boolean;`
   {*Returns true if A evenly divides B; otherwise, returns false.*}
   `begin`{*Divides*}
     `if (B mod A = 0) then Divides := true`
                        `else Divides := false`
   `end;` {*Divides*}

6. `function InOrder(A1, A2, A3: integer): boolean;`
   {*Returns true if A1 <= A2 <= A3; otherwise returns false.*}
   `begin`{*InOrder*}
     `InOrder := (A1 <= A2) and (A2 <= A3)`
   `end;` {*InOrder*}

10. `function Ran2to20(var Seed: integer): integer;`
    {*Returns a pseudorandom even number between 2
    and 20, inclusive. Uses the function Random in Figure 9.7.*}
      `var OneToTen: integer;`
    `begin`{*Ran2to20*}
      `OneToTen := (Random(Seed) mod 10) + 1;`
      {*OneToTen is a pseudorandom number between 1 and 10.*}
      `Ran2to20 := 2*OneToTen`
    `end;` {*Ran2to20*}

Chapter 10

3. **GradePoint** and **Count** are illegal because **0.0..4.0** is illegal. The rest are legal.

4. *type* Score = 0..100;
    NonNegIntegers = 0..maxint;
    List = *array*[1..10] *of* Score;

5. The loop ends with the value of **I** equal to **Last**. At that point **I + 1** evaluates to **Last + 1** and so **A[I + 1]** has an illegal index. To fix it, change the final expression of the *for* loop to **Last - 1**.

6. As written it sums the numbers between **A[1]** and **A[100]**. If the value of **A[1]** is **1** and the value of **A[100]** is **3**, then the final value of **Sum** will be **1 + 2 + 3** or **6**. The correct code is:

```
Sum := 0;
for I := 1 to 100 do
   Sum := Sum + A[I]
```

The variable **I** should be of type **integer** or, better still, type **1..100**.

Chapter 11

1. The problem is a "boundary" problem. When **I** is equal to **100**, the loop terminates without adding in the **100**. The easiest way to fix it is to change the end of the repeat loop to:

```
until I > 100
```

2. The values of **A** and **B** do not matter, but you need a collection of different values for **X**. You need one value of **X** that is greater than or equal to **5** and one that is less than **5**. You also need one value greater than zero and one less than or equal to zero. For example, the following two values of **X** will do: **5, 0**. Since some numbers satisfy more than two of the required cases, you do not need four test values. You should use other test values as well, but these are enough to fully exercise the code.

3. There are four paths, but one is impossible. One of many possible sets of values for **X** is: **5, 4, 0**. The values of **A** and **B** do not matter for testing all paths.

5. The program uses more storage than is needed for a clear program. There is no need to use an array. All that is needed is a single variable as shown below:

```
Sum := 0;
for I := 1 to 100 do
   begin
     read(Next);
     Sum := Sum + Next
   end;
Average := Sum / 100
```

The variable **Next** is of type **integer**. It is also a good idea to declare **100** as a named constant.

Chapter 12

1. 3

2. *Hip Hip Hurray*

3. For arguments of **3**, **10** and **100**, the value returned is **6**, **55**, and **5050**, respectively. An argument of **−10** produces infinite recursion and so there will be no legitimate output; however, the error message *stack overflow* is likely.

5.
```
procedure RecStar(N: integer);
   const Star = '*';
{Writes N '*'s to the screen. Precondition: N > 0.}
   begin{RecStar}
     writeln(Star);
     if N > 1 then
              RecStar(N - 1)
   end; {RecStar}
```

You should also type up and run your procedure for this exercise.

Chapter 13

1. *5 63*
   5 6

5. *ab*
   ghijkHi

7. Standard Pascal:
```
program WriteTen(input, output, NewFile);
   var NewFile: text;
       I: integer;
begin{Program}
   rewrite(NewFile);
   writeln('Writing to NewFile');
   for I := 1 to 10 do
     writeln(NewFile, I);
   writeln('Done writing to NewFile')
end. {Program}
```

UCSD Pascal:
```
program WriteTen;
   var NewFile: text;
       Name: string;
       I: integer;
begin{Program}
   writeln('Enter a new directory name.');
   writeln('It should end with .TEXT :');
   readln(Name);
   rewrite(NewFile, Name);
   writeln('Writing to ', Name);
   for I := 1 to 10 do
     writeln(NewFile, I);
   close(NewFile, lock);
   writeln('Done writing to ', Name)
end. {Program}
```

8. Standard Pascal:

```
program ReadTen(input, output, NewFile);
  var NewFile: text;
      Number, Sum: integer;
begin{Program}
  reset(NewFile);
  Sum := 0;
  while not eof(NewFile) do
    begin{while}
      readln(NewFile, Number);
      Sum := Sum + Number
    end; {while}
  writeln('The sum of the numbers');
  writeln('in NewFile is ', Sum)
end. {Program}
```

UCSD Pascal:

```
program ReadTen;
  var NewFile: text;
      Name: string;
      Number, Sum: integer;
begin{Program}
  writeln('What is the name of');
  writeln('the file from Exercise 7?');
  readln(Name);
  reset(NewFile, Name);
  Sum := 0;
  while not eof(NewFile) do
    begin{while}
      readln(NewFile, Number);
      Sum := Sum + Number
    end; {while}
  writeln('The sum of the numbers');
  writeln('in ', Name, ' is ', Sum);
  close(NewFile, lock)
end. {Program}
```

Chapter 14

2. *5 A*
   6 A

3.
```
type Sue =
  record
    Field1: integer;
    Field2: real;
    Field3: char
  end;
```

5. *type* Student =
     record
       Name: *array*[1..20] *of* char;
       QuizScores: *array*[1..10] *of* 0..10;
       MidTerm, FinalExam, FinalSum: 0..100;
       Grade: 'A'..'F'
     end;

7. Parallel arrays:

```
type StockNum = 0..Max;
     StyleNum = 0..50;
     SizeRange = 3..10;
     Style = array[StockNum] of StyleNum;
     Size = array[StockNum, SizeRange] of integer;
     Price = array[StockNum] of real;
```

Array of records:

```
type StockNum = 0..Max;
     StyleNum = 0..50;
     SizeRange = 3..10;
     Shoe = record
              Style: StyleNum;
              Size: array[SizeRange] of integer;
              Price: real
            end;
     InStock = array[StockNum] of Shoe;
```

Max is some defined constant.

8. [1, 3, 7, 8, 9], [7, 8, 9], [8], [ ], [7],
   true, false, true, true, false, true

Chapter 15

1.

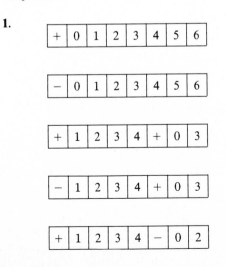

| − | 1 | 2 | 3 | 4 | − | 0 | 2 |

| + | 3 | 1 | 4 | 2 | + | 0 | 1 |

3. In each case, the largest value of type **real** is:
+0.999E+999, +0.99E+9999, +0.99999E+9

4. 7, 5, 4, 27, 22, 0.5, 0.25, 0.125, 0.625, 1.125, 5.625

5. thirty-two bit machine:

$$2^{31} - 1 = 0.2147836 \times 10^{10} \ (approx.)$$

sixty-four bit machine:

$$2^{63} - 1 = 0.9223372 \times 10^{19} \ (approx.)$$

Chapter 16

1. *type* Student =
        record
            Name: *array*[1..20] *of* char;
            Final: 0..100;
            Grade: 'A'..'F'
        end;
     GradeBook = *file of* Student;

2. X := Stuff↑;
   get(Stuff)

Chapter 17

1. *10 20*
   20 20
   30 30
   40 40

2. *10 20*
   20 20
   30 20
   30 40

3. It would not change at all.

7. There is no difference in the general form of the nodes. The difference is in the way they are used.

Index